Making Care Orders Work

Studies in Evaluating the Children Act 1989

Series editors:
Dr Carolyn Davies, Prof. Jane Aldgate

Other titles in the series include

From Care to Accommodation

Parental Perspectives on Care Proceedings

The Last Resort

Leaving Care in Partnership

Safeguarding Children with the Children Act 1989

The Best-Laid Plans

Supporting Families through Short-Term Fostering

Expert Evidence in Child Protection Litigation

Family Support in Cases of Emotional Maltreatment and Neglect

Fostering Family Contact

The Children Act Now

Placed and Paid for: Supporting Families through Sponsored Day Care

STUDIES IN EVALUATING THE CHILDREN ACT 1989

Making Care Orders Work

A study of Care Plans and their Implementation

Judith Harwin

Morag Owen

Rachel Locke

Donald Forrester

London: TSO

Published by TSO (The Stationery Office) and available from:

Online
www.tso.co.uk/bookshop

Mail, Telephone, Fax & E-mail
TSO
PO Box 29, Norwich NR3 1GN
Telephone orders/General enquiries 0870 600 5522
Fax orders 0870 600 5533
E-mail book.orders@tso.co.uk
Textphone 0870 240 3701

TSO Shops
123 Kingsway, London WC2B 6PQ
020 7242 6393 Fax 020 7242 6394
68–69 Bull Street, Birmingham B4 6AD
0121 236 9696 Fax 0121 236 9699
9–21 Princess Street, Manchester M60 8AS
0161 834 7201 Fax 0161 833 0634
16 Arthur Street, Belfast BT1 4GD
028 9023 8451 Fax 028 9023 5401
18–19 High Street, Cardiff CF10 1PT
029 2039 5548 Fax 029 2038 4347
71 Lothian Road, Edinburgh EH3 9AZ
0870 606 5566 Fax 0870 606 5588

TSO Accredited Agents

(see Yellow Pages)

and through good booksellers

First published 2003

ISBN 11 322314 5

Printed in the United Kingdom by The Stationery Office
146571 C8 12/03 19585 909709

Contents

List of figures and tables

Figures

Tables

Foreword

The Children Act 1989 was implemented on 14 October 1991. At its launch the then Lord Chancellor, Lord Mackay, described the Act as 'the most radical legislative reform to children's services this century'. Shortly after the launch the Department of Health put together a strategy to monitor and evaluate the initial impact of the Act. Taking a tripartite approach, this drew on evidence from statistical returns, inspections and research to develop a rounded appreciation of early implementation. The subsequent strategy plan was published and circulated to relevant bodies, including social services and the major voluntary agencies, in 1993. This plan formed the backcloth for a programme of research studies commissioned by the Department of Health to explore early evaluation in more depth. *Making Care Orders Work* concludes the series which is based on the 24 research studies.

The programme studies investigate the implementation of key changes introduced by the Act and evaluate the facilitators and inhibitors to the meeting of key objectives. A longer-term goal of the programme is to review the aims of the Act in the light of implementation with a view to reconsideration or amendment should this be felt necessary. Finally, a more general and important scientific aim is to consider how far change could be achieved successfully by changing the law.

There are several principles underlying the Children Act 1989 that permeate the research studies. An important strand of the Act is to bring together private and public law so that the needs of all children whose welfare is at risk might be approached in the same way. This philosophy is underpinned by the principle of promoting children's welfare. There should be recognition of children's time-scales and, in court cases, children's welfare should be paramount. To aid this paramountcy principle there should be a welfare checklist, and delays in court hearings should be avoided. The promotion of children's welfare takes a child development focus, urging local authorities to take a holistic and corporate approach to providing services. Departments such as health, education, housing, police, social services and recreation should work together to respond to children's needs. Children, the Act argues, are best looked after within their families wherever possible and, where not, the continuing support of parents and wider kin should be facilitated by avoiding compulsory proceedings whenever possible. Parents should be partners in any intervention process, and children's views should be sought and listened to in any decision-making affecting their lives. To promote continuity for children looked after, contact with families should be encouraged and children's religion, culture, ethnicity and language should be preserved.

Local authorities have a duty to move from services to prevent care to a broader remit of providing family support, which could include planned periods away from home. However, family support services should not be universal but target those most in need. The introduction of Children's Services Plans in 1996 made the idea of corporate responsibility a more tangible reality and sought to help local authorities look at how they might use scarce resources cost-effectively.

The themes of the Children Act have relevance for the twenty-first century. The concern with combating social exclusion is echoed through several of the studies, especially those on family support and young people looked after by local authorities. The value of early intervention is also a theme in the studies on family centres, day care and services for children defined as 'in need' under the Act. Further, the research on the implementation of the Looking After Children Schedules emphasises the importance to children in foster and residential care of attaining good outcomes in education. Lastly, attending to the health of parents and their children is another strand in both the family support and 'children looked after' studies.

To accompany the 24 individual studies in the research programme the Department of Health commissioned an overview of the findings, *The Children Act Now – Messages From Research*, published by The Stationery Office in 2001 in the style of similar previous publications from HMSO: *Social Work Decisions in Child Care 1985; Patterns and Outcomes in Child Care 1991; Child Protection: Messages from Research 1996; and Focus on Teenagers 1997.*

The editors would like to express their appreciation to the members of the research community; professionals from different disciplines, and service users, among others, who have contributed so willingly and generously to the successful completion of the research studies and to the construction of the overview. Without their help, none of the research would have been written or disseminated.

Carolyn Davies
Jane Aldgate

Acknowledgements

This book would not have been possible without the support and commitment of very many people. We would particularly like to thank Carolyn Davies and Caroline Thomas at the Department of Health, and Arran Poyser from CAFCASS, for their advice, help and encouragement. We also want to express our gratitude to staff at the Lord Chancellor's Department who assisted us in arranging judicial interviews and providing access to court-based data.

Under the chairmanship of Carolyn Davies, the Research Advisory Group consistently provided us with valuable feedback. The members of the group were Chris Davies, Carol Edwards, Danya Glaser, Rupert Hughes, Joan Hunt, Mike Leadbetter, Isabel Plumstead, Arran Poyser, Ruth Sinclair and Harriet Ward.

We give special thanks to Caroline Willbourne, Sally Stone and Tabitha Barran for their detailed survey of relevant case law and willingness to respond to all our requests for further information. Invaluable statistical advice was provided by Sophia Rabe-Hesketh at the Institute of Psychiatry, King's College, London.

During the course of the research we met only with help from all the participating authorities. Social workers gave freely of their time, and administrative staff ensured that documentation was made available efficiently and promptly. Liaison officers helped to smooth our entry into each authority and were available to assist in each new stage of the project. Local authority solicitors and children's guardians were equally generous in taking part in the study.

Finally, we thank all the parents, carers and children who participated in this study and were prepared to share their experiences with us.

Part

I Introduction

1 Rationale for the study

Introduction

Children on care orders are the most vulnerable children in the care system and they comprise the largest and most rapidly growing group of children looked after. Their case management raises particularly complex issues and they also demand the most intensive and expensive investment of resources by local authorities. Yet they have rarely been the sole focus of research attention.

This book reports the findings of a study that focuses exclusively on care order children. It takes as its starting-point the changes made by the Children Act to improve planning when a care application is made. Central to the study is the role of the court care plan and its influence on subsequent case management by social services. It asks how far the care plan for the court can contribute to proactive planning and to good welfare outcomes, and it explores the constraints and obstacles to both these objectives.

To answer these key questions, the study has followed up for 21 months 100 children placed consecutively on care orders in 1997. The children came from 57 families and were drawn from five local authorities covering urban and rural areas. Because of the importance of charting user views, the findings include the views of some of the children and their parents and carers as well as those of the social workers, guardians ad litem and local authority solicitors.

Practitioners' ability to plan for the future is always constrained by gaps in knowledge and difficulties in making predictions about the future; yet care orders can only work effectively if there is sound knowledge of what contributes to placement stability and good welfare outcomes. This study seeks to identify what works, for which children in which circumstances, and in this way to provide evidence that can help social work practitioners and members of the judiciary to make the most of a care order.

Chapter 1 is in four parts. First we examine the changes made by the Children Act and accompanying guidance to care planning for the courts. The second section of the chapter looks at the rationale for the study and its main objectives, and this is followed by a fuller discussion of the specific research questions. Finally, we review a range of recent developments in policy, law and practice and their relevance to the aims of the study.

The Children Act and care plans for the court

The Children Act 1989 was the first piece of legislation to strengthen the care planning process systematically and comprehensively. It made existing mechanisms of local authority review stronger for all looked-after children and introduced representation and complaints procedures. It also tried to ensure that the plans of the local authority for the children it is seeking to look after via a care or supervision order would acquire far greater significance than before.

Under the Children Act the care plan presented to the court has two quite specific roles. First, it influences the likelihood of a care order being made. Second, it sets out a framework for social services case management after the care order and it delineates the goals to be achieved and the desired outcomes for the child. In this way the care plan lays down an important bench-mark for subsequent intervention.

As early as 1981, research had drawn attention to the limited information available to courts from local authorities prior to the making of an order,[1] and in 1984 the House of Commons Select Committee recommended 'maximum possible advance indications of the local authority plans' (HC Social Services Committee 1984, para. 71). A question that remained unanswered by this proposal was what powers, if any, the courts should be given if they disliked the local authority plans. The solution of the Children Act was to introduce what came to be known as the no order principle (section 1(5)). Thus, where before the sole criterion for making a care order was proof of the grounds, the Children Act introduced a second stage to the process to enable courts to decide whether the plans of the local authority warranted the care order. Under section 1(5) the courts had to consider whether the making of an order would lead to a better outcome than if no order were made. The care plan of the local authority is the mechanism by which this decision is reached.

The cautious approach to the use of care orders in the legislation can be directly linked to the Act's underpinning philosophy that children are normally best brought up by their own parents. But it also stemmed from concerns about the capacity of the state to safeguard and promote children's well-being through compulsion. The numbers of children entering care via the compulsory route had risen sharply throughout the 1980s yet research was suggesting that compulsion provided no guarantee of good planning and that indeed 'control was often being confused with planning' (DHSS 1985). This theme, perhaps best captured by the title of the highly influential study *Lost in Care* (Millham et al. 1986), led to a new balance in the powers and duties of the family, the state and the child and was one of the reasons behind the no order principle.

Enhancing the role of planning in general, through care plans presented to the court, was another objective of the Children Act 1989.

As early as 1971, in a National Children's Home Convocation lecture, Professor Roy Parker noted that 'many children in care have no assurance of continuities, and their futures are, for them, not easily forseeable' (Parker 1971). He made a special plea for proactive planning on a number of grounds that remain important today. One argument was about local authority accountability and the need for practitioners to have a clear framework for intervention, but Parker also made a link between planning, children's rights and welfare. He argued that children in public care lack the opportunities available to most children growing up in their own families to plan ahead with their parents and to discuss different options and exercise choices. Because of their histories of uncertainty and disruption, Parker argued that good planning was especially important for looked-after children, as was their active participation in the process as a preparation for life. Subsequent research has suggested that there may indeed be a link between children's involvement in the planning process and outcome. A longitudinal study has shown that children brought up in institutions were unlikely to believe they could influence their life prospects through planning. They were therefore more likely to act impulsively over decisions such as choice of marital partner and career, often creating further risks for themselves (Rutter 2001).

Research objectives

These general considerations helped shape the study objectives, which are outlined as follows.

Monitoring the effectiveness of the care planning framework laid down by the Children Act 1989, with specific reference to the role of the care plan presented to the court for children on care orders

The care plan influences the likelihood of a care order being made or not. To help courts exercise their powers under section 1(5) of the Children Act 1989, they need to know the plans of the local authority in order to determine whether the making of an order will promote the child's welfare better than no order. The care plan, which sets out the way in which the local authority intends to care for the child if a care order is granted, is the mechanism for doing this. If the court does not like the care plan it may refuse to make the care order. Second, the care plan provides a framework for local authority case management and, as already mentioned, it delineates the goals to be achieved and the desired outcomes for the child. In this way the care plan lays down an important bench-mark for subsequent intervention.

The emphasis on care planning within the Children Act was an important response to the body of research published throughout the 1980s that drew attention to the disturbingly poor welfare outcomes of children in the care system and to the pattern of drift and delay in planning for their futures (DHSS 1985). Providing feedback to policy-makers, courts and social services on the extent to which care plans for the courts can help promote a proactive approach to planning for children on care orders was therefore a major objective of the study.

Helping to clarify the status and quality of care plans

When the Children Act became law the care plan was not enshrined in primary legislation. Although this has now been remedied,[2] the influence of the care plan is nevertheless subtle and complex. Provided that it is reasonable and does not mislead the courts, there is no binding obligation on the local authority to adhere rigidly to the care plan as originally drawn up at the time of the application for the order. Nor did the Children Act lay down specific criteria to determine what constitutes a 'good enough' care plan, although guidance by the Department of Health set down the areas to be covered. Instead it was left to guidance, case law and good practice to help clarify expectations as to the status and quality of care plans. However, an early study into interim care orders found that social workers were unsure about the extent of detail that should be provided in care plans (Plotnikoff and Woolfson 1994). The researchers also found that some social workers considered that planning could only begin following the making of an order – a finding that suggested some misunderstanding of their role and purpose. By a detailed examination of care plans in a larger sample of cases than was studied by Plotnikoff and Woolfson, the present study sought to examine content, level of detail provided and clarity of objectives and to help enrich understanding of what constitutes a 'good' or 'bad' care plan. Such findings could usefully inform the development of any future guidance and training.

In addition, there were some indications in the early days of the legislation that there was some degree of mismatch between the expectations of courts and social services in relation to the status of the plan, with attendant doubts about its ability to guarantee that particular resources would be made available or ensure that the recommendations would be fully implemented. The present study aimed to address this issue in two ways. First, it explored practitioner views on the status of the care plan. Second, it provided an examination of reasons for varying care plans and considering whether variance is due to unforeseeable changes of circumstance or to poor quality care plans at the time of the application to the courts.

Offering feedback to courts, children's guardians and social work personnel on the results of their decisions

Courts have expressed their concern at their lack of ability to obtain feedback on their actions relating to individual children. In particular they wish to know whether their recommendations have been implemented, but they also wish to learn more broadly whether their own decisions were well founded. Before the Children Act, High Court judges were able to receive some feedback through their ongoing responsibilities in wardship cases, although this was not true for magistrates or others involved in carrying out the Children and Young Persons Act 1969. At present children's guardians and courts normally only find out what has happened after an order if there is a fresh application. But cases that return to court are not necessarily representative of the generality of cases where children are placed on care orders. This research aimed to help fill the gap by providing feedback to the courts on the generality of care order cases. As part of this feedback it sought to consider the extent to which practitioners had anticipated any difficulties that might materialise in implementing the plan. (Since the study was prospective, it was possible to do this by asking the social workers and children's guardians for their predictions at the time of the first interview.) This kind of information can help inform individual decision-making both in terms of the value of making an order in the first place and the kinds of interventions which are more or less likely to promote the child's welfare if an order is made.

Tracking social workers' ongoing support for parents and carers when children are subject to care orders

As already mentioned, research carried out prior to the Children Act 1989 demonstrated that the making of an order was no guarantee of continuing careful social work planning and follow-up. To address this point, the study aimed to track social services' interventions following the making of the care order; but the Children Act also increased the challenge of working with children made subject to a care order because it emphasised partnership with parents and the promotion of the upbringing of the child by the family (section 26(3)) – except where this would be detrimental to the child's safety and welfare. In the first years of the operation of the Children Act 1989 the legislative aim of continued social work partnership following the making of an order appeared not to be fully understood. Court orders tended to be sought only when partnership had broken down, suggesting that the two processes were seen as mutually exclusive (Hunt et al. 1999). Through interviews with parents and carers, as well as analysis of care plans and their implementation, this study aimed to investigate the reality of partnership in the aftermath of a care order and the factors that enhance or decrease it.

Making a contribution to outcome-focused research for children

The concerns over the poor welfare outcomes of children in the care system have led to a heightened interest in monitoring children's welfare progress as well as case disposal. The Department of Health has funded a major programme on assessing outcomes in childcare (Ward 1995). One element of this programme was the production of the 'assessment and action records' (AARs), which in the first instance were designed as tools to enable social work practitioners to measure children's welfare but have subsequently also been used to provide management and research information. Since a central aim of the current research was to explore welfare outcome, the considerable interest in the Looking After Children materials led to a more specific aim of using this conceptual framework in the study, and a methodology was developed that enabled us to use it as a means of tracking children's welfare progress and final welfare status. (See Chapter 2.)

Providing evidence to inform debates on the boundaries between judicial and social work decision-making

The Children Act made some important alterations to the boundaries between judicial and social work decision-making. With the loss of wardship in all but exceptional circumstances, the High Courts lost their former powers to provide scrutiny and monitoring of complex cases managed by the social services. The loss of wardship powers was fiercely opposed by some members of the judiciary and the Official Solicitor's Department during the Act's passage through Parliament. At the time this study was funded, there was continuing concern among some members of the judiciary about whether the Children Act 1989 redrew the boundaries between courts and social services correctly or whether the courts should be given any powers after the order has been made. The present study can contribute to this debate in two main ways. First, it provides evidence on the extent to which plans are implemented after the order in line with the care plan submitted to the courts. Second, through an analysis of reasons for variation or non-fulfilment, it aims to provide information on the extent to which the courts would be able to remedy the problems relating to non-fulfilment of plans.

Specific aims of the research

The broad considerations outlined above led to the development of three specific questions to be answered by the research:

1. To what extent are care plans for the court implemented according to the agreed plan?
2. What factors influence fulfilment or non-fulfilment?
3. What is the relationship between plan implementation and welfare outcome?

The first of these questions was posed in order to give a factual picture of implementation rates in the five authorities and to help fill a gap in information at local and national level. The second question followed logically from the first. Once the implementation rate had been established, it was important to be able to explain what lay behind the figures. This information is essential to help inform any policy and practice recommendations by pinpointing the range of factors that need to be taken into consideration. With regard to the third question, as already argued, there are many reasons why plan implementation may be important: for example to promote stability, to honour children's rights and to ensure local authority accountability. Establishing the links between care plan implementation and children's outcomes would enable us to see whether implementing a care plan is also important for children's well-being.

These three main questions gave the study its overall focus and direction but each question generated a series of further areas to be explored by the research.

To what extent are care plans for the court implemented according to the agreed plan?

- To answer this question it was necessary first of all to identify the core ingredients of the care plan in order to decide which aspects of implementation needed to be followed up. A researcher judgement was made that placement, contact and services constituted the core ingredients of the plan.
- To measure the overall success of placement implementation, we decided to note whether children were in the preferred type of placement at the end point of the study. A distinction had to be drawn between implementation and fulfilment. Some plans were implemented but not fulfilled, in the sense that children entered the proposed placement but it later broke down.
- The study of fulfilment required a description of each of the three core ingredients, and it was also necessary to track the timing of implementation.

What factors influence fulfilment or non-fulfilment?

- Aspects regularly examined included the impact of initial assessments, children's age, their difficulties, the number of moves made and the timing of placements.
- It was hypothesised that a range of factors would influence fulfilment and these were grouped into four categories:
    - child factors;
    - family factors;
    - organisational factors; and
    - the quality of the care plan.

This classification was developed to take account of the broader influences that may lead to plan variation. The child's own wishes and feelings, and age or personal history, may lead to plans not being fulfilled in the way that was originally expected. Changes within the family or the extended family may exert a similar influence, as may the nature of the parents' problems. The research also wished to explore the possibility that resource constraints might be a significant obstacle to successful implementation. Finally, it was important to explore the possibility that the quality of the plan itself could influence fulfilment.

What is the relationship between plan implementation and welfare outcome?

- Two measures were developed for the recording of welfare outcome – welfare progress and welfare status (see Chapter 2).
- These outcome measures helped to answer the main question that the research set out to investigate – whether care plans that are implemented successfully are associated with better welfare outcomes for the child and, if so, whether the converse holds true.
- A subsidiary question was: Since good and bad outcomes are likely to be represented across the board, is it possible to identify risk and protective factors that contribute to welfare outcome whether or not the court plan is fulfilled?

Figure 1.1 demonstrates the framework for the analysis and the possible links between plan fulfilment and child outcomes.

The continuing relevance of the study

Since this study was commissioned there have been a number of developments in law, policy, practice and practice relating to children on care orders in general and care planning in particular. All these developments increase the relevance and timeliness of this study.

Care order children are the fastest growing group in the looked-after system and have high levels of need. The numbers of care orders have almost doubled since 1993 with a particularly rapid increase between 1999 and 2000 (DoH 2001b) and they are still continuing to rise – up by 19% since 1998 (DoH 2002a). Children who entered the care system via a section 31 order now

Figure 1.1 ***Framework for the analysis***

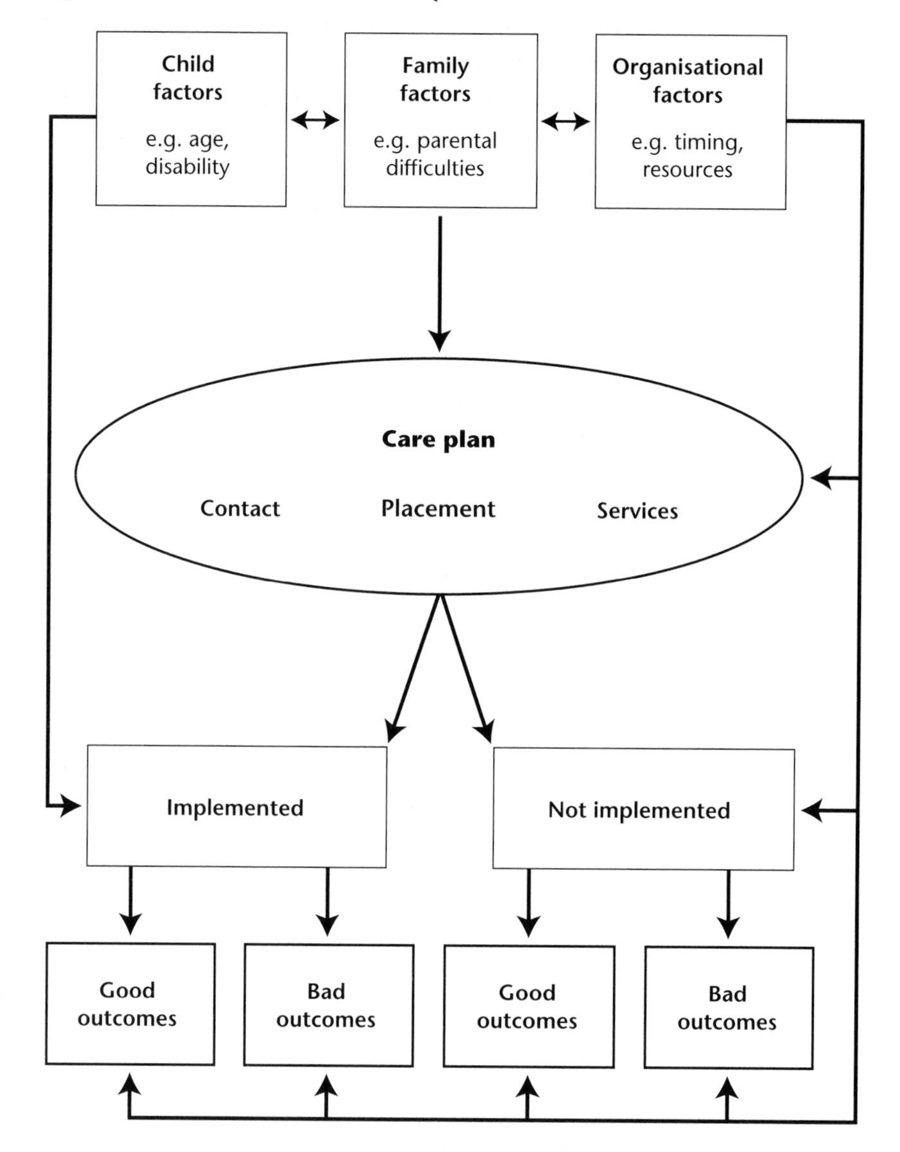

comprise the largest proportion of all children looked after – 64% of all those looked after at 31 March 2002. Meanwhile the 'volume' of care provided under care orders has risen by 25% since 1996 compared with a decrease under voluntary arrangements over the same period (DoH 2001a). Care order children are also staying in care longer.

These trends alone make children on care orders a particularly important group for people to study intensively. But they are also a very needy group. Although some studies have found little to distinguish children on care orders from those who are accommodated (Packman and Hall 1998; Brandon et al. 1999), they undoubtedly place substantial extra demands on social services in terms of preparation for legal proceedings and their associated costs. Their case management raises particularly complex issues, especially with regard to achieving placement stability.

Continuing debates about the status and quality of the court care plan

Debates about the status and quality of the court care plan are no less relevant today than when the study was commissioned. The picture remains mixed with some clear evidence of efforts to tackle some of the concerns as well as equally clear evidence of persisting concerns.

A study of the quality of care plans by the SSI (DoH 1998b) conveyed precisely this mixed set of messages. The study identified a broad consensus among the judiciary that plans had improved since the early years of the legislation, but found that concerns persisted over their variability with respect to scope, detail, clarity of aims and use of contingencies. Similar concerns emerged in Hunt and Macleod's research investigating the implementation of care plans in a range of statutory proceedings (Hunt and Macleod 1999). Case law provides another indication of the kinds of cases that have provoked concern. In an overview of case law carried out by members of the judiciary for the present study, some of the issues singled out were time-scales, the availability of evidence and the avoidance of delay.

The persistence of concerns is not the result of lack of effort on the part of judiciary and government to clarify expectations of care planning and improve their quality. The Children Act Advisory Committee produced a useful report for the year 1994/5 (LCD 1995). A new *Handbook of Best Practice in Children Act Cases* was issued by the Children Act Advisory Committee in June 1997 (LCD 1997b), which brought together all previous decisions of the courts and outlined very clear judicial expectations of what care plans should contain. Government also issued new guidance in a 1999 circular (DoH 1999b), which provides a more coherent framework for care plan preparation than was found in the 1991 guidance.[3] Our study was not of course able to assess plans against this new framework, but its analysis remains wholly relevant because the latest circular incorporates all the dimensions from the 1991 guidance.

Steps have also been taken to clarify the status of the plan. Since the Adoption and Children Act 2002, the care plan now has statutory status and a care order cannot be made without considering a section 31A care plan. This amendment plugs a gap in the Children Act, but it seems unlikely to generate change by itself since consideration of the care plan has become routine over the last decade. In essence, this change simply brings law into line with practice.

Finally efforts have been made to increase the accountability of the social services when a care plan is agreed in court. The LAC circular mentioned above (DoH 1999b) introduced an obligation on senior officers in social services to endorse the care plan for the final hearing 'as an authority wide statement of its commitment to the plan' (para. 21). This measure was intended to address concerns among the judiciary that care planning was inappropriately devolved to individual frontline social workers. While the measure went some way to increasing the accountability of the local authority, it has not been sufficient to stem the calls to give courts greater powers to oversee implementation through post-care order reviews.

Efforts by government to enhance welfare outcomes for children in the public care

Since this study was launched there has been a major drive by government to improve the standards of care for looked-after children and to improve their welfare outcomes. This needs to be seen in the context of mounting concern over the life chances of looked-after children (Utting et al. 1997; HC Health Committee 1998). The 1998 report of the House of Commons was particularly uncompromising in its conclusions. While acknowledging that children arrive into the care system with acute and chronic difficulties, the House of Commons Committee concluded that the system itself must be held partly accountable.

> The extent to which the outcomes of looked-after children fall short of those of their peers in the general population is very worrying and it is difficult to resist the conclusion that the system itself is under-performing ... It would be a betrayal of looked-after children to suppose that significant improvements cannot be made with regard to outcomes (HC Health Committee 1998, p. xvii).

Current government policy has built on this analysis and its central thrust is to try and raise the standards of health, education and well-being of looked-after children and to bring them more closely in line with those of their peers.

These aims, first outlined in broad terms in *Modernising Social Services* (DoH 1998d), were formulated in detail in the Quality Protects programme (DoH 1998e). Quality Protects significantly increased expectations upon social services to help raise the standards of care for children who are looked after. For the first time national objectives had been set, aimed at improving children's life chances. What makes Quality Protects stand out from any of its predecessors is the explicit focus on developmentally based outcome measures of well-being as the basis for evaluating the performance of local authority social services. These include targets for health, education and emotional well-being, which could provide a basis for obtaining more consistent practice in the local authorities.

The impact of the Quality Protects programme is potentially far-reaching. Above all it demands a new mindset requiring practitioners and managers to plan services explicitly with a view to enhancing children's social functioning in all key domains. The role that the court care plans may play in enhancing children's welfare outcomes is a key question that is addressed in this study.

Debates about the need to establish a system of post care-order review and the influence of the Human Rights Act 1998

In its annual report of 1994/95 the Children Act Advisory Committee drew attention to the difficulties experienced by courts because of their inability to attach conditions to a care plan or to review its progress. However, at that time the Children Act Advisory Committee did not feel it had the evidence to warrant any changes in court powers being considered. The matter has not rested there. A continuing concern that plans may not be implemented, or that implementation may proceed too slowly, fuelled interest in the possibility of extending court powers after the making of a care order. So has the frustration felt by some members of the judiciary that their options under existing law are very limited. In principle they can refuse to make the order if they do not like the plan, but in reality this may leave children unprotected.

Substantial attention was given to this issue and to the advantages and drawbacks of introducing change in court powers at the President of the Family Division's 1997 Inter-disciplinary Conference at Highgate House (Thorpe and Clarke 1998). Some detailed practical steps were drawn up to suggest a way forward but it was recognised that this would require legislative change. The Prime Minister's Review of Adoption in July 2000 (Cabinet Office 2000) also took up this theme and recommended consultation on the merits and drawbacks of extending court powers after the making of a care order.

The first serious challenge to extend the role of courts post care order came from two cases that went to the Court of Appeal[4] and then to the House of Lords for judgement.[5] The cases were brought under the Human Rights Act 1998 and the powers and duties relating to care plan formation and implementation were central to both cases. As a result of the Court of Appeal judgement, for a brief period, courts were given extended powers under a starring system, which set out a framework for returning cases to court if there had been a violation of Human Rights. The guardian was to play a key role in this process. However, the House of Lords overturned the Court of Appeal decision and upheld the boundaries between the judiciary and the executive that were laid down in the Children Act, at least in part because it argued that such a radical departure from existing law would require a return to Parliament. But a warning note was sounded when the House of Lords stated: 'One of the questions needing urgent consideration is whether some degree of court supervision of local authorities discharge of their parental responsibilities would bring about an overall improvement in the quality of childcare provided by local authorities (HL 2002, para. 106).' It recognised that this question could not be answered by a court but recommended that it should be 'conducted without delay' (HL 2002, para. 106).

The Adoption and Children Act 2002

At the time of writing, no review on the lines suggested by the House of Lords has been conducted. Instead, the Adoption and Children Act 2002 has been used as a route to remedy some of the problems identified by the Court of Appeal and the House of Lords. What has been introduced might be seen as a 'halfway house'. Reviews are to be chaired by independent reviewing officers to strengthen their rigour and introduce a greater degree of independence into the process. A route back into court has also been created through the powers given to reviewing officers to reinvolve a Children and Family Court Advisory and Support Service (CAFCASS) officer.

At the time of writing, this is where matters stand; but the settlement seems fragile and the need to establish whether the court could exert a helpful role post-order remains as pertinent as ever. Identifying the obstacles to plan implementation should help to show whether courts will be better placed than social services to overcome the constraints.

The impact of the Human Rights Act 1998

As already noted, the cases referred to above were brought under the Human Rights Act 1998. The specific questions to be tested by the cases were over the right to a fair trial (Article 6) and the right to family life (Article 8). The answers from the House of Lords have upheld the rights of legal redress afforded by the Children Act 1989 and have clarified that non-implementation of a care plan is not *per se* a breach of human rights. Even more basically, the House of Lords judgement has confirmed that the Children Act 1989 is fully compatible with the Human Rights Act.

At this point no other cases have been brought to test the impact of the Human Rights Act on care plan implementation and it is far too soon to judge its potential impact. But it also needs to be recognised that the decision to introduce a system of starring through the use of the Human Rights Act 1998 was in some ways a device to address the wider concerns among the judiciary that the childcare system itself was failing children in public care. Indeed Lord Mackay observed in relation to the House of Lords judgement: 'When I suggested that a starring system should be considered it was in order to address these problems generally rather than problems with Human Rights that I had in mind' (HL 2002, para. 111).'

Even though the challenge to local authorities foundered, the test cases have already been important in bringing to the fore a central question, which as yet remains unanswered – what does constitute a human rights breach in respect of care planning?

Finally, the cases have once again demonstrated the importance of getting the care plan right during its formative stage. Understanding the relationship between care plan formation and implementation – one of the aims of this study – continues to be a key matter for practitioners, managers and policy-makers.

In short, all these considerations based on practice, law and policy give the study continuing relevance today. Moreover, despite the considerable attention given to care plans recently, some basic questions remain unanswered. How do we recognise a good care plan? Are children with difficult histories and profiles less likely to have their plan fulfilled than those who are undamaged? What kinds of factors influence placement choice and are some placement choices linked with greater stability or better child outcomes than others? What do parents, children and carers have to say about the care planning process and how satisfied are they with the final plans and their implementation? These are just some of the questions this study explores.

Summary

1. This book presents the findings of a research study of 100 children placed on care orders and followed up for 21 months. Children made subject to care orders are the fastest growing contingent of all looked-after children and they have high levels of need; yet there is very little research focused exclusively on care order children. This study aims to identify what works, for which child and in what circumstances.

2. The Children Act 1989 strengthened the planning framework for all looked-after children. By outlining how the local authority plans to look after the child if a care order is granted, the care plan acquired a role in helping courts decide whether or not to make a care order. It also provided a blueprint for later action by social services.

3. The main purpose of the research was to examine the influence of the court care plan on case management and child outcomes. It set out to explore the extent of care plan implementation, the reasons for non-fulfilment of the plan, and the relationship between implementation and outcome.

4. Since the introduction of the Human Rights Act in 1998, the care plan has been the subject of judgements by the Court of Appeal and the House of Lords. Concerns have focused on the extent, nature and effects of non-implementation of the plan.

5. The Adoption and Children Act 2002 made care plans mandatory. It also introduced a possible route back to court through the appointment of reviewing officers with a link to CAFCASS; but there are continuing discussions about the boundaries between judicial and social work decision-making.

6. The Quality Protects programme, with government support, has increased the amount of attention paid to welfare outcomes for looked-after children. It is therefore particularly important to identify the part that the court care plan can play in promoting children's welfare.

[1] The conclusion of the research report *Social Workers and Solicitors in Child Care Cases* (Hilgendorf 1981) was: 'We have argued that the system as it is currently organised and operated gives little encouragement to social workers and social services departments to place greater emphasis on developing plans for the child's future, or to consider carefully what will be achieved by obtaining a care order ... The system itself is geared towards placing an emphasis on the justification for intervention rather than what intervention would achieve.'

[2] Section 118 of the Adoption and Children Act 2002 lays down that no care order may be made until the court has considered a care plan from the local authority. The care plan is now known as a section 31A plan.

[3] The Children Act 1989: Guidance and Regulations, Volume 3: Family Placements (DoH 1991a) and Volume 4: Residential Care (DoH 1991a, paras 2.43–2.62).

[4] *Re W & B (Children)* and *Re W (Children)*, Court of Appeal, 23 May 2001.

[5] House of Lords Judgements: Re S (FC); Re S and others; Re W and others (First Appeal) (FC); *Re W and others* (Second Appeal) (Consolidated Appeals), 14 March 2002.

2 Methodology

Introduction

As mentioned in Chapter 1, the research reported in this book was a prospective study of 100 children from 57 families. The children came from five local authorities, and they were all made subject to care orders consecutively between March and September 1997. A mixture of quantitative and qualitative methods were used in analysis of the data.

This chapter begins with a profile of the local authorities that took part in the research, then moves on to describe the two main phases of the study design. Because of the importance attached to children's welfare outcomes, the next section is devoted to an outline of our conceptual approach, which was based on the seven dimensions of the 'Looking After Children' (LAC) framework. This is followed by an explanation of our two measures of welfare outcome – first of all the dynamic measure of welfare progress, which tracks changes over time, and then the more static measure of welfare status, which records the standards reached by children at the end point of the study.

Profile of the local authorities

Of the five local authorities that took part in the study, three were inner cities, one was a large rural county and the last one comprised a suburban area on the fringes of a large city.

Three considerations guided the choice of authorities. First, areas that had implemented the LAC schedules were chosen. Second, an attempt was made to include a range of authorities with varied socio-economic profiles and a mixture of urban and rural areas. Third, authorities were chosen whose social work practice – as assessed by key indicators such as the number of children coming into care and numbers of children on the child protection register – was broadly within the normal range for England and Wales.

Another way of exploring the representativeness of the authorities is by reference to the 'York index' (Carr-Hill et al. 1997; DoH 2000b). This is a measure that is used to provide standardised information on comparative levels of disadvantage. It takes into consideration the number of children living in families on income support, children with long-term illness, children living in flats, population density and children in single parent families. As this is a recently developed measure the only figures available relate to 1999. However, it is unlikely that there has been a substantial shift in the relative levels of disadvantage in any of the authorities during the last few years.

Using this measure, our authorities encompassed the full range from the most to the least disadvantaged (see below). In terms of the children in the sample, there was also a good spread on this measure. Forty-four children from 25 families came from authorities ranked in the top 10–20% of disadvantage while a further 43 children from 23 families came from an authority ranked in the 10% least disadvantaged authorities.

Authority 1

Authority 1 is a comparatively small suburban area on the fringes of a large city with an estimated total population of 175,000, including just under 40,000 children. Approximately 8.5% of the child population is from ethnic minorities, with Asian and 'Other Groups' being by far the most common ethnic minority groups in the 1991 Census. The population density is considerably lower than for the large city it abuts. Parts of the borough are relatively affluent, with a large number of commuters; however there are still some areas of relatively high deprivation. In these areas there is a higher concentration of ethnic minority families and of children living with lone parents. On the York index Authority 1 was close to the average for the 149 local authorities in England. Five children in five families from this authority are included in the sample.

Authority 2

Authority 2 is an inner-city with an estimated population of 165,000, including 28,500 children. The borough embraces extremes of wealth and deprivation. There are some areas of expensive, privately owned housing, while other areas feature large council estates, high levels of poverty and other factors associated with social exclusion. There is a substantial black population, approximately one-quarter of the total population, and this is concentrated in the areas of greatest poverty. Most of the black population is black British, Afro-Caribbean or African in origin. Authority 2 is one of the ten most disadvantaged local authorities in England according to the York index. Fourteen children in eight families from this authority are included in the sample.

Authority 3

Authority 3 is a densely populated, medium-sized coastal city with a total population of just over 200,000 people, of which approximately 45,000 were children at the time of the 1991 Census. While there are several areas that are among the most affluent in the region, the five poorest wards within the city are among the poorest 10% of wards in England and Wales. The city is predominantly white, with less than 8% of children being non-white (the majority of these being of Asian origin); however, the black and Asian population is highly concentrated in the poorest wards. Authority 3 is in the most disadvantaged 20% of local authorities according to the York index. Thirty children in seventeen families from this authority are included in the sample.

Authority 4

Authority 4 is another medium-sized coastal city, with a total population of 175,000 and just over 50,000 children. The city has had a fairly low level of unemployment in the 1990s. However, this disguises a high level of poorly paid employment, which is largely the product of recent major adjustments within the industrial base of the city. Authority 4 is very densely populated, with an old and run-down housing stock. The population is largely white, with less than 2% of the population being from ethnic minority groups (substantially of Chinese and Indian origin). Authority 4 is very close to Authority 3 in disadvantage as measured by the York index – though it is just outside the most disadvantaged 20% of authorities. Eight children in four families from this authority are included in the sample.

Authority 5

Authority 5 is a large, mainly rural local authority with some small towns and coastal resorts. The total population is over 1.1 million people, with almost 300,000 children according to the 1991 Census. The county is very affluent (with less than 2% of the population on income support) and is largely white. (Only 2.5% of the total population, and less than 1.5% of children, come from non-white backgrounds.) There is considerable disparity of income, with the areas of council housing and the highest rates of unemployment concentrated in a small market town. In contrast with the other authorities, Authority 5 has a score on the York index that places it in the least disadvantaged 10% of English authorities. Forty-three children in 23 families from this authority are included in the sample.

The research design

A small number of interviews were held at the outset of the study with members of the judiciary, to explore their views on the care planning framework and how well it was working. This was to ensure that the research would take account of issues of particular importance to the judiciary as well as to social service personnel and policy-makers.

For the research itself, a prospective design was chosen so that new cases could be followed up from the point at which the order had been made. The use of consecutive cases was considered an important feature of the study design. Although it resulted in an imbalance of cases between the five authorities, this disadvantage was more than offset by the knowledge that the cases represented the generality of all care orders made within a particular time period. This increases their value in informing practice.

The first phase

Phase 1 of the study started with an examination of the court case files to establish the background to the case and the reasons for making the care order, and to scrutinise the care plan. The study of the court files was followed by semi-structured interviews held with social workers with case responsibility, and then with the children's guardians and local authority solicitors who had been involved in the cases during care proceedings. These interviews had a number of objectives. They aimed to identify the main sources of concern about the child, to study the development of the care plan and the input of different personnel, and to determine the opinions of the three sets of professionals about the prospects of the plan being implemented successfully. Finally, the interviews also sought information on the child's welfare profile at the time the order was made.

On the basis of the information collated from all these sources, the researchers drew up a profile of the child's initial functioning using a modified version of the Looking After Children schedules specially adapted by the researchers. (This is explained under 'welfare outcome' later in the chapter.) Children's initial difficulties were classified according to the seven dimensions covered by the LAC materials (health, education, identity, family and social relationships, emotional and behavioural development (EBD), social presentation and self-care skills) and this provided the initial baseline against which change could be measured at the end of the study.

The second phase

In phase 2 of the study, an examination of social services' files was carried out to track the major developments in the case from the care order to the 21-month point, and also to construct a picture of the child's functioning based on review data, reports of planning meetings and health or education reports. The Looking After Children assessment and action records were also consulted where they had been completed at reviews, although they proved a rather patchy source of information. At their best, they provided a valuable picture of children's progress, but more frequently the data were incomplete either because the assessment and action records had only been partially filled in or because they had not been updated regularly. The difficulties in using the AARs to obtain consistent information raise some important general issues, but in terms of the effects on the research, access to other sources helped meet the gaps. Nor had it ever been the intention of the study to rely exclusively on the AARs for data collection.

In addition to the file studies, semi-structured second stage interviews were held with social workers with case responsibility at the 21-month point. The interviews aimed to provide an up-to-date picture of the case, to establish the worker's judgement about success in implementation and to explore reasons for non-fulfilment. The final function of the interview was to determine the social worker's assessment of the child's progress on each of the seven dimensions of the Looking After Children schedules compared with the child's initial state at the time of the care order.

Second stage semi-structured interviews were also held with current carers, children over the age of 7 and birth parents. These interviews explored the views and experiences of all three groups concerning the care plan and care order. Current carers were asked to provide an assessment of the child's functioning according to the seven LAC dimensions and to rate progress since they had begun to care for the child. They were also asked to complete a short standardised questionnaire, the Strengths and Difficulties Questionnaire

(SDQ), which measures emotional and behavioural functioning in children aged 4–16. (See Appendix 2.) This instrument was chosen first because of its proven reliability, because of its speed and ease of completion, and because its framework, as with the LAC materials, identifies strengths as well as difficulties. The self-report version of the SDQ, which has been designed for use by 11–16 year olds, was completed by all those who came within this age band and agreed to be interviewed (Goodman et al. 1998).

For the purpose of providing a mental state assessment, parents and carers also completed the GHQ12 – a brief version of the General Health Questionnaire (Goldberg and Williams 1991). This is a well-established standardised psychiatric screening questionnaire, which is widely used in surveys. (More details are to be found in Appendix 2.)

Finally, the researchers collated all second stage data on the child's functioning at the 21-month point in order to derive a score of welfare change over the period, and also to determine the number and severity of deficits in each of the LAC seven dimensions compared with the standards implicit in the materials.

Access and consent

The researchers wrote letters to parents and carers, which were sent with a covering letter from social services explaining the purpose of the study and inviting them to take part. A contact number for the researchers was provided so that those willing to participate could opt in to the study. A follow-up letter was sent out to those who did not respond the first time but no further contact was attempted thereafter. Parents and carers chose the interview venue and the majority of the interviews were held in people's own homes. All carers were assured of confidentiality and that their comments could not be traced back to them.

Before the child sample could be contacted agreement had to be obtained from the Lord Chancellor's Department and it was on this basis that a lower age limit of 7 was established. A number of safeguards were also required by the LCD, which were also agreed jointly with the Department of Health:

- All children were to be given the opportunity to be accompanied by a person of their own choosing.
- Children could stop the interview at any time.

- Children were to be given the opportunity to refuse the use of a tape recorder.
- Extra time was built into the interviews to help children with learning difficulties.
- All respondents were assured that interview material would be totally anonymised.

Permission to interview children aged 11 or under was negotiated first via current carers and with birth parents wherever practicable, whether or not they had consented to be interviewed themselves. If adult consent was forthcoming, the child was contacted. Those aged 11 or older were contacted directly but their carers were also notified simultaneously. Two versions of the letters were prepared, to cater separately for the younger and older children, and a young person contributed to their design, content and style. The letters included common questions that young people might wish to be answered before giving consent and an opportunity to discuss the issues was provided by the researchers before the young people decided whether to take part in the study. Two versions of the interview schedule were also used to take account of the age structure of the children and young people.

Response rates

The professionals

The response rate among social workers was excellent. All social workers with case responsibility for every case took part in both phases of the study. The response rate was also high among children's guardians. Twenty-five guardians were interviewed, giving information on 89 children from 53 of the 57 families; only two guardians were not interviewed. All local authority solicitors who had been involved in the proceedings were interviewed.

Service users and providers

Table 2.1 provides information on the response rate among current carers; these were the carers who were looking after the child or a group of siblings at the end of the study. As can be seen, there was some variation in the response rate but the overall average was good and it was a clear advantage that the current carers covered all placement options. (Some interviews were also held with previous carers, which provided useful additional qualitative material.)

Table 2.1 ***Current carers who were interviewed***

Current carers	Eligible for interview[a]	Interviewed	Response rate %
Adopters and prospective adopters	18	11	61
Foster carers	27	18	67
Kinship carers	12	10	83
Residential carers	7	6	86
Birth parents in a caring role[b]	6	3	50
Total	**70**	**48**	**69**

[a] Five young people had disappeared by the end of the study or were living independently so that no carers were therefore available for interview.

[b] In our classification, the birth parent is the person who looked after the child from birth onwards. Non-resident fathers who had just taken over the care of the child were classified as 'kinship carers'.

Interviews were also held with birth parents not currently caring for their children. The response rate here was poor – only nine took part (18% of those eligible) – which is likely to be explained by a variety of factors, though we can only speculate. The timing of the interviews, 21 months down the line, may have been one factor. Parents, who were already demotivated at the time of the final hearing, may have not wished to go over painful ground. Others may have lost interest in taking part in an inquiry which at that point may no longer have seemed relevant to their situation. Some were difficult to trace. In some cases the placement of children at home had only recently broken down and parents were probably distressed.

The response rate among children

A total of 49 children were eligible for interview and of these 26 (53%) took part. Only four children refused to be interviewed and another three were difficult or impossible to track down. (Two had absconded and the whereabouts of a third was not clear after he had left care.) However, the most common reason for children not being interviewed was that carers refused to allow them to take part. This affected sixteen children. It related entirely to younger children and usually to those who were in a placement that was considered permanent, whether that was with their mother (five children in two families), the wider family (three children in two families) or an adoptive placement (seven children in three families). By contrast, all eligible children bar one placed in foster care were interviewed, although in some cases the interviews were delayed owing to foster carer related circumstances.

The children and young people interviewed included almost all those in residential care, most of those who had moved on to independence and the majority of those aged over 7 living in foster care. As a result, the children interviewed – and therefore their opinions – are not necessarily representative of the sample as a whole. However, the corollary to this is that they provide good information on some core elements of social work – foster care, leaving care and residential care. Children and young people living in less permanent placements were also over-represented and this too needs to be noted.

Finally and importantly, it should be noted that all names have been changed and very exceptionally minor case details have been altered, to preserve the anonymity of the children, parents and carers. Place names too are fictional.

Limitations of the research design

Welfare outcome

The analysis of welfare outcome relied heavily on secondary data, as outlined above. The feedback from the panel considering the research application had raised the question of whether it would be possible to conduct child interviews at the start and endpoints in order to measure welfare outcome more robustly. It is acknowledged that this approach would have been more satisfactory than reliance on secondary sources. However, it was argued that such an aim went beyond the resources and scope of the study and this point was accepted by the Department of Health.

Feedback from carers, parents and children

Funding for this component of the study was given several months after the initial grant. It was therefore not possible to obtain immediate feedback following the making of the order and to tie in the views of users systematically with those of the professionals. The timing of the interviews with users is also likely to have reduced the numbers of birth parents who were able and willing to participate. However, the advantages of being able to tap into the experiences of users, even if only at the end point of the study, was considered to outweigh the methodological limitations that have been identified.

Children's welfare outcome: our conceptual approach

Our starting-point in measuring children's welfare was that it is necessary to separate welfare outcomes from 'service outcomes' such as the implementation of the care plan. It was recognised that these two types of outcome are different, and they need to be kept separate so that they can be compared with each other. It was also recognised that the same events may result in different welfare outcomes for different people including birth parents, other relatives and carers. The impact of the care order on adults has not been ignored, but in keeping with legislation and policy, our main focus has been on the welfare of the child.

The Looking After Children framework

The study drew extensively on the 'Looking After Children' (LAC) framework as a basis for evaluating child welfare outcome. This framework was originally developed as a result of discussions held by members of a Department of Health Working Party on Assessing Outcomes in Child Care (1987–91). The Working Party identified seven developmental dimensions along which children need to make good progress if they are to achieve long-term well-being in adult life. These dimensions are health, education, identity, family and social relationships, social presentation, emotional and behavioural development and self-care skills. The working party took the view that children will only be able to make good progress if their needs in each of the seven dimensions are met.

The distinctive features of the LAC framework are first that it emphasises child development in the evaluation of welfare outcome, and second that it takes a multi-dimensional view. The LAC materials ask: What does the child need? Who should meet those needs and how? Is the child receiving what might be expected of a 'reasonable' parent? By collecting data on service inputs and on children's progress over time, it is possible to review how satisfactorily the service inputs have met the child's needs.

Uses of the LAC framework

The Working Party generated a set of tools known as 'assessment and action records' to help practitioners plan and review interventions with children and to monitor progress along each dimension. Although designed initially for monitoring individual progress, the AARs have also been used for management information purposes. When aggregated, the data can generate information on how effectively the service is meeting the needs of looked-after children.

The LAC framework has proved highly influential on current government policy and practice. The conceptual approach based on child developmental domains has influenced the formulation of objectives in the Quality Protects programme and the associated indicators to monitor children's welfare outcomes. While the LAC framework was originally developed to help monitor service efficacy and the progress of children who were being looked after by the local authority, it can be used in a variety of parenting contexts and it has since been extended to children in need. The seven domains underpin the *Framework for the Assessment of Children in Need* (DoH 1999c), and the more recent Integrated Children's System (Rose 2002), which has been developed to apply to all children in need including those who are looked after. The latter will also strengthen the link between information gathered on individual children and aggregated data.

Reasons for using the LAC framework in the current study

There were three main reasons for deciding to use the LAC framework in the present study. First, the aim was to ensure that our own approach to the conceptualisation of welfare outcome was soundly based in professional thinking. Second, we felt that the findings would be more readily transferable if we tapped into the main frameworks used by government, policy-makers, service managers and practitioners. Third, it was hoped that the assessment and action records completed in the local authorities would provide a valuable source of data for tracking the progress of individual children and that these materials would be more systematic and comprehensive than any traditional evaluation tools. To maximise the prospects of obtaining good data from the AARs, one criterion for the initial choice of local authorities in this study was their familiarity with and use of the materials.

Adapting the Looking After Children framework for research purposes

Since the LAC framework and its associated materials were not designed for researchers, the exercise of using the framework in this study presented a number of challenges, which had to be overcome. The way in which they have been overcome is not above criticism, but our experience may contribute to the development of other research methodologies in this area.

Although a few studies have experimented with using the LAC framework for outcome measurement,[1] its use as a research tool is still in an early stage of development. At present, with the exception of the measures used for collecting information on emotional and behavioural development, the tools have not yet been validated, and there are no longitudinal data to indicate whether certain dimensions of child functioning play a greater or lesser role in optimising children's welfare during childhood or in later life. Within a given dimension of child functioning, too, there is no available research to identify whether some areas of performance are more important than others. As a result, it was not possible in this study to draw on any existing research methodology using the LAC framework or to know with certainty whether to attach greater priority to some themes than to others. We attempted a 'balancing act' when dealing with a cluster of themes on any one dimension, but we followed the priorities of the main LAC model as far as possible and our parameters for judging welfare outcome were performance on the seven dimensions of child well-being.

Keeping the focus on child developmental outcomes

The research began with an examination of court files, which contained a great deal of important information. However, the LAC framework does not fit easily alongside a problem-based categorisation grounded in the concept of 'significant harm' or 'beyond parental control'. In drawing up the baseline profile of children's welfare at the time of the care order it was necessary to reframe some of the descriptions of children's difficulties into unmet developmental needs so that they could provide a baseline account for the final welfare progress comparison. This ensured consistency between the initial baseline and endpoint profile but it also meant that some specificity of information was lost. People may wish to know quite precisely how far a care order has been able to reduce offending behaviour, school exclusions or teen pregnancies; but according to the LAC model these issues are categorised respectively as unmet needs within emotional and behavioural development, education or health. It is only when the categories are unpacked that these issues can be more thoroughly explored.

Separating inputs from welfare outcomes

Because the AARs were initially developed as tools for practitioners, the materials cover both inputs and welfare outcome data within their objectives. For example, the LAC AAR for health lists five assessment objectives, which cover both direct child welfare outcomes such as 'the child is normally well' and process indicators or inputs such as 'all ongoing health conditions and disabilities are being dealt with'. When drawing up the criteria for measuring outcome in the study, we decided to exclude inputs and process indicators as far as possible because service delivery was being analysed separately. In our use of the materials, the sole focus was on actual child functioning.

Distilling themes that would be applicable across all the age bands

The AAR materials use an age-related approach. There are six booklets, each intended for a specific age group: children aged under 1; 1–2; 3–4; 5–9; 10–14 and 15 and over. Although these all have in common the collection of data on each of the seven dimensions, the specific indicators vary according to the age of the child. For instance, the list of sub-objectives for education in the booklet catering for 3- and 4-year-olds includes communication skills and readiness for school. Hardly surprisingly, the educational criteria for 5- to 9-year-olds are very different, focusing on educational attainment and skill acquisition. In our own study we needed to remain sensitive to these age-related differences in children's experience as well as levels of performance, but it was neither desirable nor feasible to modify the outcome criteria specifically according to the age of the child as this would have resulted in excessive fragmentation of the sample. What seemed to be needed was a classification that would distil the key themes from each dimension to ensure that there would be a common way of comparing children's welfare outcome across the entire sample. The themes were distilled as follows:

Health:

- illnesses;
- disabilities;
- lifestyle; and
- safety;

Education:

- attendance;
- achievements; and
- development of skills and interests;

Identity:

- understanding of current situation;
- acceptance of current situation; and
- self-esteem;

Family and social relationships:

- continuity;
- attachments;
- family relationships; and
- friendships;

Social presentation:

- appearance; and
- behaviour;

Emotional and behavioural development:

- signs of disturbance or well-being;
- maturity or immaturity; and
- delinquency;

Self-care skills:

- What can the child do for himself/herself?
- Is it what is expected at this stage?

The basis for selection of sub-themes was threefold. First the themes chosen were considered the most important aspects of functioning within a given dimension. Second, they were measures that could be substantiated with supporting evidence to inform our judgement. Third, they applied to all ages and therefore covered the entire sample.

Because it was recognised that an element of subjectivity might bias the choice of themes that undoubtedly reflect the researcher's values, discussion was held with researchers involved in validation of the SDQ measures and in the development of the AARs. These researchers confirmed the overall choice of themes as sound. The caveat remains, however, that at present no research has been done to establish whether some themes are more important than others.

Measures of welfare outcome

Measure 1: Children's welfare progress

The study was specifically designed with a follow-up period to ensure that it would be possible to track change over time. To achieve this objective, the first measure of welfare outcome was concerned with the child's progress in all seven dimensions from the making of the order to the close of the study 21 months later. Change was measured against the child's individual starting-point. Four possibilities were identified:

- *Normal progress* The child entered the study with no problem in a given dimension and normal progress was maintained.
- *Amelioration of problems* The child entered the study with difficulties in a given dimension and improvement was detected by the end of the study.
- *Persistence of problems* The child entered the study with difficulties in a given dimension and the difficulties persisted.
- *Deterioration* The child entered the study with or without difficulties in a given dimension and the existing difficulties increased or new ones developed over the follow-up period.

When these categories were devised, due attention was paid to the risk of circularity. The question was asked: Do all children have access to good or bad outcomes? It will be seen that children with no initial problems could end up in Categories 1 or 4, whereas those with initial problems could have outcomes 2, 3 or 4. In the rating of welfare progress on each dimension, however, only two types of outcome were considered – that is, good (Categories 1 or 2) and poor (Categories 3 or 4). Since children with or without problems could have either outcome, the problem of circularity was removed.

Progress on each dimension was rated separately as 'good' or 'poor', then a composite judgement was arrived at by collating these performance ratings in each of the seven dimensions. The child's overall performance was calculated out of a score of seven. This was called the measure of the child's welfare progress.

As previously mentioned, the judgement on any given dimension involved a balancing act whereby progress across sub-themes was taken into account. For example, if a child had made considerable progress in attaching to a new carer and making friends, this would to some extent compensate for poor relationships with the birth family. As a result, the child might be said to have made progress on the dimension of 'family and social relationships' in spite of some deficits.

Measure 2: Children's endpoint welfare status

It is clearly essential to know whether a care order can improve children's life chances and, as we have seen, this question is best addressed through tracking changes in individual welfare over time. However, children can improve over 21 months and still fall short of a reasonable standard of welfare. There is a great need to define standards, not simply as a means of improving care in the public services but as a step towards comparing the welfare of looked-after children with that of their peers who are not looked after. A discussion of criteria for evaluating the welfare outcome of children in public care is contained in the House of Commons Health Committee's *Children Looked After by Local Authorities* (HC Health Committee 1998, Vol. 1) and it highlights the importance of using both an individualised and a comparative approach.

To ensure that the child's final welfare status was represented in the present study as well as progress made over time, a second measure of welfare outcome was developed based on the welfare standards implicit in the LAC framework. Information was collected on children's endpoint status in each of the seven dimensions to see how far the child had reached the optimum position laid down in the schedules. Failure to reach the required standard meant that the child had unmet needs or 'deficits'. Once again there were four possibilities on each dimension:

- no deficit;
- mild deficit;
- moderate deficit; or
- severe deficit.

The overall aim of the analysis, both of welfare progress and of welfare status, was to arrive at welfare scores for each child, but the collection of data by dimension also allowed for outcome to be looked at by dimension. There were two main reasons for this. In the first instance it allowed for the possibility that children might make uneven progress. Second, the collection of data by dimension as well as by child allowed us to ask how far care plan implementation was associated with vulnerabilities in any given domain and how far individual placement options were able to meet the children's diverse needs effectively. Third, it enabled us to look at the links between different aspects of welfare.

The researcher judgement

All sources of data were used to arrive at a researcher categorisation of the two welfare outcome measures to increase the reliability of the results. Where it had not been possible to interview children or carers, the researcher judgement was based on interviews with social workers and social service files, which frequently included school and medical reports as well as information held by social services.

Where there was any conflict of information gathered from different sources, the researchers considered the strength and extent of the evidence to decide which source to prefer. Data derived from the SDQ was not necessarily given a greater weighting because it was standardised; the SDQ simply formed a part of the total picture and could be over-ridden, as the aim was to form a researcher view using all sources of evidence. This precise point was discussed and agreed with the author of the SDQ as a correct way to proceed.

To test the reliability of our approach to the analysis of the two welfare measures, a number of cases were independently rated by three of the research team. Thirty-three cases were independently rated to assess the direction of change and a high level of agreement was found on each of the four options. But when further efforts were made to rate the degree of change in more detail, to see if the sensitivity of the change measure could be increased, agreement proved far less common. For this reason the final measure of welfare progress remained as outlined earlier.

A similar exercise was carried out to test inter-researcher reliability for the welfare status analysis. Independent judgements were made in 24 cases and high inter-rater reliability was achieved (a correlation of 0.6 for six of the seven dimensions). Inter-rater reliability was even higher for ratings of severity in the deficits (0.894). The only significant discrepancy occurred in the rating of self-care skills, and this was a result of different interpretations of the concept. It was dealt with by clarification of the definition.

Statistical analysis

Statistical tests were carried out to discover whether certain selected variables (such as age, children's problems and the number of moves made after the order) were associated first with implementation of the placement plan and second with our two measures of welfare outcome. Details of the tests are given in Appendix 1. Statistical analysis of contact arrangements was also carried out to investigate their relationship with implementation of the placement plan and outcome. It was not possible to analyse service aspects of the plan statistically because of the diversity of the provision and the small numbers receiving different types of service.

Length of follow-up

The length of the follow-up period in the study was 21 months. There is always a degree of arbitrariness in any follow-up period and it is well known that outcomes measured at a given point may not be stable over time. It needs therefore to be recognised that results might differ if the study were replicated at a later stage. The 21-month period had advantages and drawbacks. It was long enough to show up change in some dimensions such as family and social relationships and self-care skills, but it was quite a short time-frame for witnessing improvement in emotional and behavioural difficulties. A study that aimed to provide a truly comprehensive analysis of welfare outcome would have to pursue children into adulthood, and this is presumably more than the patience of funding bodies would allow.

Summary

1 The study was designed as a prospective study of 100 children from 57 families. The children came from five local authorities, and they were all made subject to care orders consecutively between March and September 1997. A mixture of quantitative and qualitative methods were used in analysis of the data.

2 Of the five local authorities that took part in the study, three were inner cities, one was a suburban area on the fringes of a large city and the fifth covered a large rural county. All the authorities selected were familiar with the LAC schedules. They presented a range of socio-economic profiles covering differing levels of social disadvantage.

3 Phase 1 of the study started with an examination of the court case files to establish the background to the case, the reasons for the care order and details of the care plan. This was followed by semi-structured interviews with social workers, children's guardians and local authority solicitors. Apart from helping to identify the main sources of concern and charting the development of the care plan, the interviews helped to build up a picture of the child's welfare profile at the time when the order was made.

4 In Phase 2 social services files were examined to track major events and changes in the child's welfare during the 21-month follow-up period. Semi-structured interviews were held with social workers who had case responsibility at the end point. Interviews were also held with current carers, children over the age of 7 and birth parents, to take account of their experiences. Short standardised questionnaires (the SDQ and the GHQ) were used to help identify the child's strengths and difficulties and the degree of stress experienced by the carer.

5 Children's welfare outcome was conceptualised as in the Looking After Children framework. This meant that children's progress was assessed according to seven dimensions – health, education, identity, family and social relationships, social presentation, emotional and behavioural development and self-care skills. To structure the analysis of outcome still further, several themes were distilled from each dimension. This framework was used in assessing children's welfare both at the start and at the end of the study.

6 The study developed and used two measures of welfare outcome. The first, which was called 'welfare progress', was a dynamic measure indicating the direction of change over the follow-up period. The second, 'welfare status', was concerned with the standard reached.

---

[1] See for example Monck et al. (2003); Sinclair et al. (2003); Bailey et al. (2002); Ward and Skuse (2001a); Maluccio et al. (2000); Brandon et al. (1999).

3 Description of the sample

Introduction

In this chapter information from the court files has been supplemented with information drawn from the first stage interviews with social workers and guardians and confirmed from social work records. The chapter starts by outlining the demographic characteristics of the children and their families, before moving on to describe children's needs and difficulties and the adult problems that underpinned the need for the care order. The final section documents previous input to the family in the form of child protection registration and previous social work involvement.

The information drawn from the study of court files was rich in some areas and poor in others, because the social workers' reports to the court reflected the reasons why they had been written; they presented details of the previous history of the family, the events that provoked care proceedings, and evidence that children were suffering (or were at risk of suffering) significant harm. This evidence tended to be concentrated on parental difficulties and parental behaviour. There was much less emphasis on children's experience and children's difficulties – except where information about the children's own actions was brought forward to prove allegations of 'beyond parental control' – and consequently much of the information about children's initial problems has come from social work sources. However, it is interesting to note the material selected for attention in the judicial setting.

The characteristics of the children

Age and gender

The average age of the 100 children was 5.7 years at the time of the final hearing. Exactly half the sample was less than 5 years old while half was 5 years or over. Table 3.1 presents a breakdown by age using the LAC age categories, as this framework guided much of our analysis.

In terms of gender the proportions were fairly evenly balanced, although there were slightly more girls than boys.

Table 3.1 ***Age and gender of children at final court hearing***

Age[a] (yrs)	Boys	Girls	Total
<1	7	5	12
1	5	7	12
2	3	7	10
3	6	3	9
4	4	3	7
5	3	3	6
6	5	2	7
7	1	2	3
8	1	3	4
9	3	3	6
10	1	1	2
11	–	5	5
12	2	1	3
13	4	2	6
14	1	2	3
15	–	5	5
Total	**46**	**54**	**100**

[a] The ages are grouped according to the LAC age bands.

Comparability of the sample

In 1997/98 the national picture was that 14% of all children who started to be looked after were on interim or full care orders, while in the sample authorities a year later the range varied from 9% to 17% – broadly in line with the national average. However, as can be seen from Table 3.2, our sample was more heavily weighted towards young children. It seems unlikely that this bias was a result of a substantial over-representation of young children in the study areas. More plausibly, it may suggest a more proactive approach by the social services departments to the seeking of parental responsibility – but this is unproven.

Table 3.2 ***Age distribution of sample children and all children placed on section 31 full care orders in England and Wales in 1997/8***

Age bands (yrs)	Children made subject to care orders in England and Wales[a] %	Sample children %
< 1	12	12
1–4	24	38
5–9	25	26
10–15	26	24
16 and 17	11	0
	(n=1100)[b]	**(n=100)**

Source: DoH Personal Social Services Local Authority Statistics (1998) *Children Looked After by Local Authorities: Year Ending 31 March 1998 England*

[a] Figures have been rounded.

[b] Discrepancies in national figures derive from there being different local authority collection sources from those used by central government.

Ethnicity

Fourteen of the 100 children and young people from nine families (16% of the families) in the sample came from minority ethnic backgrounds, a rate that is similar to the 16% found by Brophy (2000) in a sample of children going through care proceedings in 1993–4.[1] Of the fourteen children, nine children were of dual heritage of whom four were White/African and four were White/Asian; the remaining child had a white mother and an Arab father. The remaining five were black children whose parents were both of Afro-Caribbean origin. Despite the very small sample size, the higher numbers of children from dual heritage families appears in line with other studies (Hunt et al. 1999). There were no asylum-seekers in the sample and all children had English as their first language. Ten of the fourteen children were boys whereas in the White British sample girls outnumbered boys (50:36). Exactly half the minority ethnic sample was four or under, the same pattern as for the white children.

Sibling group membership

The composition of sibling groups is represented in Table 3.3. It can be seen that while only six families (9.5% of the total) had four or more children in the sample, these families account for 29% of the total number of children. Seven of the children were in multiple birth groups (two sets of twins and one of triplets).

Table 3.3 ***Composition of sibling groups***

Number of children in one family made subject to care order	Number of families	Total number of children
1	38	38
2	6	12
3	7	21
4	3	12
5	2	10
6	0	0
7	1	7
Total	**57**	**100**

Household composition

As Table 3.4 shows, at the time of the action that led to care proceedings, 29 of the 57 sample families were lone parent households and single mothers headed 27 of these – accounting for 54 of the children. Two children in two families were living with their fathers. The remaining 44 children in 28 families were living either with both their natural parents or with one parent (usually the child's mother) and a step-parent or cohabitee.

Table 3.4 ***Households in which children were living before care proceedings***

Main carers	Number of families	Total number of children
Mother only	27	54
Father only	2	2
Both natural parents	14	23
Mother and partner	12	19
Father and partner	2	2
Total	**57**	**100**

Out of the 28 families that began care proceedings with two parental adults, nine (that is, roughly one in three) had been reduced to single-parent households by the time the care order was made. Marriages were no more stable than cohabiting relationships in this respect since both suffered casualties; but the partnerships that broke up had been 'on the rocks' for some time and the increase in tension undoubtedly contributed to the initial risks to the child. A few partners who had good relationships with the mother supported her at the start of care proceedings; but they tended to move away when they were faced with responsibilities they had no wish to undertake. In two cases these moves may have been strategic as the mothers' solicitors were suggesting that the women might stand a better chance on their own, and the couples reunited after the care order was made. In one case a partner was persuaded to leave at an early stage so that rehabilitation might be officially considered.

Table 3.5 shows the household composition in terms of main carers at the time when the care order was made. This represents the situation at the point when our follow-up period began.

Table 3.5 ***Household composition at time when care order was made***

Main carers	Number of families	Total number of children
Mother only	36	72
Father only	2	2
Both natural parents	10	14
Mother and partner	7	10
Father and partner	2	2
Total	**57**	**100**

In the majority of sample families the mother was not working and was dependent on state benefits. Council housing predominated, and the overall picture, in common with that revealed by other studies of children on care orders (Bebbington and Miles 1989), was one of material deprivation. The most obvious exceptions to this pattern were two of the cases involving allegations of sexual abuse. In these cases the families were headed by two parents living in their own homes with above average earnings.

Children's needs and difficulties

As far as children's needs are concerned, there is a discrepancy between the highly focused information presented to the court and the information available from all sources. For the sake of completeness, both views are presented here.

Children under 5

The needs most commonly reported to the court in this age group were health needs and developmental delay. The incidence of one or other of these in the court reports was 36%, though information from all sources suggests that this figure should be nearer to 50% if all conditions requiring treatment are included. Asthma, eczema and speech difficulties were common in young children, along with defects of sight and hearing that required specialist attention.

Educational needs or learning difficulties were mentioned in the court reports in 22% of pre-school cases, although later information suggests that they were present to some degree in 46%. When educational needs were related narrowly to school performance there was little reporting of the child's progress at playgroup with the exception of social experience, and little attention was sometimes paid to the child's failure to develop skills and interests as a result of neglect and understimulation. Emotional and behavioural difficulties were also under-reported in court reports for the under-fives – particularly the degree of disturbance shown during care proceedings by children aged 3 and 4, when they had suffered the loss of significant adults. (Sleep disturbance, rocking and moaning were reported.) There was, however, adequate documentation of the risks relating to foetal alcohol syndrome in babies. For three very young children this led to the identification of potential learning difficulties and behavioural problems. In three other cases, where the mother had abused drugs during her pregnancy, there was some discussion of drug withdrawal symptoms in the child. These concerns were probably advanced primarily to provide evidence of significant harm. None of the placements were unduly delayed by the concerns and there is no later evidence of damage – at least within the time-scales of our study.

Children between the ages of 5 and 9

In the 5–9 age group school problems and emotional and behavioural difficulties began to be more prominent in the court reports, although there were no primary school children who had actually been excluded from school and there was no offending behaviour. Once again health needs were apparently underestimated in the reports; but even when measured by the more exacting LAC standards there was a lower level of health difficulty in this age group. Acording to the LAC measures 30% were rated as having initial health needs, compared with 50% of under-fives and 54% of children over 10. However, the children in this age group carried a huge burden in terms of disrupted family and social relationships. There were 96% of them who started the care period with problems in this area, as opposed to 64% of under-fives and 87% of those over 10. The importance of making adequate plans for contact in this age group is underlined.

Children over 10

In the court file studies the children who were aged 10 and over, and particularly those of 12 or over, present a markedly different picture from the other groups. Fourteen children over the age of 12 were reported to have emotional and behavioural difficulties, and this is identical with the figure culled from other sources such as interviews and social work files. Their behaviours included self-harming, eating disorders, aggressive behaviour, persistent offending and a range of other indications of distress. Most had difficulties at school. Seven had been expelled or suspended and the same number had a history of offending. A large proportion of these older children were teenagers who were often both troubled by their own abusive experiences and considered troublesome to others in their challenging and difficult behaviour. (See also DoH 1996a.)

The LAC framework draws our attention to the accompanying health risks. Twelve teenagers were found to be running serious risks as a result of unhealthy lifestyles, which included smoking, drinking or unsafe sexual activity – or else because they had chronic infirmities such as heart disease but refused to have medical examinations and treatment.

Children's initial problems: the baseline picture

To form a baseline against which future changes could be measured, from the time when the care order was made, information from all sources was collated and analysed according to the seven dimensions of the LAC framework. Figure 3.1 shows the number of difficulties that were recorded on each dimension. These data will be referred to again in the measurement of welfare outcomes.

Figure 3.1 ***Children with initial difficulties in each LAC area of welfare***

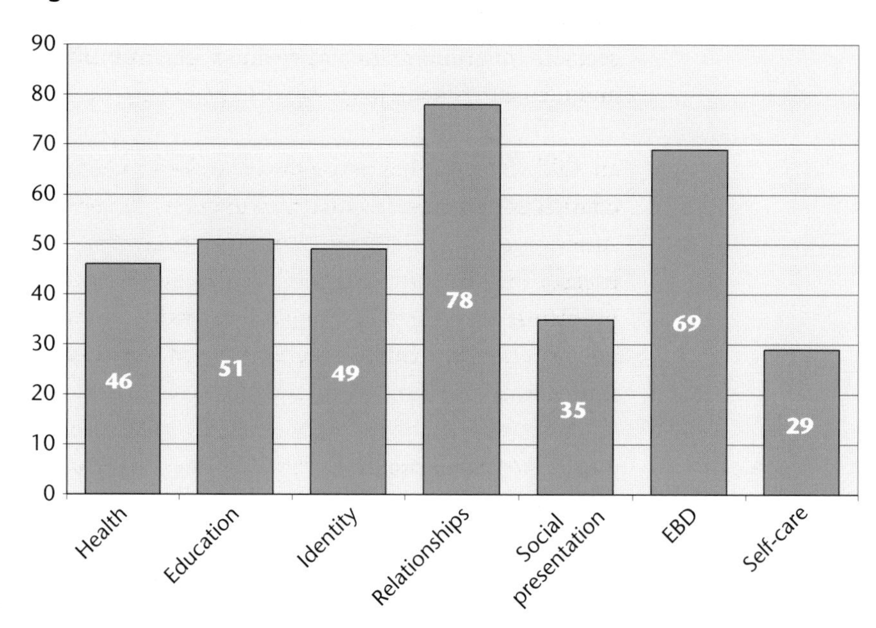

No distinction has been made between mild and serious problems because the quality of the data available at the start of the care order would not have allowed us to make these distinctions. For social workers as well as ourselves, knowledge of the children's needs and difficulties improved over time. However, the available evidence suggests that situations described as 'initial problems' at the start of the care order were sufficiently serious to interfere with children's everyday functioning. It was reasonable to expect that some of them would be improved by good parenting, although for others remedial action of some kind would be required.

Adult problems

Which adult difficulties were particularly important in the making of the care orders?

Previous studies have reported high incidences of mental illness, substance misuse and domestic violence in the carers of children on the child protection register or subject to care orders (Cleaver et al. 1999). However in our study we wanted to distinguish whether a particular difficulty was one of the key reasons for the making of the care order or whether its presence was merely contributory. For instance, in one case the concerns about the effect of the mother's manic depressive illness on her ability to care for her children were central to the evidence. In other cases where social workers considered mothers to be depressed, the extent or cause of the illness was unclear. It seemed important to go beyond the apparent incidence of parental difficulties and identify those that appeared to be key factors.

In Table 3.6 parental problems have been rated as 'major' factors where the court reports suggested that they underlay the principal reasons for the child suffering or being likely to suffer significant harm. (The number of families exceeds 57 because some concerns overlap.) As with children's initial problems, the judgements were independently rated by researchers working on the study and cross-checked with information from the first social work interviews.

Table 3.6 ***Adult problems that were major factors in care proceedings***

Type of problem	Number and percentage of families[a]	Number of children[a]
Alcohol misuse	11 (19%)	21
Drug misuse	7 (12%)	18
Alcohol and drug misuse	5 (9%)	5
Mental ill health	8 (14%)	14
Learning difficulties	13 (23%)	25
Domestic violence	11 (20%)	25

[a] The number of children exceeds 100 because they sometimes appear under more than one category.

The analysis of major adult problems once again highlights the importance of parental substance misuse within the sample. Drug or alcohol misuse or both was a major factor for 23 families involving a total of 44 children. Learning difficulties and domestic violence were also very important, each affecting one-quarter of the sample children. Mental illness appeared to be a major factor in eight families. In a few cases experts disagreed about whether a parent could be classed as mentally ill. In others a pre-existing illness had decreased or disappeared, or else depression was assessed to be a result of proceedings rather than a focus of concern in itself.

The analysis of adult problems by family found that eighteen families had no major problems of the type described (although they had other problems, for example with parent–child relationships or parenting skills). Twenty-one families had one major problem and eighteen had two or more. Alcohol misuse was strongly related to drug misuse and to domestic violence, and in two families where the parents had learning difficulties there were concerns about mental illness as well.

Previous input to the families

Child protection registration

Eighty-six of the children were on the child protection register prior to the final hearing. The fourteen children not placed on the child protection register (CPR) were either older children where the concerns focused on the child's behaviour rather than abuse (3), or younger children removed at birth or when very young with no plans for return home (6), or unusual cases (5). The unusual cases included one child who had serious disabilities, two where the mother's disability led to her not being considered to be able to care for her children, one teenager who wished to come into care because of his mother's drinking and one child who had been passed around her family a great deal and for whom this was the focus of concern.

The data on category of registration are not quite complete, as information was present for only 84 of the 86 children on the register. The distribution of categories is set out in Table 3.7. (NB Children were often registered under more than one category.)

Table 3.7 ***Children on the child protection register, by category of registration***

	Neglect	Physical abuse	Sexual abuse	Emotional abuse
Number of children[a]	50	29	18	20
% of children on CPR	60	35	21	24

[a] The total number of children exceeds 84 because some were registered under more than category. There is missing data on two children.

Neglect was by far the most common category, and the percentages of children registered for neglect were in excess of national trends prior to and including 1997.[2] Neglect encompassed a wide range of behaviours and family situations, ranging from babies born drug-addicted to children living for years with parents who could not provide for their needs for a variety of reasons. Children tended to be on the CPR for shorter periods for neglect than for other categories, but eleven children had also spent periods in accommodation prior to care proceedings. There was a strong relationship between registration for neglect and parental drug misuse or learning difficulties, a finding consistent with other studies (Stevenson 1998).

Physical abuse registration was associated with longer periods on the CPR. Twenty-two of the 29 children had been worked with for more than two years and thirteen had been on the CPR for more than two years. Physical abuse was not strongly associated with any type of parental difficulty.

Sexual abuse registration was also associated with long-term social work involvement, although only six children had been on the CPR for over two years. In several families there appear to have been concerns about the possibility of sexual abuse without social workers being able to prove it. There was a strong association between registration for sexual abuse and registration for physical abuse with twelve of the eighteen children registered for both.

Emotional abuse cases had usually been known to social services department for over two years (this applied to seventeen of the twenty children), though only four had been registered for over two years and most had been on the CPR for less than six months. Parental misuse of alcohol was a major factor for eleven of the twenty children.

Previous social work involvement

As Table 3.8 shows, there had been some involvement with social services in the vast majority of the families – sometimes over long periods of time – before the care order was applied for. However, the nature and extent of the service received by the families was very variable. It is necessary to see the input to individual children against a background of work with other children and the family as a whole.

No previous input

There were only three families where there had been no involvement before the application for the care order. In all these cases referrals were received from hospitals about grave concerns. There was one case of serious non-accidental injury, and in the other two cases a previous child had died in suspicious circumstances. Proceedings were initiated more or less immediately and the assessment of the family was undertaken during proceedings.

Table 3.8 ***Length of previous social work involvement***

	Number of children	Number of families
No previous input to these children or the family	3	3
Previous input to family but not to these children	11	7
Social work input to children for less than 1 year	17	11
Social work input to children for 1–2 years	26	10
Social work input to children for more than 2 years	43	26
Total	**100**	**57**

Previous input to the family only

In all, there were seven families where a baby was removed at birth. The concerns were focused on previous children. (In most cases previous children had been removed and placed for adoption.) The other four children who received no social work input for themselves prior to the application had recently been born into families where there had been long-term work with older children.

Social work input for less than a year

There are two groups of children who had social work input for less than a year. Twelve of them were very young – less than 2 years old at the time of the final hearing – and there had only been a short period of intervention prior to care proceedings. For most of these children social work input had been ongoing since birth. The other seven children were aged between 3 and 14, and they had only recently come to the attention of social services. Their situation was particularly bad; for example one family of three children were found to be living in cold, dirty and inhospitable conditions. Their parents had a mixture of mental health and learning difficulties and they had received intermittent help from adult services, but the family had moved house frequently and the condition of the children had never really been picked up.

Social work input for between one and two years

In several of these cases there had been input to the mother as a child or as a teenager.

A common theme was that the cases were initially considered to need family support without compulsory intervention. The use of authority appeared to be particularly problematic in a small sub-sample where the mothers had been known as minors or as adults with special needs themselves, and therefore the focus of work tended to emphasise supporting them as vulnerable people.

Support services were sometimes seen as requiring less skilled intervention, and cases were initially held by social work assistants or by students. As parents withdrew co-operation or concerns increased, social workers would be allocated and then legal orders applied for. However, this switch from a supportive focus to a child protection approach was not always easy to manage, and concerns often escalated in the meantime. The behaviour of some parents became more erratic and more extreme. Others had deteriorating problems of substance abuse where there had previously been good or good-enough parenting. The need for the order became gradually more and more apparent.

Social work input for more than two years

Slightly less than half the children in the sample had been known to social services for more than two years. The interviews with the social workers for these families highlight particularly acute difficulties in the work that had been undertaken prior to the commencement of proceedings. In particular there were issues in working with sexual abuse, with violent or threatening clients and with complex, multi-problem families.

Concerns about sexual abuse were a feature of many of these cases but, despite the concerns, social workers were of the opinion that they did not have sufficient evidence to start proceedings and the children therefore remained at home. However, the possibility of sexual abuse was not the only concern. Neglect was common, as a result of poor parenting skills (sometimes linked to substance abuse or learning difficulties) and there was physical risk from violent cohabitees. The impetus for the care order applications often came when the assessment started to focus more widely on the general development and care of the children.

A common theme in all these families was a long history of resistance to social services. In some cases this took the form of direct threats or violence. Threats to social workers are noted in the court reports as making work with the family very difficult, and even when social workers did not experience threatening or violent behaviour in these families, they tended to feel that the family was resistant or collusive.

A group of nine young people in eight families in the cases worked with for more than two years can be identified as 'troubled and troublesome' teenagers. The focus of social work concern here was the behaviour of the children, though there were often related concerns about parenting that was seen to have caused or contributed to the young person's challenging behaviour. All but one of the young people aged over 13 who had been worked with for over two years, and only one teenager known for less than two years, came into this category. Thus it appears that cases involving rebellious adolescents tended to be worked with for a long time before coming to proceedings.

This group includes the seven young people for whom offending behaviour was identified by the time of the final hearing and the seven who had been excluded from school prior to the final hearing. All the young people were between 13 and 15 and there was an even split between boys (4) and girls (5). All were identified as having behavioural difficulties. These were often acute and included violent and threatening behaviour, self-harming behaviour and actual or suspected misuse of drugs or alcohol.

This group of teenagers took up a disproportionate amount of social work time and resources; yet while they account for only 9% of the children in the sample, they represent almost 20% of the families. It was difficult to devise suitable care plans for these young people, and even more difficult to make the care plans stick.

Summary

1 At the time of the action that led to care proceedings, just over half the families in the sample (29 out of 57) were lone parent households. Single mothers headed 27 of these. The remaining 44 children in 28 families were living either with both their natural parents or with one parent (usually the child's mother) and a stepparent or cohabitee.

2 The children in our sample were younger than the national average. The ages of the 100 children ranged from 0 to 15 but the average age was 5.7 years at the time of the final hearing. Sixty-two children from nineteen families entered care as part of a sibling pair or sibling group, and 29 children were in a group of four or more.

3 The sample was predominantly white (86 children). The fourteen ethnic minority children came from nine families. Nine children were of dual heritage and the remainder were Afro-Caribbean. The proportion of

ethnic minority children by child (14%) and by family (16%) was comparable to that found in other studies of care order children and so was the over-representation of dual heritage children.

4 When compared with the more exacting standards of the LAC schedules, young children's difficulties in health and education were often underestimated in court reports. There was better reporting of teenage problems such as absconding, offending and school exclusion.

5 The analysis of adult problems highlights the significance of parental substance misuse within the sample. Drug or alcohol misuse or both was a major factor for 40% (23) of the families involving a total of 44 children. Learning difficulties and domestic violence each affected 25 children – one-quarter of the sample – while mental illness in the parent affected fourteen. Sixty per cent of the children had previously been registered on grounds of neglect.

6 In the majority of families there had been previous involvement with social services. Only three children in high-risk cases were removed immediately, without attempts at other forms of intervention. In another seven families the concerns were mainly about previous children who had been removed. Forty-three per cent of the children had received social work input for more than two years, and this group contained the most hard-to-place children in the sample.

[1] In 1997–8 no national data were collected on the ethnicity of care order children to enable wider comparison and to cover identical time-frames; nor is it possible to establish whether the rate over or under-represented the communities from which the children were drawn.

[2] See *The Children Act Report 1995–1999* (DoH 2000b), Figure 3.1.

Part

II Development of the care plans

4 Decisions about placement

Introduction

The placement was considered by social services, and by most of our other respondents, to be the main ingredient of the care plan. The impact of what happened during care proceedings, and in particular the contribution of the children's guardian and the court itself, should not be underestimated; but under the terms of the Children Act 1989 the court is not empowered to impose conditions on a care order, and subsequent case law has confirmed that the selection of an appropriate placement should be regarded as within the local authority's discretion (*Berkshire County Council* v *B* [1997] 1 FLR 171). This has not been changed by the Adoption and Children Act 2002.

The first section of this chapter starts by looking briefly at the practitioners' experience of placement planning. It asks what made cases 'straightforward' or 'difficult', and it lists the issues that were considered important. The second section, which forms the main body of the chapter, explores the framework within which decisions were made. Finally, there is a section devoted to the special problems of planning for sibling groups.

Issues in placement planning: practitioners' views

Surprisingly, almost half the practitioners who were interviewed – children's guardians as well as social workers – said that the planning of the placement had been 'fairly straightforward' even when the case appeared to be extremely complex. Complexity was associated with the number of parties involved in care proceedings and other legal or medical issues, whereas the main source of difficulty cited by all practitioners was the need to negotiate sensitively and effectively with family members. By comparison with this task, the choice of the most suitable placement could seem relatively unproblematic.

The views of children's guardians about what made planning 'straightforward':

The social worker was very good, very reliable, and she had done a lot of work before she had taken proceedings. She was quite clear about where she was going.

It wasn't in a sense heavily contested by the parents; although there were problems getting Patrick out of the house in the first place, the parents accepted that they couldn't cope with him and that he did need to go to school. So there wasn't a huge conflict between the local authority, the parents and the guardian.

It was relatively clear-cut in terms of the problem for the parents. They didn't come forward to really address their difficulties, and so the situation for the child was not really in question.

It was actually quite simple because we were presented with a *fait accompli.* This was a case of two older girls and their mother had gradually retreated from their care over a number of years ... So in effect both girls were abandoned. When the case was brought to court the children were ready for intervention, and it was really a question of 'What are we going to do with them? Where are they going to go?'

The views of children's guardians about what made planning 'difficult':

The family were difficult to engage. They were difficult actually to *see.* They were difficult to deal with in every way.

It was very daunting to start with, because before our first hearing in court I was picking up from the social worker all the negative feelings about the family. The mother had in fact assaulted the first social worker who went to do the EPO [emergency protection order] and the mother had been taken to court for common assault. I was picking up also that the family were very angry and very strident, and there could be strong, you know, 'team supporters'. When we got to court the local authority and indeed the police were all hiding in a back room. It was like a sort of siege mentality.

I found it quite hard because the parents were always pleading for chances and opportunities, hope against hope, that they were going to be able to look

> after these children. I found I was sometimes very much sucked into their emotions and had to stand back from that and be quite hard at times with them, saying 'Sorry, but what you are doing is not good enough.'
>
> In terms of the difficulty, it was trying to take ahead a plan that was probably, with retrospect, going to be too difficult for the parents to manage – and it was a very difficult time for the child. That primarily was the part that I, as a guardian, found hardest. It wasn't to do with (as it is in other cases) differences of opinion between the guardian and the social services department or the difficulty of trying to get your head round particular issues or seeking appropriate advice. The difficulty I guess is inherent in a lot of our work but very poignant in this case; it was struggling with a plan that you knew a child wanted but yet ultimately, sadly, wasn't achievable.

Given the nature of care proceedings, one can sympathise with the practitioners' problems in engaging families and dealing with conflicts of interest; but in view of the fact that the choice of placement was often clear-cut, was the planning of the placement to some extent routinised once the need for the order was clear? The decision was certainly not made by rule of thumb; but a practical and theoretical model of placement planning seems to have evolved since the introduction of the Children Act 1989. The interviews showed that the preliminary discussions and the formation of the final plan itself were concerned with eight main issues:

- the degree of risk;
- the likelihood of the parent co-operating with SSD;
- the availability of carers within the extended family;
- the child's age;
- the child's difficulties;
- the child's contact needs;
- the child's wishes and feelings; and
- resources.

These issues were always seen as linked; but certain arguments appeared to dominate at different stages in the process. In the model of placement planning that emerged from our analysis of the interviews the points to be considered were clustered together, and they were usually addressed in a particular order.

The framework outlined here was not used explicitly by practitioners, but it was drawn up by the researchers because it appeared to be implicit in the process of decision-making. It is based on material from a number of sources including court files, interviews with children's guardians and solicitors and retrospective examination of social work files; but it relies mainly on social workers' accounts of their own planning. The justification for this is that the social workers were the people with the most intimate knowledge of how the plans had been drawn up and, having recently faced the possibility of detailed questioning in court, the social workers who were interviewed at the first stage of the research were well placed to give a clear account of their placement plans in addition to stating the need for the order. Unfortunately it is impossible to reproduce all their accounts, but a representative selection is included in the text.

Placement planning: the key questions

Question 1: Is rehabilitation possible?

Prediction of the degree of risk was crucial, since children could not be allowed to reside anywhere where they were not safe. Risk was usually couched in terms of 'significant harm' or the likelihood of harm, and it was construed according to the usual child protection categories – physical and sexual abuse, neglect and emotional abuse. Placement at home was considered possible if the degree of risk could be controlled, and securing the co-operation of the parent was a necessary step to controlling it.

Figure 4.1a ***The decision about home placement***

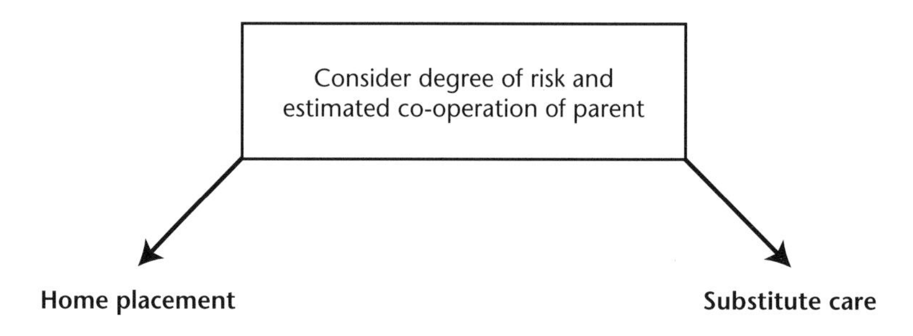

Home placement v substitute care

Without doubt, the most difficult decisions in placement planning were focused in this area of home placement v substitute care. Apart from the question of whether the child could be adequately protected at home by a mixture of monitoring and support, the decision to write into the care plan a proposal that the child should be placed at home created uncertainties inasmuch as the court might refuse to make a care order if the placement was deemed to be unsafe (*Re S and D* [1994]). A more likely outcome, however, and one that the local authority solicitors often feared, was that in the absence of strong evidence supporting the need for the care order, a supervision order would be made instead. The local authority did not usually want a supervision order, which they saw as placing responsibilities on themselves without conferring a great deal of control.

Departmental policies varied in relation to home placements when a care order was expected, and in two out of the five authorities such placements were not usually recommended in the care plan. (See Chapter 5 for more on this issue.) Case law confirms that a care order should not be made when a lesser order will suffice (*Re FS* [1995]; *re O* [1996]). Nevertheless in *Re T* [1993] the Court of Appeal observed that there will be cases where it is appropriate to make a care order even though the child has remained at home throughout the proceedings and may do so afterwards. Everything hinges on the potential benefits of home placement to the child and the degree of vigilance that will be required.[1]

The problem of alcohol misuse

What kind of risks were seen as able to be controlled in home placements, even though they justified the need for the care order? This can be seen most clearly from a scrutiny of final plans.

- In the ten families (involving 22 children) where it was planned that the children would return home or remain at home after the care order, five families contained at least one parent who had problems with alcohol misuse. Five mothers and two fathers were affected, and according to the care plans they would be caring for a total of eleven children.

The problems of alcohol misuse were long-standing and quite severe; for example one child was born with foetal alcohol syndrome. But there was only one case in the rehabilitation group where the mother was suspected of drug involvement, and that was very minor – probably not even current. Furthermore, if we consider the cases where a plan for rehabilitation was seriously considered in the early stages, although it was not carried through to the final recommendations (see Chapter 5), we find that only one family where a mother had been known to misuse drugs was included; but a further two families were affected by alcohol misuse and in one case it was present in both parents. This seems to indicate that the response to drug misuse was much stronger than the response to misuse of alcohol – perhaps because the former is illegal, but also perhaps because the latter is more widespread, more socially acceptable and more likely to engage the sympathy of professional people.

Neglect or the risk of neglect

Neglect or the risk of neglect was a prominent concern in most cases where rehabilitation was planned – not simply because of alcohol misuse but because the mother was believed to have poor parenting skills, which could be improved with regular encouragement and outside help.

- Concerns about neglect were associated with parental learning difficulties in three families involving a total of seven children.

Learning difficulties were found among the mothers who were allowed to keep their children, but not personality disorders or psychiatric disorders. Fourteen children in the sample had parents whose mental illness was sufficiently severe to contribute directly to the making of the care order, but the plan for all of these children was that they would be removed to adoption or some other form of substitute care.

Most of the children for whom rehabilitation was planned had never left home, or had entered a foster home for a brief space of time during care proceedings. In each of these cases the mother seemed to be committed to managing the problem and the children were securely or insecurely attached to her; but the care order was believed to be necessary to enforce and monitor attendance at health or treatment centres and to ensure take-up of services – including visits by the key social worker. Since in many of these families, additionally, there was threat from a violent partner who had recently been a member of the household, the care plan contained conditions about supervision of contact with this man and placed limits on his return. However, as already mentioned, the practice of placing children at home under a care order was unevenly distributed since some local authority solicitors were wary of this option. The authorities that did use the arrangement justified it on the grounds that children could be removed readily in a crisis, and hoped that the presence of the sanction would help to maintain improvements.

What the social workers said:

a) *Placement at home – the plan for a 1-year-old baby whose mother had been misusing alcohol*

I had the co-operation of the mother throughout. That was positive in terms of the rehabilitation of William at home. It was very difficult initially for his mother, because of the strong attachment she had to William ... William was a child with special needs. He was diagnosed with foetal alcohol syndrome shortly after his birth. He failed to thrive at home; it was not definite whether that was a result of the foetal alcohol syndrome or the care that was being afforded to him at home, around mum's alcohol dependency ... I felt there needed to be continued involvement from the adult side. There needed to be appropriate resources put in.

b) *Placement at home – a case involving three small children aged 1, 6 and 9; there had been a series of minor incidents, and a long period of social work involvement*

We did a comprehensive assessment to try and work out what was going on ... then looking at what we had collated, we said 'You know, this isn't on ... We are seriously concerned about the children. If we don't do something about this then they are at risk of further abuse, neglect – physical and sexual abuse.' We wanted to make the parents aware that unless they were to change what they were doing we would be forced to remove the children. So it sounds as though we were using it [the order] as a threat to a certain extent – which we were really ... It also meant that we could have responsibility and be able to say to them 'Look, we are responsible for these children as much as you are now.'

Question 2: Is there a relative who could look after the child?

When rehabilitation to the caretaking parent (who was usually the mother) had been ruled out, a search was made for suitable carers within the extended family. In accordance with the principles of the Children Act this was considered to be the second best option to rehabilitation, and if it was possible for the child or sibling group to be looked after by a relative or friend (the form of care that we have described as 'kinship care') this was usually chosen in preference to other options.

Figure 4.1b ***The decision about kinship care***

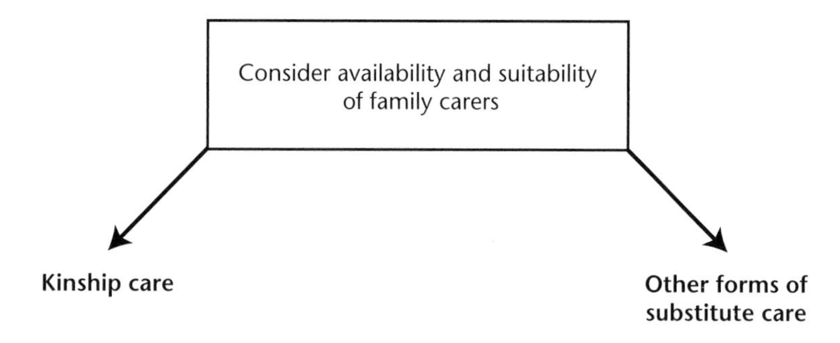

According to one local authority solicitor, the availability of carers in the extended family was regularly explored by means of a family group conference – although she had reservations about its use in every case.

> It's started to be routine in cases where we're not going to be placing the children with the birth parents and we believe that there are wider family members. If we're clear that there aren't any, it may be a case where we think: 'There's absolutely no point'; but, other than that, it's becoming standard practice.

As with placements at home, the local authorities varied in the status they gave to placements with relatives or friends and some went to greater lengths than others in attempting to find family carers. In a few cases where kinship care was eventually chosen because a relative volunteered, fostering or adoption by strangers had been selected as a first choice – and this happened before even the possibility of care by a relative was investigated.

Where it was planned, it was hoped that kinship care would maintain continuity in order to reinforce the child's sense of identity, and preserve important attachments by keeping the child within the family network. However, the grounds for the care order had an impact on the arrangements.

- The original parent was now seen as a source of risk, and the new carer had to demonstrate the ability to *protect the child from the original carer.*

Foster and adoptive parents could usually be relied on to do this, but serious questions were raised about members of the extended family who might be assumed to be sympathetic to the parent. For this reason 'kinship carers' were scrutinised to ensure that they would be able to control the child's contact with the birth parent, as well as enabling it to continue, and plans reflected these child protection concerns.

If a child was to live with relatives, the plan was commonly for the child to be moved not to a member of the mother's family but to *a member of the father's family*. The only exception to this rule was in two cases where children specifically requested placement with a maternal aunt. In five other families it was planned that young children would move directly from the mother's care to that of the father, or father plus partner. (Some people might dispute that this can be described as 'kinship care'; but since these parents had not previously been in close touch with the children and the father had not been resident in the household, the experience was substantially equivalent to care by a member of the extended family.) Other carers named in the care plans included a paternal great aunt and uncle, a paternal aunt or aunt and uncle, the paternal grandmother or grandparents, and relatives of the mother's former partner. The carers were known to the children in all cases, and in some cases chosen by them.

What was the main concern that led to a choice of kinship care?

- Ten of the eighteen children for whom kinship care was planned were considered to be at risk because of the parents' misuse of drugs.

This appears to mirror what is happening in the USA, where a national policy study of kinship care estimated that 80–99% of all cases where children were removed from their parents and placed with relatives were related to drugs (Hornby et al. 1995). Five families were involved in the current allegations. In three of them the concerns about drug misuse focused on the mother, while in the other two families both parents were involved.

- Seven of the eighteen children for whom kinship care was planned came from five families of minority ethnic status. Since the sample included only fourteen children from ethnic minorities, from a total of nine families, this means that half of them – a very high proportion – were to be placed with relatives rather than in other forms of substitute care.

Again this parallels what appears to be happening in the USA, where kinship care is said to be used predominantly for African-American families (McFadden 1998). The interviews with social workers confirm that in these cases links with the cultural community were seen as important for the children in addition to family links, and this was a major factor in the decisions that were made.

What the social workers said:

a) *Kinship care – a plan for an 8-year-old girl of dual heritage to live with her paternal grandmother*

The concerns were about late attendance at school or non-attendance, reports from the teachers about poor concentration, developmental delay in her education, falling behind ... Also the whole environment and the chaotic conditions she was living under. There was concern about her mother's lifestyle – her use of drugs and how she was financing that habit. I believe that this mother loves her daughters dearly. I just think it's unfortunate that her lifestyle has meant that she's not always been able to put her children's needs first ... The most important issue was to find somewhere secure for Terry to be. The paternal grandmother was somebody who worked well with professionals – which I can't always say was the case for the maternal side ... And we knew, even with the kind of benefits we'd given her – money, transport and so forth – that the cost both in emotional terms for Terry and in financial terms for the local authority was going to be far less than placing the child with strangers.

b) *Kinship care – the making of plans for three Afro-Caribbean boys aged 4, 5 and 6; their mother was reputed to be affectionate towards the children but extremely volatile*

There was one critical meeting ... It was about: Who will look after these children? What avenues do we explore? Do we give mother another chance at assessment? What about dad? I can remember a lot of pain around making the final decision. Mum wasn't going to get another chance, because there were no indicators at all of the likelihood of change. If we spent more time with mum it would lead to more delay, and it wasn't getting anywhere in the long run for the boys ... Then there was a debate about how dad would fare. I was probably strongest on that one; I wanted to see him get that chance – and we got it! ... These children had such complicated networks within the community. And they were so embedded. You know, they are deeply rooted here. The idea of removing them from it just seemed abhorrent ... The boys were exhibiting difficult behaviour. The foster carer was exhausted by the time they left. I think that placement would probably have broken down.

Question 3: Is the child suitable for adoption?

Once the degree of risk in the home environment had been established as too great for rehabilitation after the order, and care by other family members had been found to be impossible or deemed unlikely to succeed, the next step was to assess the child's suitability for adoption. In the case of a very young child this had to happen quickly in order to prevent damaging delays – especially when there had been late collapse of a rehabilitation plan. One solicitor said: 'My bitter experience is that we're going along down Path A, which is rehab to the parents, and then suddenly some event occurs which blows the whole thing out of the water.'

When the need for substitute care away from the family had been determined, the age of the child, the child's problems (if any) and the perceived need for contact all helped to distinguish children who needed adoption from those who would benefit most from long-term fostering or residential care; but the key consideration was age. There was a significant relationship between age and placement choice (Wald test, $p < 0.001$). Adoption and home placement tended to be selected for the youngest children, and the children for whom other placements were chosen (kinship, fostering, residential care) were significantly older. Lowe and Murch (2002) also found that age was a key factor in determining whether a child was to be placed for adoption or long-term fostering.

Figure 4.1c ***The decision about adoption***

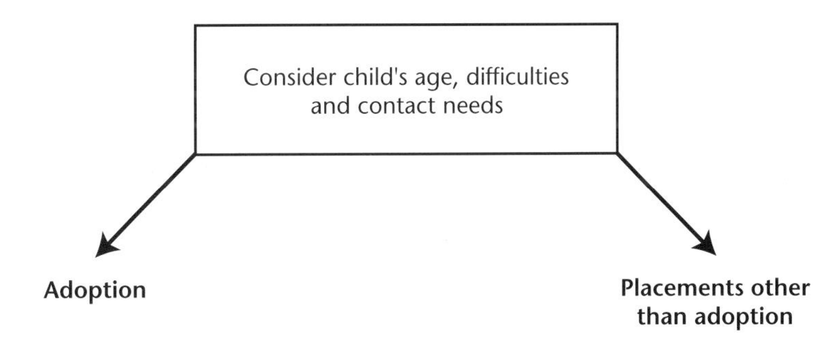

Face-to-face contact after adoption was not planned in most of the cases in the sample, and we were told that it happened rather rarely although there was no actual policy against it in any of our authorities. The reasoning seemed to be that most adopters would not welcome face-to-face contact with the birth family and, since adopters were in short supply, the plans were made to some extent with their interests in mind. The same screening mechanism was applied, though less rigidly, to children with behaviour problems. Older children were not readily brought forward for adoption because it was recognised that they could not be placed as easily as younger ones – and since older children were also more likely to need ongoing links with the birth family and to have experienced a greater degree of 'pre-care adversity', the problems and contact needs of the children were to some extent age-related.

- The presence of older age, children's difficulties (especially aggressiveness or hyperactivity) and strong birth family links together shifted the care plan in the direction of fostering rather than adoption.

This did, however, leave unresolved the problem of children in large sibling groups, who could not easily be placed together in either adoption or fostering. Attempts were made to keep siblings together; but when they had to be divided, they were usually divided along an axis that related to age, behaviour and contact needs. Often this happened when the initial placement was made, and these arrangements remained.

Parental problems in the families spanned all the categories, but the most frequently occurring problem in this group was learning difficulties, which affected parenting in seven families and put thirteen children at risk of serious neglect. Learning difficulties seldom occurred on their own, however. In cases where adoption was planned they were associated with domestic violence in three families, with mental ill health in two families, and with alcohol misuse in another two.

What the social workers said:

a) *Adoption – plans for a baby whose elder sibling had been injured, probably by the mother's partner*

> There was the option of Lucille, the mother, having him back [not acceptable]. There was the option of him going back to live with Lucille and her sister – but if Lucille had got a prison sentence, that would have been with the sister on her own. There was also consideration given to the baby being cared for by other members of the extended family, but nobody wanted that. They would have found it difficult to disassociate their feelings about Lucille from the baby. They were very angry – and they did blame Lucille. That was mixed up with a lot of guilt they had because they'd noticed things themselves, and if they'd acted sooner, it may not have had that outcome ... I interviewed several family members and they all felt the same. They felt the best option for the baby was adoption outside the family.

b) Adoption – plans for two children aged 2 and 4, after failed attempts at rehabilitation

> We had always said it would be adoption. We had said to the family 'It's not fair on these children. They have a right to a family.' We had also made a direct approach to the family members – I think it was after the rehab had failed – in order to try and organise a family group conference. We'd said to the family 'This is the problem ... What can you do?' We had an independent co-ordinator go out and seek their views. The answer that came back was that (a) they weren't in a position to help, and (b) they didn't feel able to ratify the local authority plan for adoption – because that's what they would have been doing if they came up saying no they couldn't. The sub-message that we got was that even if they felt they could help, they believed they would see great interference from Mrs Y [the children's mother] ... They are getting harder to place now by virtue of their age. Maria is leaving that window of bonding. David is slightly beyond that. I'm hopeful we can find a placement for them. It would have been great to have these children placed months ago.

Question 4: Is there a choice to be made between long-term fostering and residential care?

Where children required substitute care apart from adoption, there was a clear policy and practice bias in favour of fostering – either ordinary or specialist fostering depending on the age and needs of the child. Residential care was seen as a last resort for older adolescents.

The wishes and feelings of older children (though not necessarily those of very young children) were always sought, and when they were clearly expressed they could be influential in securing any type of placement including placement at home. However:

- it was considered particularly important to gauge young people's wishes and feelings when planning placements in fostering or residential care because they had power to abscond.

One solicitor was so pessimistic about the prospects of achieving stability for stubborn adolescents that in some cases he was reluctant to recommend care proceedings at all.

> Adolescents can vote with their feet. Usually they're very clear about what they will and will not co-operate with, and there's precious little point in saying to a

> 14- or 15-year-old 'We're going to get a care order in respect of you' because they turn round and say 'Well, you can say what you like, but I'm not gonna live with foster parents, I'm not gonna live in a children's home, I'm not gonna go to school and what are you gonna do about it?'

Availability of resources was also crucial to the planning process at this stage; but most older children had views on the basic question of whether they wanted to live in a family or in a more residential environment, and when a particular placement had been identified, the children's full agreement was needed if they were to profit from the chosen placement and not run from it.

Figure 4.1d ***The decision about long-term fostering***

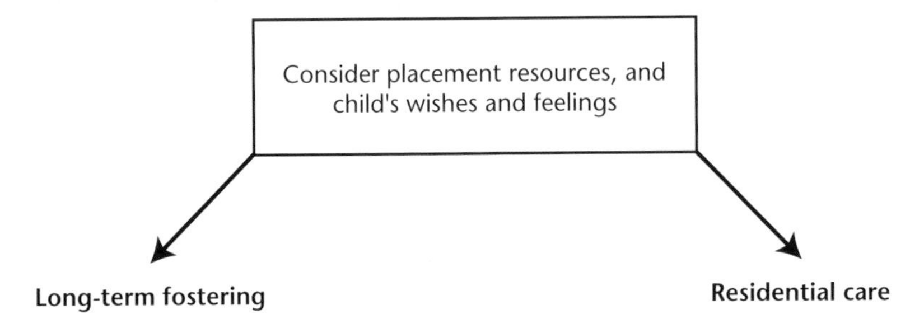

The importance of resources

For pre-adolescent children who required ordinary foster care rather than a specialist project, considerations of resources did not seem to feature highly when the care plans were being drawn up, although most practitioners were prepared to admit that serious shortages existed and that choice was often limited. More problems were expected with the supply of specialist placements.

- Specialist resources were extremely limited and they were also costly; but cost seemed less of a problem than availability.

For difficult young people over the age of 13, foster homes and residential places were in short supply. Practitioners and local authority solicitors recognised this as a problem, although they were prepared to deal with it pragmatically. Here are two quotations from solicitors' interviews:

> We have to be resource-led, don't we? So if there isn't somewhere, or it's going to take a while to find it, and in the meantime you've got a child in a medium- to short-term or medium-term placement, you just have to live with that.

> If we actually looked at what resources we had, I think in a lot of cases we'd be getting to a stage where there wouldn't be any point in taking proceedings because we wouldn't be able to achieve what we wanted to achieve.

The second solicitor said that the question of *financial cost* – particularly if there was a need for secure accommodation – had 'huge implications for social services at each stage of proceedings'; but she saw this as being a decision for social workers and their managers to make, and when the placement was being planned she simply made sure that what they were asking for 'was going to be covered financially'. Certainly if an expensive resource was really needed, whether it was a particular type of placement or therapeutic services or long-term supervision of contact arrangements, the reasoning was that it should be funded. There were only two exceptions. First, the cost of some placements was expected to be shared with other agencies (particularly where a residential placement provided education as well as a living environment). Second, questions were raised very often in relation to out-of-county placements, because of the general policy that in-house resources should be used wherever possible. With these reservations, it does appear that resources for the few children who most needed to be looked after were given due priority, and consequently they were not unduly constrained by the tight budgets within the local authorities.

What the social workers said:

a) *Long-term fostering – a case where an 11-year-old girl had been living with a mentally ill mother*

> Basically Rowena was being used as a young carer. She was being given a lot of responsibility to feed, supervise, do everything for her mother ... The mother just wouldn't work with us. She would phone us up and write letters and make complaints, but if we arranged to see her she would never answer the door or be in ... When the responsibility became too much Rowena challenged her mother about it; then there became arguments and those arguments did lead to physical violence. She loved her mum but it was becoming too much for her. We were really trying to get a balance of protecting her, but recognising that she was close to her mother and trying to establish when was going to be the best time to pull her out ... The foster parents were interested in caring for her long term, and it was clear that contact would be maintained.

b) Residential care – finding a placement for a disturbed 13-year-old girl

Vicky was sexually abused as a very young child, and the degree of emotional disturbance she's shown since then has been characteristic of the severest abuse. The relationship between her and her mother very quickly broke down and Vicky exhibited a lot of self-harming behaviour, was unable to be educated in mainstream schooling, had no close relationships, didn't seem to be bonded to anybody ... For her own safety and the safety of others we got a secure order, and it was during that time that the plan for the care order was made ... We couldn't hold this girl in one of our homes. We needed a very specialist therapeutic community for her ... We looked at endless brochures and I worked with the residential staff trying to find the right place for her. We had to ring up places and find out. They have got a central resource at the secure unit, but it's quite out of date; these places change every five minutes ... We approached various places but what was actually needed was somewhere that could offer therapy to a girl who was as badly abused as Vicky had been. We identified one in Midshire; but if I'm honest with you, she always wanted to stay in her home town ... In the secure unit she belonged. She was part of the regime. She had quite a power base among the youngsters there because she'd been there before; but because of the very security they offered her, she had nothing to fight against, so those highs – the highs that she needs when she's outside – weren't there ... It was a very structured existence. She knew exactly what was happening and she benefited from it; but we can't keep her locked up for the rest of her childhood, and that's why a residential placement had to be found.

Planning for sibling groups

The presence of siblings was not significantly associated with placement choice, but the need to cater for children in sibling groupings was a major complicating factor in social workers' decisions about placement. In nineteen of the 57 families that formed the sample in the study as a whole, more than one child was made subject to the care order at the same time. In six families there were sibling pairs, and in another thirteen families there was a sibling group of three or more children. Sixty-two out of the 100 children in the sample entered the care system with at least one other sibling or half-sibling. One practitioner said: 'I guess one started off with the writing on the wall. It was then a case of determining what there actually was for these children – and, for me, it was largely this together or apart business.'

Arrangements for contact with other siblings – at least those who had lived together and were made subject to the care order at the same time – were written into the fostering and kinship care plans; but they could not be guaranteed in adoptive placements.

- The absence of plans for post-adoption contact meant that contact between siblings had to be severed, if the group was split between adoption and other placement options.

The dilemmas are illustrated by a case involving three children aged 3, 4 and 10, where the social worker and the guardian agreed that it was in the children's interests for the group to be divided so that the youngest two would be placed for adoption and the 10-year-old would be fostered. Resources played a part in this decision, because it was felt that adoptive parents would not be found for all three children together; but resource shortages were only a contributory factor. The social worker who made the decision said that he would have 'struggled with it' if separation of the children had been likely to cause 'serious emotional damage'.[2] Separation was justifiable in this case, he felt, because the third child was less securely attached to his siblings and also required different contact arrangements with adults in the family.

Conflicts of interest

When the interests of two or more children were at stake, it was often impossible to benefit the children equally – and this applied to contact arrangements as well as to the decision about joint or separate placements. Here is what one practitioner said about two sisters aged 8 and 15 who were separated during care proceedings. Previously the older child had had a parental role in relation to the other.

> Zolda had been Catherine's substitute mum for the months leading up to proceedings, and I think Catherine was very dependent on her. She got a lot of stability and security from Zolda, who did a lot of looking after; so she was very upset at being separated from her. Zolda I think missed Catherine less, because she was relieved of the burden of caring for her – and also Catherine had been seen as the favoured child within their relationship. I think there was some resentment from Zolda which she wasn't ever allowed to express. It was certainly some relief for her that she could actually concentrate on herself.

Having admitted these advantages of separate placements and talked about the arrangements for contact, the worker went on to say:

> I think ideally they should have been together. Separation provided some relief for Zolda, but if she could have been somewhere where she could have been simultaneously relieved of caring for Catherine and given some sort of positive feedback for herself, and still be allowed to be with her, that would have been the best.

How brothers and sisters were to be divided

Out of the nineteen sibling groups who entered care together, seven were to be divided according to the recommendations of the final care plan.

- If one child was to be separated from the others it tended to be the eldest (fostered when the rest were to be adopted) or the youngest (adopted when the rest were fostered).

Adoption was often chosen for the youngest children, partly because it was felt that they would be easy to place and able to benefit from a new family, and partly because there was an understandable desire to offer the youngest child opportunities that had not been available to the others. However, out of six families in the sample where sibling groups involving more than two children were to be split up, there were five where *the eldest child* was the one to be separated from the others. It seemed that in all these families the difficulties got worse as the children got older, and for various reasons the first born was the one the mother found most difficult to cope with. Consequently this child was more neglected than the others, or scapegoated and acting out, or made to undertake an overly parental role. The eldest child was sometimes considered to be more self-sufficient, and therefore capable of surviving apart from the others. In one case, additionally, the eldest child was the only one who needed contact with the birth father.

The children's guardians usually agreed with the social workers' judgement on the necessity for separate placements. However, guardians and key social workers noted that some children could have remained together if carers had been available – not simply in sufficient numbers, but with the necessary skills to parent them.

Discussion and conclusions

In this brief sketch we have outlined the considerations that seemed to be important in shaping the placement plan, and the way in which they were considered. The model is not foolproof, however. Apart from the fact that every item in the decision-making process is open to interpretation in the light of what is known about a particular child or family, some parts of the 'conventional wisdom' itself may be open to challenge.

Figure 4.1 shows the full model of placement planning that was commonly used by the social workers.

In the cases studied, the model proved helpful and effective inasmuch as it helped to structure social work planning; but it had some disadvantages. First, it was a sequential model. There was little evidence of regular 'twin-track' planning, and when there was pressure to move quickly, the tendency was to omit one stage altogether. (For example, in one case the social worker moved directly from rejection of home placement to adoption, and the guardian complained that it had been left to her to check out the extended family.) Second, the choice of the main criteria could be criticised. Several practitioners, and especially guardians, had doubts about the inclusion of resource arguments since this could result in decisions that were not in the children's best interests (although it could equally be argued that feasibility is one of the essential requirements in planning). Third, the model works by a process of elimination, and since it depends heavily on negative reasons for ruling out placements, it lacks subtlety when it is used on its own. In cases where it worked well it was accompanied by rigorous professional thinking about the value of specific options to individual children.

The final disadvantage of the model, in terms of dynamics, is that most considerations were seen as relevant at certain stages, and at other stages they could be treated as if they were not relevant. An example can be found in cases of rehabilitation where rather limited attention was given to the effect of the child's difficulties and contact needs. In spite of the multi-dimensional view of assessment that is now generally advocated (DoH 1999c), these issues were sometimes not adequately addressed in home placements because the emphasis was on parental behaviour. Another example can be found in the lack of attention that some social workers paid to the wishes and feelings of pre-adolescent children – not because of the children's lack of competence, necessarily, but because of their lack of power.

In later chapters we shall look at the results of the decisions, to see whether any lessons can be learned from the implementation or non-implementation of the plans; but first we need to look in more detail at the development of the plan during care proceedings.

Figure 4.1 ***Social workers' decisions about placement: the commonly used model of placement planning***

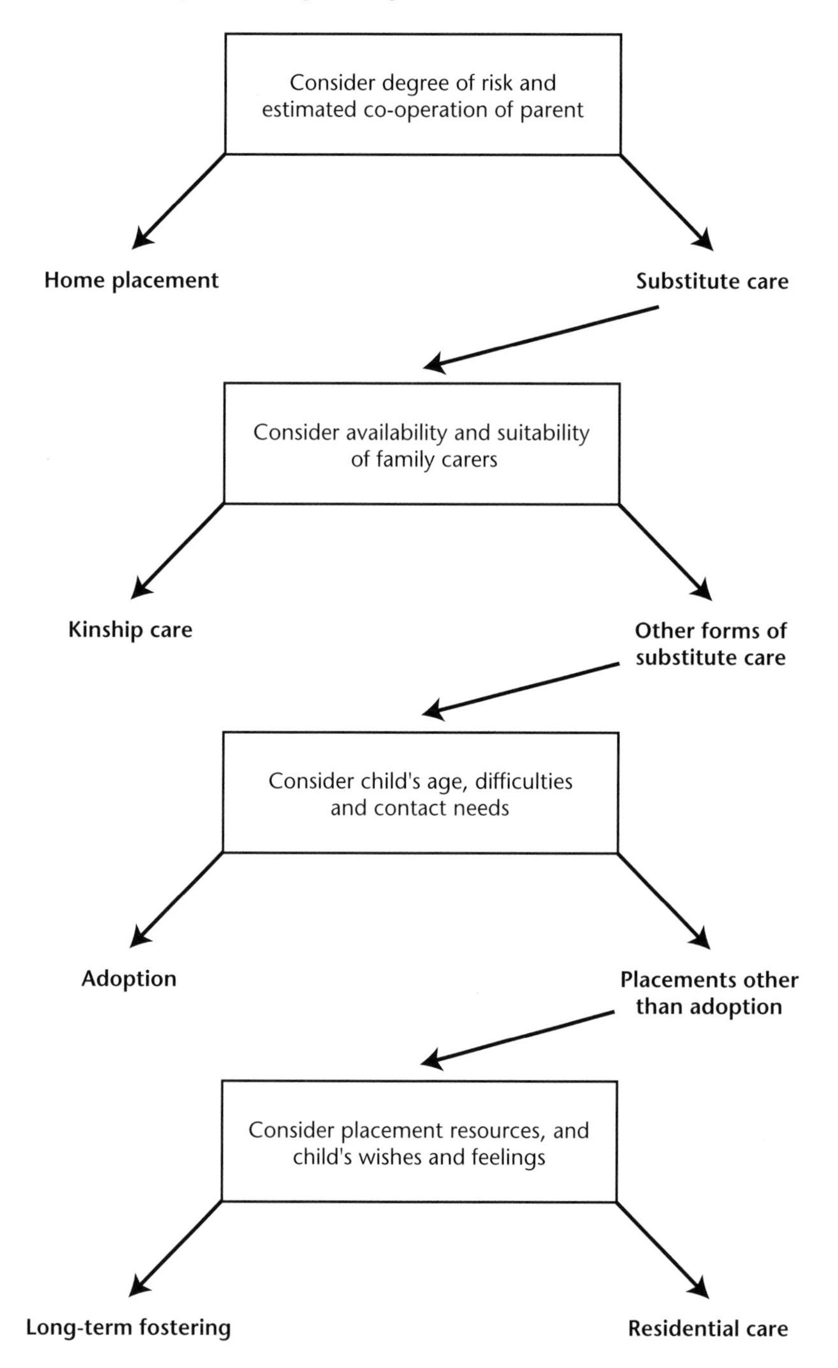

[1] This position has changed somewhat with the introduction of the Human Rights Act. If home placement is planned, it is possible that birth parents may challenge the making of the care order on the grounds of disproportionate interference in family life (Harwin and Owen 2002).

[2] Schofield (2003) reports that separation from siblings carries different meanings and consequences for different children, but for some of the people interviewed in her study the loss of role as well as the loss of an intimate relationship 'was viewed as a defining moment in their childhood when they lost faith in social workers and felt truly alone'.

5 The development of the plan during care proceedings

Introduction

Thanks to the streamlining of the care planning process in recent years, the clarity of care plans seems to have improved over time. In the study by Hunt and Macleod 67% of the social services' objectives were classified as 'contingent on developments during proceedings' and, while only 74 of the 131 children studied were made subject to care orders, the final plans for ten of these 74 children were described as 'uncertain' (Hunt and Macleod 1999). In the present study initial preferences were of course subject to change but no child was made subject to a care order without at least a placement plan.

This chapter looks at how the social workers' initial choices – which were inevitably somewhat tentative in the early stages – were shaped and modified during care proceedings. It starts by exploring how children's guardians and local authority solicitors saw their role in relation to care plans, then it outlines the extent of the changes during proceedings. After this, the chapter moves on to examine systematically the development of plans for the five placement options – placement at home, adoption, long-term fostering, kinship care and residential care. Besides documenting the changes in more detail, these sections bring forward particular dilemmas experienced by the decision-makers. The chapter concludes with an overview of the decisions made, and an analysis of key factors that had a bearing on placement choice.

The input of guardians and solicitors

Among the key players during care proceedings were the children's guardians and the local authority solicitors. They both influenced the care plans, but in different ways.

The guardians' main task in relation to the local authority's care plan was to criticise it – as one guardian put it, 'to keep at the heels of the local authority to get the plan for the child right'. They also had multi-dimensional roles in court, acting as 'overseer, mediator, negotiator, broker and indeed gatekeeper'

(Brophy 1999). In this study they seem to have initiated a somewhat higher number of changes to placement plans than is recorded in the study by Clark and Sinclair, who found only two such plans in a survey of 59 families and 117 children (Clark and Sinclair 1999). However, many factors contributed to shifts in direction, including the reports of expert witnesses and parents' behaviour during proceedings. The guardians frequently sought out and interviewed absent relatives, such as fathers, who were not normally in touch with social services. As reported by Bourton and McCausland (2001) they also played a key role in contact arrangements, but it would be hard to conclude – as did social workers and solicitors in Clark and Sinclair's study – that this role was more important than acting as an independent check on plans or helping to avoid delay and drift.

The local authority solicitors, by contrast, worked in close partnership with social services. They did not write the final care plan, as was noted elsewhere (LCD 1997a), but they usually took responsibility for checking its contents. Their main task was to obtain the care order, which one solicitor described as a 'tool' to enable social services to plan for the child's future, and they were usually at pains to distance themselves from professional social work decisions, but they were also capable of going beyond their formal role by giving advice to the social workers and managers from whom they took instructions. Because of high turnover in the social work teams and pressures on management, they felt that in care proceedings they had a considerable role in supporting social workers, as the following quotations show.

How the local authority solicitors saw their role:

> I like particularly for social workers to trust us. I'm there to help them. I'm not a sort of far off lawyer in a fancy office elsewhere. I'm an 'in house' lawyer ... and sometimes they do like to just talk matters over with us and to let fly.

> I wouldn't say I make recommendations. That's not my role. I'd say we take a very full part in the discussion and I advise the client as to what would wash with the court and what wouldn't ... I assist them in looking at the evidence they've got and what the evidence would point to – how the courts would view this type of evidence ... I say 'Please think about this in advance. Let's thrash it through now.'

> If there isn't enough detail in the plan then we'll say 'This is not good enough.' We send it back to be redrafted and extra bits done to it. But I don't

think that's the lawyer's main role really ... As long as it's all criteria to satisfy the court and the parties, I'm inclined not to intervene in it.

Our role is to look at what the options are and to give advice on that – and quite often you can give some practical advice as well. Most of the solicitors here have been doing the work a long, long time and we can use our experience in other situations to say 'Well, it might be a better idea to try this suggestion.'

Our advice is often reminding them of the real basics; for example, if they're considering care proceedings because of the care of a child, we say 'Well, is there a father? Are there grandparents? Are there any other relatives that you've considered? What assessments have been done?' ... You get social workers who'll say they just don't know who else to turn to.

They know that when they send their care plan to us we'll look at it, we'll go through it ... but I think it's really building on relationships and improving relationships, because of the turnover of staff ... It's building up a rapport and making sure staff feel confident, and also making sure that they feel confident when they actually go to court.

Changes and modifications to the plan

When application was made to the court at the start of care proceedings, the care plan was not totally open-ended. In most cases there was a pre-existing plan for the child or at least a presumption about what the final outcome of care proceedings would be. During care proceedings:

- 15% of placement plans did not change in any way (this situation was mainly found in adoption cases);
- 25% altered radically; these were plans that had been energetically pursued but then collapsed at a very late stage in the proceedings – many of them were plans for rehabilitation; and
- 60% did not change radically but became firmed up over time. ('Firming up' seems the best way to describe the process whereby the placement plan was clarified and made more definite, while necessary details were added.)

By comparing the agency's intentions at the time of the first application with the final recommendations, we can see the impact of what happened during care proceedings. As can be seen from Table 5.1:

- the greatest degree of change between the first and final hearing was found among plans for home placement and for adoption.

The number of rehabilitation plans was reduced substantially, while the plans for adoption increased. There was also some increase in plans for fostering and a small shift in plans for kinship care,[1] but the five residential placement plans remained unchanged.

Table 5.1 ***Changes during care proceedings: development of placement plans for the sample children***

	Initial preferences	Final plans
Home placement	39	22
Kinship care	18	18
Adoption	19	33
Foster care	11	22
Residential care	5	5
Total	**100**	**100**

The development of plans for placing children at home

Out of 39 children who were originally intended to be placed at home:

- Twelve were never separated from their carers.
- Ten were removed temporarily to foster care and then returned.
- Seventeen were removed for assessment and a decision was made not to return them.

The high number of initial plans for home placement is striking, even though some of them were tentative in the early stages. This pattern of preferences reflected a broad aspiration to keep families together or to reunite them in keeping with the principles of the Children Act; but, as the previous chapter showed, there were far more specific factors that influenced plan formation. Social workers' intentions to place a child at home were based on a view that the degree of risk could be controlled and that parents could be worked with co-operatively. The court process was used to test out parental commitment to improve parenting, by means of assessments and expert reports in addition to the input of social workers, guardians and solicitors.

The turning points

When initial plans for rehabilitation were subject to radical change the case details vary, but from the point of view of court processes, the reasons are not hard to find. Typically there was a social worker who was committed to working with the family under a care order, and a guardian who wanted to emphasise risk to the child. This does not mean that there was open conflict, however. Agreement was reached during the firming up of the plan and before the final hearing in all but one case, which remained embattled to the end.

The children's guardians had an enormous amount of influence in these cases. Does this indicate that the guardians were more sensitive to the risk of significant harm than social workers? Such a conclusion would be unfounded, since the design of the study did not allow us to follow up cases where the application for a care order was abandoned in favour of a supervision order or no order at all. The guardians may well have been active in achieving such an outcome. What we can say on the present evidence is that where a care order was applied for and obtained, the guardians tended to favour removal of the child to a different environment. There were, however, a few cases where the social worker and the guardian were working towards a home placement for children who had been removed and it proved to be impossible, because the family members could not meet the demands that had been set.

In one case involving two children aged 2 and 4, the guardian said:

> I suppose I was sucked into the first few months of it being just about good enough. In retrospect, looking at the wider, deeper issues and the longstanding problems mother had, it would have been easier to have said 'Look, this person is not going to be capable long-term of caring for these children.' But it was a hard decision to make because she was actually caring for them at that point, and nothing was too awful, to say that they've got to be removed.

In each of the cases where rehabilitation was abandoned late in the proceedings, there was a turning point that practitioners could easily identify. The plan changed direction when:

- parents withdrew from the assessment;
- a decision was made that parents were not making enough progress;
- attempts at rehabilitation were seen to have failed;
- risk of physical or sexual abuse was not acknowledged; or
- previous concerns were seen in a new light.

At the time of the care order ten of the seventeen children who had been diverted to substitute care had plans for adoption, while four were to remain in foster care and three were to live with relatives.

It is noteworthy that in all the cases that ended up with a substitute care plan at final hearing, the child had undergone an assessment away from home and never returned. By contrast, twelve of the 22 children whose plan at the final hearing remained home placement were never separated from their original carers during care proceedings. The rest were returned either shortly before or almost immediately after the order.

Difficulties associated with home placement plans

The decision to recommend placement at home in the care plan at the final hearing caused the most worry to social workers, guardians and solicitors. At interview these placements were sometimes rated as standing no more than 50% chance of success. This uncertainty did not come out in proceedings and it may have been obscured by lack of contest on the part of parents who sometimes agreed to the order on the condition that the child would remain at home. (Home placements had the lowest rate of contest of all placement options.) Furthermore although home placement was usually chosen for positive reasons, it also reflected in a number of cases a solicitor's view that there was insufficient evidence to justify removing the child. This view was based on a belief about how the circumstances of the case might be read by the court, since in law there is no specific ground for removal as such. It applied to two types of case in particular:

- young children whose elder siblings had been harmed, but for whom there was no evidence that they had themselves received particularly harmful parenting; and
- cases of chronic longstanding neglect that lacked any 'trigger event' for the proceedings.

Sometimes risk had been greater at an earlier point (for instance, from a dangerous partner who had moved out). Solicitors were prepared to admit that some applications should have been made earlier, and that it was less easy to justify removal of the children when there had been a long history of tolerance: 'I think some people felt: "We turned a blind eye for two or three years. We can't really just remove the children now."'

Occasionally unease was echoed in the court arena, and in one case the plan was endorsed only on the grounds that the parent had not been formally warned previously by social services of the possibility of removal.

Which rehabilitation plans were carried through to the final hearing?

For 22 children, the care plan at final hearing recommended home placement, and on the strength of these plans the care orders were made. From the court's point of view, what characterised these cases? Some influential considerations were:

- sympathy for the mother;
- respect for children's attachments;
- perceptions that the children were able to seek help when required; and
- faith in the ability of the care order to generate change.

It is understandable that among court personnel there should be genuine sympathy for the mother, who in three out of four cases was a single parent; but an equally strong factor was the children's desire for return, which in more than one case was prompting the guardian as well as the social worker to recommend rehabilitation. In cases where the mother was misusing alcohol or had learning difficulties, children of school age were seen as less at risk than younger children because social workers felt that they could seek help when required (although there were obvious constraints in their loyalty to the parent and the absence of outside contacts). The power of the care order was seen as necessary to control the children's environment and bring about change; but when the mother was pledging co-operation with the department and the children were securely or insecurely attached to her, there were strong incentives to 'give her a chance'.

Why was a care order sought in cases of home placement?

In two of the five authorities any child who was considered to need a care order was always placed away from home; but it may be asked how it was possible for home placement to be recommended at all, when the making of a care order by definition indicated that these children were at significant risk. In some cases a dangerous partner had left the house. If the main threat had been removed, why was a care order thought necessary rather than a supervision order?

In cases where an actual or potential abuser had left the house, there was often a very real fear that he would return. In these circumstances the care order was seen to provide a useful sanction, because social services could state that if this happened the children would be removed immediately.

- One objective to be achieved by means of the care order was therefore keeping abusers at bay.

More commonly, however, the current threat was seen as neglect or emotional abuse by the mother because professional concerns were focused on her parenting skills.[2] In these circumstances the care order was seen as:

- ensuring the take-up of services by parents; or
- obliging the local authority to provide services.

The first of these is a social work view, based on the notion that parents would be likely to renege on their obligations. The second was voiced by some guardians, who wanted to ensure that after they had left the case the family would be given the support necessary to maintain the placement. The advantage of the care order from this point of view is that it would place duties on social services through the granting of parental responsibility – but since it would also make more resources available, the reasoning of the guardians was not necessarily distrustful or punitive.

However, a major consideration for social workers and guardians was that there was a lot of uncertainty about risk. The order was seen as providing:

- an extended period of monitoring and support with built-in safeguards, inasmuch as the children could be removed readily without the necessity of returning to court.

Because the concerns of the professionals remained at a high level, a lot of reliance was placed on the ability to remove children quickly if things went wrong. Only a care order, it was felt, would give the local authority this power.[3]

Sadly, many rehabilitation plans were not wholly positive options. In the eyes of solicitors and guardians they were made in a spirit of uncertainty, because it would have been difficult to justify a plan for substitute care. Some could also be regarded as plans that were 'inchoate' inasmuch as radical decisions were being postponed. On some future occasion, it was felt, there might be a fresh eruption of risk, which would lead more clearly to the removal of the children.

The development of plans for adoption

The number of adoption plans increased dramatically during care proceedings, mainly as a result of the collapse of rehabilitation plans. As can be seen from Table 5.1, nineteen initial plans for adoption were extended to 33. Only one child with an initial adoption plan was diverted to another placement option (foster care). Of the others, ten children had adoption plans that were fully formed within weeks of the application date and they did not change. Another eight children started with tentative adoption plans, which were firmed up, and fifteen new children were added to the adoption list.

The 'firming up' of adoption plans

There were some commonalities in the ten 'definite' cases. Typically:

- The family history was well known.
- One or more children had already been removed.
- Rehabilitation was considered strongly inadvisable.
- There was no other relative capable of caring for the child.
- Permanent placement was seen to be needed.
- The child was young and without significant behaviour problems.

Where the family history was well known, the agency was not starting from 'square one' in the assessment process. Attention had to be paid to changes of circumstance, such as partners joining or leaving the family, and the court also had to consider the possibility that the parents had matured; but when already there was a repeating pattern which involved risk to the child as well as non-cooperation on the part of the parents, the net result was that:

- in these 'definite' cases the assessment moved very rapidly through the first three stages outlined in the last chapter. The pattern charted by social services was confirmed by the children's guardian and ultimately by the court.

In cases where an adoption plan needed extensive 'firming up', the main alternative to adoption was not rehabilitation but *kinship care*. These children tended to be slightly older than the others (typically more than 2 years old at the time of the final court hearing), and since they had experience of relationships within the birth family, the possibility of care by a relative or at least face-to-face contact after adoption had to be actively considered.

- The fact that other family members such as grandparents and fathers were putting themselves forward as carers meant that the adoption plan could not be clear-cut until all the necessary assessments had been made.

In spite of minor disagreements, there was a considerable degree of consensus between social workers and guardians in terms of the actual placement choice. There was only one case where an initial plan for adoption was not carried through to final hearing.

Was post-adoption contact considered?

In the final plans *indirect contact* was offered to relatives who needed to be kept in touch with the child by means of information exchange; but with the exception of siblings in joint placements,[4] there were almost no cases where the care plan recommended face-to-face contact between a child and any member of the birth family after adoption. The main reason given by the practitioners was that ongoing contact was not in children's interests, either because there was risk of abuse or because it was feared that relatives would undermine the placement – and in the case of small babies removed at birth, there was no pre-existing relationship that needed to be maintained. Second, there was a wish not to bind unknown adopters to commitments they might not be willing to undertake, and this was usually accompanied by a fear that children with plans for ongoing face-to-face contact would be 'hard to place'.[5] Adoption had usually been ruled out as a placement option when the child had a definite need for contact with the birth family; but there were also occasions on which contact was deliberately axed in order to facilitate adoption. One solicitor said: 'If it's clear that we're dealing with a young child and contact isn't going to be official, then normally I would just go for permission to refuse contact. It speeds things up and I think it's probably kinder to the parents as well.'

For whatever reason, *decisions to terminate contact were extremely common in adoption*, though not in other placement options. It is interesting to note that the relatives singled out for termination of contact were those who were likely to want to get in touch with the child. When grandparents made a bid for the child in adoption cases and failed, this usually provoked a definite decision to terminate contact. This was different from the pattern in other placement options, where termination of contact was only considered if there was risk of the child being abused.

Avoiding delay in adoption cases

Guardians and solicitors were anxious to ensure that cases involving newborn babies were not unduly delayed during the court process. In one such situation where an assessment had to be made of a mother's parenting and potential to change her drug habits, the guardian said: 'I think that in circumstances like this an over-abundance of openness towards rehab has to be allowed, but within a reasonable time-frame. So that's not a time-frame of a year, but it's probably a time-frame of eight to twelve weeks.'

In another case the solicitor supported formal assessment of the mother to avoid any criticism of the local authority, but the guardian thought that the social services department would have been within its rights to dispense with the assessment because of the previous history.[6] However, it should be noted that cases that shifted from rehabilitation to adoption took no longer than the others. The children who spent most time in care proceedings prior to adoption were not those whose plans changed radically, but those whose adoption plans had to be 'firmed up'.[7] Since these children tended to be more than 1 year old at the start of proceedings, and since they also spent longer in the court system because of the complexity of their cases, the age difference between them and the others was unfortunately exacerbated.

As can be seen from Table 5.2, there was a slight tendency for cases heard in the family proceedings court to be finalised more quickly than in care centres, but this difference is not really large enough to cause concern.

Table 5.2 ***Adoption plans: duration of proceedings and tier of court at final hearing***

	Time from first application to final hearing			
	Less than 6 months	6–9 months	9–12 months	12–18 months
Family proceedings court	6	8	–	–
County court	5	7	1	4
High Court	–	2	–	–

The development of plans for long-term fostering

Fostering was the main option being considered for children of school age who definitely needed substitute care. Nineteen children entered care proceedings with an initial preference for foster care, and this placement was finally recommended for 22 children. In total:

- Fifteen fostering plans were carried through to the final hearing.
- Four children had their plan changed from foster care to adoption.
- Seven children were added to the fostering list.

Foster care is of course the backbone of the care system, but it was not always seen as a positive option. Of the seven children whose names were added to the fostering list during care proceedings, five children started with a plan for rehabilitation that collapsed, while two other children had an initial plan for kinship care, but the relatives or friends favoured by the children would not agree to look after them. Adoption had usually been ruled out on the grounds that the child was too old or had behavioural difficulties or specific contact needs. As previously mentioned, some solicitors were disinclined to favour a care order with a fostering plan in situations where adolescents were likely to abscond from any placement. (This was also an issue in residential care.) However, the guardian might have stronger views about the responsibilities which the local authority should undertake.

Children's wishes and feelings

In their role as the child's representative, the guardians found themselves coping with deep anxieties while sounding out children's 'wishes and feelings' about intended placements. These anxieties made it difficult for children to agree to the plan. A guardian who dealt with two sisters (aged 11 and 12) who needed to leave a mentally ill mother said:

> They wanted to know who these foster parents were, what this foster home was going to be about ... what the expectations of them were, what part they were going to play in that home, as part of that family, how they were going to maintain contact with their mother and the extended family ... And there were the practical difficulties of, you know, how they were going to get to school ... and just getting used to a different way of life, which it would inevitably be for them.

Children's attitude to the plan could be influenced not just by a brief experience of foster care but by the manner in which the move was accomplished. Here is a comment made by a guardian who dealt with a 13-year-old boy with learning difficulties:

> Paul had this vision of foster care, because of the circumstances when the interim care order was first made, of trying to remove him from the household. It was extremely difficult and he was saying he wouldn't go; I mean he was just lifted up! Although the social worker in an ideal world would have wanted to do introductions and do it all properly, Paul just wasn't able to co-operate with any of that. So he was literally kind of lifted and placed somewhere.

Ten of the 22 children whose plan was for long-term fostering were made the subjects of *emergency protection orders* at the start of care proceedings. This is a higher usage of emergency protection orders than that found at the start of adoption cases (six out of 33) and it indicates a higher rate of compulsory removal than was found in any other placement option with the exception of kinship care (nine out of eighteen). It stands to reason that these events had an impact on children's 'wishes and feelings', and if the distress could not be dealt with during care proceedings, the viability of the plan was in jeopardy.

The guardians tried to support the child's wishes about the care plan wherever possible. However, it was not always feasible to support plans where young people said that they wanted to return to an unsuitable environment. It was impossible, too, where they said that they wanted to live on their own without any parenting at all. How did the guardians reconcile the children's wishes with their own perceptions of the child's interests? This was recognised to be an enduring problem, but the guardians felt that in many cases the *child's views shifted during the course of care proceedings* – partly because of their adjustment to the new situation through time spent in the care system, and partly because they began to accept the concerns of social services. Here is one guardian's description of this process in action. The girl she is referring to is 9 years old, and in her family she had occupied the role of a 'parental child'.

> Like 99% of the children, her views were 'Yes, I do want to stay with mum and dad'; but there were subtle messages being given out about her fears and concerns. In the beginning I felt confident that she understood what she was saying and understood the consequences. Then it changed to my wondering if that was still what she wanted, to her actually withdrawing, becoming more guarded, showing less fight about the eventual outcome.

Some children were said to remain ambivalent throughout care proceedings. Others never fully accepted the plan for substitute care, although in the opinions of the guardians they agreed to it because they felt there was no option.

The need for separate representation

Only one young person in the study was separately represented by a solicitor to whom she gave instructions. Should this procedure have been used more often? A study by Ruegger (2001) found that children did not fully understand the guardian's role or the right to separate representation, and they became frustrated if their wishes were not relayed to the court. Masson and Oakley (1999) reported that guardians' implicit decisions about children's age and competence resulted in a low level of separate representation.

The guardians in the study were very aware of the importance of this issue. One experienced guardian said that when dealing with adolescents she was alert to the possibility 'from day one'. She worked closely with a solicitor when determining the need for separate representation, both to obtain a second opinion about what the child actually wanted and to enable a judgement to be formed about the child's ability to give instructions. Partnership with solicitors who were prepared to work 'hands-on' was greatly valued and deliberately sought. One guardian said that in a case that involved possible sexual abuse of a teenage girl she engaged an experienced woman who would have 'taken her on' if separate representation had been required. Yet another changed the solicitor when she found that an adolescent boy with learning difficulties was unhappy at the idea of being represented by him.

If young people were really unwilling to accept a fostering plan that was deemed to be in their best interests, the move to the foster placement was sometimes postponed to give them an opportunity to change their minds. Three teenagers accepted a 'bridging placement' in residential care, with the proviso that a specialised foster placement would be found and entered at a later date.

Contact with the birth family in fostering plans

The continuation of contact was an important issue in fostering and the children's guardians were heavily involved in these arrangements, which affected the welfare of children during proceedings as well as in the care plans. In most cases there was a presumption that contact would continue and an implicit reliance on the ability of social services to sustain it. This was made explicit in one case, where the magistrates said that they would not make a contact order but would rely instead on the statements made in the care plan.

Because of the importance of contact in foster care, long-term plans were clearly needed. However, three considerations contributed to the fact that the plans were often short term.

- *Social workers and their managers,* in company with the *carers,* often felt that contact arrangements would have to support the placement rather than this happening the other way round.
- *Local authority solicitors* were concerned not to bind the authority too tightly, since this might result in parental applications to the court for increased contact at a later date.
- *Guardians* realised that a degree of flexibility was necessary in the children's interests, because contact plans might have to shift over time.

As a result, the guardian and the solicitor often supported the social services department in leaving future options open, and plans for contact were marked 'subject to review'. This was particularly common in fostering, though it applied in other placement options as well.

The development of plans for kinship care

As can be seen from Table 5.1, there were eighteen final recommendations for children to live with a relative or friend. This matches the number of initial plans in which preference was given to this placement option, although some changes had occurred along the way. Three children who were hoping to live with relatives had their plans changed (one to adoption and two to foster care) because the prospective carer withdrew during care proceedings, and three new children were given kinship plans when it was clear that return home was impossible.

As already reported, there were two categories of kinship carers in the final plans. They were:

- members of the extended family; and
- birth fathers.

Members of the extended family. For nine children who would otherwise have found their way into long-term fostering, the final plan was that they would be looked after by a member of the extended family. The carers selected for the task were five aunts, three paternal grandparents and one paternal great-aunt and uncle. Four of these plans were formed at an early stage in the proceedings because the relatives were already in touch with the child or arrived on the scene as soon as they heard that care proceedings were being initiated. However, the carers did not always volunteer. In two cases the relatives had to be approached by social services after the child expressed a wish to live with them.

Birth fathers. Another nine children from five families were to be looked after by a father or father plus partner. Since the strengths and weaknesses of the father were not always known, parallel assessments of both parents had to be carried out in two families. However, the interviews suggest that in these cases there was usually a pre-existing preference for care by the father, and a presumption that he would take over the care of the child as long as his assessment was positive.

The assessment of kinship carers

With the approval of the children's guardians, the suitability of carers within the family was interpreted in a very wide sense in these cases compared with those where the initial plan was adoption or fostering. The psychologically based, strongly developmental type of assessment used in adoption was replaced by one that might be described as ecological in focus. It picked up on ethnic and community links as well as family ties. The assessments were sometimes less rigorous than would have been the case in approving foster carers, partly because each of the kinship carers was being approved for one particular child, and partly because of the impetus given to the placement choice by the child's own views. One guardian who dealt with two separate cases where the children (one girl aged 4 and another aged 14) had made it clear that they would not accept fostering with strangers said:

> I think we're all aware ... that there are more difficulties sometimes when it's family than there are with neutral foster parents, although there are significant advantages for children if they can remain in their family ... In both these cases the difficulties were looked at very carefully ... but I think it was recognised, certainly in terms of Marcia [the teenager], that this was the only option for her that was going to have any hope of working ... There was an aspect of 'Well, if she's happy with it, providing there's nothing obviously wrong with this aunt, let's try it out.'

Similar sentiments were expressed by another guardian who dealt with a 15-year-old girl who had a history of absconding from residential care, and whose problems included non-school attendance, eating disorders, drug and alcohol abuse: 'She wanted to live in Scotland – very clearly wanted to. And nothing was working down here. We thought "If we bring her back here it's going to be worse. At least give it a try."'

Another problem commented on by social workers was the need to do a very rapid assessment of fathers and other relatives who had been virtually unknown to the department before the onset of proceedings, and who needed to move quickly from a standing start.

Very exceptionally care was taken on by 'significant others' who had known the child long term but were not blood relatives. There appeared to be no well-trodden route to process the assessment in these cases, and in one case the carers applied to the court for a residence order at very considerable personal expense because they wanted to 'become part of the care plan' (See Chapter 6.) It was only through the ingenuity of the guardian that they became parties to the proceedings. These problems may reflect the fact that placement with non-relatives was rarely used, as appears to be the case nationally.

The development of plans for residential care

In cases involving older adolescents, the social workers, guardians and solicitors faced difficult decisions – not simply in relation to the care plan but in relation to the need for the order and the grounds on which it might be obtained. In two cases where there were unproven allegations of sexual abuse the grounds chosen were 'beyond parental control' to avoid a contested hearing. In another case there was disagreement between one local authority solicitor and her colleague about whether it was appropriate to take care proceedings at all.

The five young people for whom residential care was planned were to be placed separately. Even in such a small group, the placement plans reflect the very wide range of residential provision available for young people. They included:

- two residential schools;
- two therapeutic communities; and
- one local authority children's home.

In two cases the children were already living in the institutions named in the care plan (one school and one residential home). In the other cases visits were made prior to the order, to try to ensure that the young people would undertake some commitment to the placement.

Because of their knowledge of out-of-county resources, the guardians could be helpful in identifying places – particularly in therapeutic communities – but resource shortages and the need to negotiate funding arrangements with other agencies made these plans difficult to firm up and finalise. One guardian who dealt with a 13-year-old boy drew attention to the fact that it is not only in adoption cases that reasonable speed is required: 'There was a lot of frustration with Moulton Hall – just waiting, waiting, waiting … meanwhile he was just out of control on the streets.'

With the support of the guardians, *secure orders* had been made on two adolescents at the start of care proceedings. The secure orders were discharged at the time when the care orders were made, and alternative placements for these two children had been found; but questions of cost and availability explain why, with the exception of bridging placements in ordinary residential homes, the plans for residential care were so few.

Placement choice at final hearing: an overview

In this final section we look across each placement option to analyse some of the key factors that seemed to be related to placement choice. *The importance of the child's age* has already been highlighted. It will be recalled that there was a strong statistical link between age and placement choice, adoption and home placement being selected for the youngest children (Wald test, $p<0.01$). Kinship care and home placements had the widest spread of ages – from 0 to 15 in the first case and from 0 to 13 in the second. Adoption was never recommended for children over the age of 7, while foster homes catered mainly for children in the middle ranges (5 to 15) and residential care was limited to young people over the age of 12. By contrast *the impact of gender was slight*; there were more girls than boys in the study overall (54:46) but the excess was more or less evenly spread across the options. *Ethnicity was most clearly associated with kinship care*, which was planned for seven of the fourteen children who were of minority ethnic status. (Four of these children were black and three were of dual heritage.)

The child's previous history was related to placement choice at final hearing. Emotional and behavioural difficulties noted in the court proceedings were most strongly associated with residential care, followed by plans for foster care (54%) and kinship care (33%) while developmental delay mentioned in court reports was mainly found in adoption plans (33%). Educational difficulties mentioned in court reports featured in all the residential care plans but they were also present in a substantial number of foster care plans (45%) – more than twice the proportions found in kinship (22%) and adoption (18%). No home placement plans at final hearing had children with educational difficulties cited in court reports.

Some links were noted between placement choice and *parental difficulties*. Alcohol abuse, as already noted, was present as a major factor in sixteen of the families, affecting 26 children. Home placements had the highest proportion of parents in which alcohol misuse was judged to be a major factor. By contrast drug abuse was most strongly associated with kinship placements. (See Chapter 4.)

Another consideration that was extremely important in planning during care proceedings was *the child's need to be placed singly or with other members of the sibling group*. Table 5.3 shows the final plans for the placement of siblings.

Table 5.3 ***Plans for placement of siblings***

	Adoption	**Foster care**	**Kinship care**	**Home placement**	**Residential**
Singletons	17	8	6	4	5
Siblings to be placed singly	2	7	3	0	0
Siblings to be placed as a pair	10 (5 pairs)	4 (2 pairs)	6 (3 pairs)	0	0
Siblings to be placed as a group	4 (1 group)	3 (1 group)	3 (1 group)	18 (6 groups)	0
Total number of children	**33**	**22**	**18**	**22**	**5**

As attempts were made to ensure that children were placed with at least one other sibling wherever possible, Table 5.3 does not reveal the full extent of the separations that children had suffered. Some points that should be highlighted are described below.

- *Home placements* were more likely than any other option to involve members of a group, and groups of three children were usually selected; but in four out of the six families who according to the care plans would have three children placed at home, there were other siblings who entered care proceedings at the same time as their brothers and sisters and who were re-routed to out-of-home care.
- Almost equal proportions of children in *kinship care* (33%) and *adoption* (30%) were to be placed in pairs according to the plan at final hearing but, once again, many of these pairs had been split off from larger groups. (This applied to three of the five pairs with adoption plans and two of the three pairs with kinship plans.)
- Siblings were especially likely to be placed separately in *long-term foster care.*

As mentioned in Chapter 4, attention was paid to the relative ages of the children when sibling groups were divided. If one child was to be separated from the others it tended to be the eldest (fostered when the rest were to be adopted) or the youngest (adopted when the rest were fostered).

Contact plans by placement option

When joint placements are included, the type of ongoing contact most frequently planned was between children and their siblings or half-siblings, either in or out of care. The adult most frequently mentioned in contact plans was the birth mother. (In these plans birth mothers outnumber fathers in the ratio 3:2.) However, contact with other relatives, though at a lower level, was deemed important in fostering as well as kinship care – and grandparents were considered to have an important role in supporting home placements.

Table 5.4 ***Plans for continuation of face-to-face contact with named individuals at time of final hearing***[a]

	Birth mother	Birth father	Step-mother	Step-father	One or more siblings	Aunt or uncle	Grand-parent
Adoption	4	4	–	–	13	–	–
Foster care	20	13	1	3	19	3	3
Home placement	22	9	–	3	20	–	7
Kinship care	17	12	4	1	15	5	5
Residential care	5	4	–	1	4	–	–
Total	**68**	**42**	**5**	**8**	**71**	**8**	**15**

[a] Indirect contact has not been included in this table because it applies to adoption only. Also, the numbers need to be read in association with the numbers of children for whom these placements were selected in the final plans. (See Table 5.1.)

Plans for ongoing contact were, as one might expect, much more frequent than plans for termination – except in adoption cases; but much of this contact would take place as the result of *joint placement*. This applies not only to sibling contact but to interaction with mothers or fathers in the home environment.

The impact of the court process

Table 5.5 contains a brief summary of the care plans made at each tier of court. County courts and family proceedings courts dealt with cases representing all placement options and the volume of work was fairly evenly balanced – but the magistrates' courts had more fostering cases, while the higher courts dealt with more children heading for adoption or kinship care. A total of seven courts were represented in the study.

Were there any instances of the court *acting of its own motion*? In view of the frustration experienced by some judges (see Chapter 1) this is a relevant question to ask. We found no cases in which the courts sent back for further consideration any plans that may have appeared ambitious or inchoate, although one court was said to be unhappy about the care plan. Nor were there any instances of senior social service personnel being called to court by the judiciary to underwrite any of the plans, for example where expensive or scarce resources were required – although solicitors cited other cases where this had happened. Some social workers actually felt that the plan would have benefited from a more thorough scrutiny by the court, at an earlier stage in the process.

Table 5.5 ***Tier of court and care plans at final hearing for the 100 sample children***[a]

Placement plan	Tier of court at final hearing					
	FPC		**County court**		**High Court**	
	Children	**Families**	**Children**	**Families**	**Children**	**Families**
Adoption	14	8	17	13	2	2
Foster care	12	9	9	5	1	1
Home placement	11	5	11	5	–	–
Kinship care	6	5	12	6	–	–
Residential care	2	2	3	3	–	–
Total	**45**	**29**	**52**	**32**	**3**	**3**

[a] The total number of families is larger than 57 as children from the same family were included in more than one placement option.

There was one case in which the court ordered a residential assessment under section 38(6), and it was deeply resented by the local authority because of the very considerable costs involved and the view that the outcome was a foregone conclusion.[8] In the only case that remained embattled to the end regarding the choice of order – a case involving an out of control teenager – the court overrode the wishes of the local authority that a care order should not be made and followed the guardian's advice. All requests for contact orders were granted, except in two cases where the initial plan had been rehabilitation.

Since these particular plans changed to substitute care at a very late stage, the court apparently decided that it would be premature to authorise termination of contact when the children and their parents had been in close contact throughout the proceedings.

Discussion and conclusions

How did the events during care proceedings affect the final plan? The most dramatic changes were in the 25% of plans that changed radically, and in most of these cases the initial preference of the agency had been for home placement. During care proceedings the number of initial plans for home placement decreased by more than one-third. Most of the children deflected in this way ended up with adoption plans, although some were heading for long-term fostering; but a wider issue raised by the research was the rationale for home placements in general and the considerable variation in local authority practices in this regard. In some cases where placement at home had been planned the care order was apparently being used as a threat, its main value being that it gave the local authority the right to remove a child quickly without the need to return to court. There is clearly a need to re-evaluate this practice.

What happened in the 60% of plans that were 'firmed up' during care proceedings? The placement choice was finalised, resources were added and in some cases interdisciplinary funding was arranged. Contact arrangements were often seen as problematic, as were the plans for the placement of siblings (see Table 5.3) and attempts were made to safeguard important relationships by means of joint placement.

The children's guardians had considerable influence in all these areas, and local authority solicitors also helped to firm up details of the plan. Everything that happened during care proceedings had an impact, including the actions of parents and children. However, there was very little direct input to the plan from the court itself.

Summary

1 At the time of application to the court, views had already been formed about the preferred plan for the child. During care proceedings 15% of these early plans did not change in any way. Another 25% altered

radically and the remaining 60% were 'firmed up'. Key players at this stage were the guardians and the local authority solicitors.

2 For 22 children, the care plan recommended home placement, and 18 of their children were in sibling groups. In these cases it was felt that the care order would provide security for the children as well as ensuring the take-up of services. However, plans for home placement were not always positive options. They were sometimes made because solicitors and guardians felt that it would be difficult to justify a plan for substitute care.

3 Thirty-three plans were made for adoption. (This number increased dramatically during care proceedings, as rehabilitation became ruled out.) All the children involved were very young (below the age of 7, with an average age of 2.5 years). With the exception of siblings in joint placements, there were almost no cases where social workers or guardians recommended face-to-face contact with any member of the birth family after the adoption placement had been made.

4 Long-term foster care was recommended for 22 children and young people. For seven of those aged 13 or over, specialist foster placements were needed. The five residential care placements, which also catered for adolescents, included two residential schools, two therapeutic communities and one local authority children's home.

5 There were eighteen plans for children to live with a relative or friend. These assessments picked up on ethnic community links as well as family ties.

6 The placement overview shows that there was a strong statistical link between age and placement choice, adoption and home placement being selected for the youngest children. Educational difficulties mentioned in court reports, and emotional and behavioural difficulties, were common in the backgrounds of young people selected for fostering or residential care.

---

[1] The changes in fostering and kinship plans are greater than the figures in Table 5.1 would suggest, since there was movement both into and out of these placement options.

[2] The tendency for concerns to be transferred from the father or stepfather to the mother during the course of investigations has been documented in child protection research (Farmer and Owen 1995; 1998).

[3] This position has become less tenable following the introduction of human rights legislation. Lady Justice Hale has argued that it is not open to the court to give the local authority a disproportionate power to intervene, so a care order may not be appropriate if the child is to remain at home. See the conference report *Care plans – the Way Ahead* (Children Law UK 2002).

[4] In two cases the adopters of other siblings were approached to find out if they would entertain the idea of another placement, or alternatively permit contact if the adopter of the new child was willing.

[5] Similar findings were reported in the study by Lowe and Murch (2002), who also reported a worry among social workers that adopters would not maintain contact arrangements once they had parental responsibility.

[6] Dame Margaret Booth's enquiry into delay in Children Act cases (Booth 1996) noted that assessments can set people up to fail unless there are real prospects for positive outcomes.

[7] In both 'definite' cases and those that showed a radical shift, the time from court application to final order varied between six weeks and nine months, and the average time spent in care proceedings was just under six months; but in the cases where an adoption plan had to be 'firmed up', the time spent in care proceedings was longer. The range was from four months to eighteen months, and the average was ten months.

[8] In the House of Lords judgement *Re C (A Minor) Interim Care Order: Residential Assessment* (1996), which upheld the right of courts to order section 38(5) assessments, Lord Browne-Wilkinson commented: 'In exercising its jurisdiction as to whether to order any particular examination or assessment, the court will take into account the costs of the proposed assessment and the fact that the local authority's resources are notoriously limited' (LCD 1997a, p. 72).

6 Care planning: the experiences of parents, carers and children

Introduction

Care proceedings are always a traumatic time for parents and children alike. Other studies have drawn attention to parents' sense of powerlessness in courts and case conferences, their feelings of anger and confusion, and the ways in which stress interferes with their attempts to participate even if the outcome is not seen to be unfair (Packman 1986; Farmer and Owen 1995; Freeman and Hunt 1998). Little work has been done on consumer perspectives of the care planning process during proceedings, however, and this topic formed an important focus in the interviews with birth parents, current carers and children in our own study.[1] Current policy and practice underlines the importance of consulting parents, giving them space to air their own agenda and helping them to make informed choices (DoH 2001a, p75), while children also need to be able to talk over their fears and feel that they have some control over events in their lives (DoH 2001a, p88).

As mentioned in Chapter 2, the number of birth parents who were prepared to take part in the study was rather small and they are not necessarily representative; but their views are nevertheless important because there is a great need to make practice more sensitive to their concerns. Carers participated from all the substitute care options, and there was also a good response from children and young people in fostering and residential care.

This chapter is divided into two parts. The first presents the views of birth parents and the different groups of carers, while the second presents the views of children and young people. At the most basic level the interviews were designed to establish people's knowledge and understanding of the court plan and to see how far they felt involved in the planning process. Many of the current carers and almost all of the adopters and prospective adopters had not been on the scene at the time of the final court hearing – but their views about the value and purpose of care planning added a useful dimension to this part of the research.

Parents and carers

Knowledge and understanding of the care plan

Birth parents

Four of the twelve birth parents interviewed had difficulty in identifying the care plan that had been presented to the court. In part, this was probably a result of the time that had elapsed since the final hearing (up to two years in some cases). In part, it was because they found it difficult to separate this plan from the series of other plans that had been made and were still being made for their children. Their views were of course coloured by the outcome of care proceedings, and in most cases the outcome had not been in their favour.

The majority of the respondents could not remember the content of the court care plan in any detail. When prompted by the interviewer they sometimes remembered contact and placement arrangements, but only exceptionally did they recall services to be offered to the child or family. Two parents said that they had not received a copy of the plan, while one was not sure whether she had seen it or not, and another said she had no knowledge of the care plan until she got to court. This was unexpected since care plans are filed in the proceedings to which the parents are parties.

The tendency to forget was no doubt reinforced by the unpleasantness of the whole experience: 'All the plans are something that has not stuck in my head; it is just like gone' and 'I wasn't able to take it in really' were two of the comments made.

It was important to have the plan explained by a sympathetic person. One birth parent said 'I've got the papers and what have you, but it's a lot of jargon ... I think things could have been explained a bit more. It just happened too quickly for me to be able to think about it.'

Confusion about the nature and content of the care plan was accompanied by confusion about its purpose. Two fathers saw it as presenting evidence to the court in support of the care order, and at the same time vindicating their own claim to the child. (One said 'I think it was to prove grounds for a care order' and the other said 'It was to dissuade the court from listening to Miss T [the child's mother] and to persuade them to listen to me.') More accurately, it was described by other parents as 'an action plan' or 'guidelines on how social services are hoping to implement the order', and its purpose was seen as ensuring the well-being of the child. One mother with learning difficulties had had the plan thoroughly explained to her, and she felt that every parent should receive a copy.

> I would like to have a copy of it so, when Lucy gets older, I could show her, if she asked you know, why was we living with people or why were we there? It would be nice to have a copy to show her – to read it to her so that she can understand more.

Foster carers

Foster carers had generally not seen the plan but they knew of its existence. They described its purpose as 'to provide information', 'to show the court what is happening to the child', 'to map out the child's life' and 'for someone to check out what's happening' (an interesting element of accountability), 'to provide a guide to the way in which a child should be brought up' and 'to give the child a normal life'. Six of the eighteen foster carers interviewed felt that it might have been useful for them to see the plan, but the issue that was most important to them was the provision of information about the children who were placed with them. They were happy for this information to come directly from the social worker by word of mouth. The information they most wanted concerned the backgrounds of the children, and particularly the details of any abuse they had suffered.

Residential social workers

Residential social workers had not usually seen the plan. Like foster carers, they wanted information on the children in their care but, since they were also social workers, they were concerned to know the circumstances surrounding the care order and the direction that children's careers had taken. Residential workers were generally happy with the information they had been given, but because of the organisational gap between residential care and the work of the area team, together with the high turn-over of staff in residential homes, there were discontinuities that could result in the care plan disappearing from sight. They said: 'The information did come back to the unit; but I wasn't there at first hand' and 'The social worker ... wasn't very forthcoming with us about what she was doing. She was an older social worker from the time when residential workers were poor relations to social workers. As a case holder, she didn't feel the need to keep us informed.'

One residential social worker who found himself caring for a difficult child after a foster-home breakdown made attempts to trace the boy's history himself. The research interviewer asked, 'Do you know what the plan was, that was submitted when the care order was obtained?' his reply was:

> No. I actually asked at one point. I was so in the dark about Kevin and his background that someone suggested that I went into the office and actually read his files. I went in and the social worker wasn't there. I walked in to have a finger pointed to a desk where there was a pile of files. 'That is what you

> want.' So I sat there. I asked if I could have a copy of the care order. I couldn't find it – and I still haven't got a copy of the care order.

Following this, the interviewer checked whether he had actually been told what the plan was. The residential carer answered 'No, absolutely not.'

Kinship carers

Kinship carers, in contrast with every other group of carers including adoptive parents, had always been involved at the time when the care order was made. This meant that, with the exception of birth parents, they were the group of adults most likely to have intimate knowledge of the development of the care plan. Like other interviewees, they often had difficulty in recalling the details, but their accounts highlight another issue – that in the initial stages of care proceedings the local authority's intentions were sometimes extremely unclear. This quotation comes from a kinship carer who was looking after one member of a large sibling group: 'They didn't know themselves [what the plans were] ... It was just a muddle, weren't it? They went around there and took all the kids that day. She [the children's mother] came marching around here crying: "They took all my kids. What am I going to do?"'

Another couple who wanted to become kinship carers were very relieved to see the documented care plan, because this was the first time they felt that the agency's intentions could be relied on: 'For us, it meant that we could actually see they meant it in black and white. All the way through it was like running a race, and we kept jumping hurdles, and every now and then they put a ditch in unexpectedly – that's how it felt.'

Adoptive parents and prospective adopters

Adoptive parents and prospective adopters felt that their experience distanced them both from the court hearing and from the initial actions of social services. They were keen to have information on children's difficulties and how these might be caused, mainly so that they could predict and deal with any problems that might occur in the future, but they did not usually feel that they were entitled to detailed information about the past and were duly appreciative when it was provided by social services. (One adopter said: 'There was a lot of helpful information about his birth family, which was given to us in the strictest confidence.') They knew that the plan presented to the court at the final hearing had recommended adoption, but they did not know what services had been planned or what time-scales had been proposed – even though it might have been in their interests to be given this information. In two cases they knew that the initial contact arrangements had been changed.

Only three adopters had actually seen the plan but, of the others, only one couple said that they would like to have seen it. Most people did not think it relevant:

> I would always say a written brief is useful – but I think we had that much verbal contact with the social workers, it wasn't really necessary.

> I don't think we would have had much control of that [i.e. what happened during care proceedings]. It is in their system to protect them, so adoptive parents coming into it is another branch of it. They don't marry up necessarily. You have to go through completely different procedures to get to the children.

A single adoptive parent who took over care of a small baby said:

> All I can remember of the care plan was when they came and said to me 'What did he do?' 'What was my routine with Joseph?' ... I made up my own care plan and routine, which I kept on the fridge door, so that anyone who came to stay or look after him knew from hour to hour what I did with Joseph. The only bit of the care plan that I can remember was what was going to happen in the future.

Views on variation

Did the respondents think it was permissible for social services to vary the plan? The group of birth parents was evenly divided on this topic, half being in favour of flexibility in response to changing circumstances while the other half wanted the plan to be rigidly maintained (One father said 'It's legal and binding. They can't back off at all – no way.'). Two parents made the interesting and important point that if plans were to change, parents should be consulted. There is little evidence that they were routinely consulted, or that they understood the legal options available to them.

Foster carers, residential workers and adoptive parents were generally in favour of flexible planning. There were only three foster carers and one adopter who thought that the plan should be followed rigidly, and one foster carer who felt that the court should be informed if the plan changed direction. However, some caution was expressed about the extent of any changes. One adoptive parent said that a plan should not need to be changed 'if social services have done their homework and research properly ... On the whole I expect them to carry on the process they've started. The child always comes first – I accept that – but I would be most upset if I'd been built up and prepared for it and they say "We've changed our mind."'

Involvement in the care planning process

The principle of 'partnership' underlies the Children Act 1989, and one aspect of this principle in action is that parents as well as children should be consulted before decisions are made about children's futures. When compulsory powers are used, some conflicts may be inevitable; but the Department of Health Guidance (DoH 1991b, Vol. 3) urges local authorities to reach agreement with parents wherever possible, and it is clear that this is envisaged as a continuing process: 'A child's interests are likely to be served best if the parents are encouraged to keep in touch and take an active role in planning for the child. This will be the case even where the long-term plan for the child is that he remains in care.'

Two sets of birth parents in the study said that they had been fully involved in the planning process during care proceedings and that they had been shown all the relevant documents, but they felt that their views mattered much less than their children's views. For two other parents, the priority given to their children's views made them feel excluded from the process. One reported that she was made to feel 'an unstable person' and the other 'a drug-crazed monster'. They avoided meetings for a period during proceedings because they thought that the situation was completely hopeless, and consequently they did not know the plans for the children at the time when they were drawn up. In two other cases fathers felt strongly that the system favoured mothers: 'As I see it, they don't give fathers a chance at all. You know it is not always the father's fault.'

Most birth parents could identify at least one professional who had listened to them during the course of the proceedings, but they were much less sure of their ability to influence decisions. The guardian most consistently came in for praise. Here are three different parents speaking: 'She was fantastic. She listened to all that I said. I saw her as the "guardian angel" and said "Would you tell the children this ..."', The only person who was interested was the guardian' and 'They listened to all that I said were my problems and what not.'

Views of the helpfulness of solicitors were more variable. Even those who were acting for the parents were sometimes deemed to be in league with social services – or simply ineffective. But two parents singled out the judge for special praise. (One father said: 'The judge know what he is saying. He ain't no fool and nobody can bribe the judge!') The study by Freeman and Hunt (1998) also found that there was a tendency for judges and magistrates to escape strong criticism. Given the nature of the proceedings, it is perhaps unsurprising that social services were seen less positively than the court itself. The use of power by social services was not always found to be problematic, however. One parent with learning difficulties was happy enough for social services to take decisions on her behalf – although in this and other cases there was evidence of work being done by social workers to increase the parent's understanding of the care order and its impact. Another mother who had a disabled child was ambivalent about social services involvement, as she wanted someone to take responsibility for her daughter but resented the fact that she was pushed into certain decisions by the social worker. At the extreme edge, one father felt totally shut out and unable to contribute.

Relatives and 'significant others' who had put themselves forward as kinship carers had some strong views about the way in which they had been involved. The most frequent complaint was that social workers had not made enough effort to find out about their existence, and consequently they had not been contacted soon enough. Since the primary reason for the social services departments to contact members of the extended family at the start of care proceedings was the hope that they might accommodate one or more children, it appears that relatives were not routinely consulted about placement decisions – unless there had previously been a family group conference, which was unusual in the cases studied.

> They didn't know about us when it all first started. They knew about Ann and Hannah but they didn't know there was an Uncle Robert. His name came up one day and they said 'What about Robert? Why can't one of them go and stay with Robert?' And that is when they phoned and we came into it.

A grandparent who volunteered to look after the child as soon as he heard that care proceedings were being initiated said: 'We didn't realise the degree of involvement that there was with social services ... They definitely should have had some liaison with us – not least because it wasn't a spur of the moment decision to remove him.'

The people who felt most marginalised in the planning process were often women not directly related to the child. They had taken on a caring role because they were the partners of fathers, uncles or grandfathers. (All of these were represented in the study.) One woman who had cared extensively for her partner's children when they were neglected by their mother, and who regarded them almost as her own children, felt spurned by social services when placement plans were being discussed.

> They [the social services] said: 'The boys are fine. They are in care, but we need to talk to their dad.' I said 'Well, I have been looking after them; why can't you talk to me?' They said 'Because you are not a blood relative.' Which I think is wrong because if there are people out there willing to look after children and do everything for them, why can't social services talk to them about it?

Because of her lack of involvement in the planning process, the woman in the above case felt that she was likely to lose out in favour of an adoptive parent.

> That is what makes me so angry. Adoptive parents, yes, are fine for kiddies who have not known someone else in their life, but I was a role model in them two boys' life and I still am. To put them up for adoption when I love them to bits and they are like my own – why should they want to put them up for adoption when I am capable of looking after them?

Did parents and carers agree with the plan?

Parents

In the sample as a whole, exactly one-third of the cases were contested (19 out of 57), and in the two-thirds of the cases that were not contested, there was agreement on the need for both the order and the plan. The interviews show that this agreement was often superficial. One parent 'went along with it' because she felt that the order was inevitable and the fostering plan would at least guarantee her access to the children. Another said that she 'agreed with all of it' because it was a time of great stress and she saw that the care order would be a source of help: 'It was so upsetting; I just say yes, yes, yes to everything they said. I just wanted somebody to help me look after my child.'

The prospect of rehabilitation was a particularly strong incentive to ignore everything else in the plan: 'I didn't disagree, no … if anything because I was so desperate to have him come home. So I didn't really care what they said. I just wanted him home.'

Sometimes the decision not to contest was reported to be the result of advice from the parent's solicitor: 'We had a solicitor … and he said it was best if we work with social services rather than against them', 'As long as you didn't contest anything, they were all hunky dory with you', 'I was told if I didn't concede the care orders then it would be more difficult to have access ... and rehabilitation and things like that.'

There is also evidence that some parents agreed to the plan and the order because they had simply given up. One parent of a teenage girl who had previously been accommodated in a residential home felt that her daughter had taken the initiative: 'I think it was a foregone conclusion ... because Kate had her mind set on a care order. There were quite a few other children there with care orders, and I think she wanted to have a care order.'

Another mother of a 3-year-old boy had clearly been depressed at the time of care proceedings. Having struggled for a long time with drug-taking and marital violence, she did not contest the order or the plan: 'I felt I'd lost John – and I didn't think I deserved him anyway, after what I felt I'd put him through.'

Foster and residential carers

Foster carers and residential carers generally agreed with the plan, and one reason was that they sometimes had an opportunity to contribute to assessments by means of observational evidence. This comment comes from a residential carer whose agency had contributed to plans for a 13-year-old boy with learning difficulties:

> The plan came to fruition through different reports and assessments, and part of this was our experience of the access visits ... We also did an overall assessment of how Peter was coping here, what his skills were, how we saw him as a young person within our system. It was contributory, I suppose – especially the fact that he was succeeding here and his schooling had improved.

Most of the foster carers interviewed had not been caring for a child in the sample at the time of care proceedings; but they tended to accept the recommendations of the care plan as offering the best way forward at the time when they were made: 'It seemed like the logical plan to go for', 'I think we were part of it, really' and 'Yes, I did agree. I just wanted what was best for the girls.'

One dissenting view was focused on an adoption plan, where the foster carer felt that adoption was unlikely to succeed and that long-term foster care would have been a better option: 'In some cases I agree with adoption ... In this case I didn't feel that it was really the best way to go. But you don't say anything; you go along with the plan.'

Foster carers were of course part of the care system itself and (with a few notable exceptions) they had faith in the judgements of the professionals. If they had criticisms, these were usually concerned not with the original plan but with the way in which it was being implemented – for example, if there seemed to be undue delay, or if they disliked the particular people chosen to adopt the child.

Adoptive parents and kinship carers

Adoptive parents agreed with the plan because it was consistent with the information they had been given about the child's past, and more importantly because it had enabled them to have a child. Kinship carers had mixed feelings. Although they saw that the care plan and the order had been necessary, they were also in close contact with the previous carer, who was usually the child's mother: 'She was a brilliant mother and she just went downhill … She got in with the wrong fellow and got into the wrong stuff. But towards the end of it, it was my mum doing all the work; so they were better off out of there.'

They also knew that the task they had undertaken in response to the plan was an onerous one, which was sometimes ill-rewarded: 'We were thinking about all sorts of things to do for the next twenty years of our lives. But trying to bring up a badly damaged child was not what we were planning to do with our lives.'

One couple were so determined to become kinship carers that they engaged a solicitor and applied to the court for a residence order, with the help of the guardian and at very considerable expense to themselves. Eventually, they said, the judge gave qualified approval to the care plan as long as the child stayed with them: 'We relaxed a bit then – and we became part of the care plan, for Josie to stay long term.'

The children

Like the adults, the children who were interviewed often confused the court care plan with others to which they had been subject. At the time of the interviews the court hearing was in the past, and if they saw and understood the value of planning (which was by no means a universal experience)[2] children were most concerned with the current plan for their care. Their experience of planning during care proceedings was still a live issue, however, and children were given an opportunity to talk about it during the research interviews.

Most of the children had significant things to say about their experiences of court, about the planning process and about ways in which things could be done better.

Knowledge and understanding of the care plan

When children's placement plans had been fulfilled, they had a fairly clear idea of what recommendations had been put before the court. When the plans had not been fulfilled, on the other hand, clear recollection was unusual. Children rarely remembered what contact arrangements had been suggested, although contact was important to them. The aspect of the plan that was commented on most often was the need for the order and/or their removal from parents.

The making of the care order had advantages and disadvantages. As one adolescent boy put it:

> I didn't want the care order. I did and don't. There were certain things I liked and certain things I did not like, as in they have parental rights as well as my mum and I didn't like that. If I wanted to do something and my mum said yes and they said no, I couldn't do it, unless I did it myself.

Particular resentment was felt about the care order in the few cases where the grounds had been 'beyond parental control'. One young person who had run away from home, and who at the age of 14 was living with an older man with mental health difficulties, felt that the order provided no more control than not having one. She remembered 'going absolutely ballistic' when the order was made, and felt that it had made matters worse: 'I was more determined to stay away by then. I actually started staying at other peoples' houses and they weren't finding me.'

Looking back from the age of 17, this young woman suggested that a more co-operative approach might have worked more effectively:

> I don't think I would've gone for a care order ... I would have done what the leaving care have done for me now – I would have been a friend to the person, been someone that I could talk to, you know, so they could come and they could talk to me. That is what I would have done.

Another young person who had initially welcomed care proceedings had regrets by the time of the interview, because she had not fully understood the difficulties associated with discharge.

What most children wanted, at the start of care proceedings, was to be allowed to go home – and they were usually prevented from doing so. This meant that 'information-giving' was never a passive process. Explanations had to be offered and discussed, if children were to understand the actions of social services and contribute to the plan itself. The explanations given to children were not always assimilated at the time of care proceedings and, understandably enough, children's emotional needs could get in the way; but there is evidence that as children matured, the information they had been given began to make sense. Many children and young people had gained a new perspective by the end of the study, when the distressing events of care proceedings had slipped into the background. Here is part of an interview with an adolescent girl, 21 months after the care order:

> *Interviewer:* Did they talk to you about what was going to happen or what you thought?
>
> *Young woman:* Oh yes, I think they did explain to me, but I wasn't bothered really. I didn't really know what was happening. All I was being told was all these big words … and I was like 'OK, whatever.' They don't really explain much – just basically what they feel you need to know. Even so, you can't properly understand – and then when you get a bit older you think 'Oh, so that is why they did that', and you are like 'Oh right.'

One young man in a residential home admitted that at the time of care proceedings he had deliberately screened out what was said to him, although he had ulterior motives for doing so.

> *Interviewer:* Do you remember when you came into care? Did anyone tell you what the plan was for you then?
>
> *Young man:* When I first came in here I didn't really listen to what they said.
>
> *Interviewer:* So you don't remember. What made you start listening to what they said?
>
> *Young man:* The first time I saw my mum and dad again they told me how important it was and if I co-operate with them they will probably do more things and I will probably get home quicker – and that was what made me start listening.

In spite of the various factors that lessened understanding, it is encouraging to note that most children were able to quote the reasons why the order had been necessary – even when they had disagreed with the plan.

> *Interviewer:* Do you remember whether you were happy with the plan [for foster care]?
>
> *11-year-old child:* No, because I wanted to stay with my mum.
>
> *Interviewer:* Did anyone explain to you the reasons why they felt you couldn't?
>
> *Child:* Yes. It was because she weren't ever home. It was always my step-dad that was at home.
>
> *Interviewer:* Did you understand those reasons?
>
> *Child:* Yes.

Another child, who had been 6 years old at the time of the final court hearing and whose mother was involved in drug-trafficking said: 'If I went back home my mum would only smack us and sometimes she would hit us with a stick or she would twist our ankles and our wrists.' He was one of the few children who had actively wanted to be removed from a damaging environment. His half-sister, who had been 9 years old at the time of the court hearing and who had different experiences of the same parent, said in answer to a question about the care order: 'I knew it was because my mum had done stuff wrong, but I still wanted to stay there.' In this very concise statement she showed that she was capable of separating her own feelings from the reasons she had been given for the care plan; and 21 months down the line she was capable of recognising and accepting the importance of both.

Involvement in the care planning process

Apart from the receipt of information – which, as we have indicated, was never an entirely passive process – children were more actively involved in care planning through consultation. The professionals needed to 'ascertain and give due regard to children's wishes and feelings', as required by the Children Act.[3] Rather more rarely, children participated by means of attendance at planning meetings and eventually at the court itself.

As other research has reported, children can be worried and distressed by court hearings, being uncertain about the nature of the proceedings and their own role in them – particularly as the association with the criminal justice system can easily lead to children forming negative images of themselves (Thomas and Beckford 1999). Most of the children interviewed had not been present at the court. One of those who attended found it 'boring'. A second remembered 'making the judges laugh', but had little recollection of anything else. Two of the young people had been angry because they felt that there was no need for a care order. A fourth girl had wanted to be in court at the time but, looking back, was glad that the social worker and her parents had agreed that it was inappropriate for her. ('It would have destroyed me.') A fifth who had been given leave for separate representation changed her mind before the final hearing and absconded. Nevertheless, wanting to know what was going on in proceedings was important and this could include access to court reports. One young person said: 'I felt strongly about things like I ought to be allowed to see the report in its entirety … I ought to be allowed to know what was going on …'

In the accounts of young people over the age of 11, there is often a tension between the desire to participate actively and the wish not to be hurt by it – particularly if sensitive information was being aired in what appeared to them to be a very public forum, in an atmosphere of blame. Since the children's attitudes varied with maturity, confidence, cognitive ability and the extent of their vulnerability in relation to personal circumstances, it would be wrong to overestimate the importance of chronological age; but in general the children of primary school age were happy to have difficult matters discussed with them in private and to know that their interests were represented, while older children were more concerned about the prospect of major decisions being made by adults in their absence.[4] Planning meetings could be just as stressful as the final court hearing and in some cases more so. It was not usual for children to attend them; but it did not always help for the children to be offered partial attendance at meetings, as other researchers have also found (Farmer and Owen 1995; Grimshaw and Sinclair 1997) and as this quotation shows:

> I said I should go to the meetings and she [the social worker] said 'No, because they are too heart-breaking'. But I could hear from the next door, and if they were heart-breaking I would have cried! I want to go in there and be in the conversation. I don't want to stand outside. Gosh.

Another young person who had initially wanted to attend court but changed her mind said:

> I felt that a lot was being kept from me. I can see now that I wouldn't have been able to handle it; but at the time I was really indignant. I thought: 'They can't do this! I want to know what's going on!'... I also knew that it would hurt like hell.

Often what was important to the children who wanted to attend court was knowing what was said about them, rather than participating in the full sense of the word. One teenager who insisted on attending court said: 'I wasn't going to have any of these people slagging me off when I wasn't there.' Another said that she would like to have attended 'if I could have just sat there and not said anything'. These responses are not particularly surprising, given the system for dispensing justice in childcare. The court is not a child-friendly forum, though child-centred in its philosophy, and as other writers have pointed out (Owen 1992; Thomas and O'Kane 1998; Alderson 2000), the 'best interests' principle is adult-dominated and to some extent paternalistic. The most effective way for children to participate in care planning was not by attending court but by making their views known to the guardian ad litem beforehand.

Some adolescents knew exactly what the respective roles of court and social services were, and they wanted the care order to take power away from their parents (which they saw as a source of freedom for themselves, although the experience of freedom did not always live up to expectations). However, these young people were the exception rather than the rule. For most children the process was shrouded in uncertainty, and in their retrospective accounts there is a blurring of responsibility between courts and social services.

> *Interviewer:* What do you think a care order is?
>
> *Child:* I don't know – a piece of paper with writing on it.
>
> *Interviewer:* What do you think that paper says?
>
> *Child:* Tells me where I am going to stay.

To have any real feeling of involvement in this adult-dominated system, it was essential for children to have the help of an adult to whom they could relate and whom they could trust to take their part. Most children had vivid memories of the professionals involved during proceedings – in particular the social workers, guardians and their solicitors.

Children's views about social workers

Since their wishes were seldom granted in full, it is surprising to find that many of the children were positive about the social workers they had had at the time of the care proceedings. They valued their commitment and reliability and thought that they were good people to talk to. For instance, one 17-year-old girl said:

> I think the main thing was that my social worker was great and that's what you need really ... She was there if there was problem, especially in the foster home she would come immediately and she insisted on coming anyway, which at first I found a bit of a bore, but she said, she always said, 'Let's not leave things till they get to the point where I need to see you. Let's make it so I'm seeing you anyway, and then if something arises then you know I'm coming in a week or two' – and I found that very helpful.

The quality the children prized most highly in their social workers was personal commitment (see also DoH 2001a, p.93). They desperately needed to feel that this person was on their side. This need was so acute during care proceedings that some children became distressed if the worker spent a long time talking to their parents or foster carers – especially if these people were expressing criticisms of the children's behaviour. Once they had formed a judgement that the social worker was 'two-faced' it was difficult to regain the relationship.

Along with commitment, the children looked for evidence of empathy and genuine understanding of their experience. They were remarkably astute in identifying whether these qualities were present or absent, as these quotations show:

> You can tell that they are listening and they don't laugh at you. They just try their best to sort out what you want. They try to feel what you feel. If I'm upset then they'll be upset. If I'm happy then they will be happy.

> There's so much difference between appearances and reality, and all too often social workers allow themselves to be satisfied with the appearances [of life in the foster home] ... They're not there long enough, or they don't look deep enough, to find the reality.

> I hated her [the previous social worker] ... She was trying to act like she was a teenager and like trying to be my friend and trying all different approaches, and none of them were working because I could see through it. She was really

> trying to be my buddy and things like that ... She should have acted like a social worker.

Reliability showed itself in the ability to carry out what had been promised. The issues that children were concerned about were often minor and very short term by comparison with the central concerns of care proceedings – the provision of a taxi for contact arrangements, for example, or the sensitive timing of a visit home. If an agreed plan could not be met because of resource shortages, children were capable of understanding these difficulties – provided that the social worker was straightforward in giving explanations (which could mean accepting blame where blame was due).

> Just on a personal level you need someone who's not going to treat you like a 6-year-old ... but you also need someone who can see what you need and get around to getting it. Francesca [the social worker] fought every step of the way ... She'd phone me up and say: 'I'm having a bit of trouble with finance; I keep promising all these things and I forget about the money!' But if she saw that you needed something she'd absolutely ensure that you got it.

What mattered more than resources, however, was being there in an emergency. This was the same adolescent's description of her social worker's response when the fostering placement broke down.

> She [the foster carer] must have phoned her at half seven and she [the social worker] was there for eight thirty. She took me in her car and brought me back and said 'Well, what are we going to do?' And I know if she hadn't have been there then – if she hadn't have kept coming down to check I was all right – I'm not sure I could have made it.

Children had high expectations of their social workers – although they were also capable of appreciating the stresses they were working under. Some were ambivalent towards them, and we can sympathise with the residential worker who said 'When things are going wrong, the social worker isn't the flavour of the month.' Nevertheless an especially heavy load was carried by the key worker during care proceedings, and children were grateful when it was carried well.

Children's views about guardians

The attributes valued in social workers, such as being friendly and reliable, were also valued in guardians. When asked if she remembered her guardian, an 11-year-old girl commented: 'Yes, that is who I was talking about, with the red hair, the guardian ad litem. She was really kind and nice.'

One boy valued the way in which his guardian had expressed his views in court, even though he felt that the court did not listen to them. A 17-year-old girl thought that the guardian had treated her as an individual: 'She was all right because she was interested in me, not what should be happening, but she was interested in what I would want happening, what my needs were.'

However, some of the children were not quite so positive about their guardians. One child felt that the lady had been somewhat hypocritical – and this mirrors the criticism of social workers who had been somewhat clumsy in their attempts to perform a mediating role.

> I didn't find her trustworthy at all. She tended to contradict herself a lot of the time. One minute me and my mum were arguing profusely about something yet she would go and sit with my mum and agree with everything my mum said. Then she would come and sit with me and agree with everything I said.

Another thought that her guardian would have been better if she had been more 'detached'.

A more common issue was that children felt that they had not seen enough of the guardian to establish a relationship of trust. This appeared to be particularly true where children had spoken positively about their relationship with their social worker. Typical comments include: 'I can remember a little bit about her; she used to come about every six months and used to talk about what was going on … It was quite difficult because I didn't use to see her often' (a 12-year-old boy) and 'I don't know if I could have spoken to that guardian ad litem and the solicitor as well because I didn't really sort of know them, whereas my social worker I would have known for quite a while' (a 15-year-old girl).

Children's views about solicitors

The solicitors were key sources of information about the process, but young people sometimes had difficulty in understanding and accepting the solicitor's role in court. One teenager said: 'I just remember my solicitor and my mum's solicitor. They hated each other in court and then would go for coffee afterwards, and I couldn't understand that relationship.'

Many of the children, particularly the younger ones, had little recollection of their solicitors during proceedings. However those who did remember them as individual people usually spoke very positively about them and it is clear that they could be regarded as sources of support as well as information. One 11-year-old girl said that her solicitor had sent her weekly letters about what was going on. A 17-year-old said that she could talk to her solicitor and that he was 'really helpful'.

> ...because he would try and explain. Even if he couldn't properly *properly* explain he would like do his best to explain all these words they were using and sort of. He told me more about, he told me basically not what was happening at the time, but more like you will probably be on it till you are 18 till you can apply for anything different. Or if you or anyone feels the need for you to come off it or whatever ... he was just explaining all that business to me.

Another 17-year-old said:

> My solicitor Peter was brilliant as well ... they were there for me and also they would explain to me in normal language what was going on. If they felt something was wrong, or if they felt I was being out of line they would say 'You can't do that.' They also felt that if someone else was being out of line they wouldn't stand there and take it.

Although the children's memories of the care plan were somewhat hazy and they had sometimes disagreed strongly with the need for the order, their accounts suggest that they had managed to find support in at least one of the professionals around them. There was also a sense that in many of the present placements progress was being made. The children seemed to have acquired an incremental view of planning that paid little attention to what was said at the court hearing, because they saw that planning was now ongoing through social work visits and the system of reviews.

Discussion and conclusions

The interviews with parents, carers and children reveal a great deal of uncertainty about the contents of the care plan; but they also reveal some of the obstacles to understanding and remembering, such as lack of clarity in the original plan, poor communication and (especially in the case of birth parents) lack of emotional support, which would have lessened the whole trauma of care proceedings. Parents were very aware of the power imbalance between themselves and social services, and it is sad to have it confirmed that many of them agreed to the plan either as part of a 'trade-off' for perceived benefits or because they were under duress.

Both parents and children needed a sympathetic person who would listen to their concerns with real understanding. It is interesting to note that the guardian was frequently seen in this light – not merely by children but by parents as well. The perceived independence of the guardian was clearly an advantage. However, children sometimes preferred to talk to social workers whom they knew and trusted. The important factors from their point of view were, first, that their views were heard and, second, that they were helped to participate in an adult-centred process by means of a friendly and reliable adult who was seen to take their part. Children who wanted to attend court needed particular support in order to do this, but the children who attended court did not regret doing so; if these children had been prevented from attending, their experience of participation would have been incomplete.[5]

The interviews also highlight a number of issues concerned with assessment and continuity. Who needs to be consulted in the initial stages? Priority should clearly be given to people who know the children and have their interests at heart, and these may include non-relatives as well as members of the extended family. Second, who needs a copy of the plan and for what purposes? Parents had a justifiable claim to receive a copy, not only because their interests were materially affected as well as the child's but because the sharing of responsibility with the local authority should allow them to monitor changes in the aftermath of the care order. With the exception of residential social workers, current carers were not particularly interested in the court plan as long as they were given details of the child's background and difficulties; but from the point of view of continuity in planning, all these groups might benefit from knowing the contents of the care plan presented to the court – particularly in cases where it could act as a bench-mark for contact and service arrangements.

The interviews show that a sense of involvement increased people's acceptance as well as understanding of the plan. However, all plans have a limited shelf life, and if there is continued movement towards implementation, there will come a time in the care-career of every child when the value of the care plan presented to the court is mainly historical. Moreover the children's interviews remind us of the distress that children experience when information about their private circumstances is given to others. (The phrase 'I forget' often implied 'I do not want to discuss'.) It is one of the established tenets of social work that sensitive information should not be spread except on a 'need to know' basis, and that the confidentiality of records must be respected in the interests of children's privacy.

If children are involved as fully as possible in planning for their own futures, and at the same time given reasonable guarantees of privacy afterwards, this is perhaps the best way to ensure that children's basic rights are met.

Summary

1 Four of the twelve birth parents interviewed had difficulty in identifying the care plan that had been presented to the court – in part because they found it difficult to separate this plan from the series of other plans that had been made and were still being made for their children. Current carers also had very little direct knowledge of the care plan, although they knew of its existence, and some did not feel it was relevant for them.

2 The group of birth parents was evenly divided on the question of whether it was right to vary the plan, half being in favour of flexibility in response to changing circumstances while the other half wanted the plan to be rigidly maintained. Foster carers, residential workers and adoptive parents were generally in favour of flexible planning. There was only one foster carer who felt that the court should be informed if the plan changed direction. However, some caution was expressed about the extent of permissible changes.

3 Two sets of birth parents in the study said that they had been fully involved in the planning process during care proceedings, but they felt that their views mattered much less than their children's views. For two other parents, the priority given to their children's views made them feel excluded from the process. Birth fathers occasionally complained that the system favoured mothers.

4 In the sample as a whole, one-third of the cases were contested (19 out of 57), and in the two-thirds of the cases that were not contested, there was agreement on the need for both the order and the plan. The interviews show that this agreement was often superficial, however. People felt that the order was inevitable, or agreed to the plan because they saw that they would not lose contact with their children.

5 When children's placement plans had been fulfilled, they had a fairly clear idea of what recommendations had been put before the court. When the plans had not been fulfilled, clear recollection was unusual. The aspect of the plan that was commented on most often was the need for the order and/or their removal from parents; but the children remembered individual people who had been helpful and supportive to them during care proceedings.

6 Children were sometimes ambivalent about attending court. In the accounts of young people over the age of 11, there was a tension between the desire to participate actively and the wish not to be hurt by it. In general the children of primary school age were happy to have difficult matters discussed with them in private and to know that their interests were represented, while older children were more concerned about the prospect of major decisions being made by adults in their absence. In both situations, they needed to identify a sympathetic adult among the people surrounding them.

---

[1] As outlined in Chapter 2, interviews were held with eleven adopters or prospective adopters, eighteen foster carers, ten kinship carers, six residential social workers, three birth parents who were currently caring for their child and a further nine parents who were no longer caring for their child. Twenty-six children were interviewed.

[2] One young person said that she did not see the point of planning, since she saw the future as completely unpredictable. ('You don't know what's going to happen, do you?') She also said that she was capable of changing her own mind 'about twenty times' and that social workers would always be obliged to abandon plans for this reason. (See Chapter 1; also Parker 1971 and Rutter 2001.)

[3] The provisions of the Children Act built on Article 12 of the UN Convention on the Rights of the Child, which states that the child shall be provided with 'the opportunity to be heard in any judicial and administrative proceedings affecting the child, either directly or through a representative or appropriate body'. (See Lowe 2001.)

[4] Age is a highly significant factor in children's wish to participate. Grimshaw and Sinclair (1997) report that children's attendance at meetings gathers momentum as children reach the age of 11. They found that the majority of 11 to 15-year-olds, and nearly all 16 to 18-year-olds, attended review meetings.

[5] At present there is no automatic right for children to attend the final hearing in care proceedings – a fact that may contravene Article 6 of the European Convention for the Protection of Human Rights and Fundamental Freedoms (now part of the Human Rights Act), dealing with the right to a fair trial (Fortin 1999).

7 The final shape of the care plans

Introduction

At the end of the care planning process, what did the final care plans look like? What level of detail was provided for the courts? Did the plans serve a useful purpose? To answer these questions, a content analysis of care plans was undertaken at the close of the first phase of the study. The analysis was based on the list of items outlined in Vol. 3 of *The Children Act 1989: Guidelines and Regulations* (DoH 1991b) since this framework had been adopted by all the local authorities in the study. The information was originally recorded as separate items (see the summary table at the end of this chapter), but since there are common themes, the items have been grouped together here into four categories:

- children's needs and how they may be met;
- aims and time-scales;
- the details of placement, contact and services; and
- the roles of parents and children.

The central part of this chapter describes and examines the material presented in each of these categories. Before looking in detail at the content of the plans, however, it is necessary to ask how they can fairly be evaluated. Are there any agreed standards by which care plans may be judged?

How care plans may be judged

As mentioned in Chapter 1, debates about the role, status and quality of the court care plan are no less relevant today than when the study was commissioned. In the late 1990s concerns about the variability of plans were raised both in a study by the Social Services Inspectorate (DoH 1998b) and in Hunt and Macleod's research investigating the implementation of care plans in a range of statutory proceedings (Hunt and Macleod 1999). Accountability was increased by the 1999 LAC circular (DoH 1999b), which made it obligatory for senior officers in social services to endorse the care plan for the final hearing, while the Adoption and Children Act 2002 made provision for the appointment of reviewing officers with a route back into court by way of CAFCASS. At the same time the Adoption and Children Act made care plans mandatory. These measures have increased the reliability and importance of care plans, without necessarily making it easier for courts and other people to determine whether a particular plan was good or bad.

What bench-marks can be used to evaluate plans? The judges, solicitors and guardians whom we interviewed had clear expectations, and there is also guidance to be found in case law. We know, for example, that wherever possible evidence in support of the plan should be made available to the court (*Re J* [1994] 1 FLR 253) and that this evidence should include placement details if they are available. The recommendations are quite precise; *Re J* says that in adoption cases it may be sufficient to give general evidence about the ease or difficulty of finding a placement (to avoid the local authority having to identify named adopters before the principle of care leading to adoption has been established). However, when foster care is planned, the local authority should be able to put forward a written statement describing the placement and the foster carers by a worker who has interviewed them and knows them sufficiently well to satisfy the court that the placement is suitable. From other law reports we know that the local authority may be criticised for reacting to events within families instead of having 'clear goals and expectations' (*Re CD and MD* [1998] 1 FLR 825) and that if the plan is not implemented properly the care order may be discharged (*Re O* [1999] 2 FLR 119) – so clarity and feasibility are two of the issues that have to be addressed. Finally, there has been judicial support for the notion of 'twin tracking' (*Re D and K* [1999] 2 FLR 872), which relates both to time-scales and to contingency plans.

There are more official bench-marks for quality control in the form of Department of Health guidance (*Reporting to Court under the Children Act*, DoH 1996b, and Local Authority Circulars) as well as in the principles of the Children Act itself. The report of the Children Act Advisory Committee *Handbook of Best Practice in Children Act Cases* (LCD 1997b) would not have been available to the social workers in our study; but it makes six recommendations about the care plan, all of them concerned with promoting thoroughness in the preparations for court. This thoroughness extends not only to the drafting of the care plan but to the actions that need to be taken in order to ensure speedy implementation – for example preparing the ground for family placement 'without pre-empting the court's decision', seeking the approval of the adoption and fostering panel before the order, and making plans for any necessary assessment or therapy with identified placements, professionals, time-scales and funding. It is suggested that the care plan should be 'fully researched' to enable the parties to know what case they have to meet.

Approaches to evaluation used in the study

The main principle underlying the current evaluation is that the care plan had to serve the purposes for which it was intended. First, it had to give the court appropriate information on which the decision to make or refuse a care order could be based. Second, it had to provide a suitable framework for social services case management after the order; and third, its provisions had to reflect the fact that social services would work in partnership with parents and children wherever this was possible.

Since much of the existing criticism has been focused on the amount of detail in the plans, and particularly on the pieces of important information that might be left out, we felt that it would be useful to study the amount, quality and relevance of the information provided in the care plans in the light of the objectives mentioned above. The criteria that were used in the classification of detail are as follows.

- *Omitted altogether* means that there was no reference to this item, either under the expected heading or anywhere else in the care plan.
- *Mentioned briefly* means that the information was given without supporting detail, apart from what could routinely be supplied (for example information about procedures, or generalised statements about placement type).
- *Mentioned with detail* means that information was given with specific supporting detail such as:
  - a named resource or carer;
  - tasks to be performed; and
  - justification of options.

Since the primary intention of our analysis was to uncover the actual content of the plans rather than to look at the way in which the headings were used, points of detail that occurred more than once in each care plan were recorded whenever and wherever they appeared.

The content of the plans

Children's needs and how they may be met

Children's identified needs, which headed the care plan agenda, usually carried a clear line of continuity back to the welfare checklist, which appeared in earlier social work statements. However, in the official framework 'the child's identified needs' are subdivided, first into needs arising from the child's race, culture, religion or language, and second into special education or health needs.

Needs arising from the child's race, culture, religion or language

Somewhat surprisingly in view of the fact that the Children Act emphasises the need to take account of these issues, *racial or cultural needs* were mentioned in only ten of the 100 care plans. The sample contained fourteen children who were black or of mixed parentage, and yet for half of these children the subject of their ethnicity was not mentioned.

The nine care plans in which the issue was given brief mention referred simply to the need to match the child's ethnicity in substitute placements. Of these children four were Afro-Caribbean, one was of mixed Irish/Afro-Caribbean parentage, one had a white father and an Asian mother, and the remaining three were white European. In one other case involving an adolescent of dual heritage the care plan stated that work was required to help this young person to acknowledge his cultural background and to feel positive about his own identity.

In six of the nine cases where ethnic matching was said to be required as part of the placement plan, the proposed plan was for the child to be placed with relatives – and this reinforces the view that ethnicity may have been a powerful factor in the selection of kinship care as an option. In four more cases where racial or cultural needs were not mentioned but clearly treated as significant, Afro-Caribbean children were also destined to be placed in kinship care. Three adolescent children of Asian or white/Asian parentage were heading for foster care, but their cultural needs were not mentioned in the care plan and there is some evidence that the agency did not treat these needs as particularly relevant.

Religion and language were not mentioned at all in any of the care plans, except for a few adoption cases in which the importance of religion was discounted.

Special educational or health needs

For almost three-quarters of the children, health and educational needs were specified in some detail (although they were not always 'special'), and in more than half of the eleven cases where no reference was made to them, the child was a very small baby whose development was believed to be normal. In the seventeen cases where the issue was mentioned briefly, the child's needs were said to be those of any child of this age.

The needs most frequently mentioned were generalised *developmental needs*. The requirements of young children were commonly described as stability, security, permanence, physical care, stimulation, affection, consistency of care and 'boundaries'. Somewhat less often (worryingly, in view of research findings such as those of Quinton et al. in 1998) there was reference to the need for warmth and responsiveness on the part of the carer. However, the detailed statements of need that stood out as being different from the others were particular to the child and identified him or her as a person who was known to the worker.

In detailed care plans the needs of siblings were usually carefully differentiated, and the effect of sibling group membership was not ignored. Many of these detailed plans catered for older children. *Educational needs* were less well documented than those concerned with health, particularly in the case of young children, but the need for some form of help with education (including skill development) was mentioned in seventeen cases and in twelve of these it was suggested that there might be a need for special schooling or a placement with education. In some but not all of the cases where it might have been appropriate, reference was made to children's difficulties that might pose possible problems for carers and teachers.

Protection from physical, sexual or emotional abuse was said to be needed if this had been experienced in the past. Six children were said to need an environment that gave protection from *domestic violence*, and this would presumably help to ensure that in the assessment of new carers special attention would be directed to this issue. There was also recognition of needs that stemmed from past abuse or neglect, and which might demand remedial action.

How those needs might be met

In the nineteen cases where strategies for meeting needs were dealt with only briefly, reference was made simply to the proposed placement type. In other words the child's needs were to be met by birth parents or relatives in a parenting role, or else by adoption, long-term fostering or residential care. The implication seemed to be that the placement would fulfil all the complex needs listed above, and act as a cure-all for any problems that might be encountered.

The more detailed responses fell into three categories. First there were those that expanded the notion of placement, giving details of the preferred locality or the skills and qualities that would be required of carers. This was useful information, although it sometimes duplicated material that appeared under other headings. Second, and entirely appropriately, there were some responses to 'how the child's needs might be met', which made a link between placement, contact and services, showing how they would work together to meet the child's needs. Regrettably, these responses accounted for not more than 12% of the total.

Third, there were some interesting responses that discussed very briefly the pros and cons of different placement options. This seemed helpful as an aid to future planning and also as a way of explaining to the court why particular choices had been made. Some workers began the discussion of options with a brief statement of why the child's needs could not be met by the birth family, and this provided a useful summary of the issues that had been discussed in court as well as making the care plan a more free-standing document. It was less helpful, however, in the few cases where workers began once again to argue the case against rehabilitation, as though this was the main issue that the care plan had to address.

Continuity and understanding of the rationale for decisions is important, and the care plan has value as a planning document within social services departments as well as in the courtroom – as is shown by the increasingly common practice of detaching the care plan from its surrounding literature in order to include a copy in the child's current file. The information about how children's needs may be met is extremely valuable in that context.

Aims and time-scales

The aim of the care plan, which should have been one of its main features, was dealt with in a fairly rudimentary way in approximately one-half of the cases; but it occupies a strange position, quarter-way down the list, and in the revised layout it should receive more of the attention it deserves.

Aim of the plan

Once again, the briefest responses in this section mentioned placement only. The aim was 'to place the child for adoption' or 'to identify suitable foster carers'. There were some more detailed entries that took a wider view (for example, 'to place the child with a permanent substitute family, preferably by means of ...') or else a longer-term view ('a bridging placement with a view to ...'). It was useful to have it recognised that not all the parts of the plan could be realised at one go.

Not every care plan was capable of being conceptualised in stages, of course, and this approach was more common with older children – for example where a young person needed a period of preparation for independent living. Wherever it was possible to make them, statements of short and medium-term goals seemed particularly valuable as an aid to future planning when they were related to long-term targets that could be worked towards.

Sometimes the aim of the plan was mapped out in terms of shifting responsibilities. For example, the aim was 'to take responsibility for the child' or 'to share responsibility with the parent' (a clear reference to the effect of the care order). Less frequently, there was some reference to how responsibility might be shifted again in the future – for example by encouraging the carer to apply for a residence order, or by applying to have the care order discharged. In most cases the 'aims' dealt solely with the child's entry to the care system. It seems equally important to consider how exit can be achieved.

The 'aim' section of the care plan presents a unique opportunity to incorporate *legal targets*, which – if they were used more – would not only tighten up social services planning but prepare the court for applications likely to be lodged in the future.

Time-scale

In view of the importance of avoiding unnecessary delays in the placement of young children, it is surprising to find that time-scales were omitted altogether in almost half the cases and dealt with very briefly in twenty others. These brief references included phrases such as 'within a reasonable time-scale' or 'in the forseeable future' but they usually consisted of some variation on the theme 'as soon as possible'.

The detailed responses gave time-scales in weeks or months. Usually the time quoted was from the care order to the start of placement, though in one case where children were to be placed at home there was a time set for review of improvements (one year). For three children who needed a long-term foster placement, the one-year point provided a convenient marker. However, timescales were given in only one-third of fostering cases, probably because there was a lack of certainty about whether some children would have to move on.

The most carefully timed programmes covered the gradual reduction of parental contact where adoption was planned (for example, decreasing from once a week to once a fortnight during the first two months, and then at monthly intervals till placement). But in roughly half the adoption cases it was uncertain when the adoption panel might be approached, when suitable adopters might be identified and when the child might be expected to enter the new home. Where a time from care order to adoption placement was given, the expected timespans ranged from twelve weeks to 38 weeks and the average was about five months. As can be seen from later information, the timespans given in the care plans were regularly exceeded.

Placement, contact and services

There was a good rate of completion when information was requested on these core elements of social services planning – placement, contact and services, but there were some regularly occurring gaps, as our analysis uncovered.

Type and details of the proposed placement

The placement was the section of the care plan that received the most thorough documentation. Sixteen per cent of the social workers' responses stated no more than the preferred type of placement but 84% gave fuller details. The information included named carers or a named residential unit where these had been identified – although in the case of foster care as well as adoption the named carers were usually short term and a further placement would have to be selected later.

Carers were always known in kinship care and home placements, of course. Where the identity of the future carers was not known, the skills or qualities required of the carer might be listed. For example, in some adoption plans reference was made to the ability to cope with difficult background information about the birth family (especially where a previous child had died), to deal sensitively with children's problems such as possible learning difficulties, and to maintain indirect contact.

Geographical locality was regarded as important, and it was mentioned in 15% of care plans. If it was planned that the child would be living in foster care, proximity could help to facilitate contact with parents and siblings, and it was also possible that lack of proximity could be used to restrict it. (This appeared to be a deliberate objective in at least two cases.) In placing children for adoption a degree of distance might be required to prevent the child from being recognised; but on the other hand the selection of locally based adopters would ensure continuity of input from the child's social worker and family placement officer, and perhaps lower costs for the agency as well.

Future family structure was occasionally mentioned – for example if it was felt advisable for a child to be the eldest or youngest in a new family – and in two cases it was noted that consideration would be given to placing the child with a sibling already adopted. However, it was not always stated that children entering care together would be placed together, even where this appeared to be the intention of the agency. We have no means of knowing whether the joint placement was simply assumed, or whether there was a wish not to bind the agency in this respect because of the difficulty that might be experienced in placing sibling groups.

Services by local authority or other agencies

There was a detailed response under this heading in 80% of care plans. Where the subject of services was mentioned only briefly, the type of provision most commonly mentioned was 'placement-finding' or 'social work support'; but in a few cases the provision was seen as totally open-ended and the social worker simply said that services would be 'as needed'.

Potentially there was a great range of services that could be offered, since the recipients included birth family members and carers as well as children, and the services that could be provided covered not only psychiatric benefits such as counselling and therapy but practical assistance with housing, finances and transport. In the better integrated plans the services offered linked up with the children's identified needs, particularly in the realms of health and education. The fact that this did not always happen may in part be because of the 'laundry list' approach encouraged by the care plan format, but it also owes something to the belief that children's essential needs would be met by the placement. Another possible criticism is that some plans did not make it clear whether the services were likely to be acceptable to the people for whom they were intended (presumably because this had not been discussed), and they were not always specific as regards resources.

The term 'services by local authority or other agencies' might be taken to imply that there was some kind of interagency agreement, or perhaps even a joint forum, which would enable agencies to share responsibility for the provision of services. In fact there was no such forum in any of our authorities, with the possible exception of child protection committees, which usually ceased their activity (except in home placements) as soon as the order was made. As a result, social workers would find themselves responsible for making referrals to other agencies in a great many cases; but the only services that could be promised with confidence in the care plan were services that were under the control of social services, or which could be supported by agreements already in place. However detailed the care plans, therefore, it was clear that in the last resort the main burden of service provision would rest with social services.

Arrangements for contact and reunification

Reunification was not usually stated as an aim in care plans, except where the child had left home briefly during care proceedings and was due to return immediately after the order because the plan was 'placement at home'. In addition to this, the interviews with social workers suggest that there were five or six fostering cases where rehabilitation at some future date had not definitely been ruled out, and some workers were willing to say that it should never be ruled out as long as the child was in substitute care without plans for adoption; but reunification was not targeted in the care plans, probably because the possibility of an immediate return had been considered and dismissed during care proceedings. Most of the entries in this section of the care plan were therefore concerned with contact only.

Contact plans were multi-faceted. They included the names of individuals with whom contact was to be terminated or continued; but they also included details of frequency and duration, and sometimes strategic or administrative arrangements concerned with supervision, venues and the provision of transport. The amount of detail in the plans varied enormously. Long-term plans (even including 'indirect contact') were missing for approximately half the children in the sample, and the only comment made to the court about family contact for these 50 children, beyond the initial stages of the care order, was 'subject to review'. Short-term plans received fuller documentation, and they were reasonably well detailed in two-thirds of cases.

Support in the placement

The lack of detail under the heading 'support in the placement', when combined with the information about services, suggests that rather a low priority was given to supporting foster carers. The most frequent response in this section was 'statutory visiting' or 'visits by the social worker and family placement officer'. In the responses that were more detailed there were references to financial and material help (which included the provision of equipment), help with housing and respite care. However, these benefits were usually earmarked for new carers, and especially kinship carers. There was one reference to a 'shared care' arrangement that would enable the mother to share the burden of looking after the child.

Likely duration of placement

Duration was specified in 12% of cases and in 20% it was mentioned briefly. In the other 68%, this item was ignored. In many of these cases it was expected that the final placement would be permanent, and the heading may have been considered inapplicable for that reason. On the other hand a great many children were in temporary placements, and the lack of information here may represent another aspect of the tendency to omit detailed time-scales in care plans.

Contingency plan if the placement breaks down

Along with time-scales, contingency plans were recognised by judges and guardians as important ingredients of the care plan. These expectations do not seem to have been entirely fulfilled. In 27% of cases this item was omitted altogether. In the contingency plans with brief detail, which were found in almost half the cases, the contingency mentioned was a purely administrative one; in other words a meeting would be held or the situation would be reviewed. Alternatively, a search would be made for another placement of the same type.

The more sensitive plans set out the options, and recognised that in the event of a breakdown the child should be enabled to return (albeit temporarily) to the care of people who were previously known and liked. Former foster carers could serve this purpose, and it is clear that in some cases this arrangement had been discussed in advance. Alternatively family members could be consulted and involved in the decision. In view of the fact that most parents still held some degree of parental responsibility, at least in legal terms, it is surprising how seldom this option was mentioned. However, the main deficiency in this section of the care plan is probably the heading itself. In some circumstances, and particularly in the case of older children for whom adoption was planned, the main contingency that had to be faced was not placement breakdown but the likelihood that a suitable placement would never be found.

Some heart-aches could perhaps be avoided if contingency plans were made with this in mind, and if the contingency plans were accompanied by a time limit by which they should be instigated.

The role of parents and children

The effect of section 2(6) of the Children Act is that parents do not lose parental responsibility when the local authority obtains a care order; but section 33(3)(b) provides that the authority has the power to determine the extent to which a parent or guardian may meet his parental responsibility, insofar as it is necessary to safeguard or promote the child's welfare. It is interesting to note how the writers of the care plans interpreted these issues – and also to examine the extent to which the care plans reflect the duties laid out in section 22 of the Act, which says that 'before making any decision about a child whom they are looking after or proposing to look after, a local authority shall, so far as is reasonably practical, ascertain the wishes and feelings of the child, his/her parents, and any other person whose wishes and feelings the authority considers to be relevant.'

Responsibility for implementation

Responsibility for implementing the plan was usually allocated to the social worker or social work agency, unless there was some reference to tasks in which the parent might be involved. Parents were not generally given any responsibility for implementing any part of the plan if the child was in substitute care. Where children were being placed at home, on the other hand, the burdens and expectations being placed on parents could be clearly set out.

In a few other cases where the plans were detailed the tasks were divided between different professionals, and the social worker was given an overall co-ordinating role. Children were not generally seen as responsible for implementing any aspect of the care plan, although their capacity for disruption was considerable.

Parents' role in day-to-day arrangements

The entries in this section confirm that the parents' role in care order cases was usually seen as passive and reactive. In most cases where the parent was not actually in charge of the child, the parent was to be 'advised of progress' or 'informed and consulted'. In home placements the parent was to be 'monitored and assessed'. The maintenance of contact was occasionally mentioned, and the opportunity to attend meetings and reviews; but there is only one case in which the plan states that the parent is to be involved in the child's introduction to long-term foster carers and given opportunities to develop the links.

Wishes and views of the child, parents and other interested people

The response to this heading was detailed in 68% of cases, although not all the entries actually gave the wishes and views of children and adults. In some but not all of the cases where children's views were omitted, the child was very young – usually below the age of 7. In 35 cases the parents' views were given but not the child's. In six cases (all involving adolescents) the child's views were given without the parents' views being quoted. In 27 both were documented.

In the remaining cases there was no reference to family views, or else the subject was briefly mentioned in a statement such as 'the parent is contesting the order'. There were no references to the views of other interested people, with the exception of grandparents where the grandparent had taken an active part in the proceedings. A fuller statement of views might sometimes have been valuable to the court, as this was the only part of the care plan in which the feelings of the child's family and friends could be noted. However, it would have been even more useful if the plan had regularly given reasons why the views of children or family members had been overruled.

Arrangements for input into decision-making by parents, the child and others

From here onwards, the responses to headings on the care plan were fairly routine. The usual response to 'inputs into decision-making' was to mention reviews or planning meetings. A few plans mentioned that representations could be made by way of the social worker, and in two cases solicitors were mentioned.

In addition to being treated fairly routinely, the headings in this section of the care plan all had a poor completion rate. 'Arrangements for notifying disagreements' were mentioned in only 25% of care plans, although this might have been one of the things the parents really wished to know. The section on 'arrangements for health care', when it was completed, gave brief information about responsibility and consent for treatment and sometimes named the individual professionals who would be involved. 'Arrangements for education' in most cases gave the name of the school or playgroup which the child would be attending, and in very brief responses the educational information was simply 'local authority provision'. The standard distance between reviews was quoted in 'programme for reviews', and in two cases (helpfully) the date of the first meeting was given.

Discussion and conclusions

Table 7.1 lists the main ingredients of the care plan, the percentage of 100 individual children for whom each item was mentioned or not mentioned, and the degree of detail.

In discussing the role of the care plan, some social workers had been willing to identify it as a 'parents' and children's charter' – a document that would set out not only the local authority's proposals but the views and the rights of family members, including children. Such a document, they argued, would make it possible for the local authority to be challenged at a later date if promises were left unfulfilled, and it would also set the scene for social workers to work in partnership with parents and children. The possibility of challenge certainly exists, as was shown by the fact that two test cases recently brought under the Human Rights Act went to the Court of Appeal and then to the House of Lords for judgement. (See Chapter 1 for details.) However, the plans in our sample cases suggest that even where home placement was planned, the official role of the parents post-order would be strictly limited. The evidence for this is not simply in the content of the plan, but in the limited amount of detail devoted to parental tasks.

Does the care plan perform its main role of giving the court information that will contribute to the making of the order? On this evidence it does, as long as courts are content to receive the most basic information about placement planning. There were serious gaps in the detail of how potentially difficult placements were to be achieved. (Time-scales and contingency plans were notable omissions.) Even more fundamentally, the general aims of the plan were often unclear, and there was little consideration of how children might be allowed to exit from the care system at a later date.

The need for the child to be protected from harm, in most cases by the provision of substitute care, was made very clear – but it was sometimes less obvious how children's other needs were to be met. The short-termism in contact plans is especially worrying, since in approximately half the cases in the sample the court would have been given no definite statement of long-term contact plans.

Table 7.1 ***Summary of the content analysis of care plans***

	Mentioned with detail %	**Mentioned briefly %**	**Omitted altogether %**
Needs arising from child's race, culture, religion or language	1	9	**90**
Special educational or health needs	**72**	17	11
How those needs might be met	**74**	19	7
Aim of the plan	**58**	42	0
Time-scale	31	20	**49**
Type and details of proposed placement	**84**	16	0
Services by local authority or other agencies	**80**	17	3
Arrangements for contact and reunification	**60**	36	4
Support in the placement	5	**70**	25
Likely duration of placement	12	20	**68**
Contingency plan if placement breaks down	28	**45**	27
Responsibility for implementation	13	**50**	37
Parents' role in day-to-day arrangements	10	**46**	44
Wishes and views of the child, parents and other interested people	**68**	7	25
Arrangements for input into decision-making by parents, the child and others	5	45	**50**
Arrangements for notifying disagreements	0	25	**75**
Arrangements for health care	19	36	**45**
Arrangements for education	25	37	**38**
Programme for reviews	2	47	**51**

This is perhaps offset by the fact that the court has power to make a contact order if this appears to be appropriate, and some legal safeguards exist inasmuch as the parent who is dissatisfied can return to court at a later date to seek extension of contact – but there is no guarantee that children's rights can reliably be upheld in this way.

From the point of view of social services planning, the content analysis has highlighted the priority given to the placement plan. This sometimes led to other ingredients, such as contact and services, being understated and perhaps undervalued. However, we must beware of extrapolating too much from what is essentially a paper exercise. Some plans, as we have seen, lack detail; but this need not necessarily result in a worse outcome.

In later chapters we shall look at how far the expectations raised by the care plan were fulfilled, and how far the implementation of the plans was related to welfare outcomes. The dimensions of outcome chosen for the Looking After Children schedules, on which our analysis of outcome is based, go far beyond the provision of placement to touch on important aspects of the child's development. If the court care plan is to have any validity as a social services planning document, it must relate positively to these outcomes.

Part

III Implementation of the placements

8 Placement patterns: an overall view

Introduction

After the order, social workers set about the task of implementing the care plan that had been presented to the court.

The core of the plan was a placement choice. The first part of this chapter examines the extent to which the placement plans were fulfilled, and the factors that may have contributed to fulfilment or non-fulfilment. The second part looks at the actual situation of the children at the end of the study. It documents where the children were living at the 21-month point, and it explores patterns of stability and permanence in the implementation of the placements.

The implementation of the placement plans

How many plans were fulfilled?

To measure the overall success of placement implementation, we noted how far children were in the preferred type of placement at the end point of the study, 21 months after the order.[1] We have called this the 'fulfilment rate' and we have also referred to fulfilment as 'successful implementation'. (Some plans were implemented but not fulfilled, in the sense that children entered the proposed placement but it later broke down.)

Figure 8.1 shows the number and proportions of children whose placement plans were fulfilled at the end point of the study. Across the sample as a whole, 60 of the 100 children were living in the placement type specified in the court plan. The rate of fulfilment was highest for kinship care (78%). It was lowest for children who had been living at home (41%). Sixty-eight per cent of fostering plans were implemented successfully, and three of the five residential care plans were fulfilled.

The adoption rate needs special comment. Fifty-eight percent of plans were achieved during our time-scale, but a further six children were due to move to adoptive parents shortly after the period of data collection ended; we were also informed that adopters had been identified for two more children a few months later. Follow-up studies always involve a somewhat arbitrary cut-off point, and the adoption result reminds us that we are dealing with a moving picture, which can change at any time. However, most practitioners would agree that it is reasonable to expect a child to be placed for adoption well before the 21-month point, and if this does not happen the situation is far from ideal.

Figure 8.1 ***Placement plan recommendations at final hearing and fulfilment at 21 months***

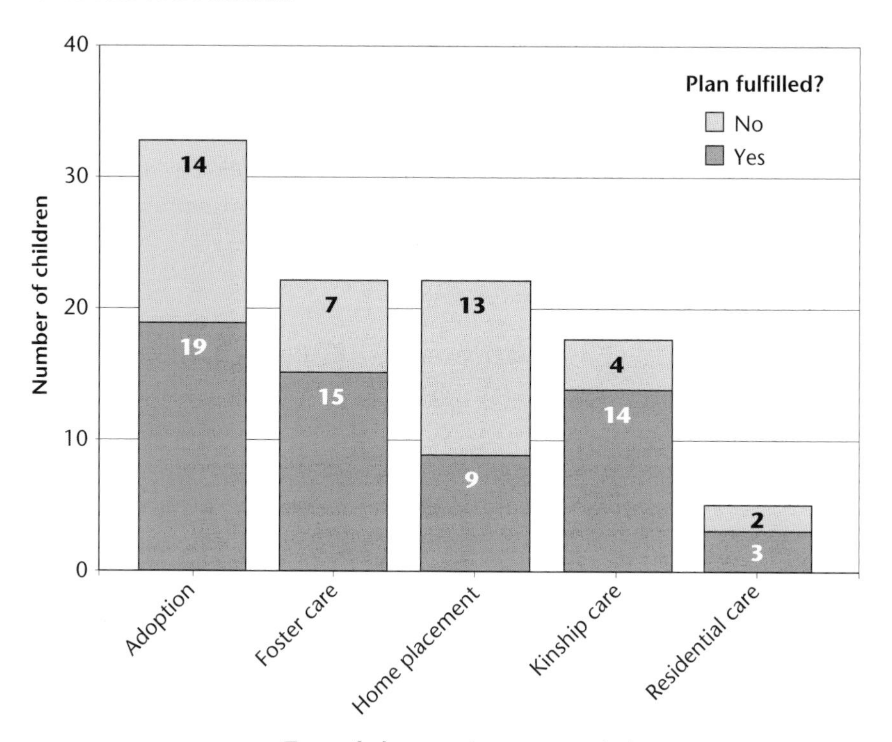

More generally, the variation in fulfilment rates leads us to ask why some options were more likely to be carried through successfully than others. There were two main situations in which care plans were not implemented as fully as expected: either the child never entered the placement or the placement broke down. Individual reasons vary with the type of placement, but some overall patterns are revealed by statistical analysis of the data.

What factors were associated with fulfilment or non-fulfilment?

Quantitative analysis isolated four factors that were statistically associated with placement plans being fulfilled or not.

- The greater the number of children's initial problems, the lower the chance of fulfilment, especially if educational difficulties or developmental delay were mentioned in the court report ($p = 0.004$).
- Placement plans were more likely to be fulfilled when contact was continued or terminated with named individuals as stated in the care plan ($p = 0.015$), and when the duration and frequency of contact were in line with the care plan ($p = 0.022$).
- Parental alcohol abuse was a prominent risk factor in home placement. (This fell just short of statistical significance; $p = 0.052$.)
- The court that dealt with the case in care proceedings was a significant predictor of care plan implementation ($p = 0.03$). Cases heard in the family proceedings courts were less likely to be fulfilled than those heard in the higher tiers of court.

Children's initial problems

The links between plan fulfilment and children's difficulties confirm that the more difficulties a child faces, the greater the obstacles to implementation. Children who failed to enter the recommended placement, or whose placement broke down, were significantly more likely to have three or more initial problems according to the Looking After Children framework.[2] These included emotional and behavioural difficulties, problems in family relationships and in self-care; but for children who never entered the placement, there were additional problems in the areas of health and education. If we consider only the children's difficulties that were cited in court reports, the best predictors of non-fulfilment are educational needs and developmental delay.

Contact

It is useful to know that there is a link between contact and placement fulfilment, although there were many plans to terminate contact (particularly in adoption cases) as well as plans to maintain it. The finding that the fulfilment of contact plans was significantly related to placement implementation, both in terms of contact with named individuals and in terms of duration and frequency,[3] reinforces the belief that contact is an important ingredient in the care plan and that good organisation of contact can help to stabilise placements. However, there was a tendency for changes in the contact plans to follow placement changes – so the statistical analysis may indicate that placement implementation has a strong effect on contact, rather than the effect being the other way round.

Parental alcohol abuse

Alcohol abuse by the parent was almost statistically significant in relation to placement implementation. Other types of parental problem were not significant predictors of whether or not the placement plan would be fulfilled, and we may well ask why there is no statistical link here with drug abuse or serious deficiencies of mental health. The answer probably lies in the fact that:

- Alcohol abuse was less seriously regarded than drug abuse or mental health problems. (See Chapter 4.) As a result, the children of alcohol-abusing parents had been left at home for a longer time, and when they entered the care system they were more likely to be placed at home.

Alcohol relapse was only one of many reasons why home placements failed, but some plans had been over-optimistic with regard to parental motivation and attendance for treatment.

Tiers of court

Seventy-three per cent of the plans made in county court cases (38 out of 52) were fulfilled, as opposed to 44% of those presented to the family proceedings court (20 out of 45). Two factors help to explain these rather surprising results, although considerable care should be taken with the findings because the numbers are very small. First was the influence of age. The family proceedings courts dealt with a somewhat lower proportion of children aged 5 years or under compared with the higher courts, and they also had fewer children aged 2 or under with adoption plans. At the same time they had a larger share of children and young people aged 11 or over.

Second, the children whose cases were heard in the family proceedings courts were reported to have more of the problems that were associated with poor plan fulfilment – particularly educational difficulties and developmental delay. In spite of this imbalance, implementation rates were slightly higher if the case involving educational needs or developmental delay was heard in the care centre. However, the analysis by tier of court should not detract from the bigger picture which has shown some important commonalties as well as differences. Child characteristics such as being aged 3 or over were a risk factor affecting the likely success of adoptive placements at all levels of court and, as we have seen, fulfilment rates across the board were lower if the child had a large number of initial difficulties. The way in which proceedings began may also have had an effect on implementation rates, since:

- there was an apparent association between the issuing of emergency protection orders at the start of care proceedings and plan fulfilment.

Altogether 25 emergency protection orders were made at the start of proceedings, and in nineteen of these cases the plan was fulfilled – a success rate of 76%. Serious child protection considerations were likely to result in cases being heard in the higher tiers of court, and more of these plans may have been fulfilled because of the nature of the perceived risks.

Differences between the two groups of children with unfulfilled plans

When the two sub-groups of children whose plans were unfulfilled were compared directly with one another, the most significant difference was that children who failed to enter the recommended placement were more likely than children whose plan broke down to have initial educational problems (odds ratio = 11.0, $p = 0.02$). They were also more likely to have problems in health.

Once again the importance of educational needs is highlighted, but the analysis shows that these needs were mainly concentrated in *children who failed to find a placement*. Approximately two-thirds of the children with educational needs had learning difficulties, often combined with developmental delay in other areas. Slow learning and poor school achievement lessened young children's chances of finding an adoptive placement, especially when combined with sibling group membership, while in the case of older children the likelihood of finding a suitable foster placement was limited by different educational problems such as non-school attendance or school exclusion. At the same time many of the children with learning difficulties were found to be rewarding by their carers, and they settled in foster homes or residential institutions without moving on to the placements originally intended for them. This helps to explain why educational needs were associated with non-fulfilment of the plan, without apparently making breakdown more likely.

The children whose placements broke down, by contrast, had fewer initial problems than the children who never entered the recommended placement – although we should note that this difference is not statistically significant, and that since our categories of initial problems are really 'umbrella categories', there are qualitative differences in the type of problems experienced by the children and the reasons for them. Pre-existing emotional and behavioural difficulties were common in both the non-fulfilled groups, but they were also common in children whose placements were fulfilled. Initial problems in the area of self-care skills, when found in the non-entry group, were associated with learning difficulties. (For example, one 10-year-old boy could not be relied on to visit shops on his own.) In the group that experienced breakdown of the placement, on the other hand, initial difficulties with self-care skills were more clearly linked to physical or emotional neglect. Initial problems in family and social relationships were again common to both the non-fulfilled groups; but more of the children in the breakdown group had been actively rejected by their carers – a factor that has been shown to be extremely damaging for children joining new families (Quinton et al. 1998).

The precise form taken by children's problems was age-related – although it should be noted that age on its own was not a significant predictor of placement fulfilment or non-fulfilment. The summary presented here is necessarily brief, and the issues will be explored in more detail in later chapters dealing with individual placement types.

The link between the amount of detail in the plans and placement fulfilment

Where the items in the care plan were well detailed, there was no automatic link with placement fulfilment. There appear to be two reasons for this. First, some of the items listed in the care plan (such as contingency plans) had no possible bearing on the fulfilment of the recommended placement, although they were important for other purposes. Second, some items were well detailed in precisely those cases that were problematic and therefore most difficult to implement. Two items in particular come into this latter category. 'Special educational or health needs' were well documented in 72 plans, out of which only 38 were associated with fulfilled placements – a success rate of 53%. The 'wishes and views of the child, parents and other interested people' were well documented in 68 plans, out of which only 35 were associated with placement fulfilment, and this is equivalent to a success rate of 51%. Since the average rate of placement fulfilment across the whole sample is 60%, these results are below average, and it is not difficult to understand why. If the child had special educational or health needs that required to be set out in detail, or if there was strong disagreement between the parties that had to be recorded, the chances of implementing the placement plan were lessened. It can, however, be argued that the care plan was fulfilling its function well if it set out the possible impediments to fulfilment.

There are only four items in the care plan that, when they were recorded in detail, were associated with an above-average success rate in terms of fulfilled placements. They are outlined in Table 8.1.

Table 8.1 ***Relationship between detailed plans and fulfilled placements***

	Placement fulfilment rate where this item was well detailed in the care plan
Type and details of proposed placement	53 out of 84 (63%)
Arrangements for contact and reunification	37 out of 60 (62%)
How the children's needs might be met	45 out of 74 (61%)
Services by local authority or other agencies	48 out of 80 (60%)

It is easy to see why these particular headings were linked to plan fulfilment. Detailed completion of the parts of the plan relating to placement, contact and services demanded positive forward planning, and they also invited action to ensure that the necessary arrangements would be in place. (For example, 'type and details of proposed placement' could not be completed adequately without the identification of named carers – or at least some indication that the social services department had considered specific requirements.) It is particularly interesting to note that:

- careful completion of the section on 'how the children's needs may be met', which had a distinctly practical orientation, was associated with a much better rate of implementation than the statement of needs on its own.

The care plan presented to the court had to serve many purposes, and there are many reasons why detail was required – including accountability and the need to provide information for the court; but from the point of view of forward planning in social services, the four items mentioned above seem to deserve special attention if the chances of fulfilling the placement plan are to be maximised.

How helpful were the contingency plans?

Contingency plans were not mentioned in the cases of eleven of the 40 children whose placements were not fulfilled. Sixteen of the 40 children had brief contingency plans and thirteen had more detailed ones.

When we consider the careers of the 29 children who were given contingency plans and who appeared to need them, inasmuch as their placements were not fulfilled, we find that the contingency plans were to a greater or lesser extent implemented for 24 children. There were only five cases in which they were not used at all. However, in fourteen cases the implementation was only partial, and in another three cases it was unhelpful. This means that there were only seven children on whose behalf contingency plans were listed in the care plan and used successfully when the need arose.

Contingency plans successfully implemented

In each of the seven cases where contingency plans were implemented, the child entered foster care after the breakdown of another placement. All except two of these children would have to move on to other placements, however – and since the further placements were not named in the contingency plans, which mentioned only the move to foster care and the need for review, implementation could be said to be guaranteed by the vagueness of the original plan.

Contingency plans implemented with changes

In some care plans – and especially those with rather brief details – the contingency plan was focused on administrative arrangements. For example, it said that a meeting would be held and the situation would be reassessed. Because breakdowns tended to happen in emergencies, however, the first step was usually to remove the child. A further discrepancy was that family members were not given the status accorded to them in the care plan. In two cases where it was said that family members would be consulted about alternative arrangements, they were not consulted until after the child had been removed and alternative plans had been drawn up. In one case where a family group conference was named as the forum for reassessment, the conference was not held until ten days after a planning meeting at which the fate of the children was decided.

Another discrepancy was that there was variation in the time when the contingency would be brought into play. For example, in one case where the children were to be removed 'if no progress was made within one year', the review that should have been held at the one-year point was omitted and the children were removed after an incident at nineteen months.

Contingency plans that were not used

In the five cases where the contingency plan was not used at all, the social services department had misunderstood the likely nature of the contingency. Typical cases were those of three young children (from separate families) bound for adoption. The contingency plan said that in the event of breakdown another adoptive placement would be sought; but in fact no adoptive placement was ever found, and the children were allowed to remain with foster carers to whom they had become attached.

Contingency plans that were used but found to be unhelpful

In three cases where the contingency plan proved to be unhelpful, one line of approach was continually repeated in the face of evidence that the plan was not working. In the first case of this sort, the plan for a 13-year-old boy was that a recovery order would be sought if he absconded from residential care. It was only after he had absconded and been brought back several times that the plan was changed so that he could live with relatives. In the second case specialist fostering was attempted over and over again for a 15-year-old girl, although the young person concerned spent very little time in the placement, and the plan was eventually changed to independent living. Third, a 9-year-old boy absconded from his foster placement and was brought back so often that the social services department was accused of wasting police time. Rehabilitation was tried for this boy, although it had been expressly ruled out as a contingency in the care plan, and when this failed he ended up in residential care.

The difficulties in all these cases were accentuated by resource shortages as well as children's initial problems; but it is worrying to discover that the contingency plans contributed so little to planning at the time when they were most required.

The children's situation at the end of the study

Where were the children living?

Table 8.2 shows where the children were living at the end of the study. Inevitably, the 40% non-fulfilment rate means that at this time 40 children were living in placements that had not been intended for them. It is interesting to note where these children went.

Table 8.2 ***Placements of children at close of study***

	Number of children	Number of children for whom this placement had not been intended
Adoption	20	1
Foster care	42	27
Home placement	10	1
Kinship care	16	2
Residential care	7	4
Other	5	5
Total	**100**	**40**

Very different routes were taken by adolescents and younger children when placements broke down or were unavailable. Young children who were removed from home moved to foster care or adoption; but older children were transferred from one foster home to another, or else they moved out of foster care altogether into residential accommodation. The category described as 'other' consists mainly of older adolescents who failed to find a place either in specialist fostering or in residential communities. Most of these children found their way into independent living.

One of the most striking points to emerge from these findings is the importance of foster care as a collecting ground when placement plans for younger children run into difficulties.

- A total of 42 children ended up in foster care although it had been planned only for 22. Since seven of the original 22 children had found placements elsewhere, this means that foster care drew in an extra 27 children for whom it had not been planned.

Eight of these children were waiting for adoptive placements, three had been returned to foster carers after suffering adoption breakdowns, and another three were children who had lingered in foster care and become attached to their carers. The other thirteen had entered fostering after the breakdown of other placements – eleven from placements at home and two from kinship care. The composition of the group is presented visually in Figure 8.2.

Figure 8.2 ***Children in foster care at end of study: composition of group in terms of original plans***

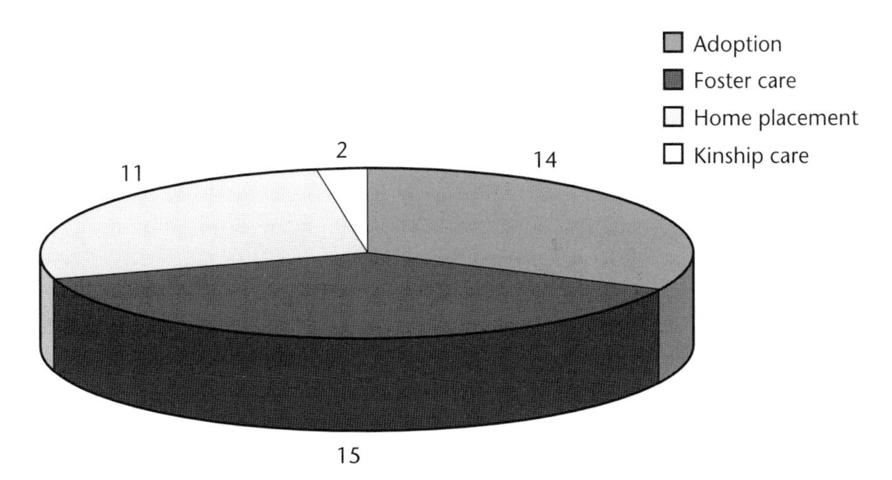

Some of these children were still on the move. At the time when our study ended, they had fairly recently been removed from home or kinship care and new plans were being actively pursued. But for six of the 27 children who had been unexpectedly added to foster care during the course of our study, the likelihood was that they would spend a substantial part – indeed the greater part – of their childhood in foster care.

The importance of foster care is not surprising – for in reality the alternative options are very narrow; but the figures highlight how important it is to have a large stock of suitable foster placements that can cater for children with a wide range of needs, including emotional and behavioural difficulties and developmental delay.

How often had the children moved?

Encouragingly, there was a high degree of placement stability, whether or not the plan was fulfilled. Figure 8.3 shows the number of times the children moved during the 21-month follow-up. Thirty-seven children – more than a third of the sample – remained in the same placement they had entered before the care order was made. Thirty-four moved once, and many of these were children for whom one move was unavoidable because they had to enter an adoptive placement. A further eighteen moved twice. A small group of eleven young people found themselves moving on three times or more. Children who experienced breakdowns in foster care, kinship care and especially in residential care were involved in this pattern of frequent moves.

Figure 8.3 ***Number of times children moved over the 21-month follow-up period***

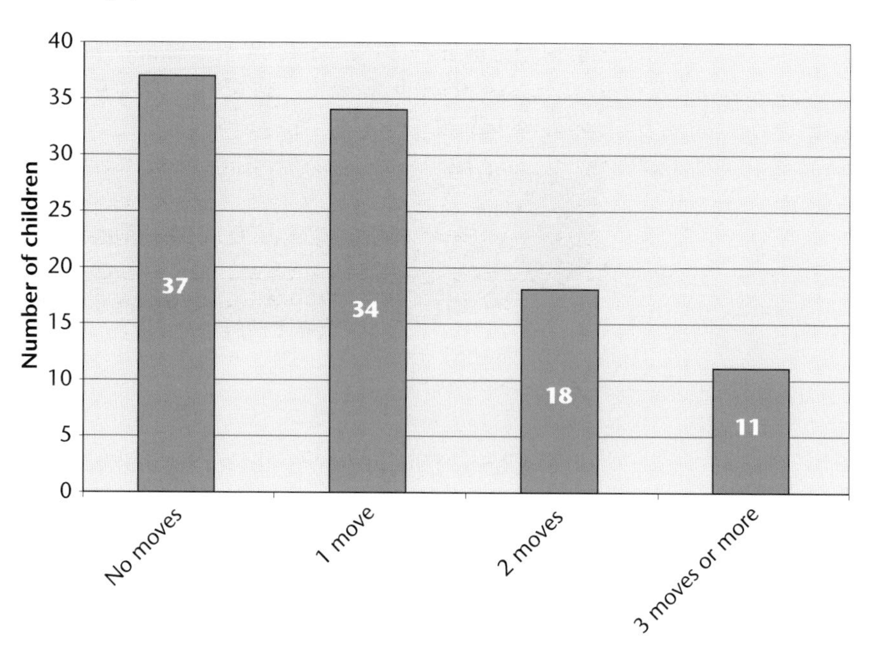

The significance of individual moves varied, and many were made for positive reasons. However, counting the total number of moves is one kind of benchmark of stability, and indeed there is a National Priorities Guidance target on this subject. In view of the fact that the proportion in our sample who moved three or more times in a year was fairly low (just over 10%), our figures suggest a definite attempt on the part of the authorities to keep disruption to a minimum after the care order was made.

How permanent were the final placements?

In addition to recording the number of moves, the researchers developed a six-point scale to measure the permanence of the placements. In the upper half of this scale are three categories of placement that offered children a certain degree of permanence at the end of the study.[4] The first category consisted of placements that had been officially confirmed as permanent (for example by the court in the form of an adoption order or residence order, or by the agency's permanence panel in the case of long-term fostering). The second category contained placements in which permanence had been applied for, and the third consisted of placements that were informally considered permanent and treated as such.

The next three categories on the permanency scale contained placements that could not be described as permanent at all. In the first of these, the current placement was temporary but new carers had been identified and the child was about to move. Next there was a small group of short-term placements that might possibly become permanent if the carer could be persuaded to continue looking after the child. At the bottom of the scale were placements from which the child would definitely have to move on.

Table 8.3 ***Relationship beween implementation of plan and permanence***

	Number of children with fulfilled plans	Number of children with unfulfilled plans
Permanence confirmed	16	2
Permanence applied for	21	1
Placement considered permanent but not confirmed	18	10
Permanent placement identified but not yet entered	0	6
Possibility of current placement becoming permanent	1	4
Temporary placement	4	17
Total	**60**	**40**

The most salient finding is that children who were living in the placement type specified in the court plan were much more likely to be living in a placement that matched one of our three categories of permanence. By contrast children whose plans were not fulfilled were more likely to be living in placements that were temporary to a greater or lesser extent. (See Table 8.3.) Sixty-eight per cent of the placements had some degree of permanence at the 21-month point whether the plan had been fulfilled or not; but there were still only eighteen children in the whole sample for whom permanency had been confirmed, and one in five children were in completely temporary placements.

The placement choice was strongly correlated with these results. Children with fulfilled adoption plans were most likely to have achieved the top two rungs of the permanency ladder; in the case of seventeen of the nineteen children who had been placed, either an adoption order had been made or an application had been lodged with the court on their behalf. Kinship care too did well in this respect although there were fewer children in Category 1 (which in this placement option indicated that a residence order had been made) and the majority were in Category 2 (residence order or adoption order applied for). In foster care there were relatively few placements that had been officially designated as permanent. Even among children whose fostering plan had been fulfilled, one in four were in temporary placements, and the biggest proportion of those whose placement was considered permanent fell into Category 3 – which could have meant that although there were no plans to move the children, the status of the placement was constantly up for review.

Thirteen children were in permanent placements although their plans had not been fulfilled, because the original plan had been varied at least partly for positive reasons such as attachment to the existing carer. However, there were only five children (four in foster care and one in a residential placement) who were still temporarily placed although their plans counted as fulfilled. Overall, therefore, it can be seen that there is a close association between care plan fulfilment and permanence.

How long did it take?

The time taken to reach a permanent placement varied according to the placement type. On average it took about two months for kinship care, six and a half months for long-term fostering and just under ten months for adoption. These average figures conceal a great deal of variation, however, as Table 8.4 shows.

Table 8.4 ***Time taken to reach a permanent placement***

	Shortest time	Longest time	Average
Adoption	1 month	21 months	10 months
Foster care	Immediate	21 months	6.5 months
Home placement	Immediate	–	–
Kinship care	Immediate	16 months	2 months
Residential care	Immediate	–	–

Figure 8.4 shows the number of children who were in a placement considered permanent by length of time post care order. By the end of the study 68% of

the children were in placements considered permanent; but 21 months is a comparatively long period for follow-up, and it might be reasonable to expect that most children would be in a permanent placement after six months or at least by the end of the first year. The following bar chart shows that only 50% of the children were in a placement considered permanent by the twelve-month point.

Figure 8.4 ***Children in a placement considered permanent by length of time after care order***

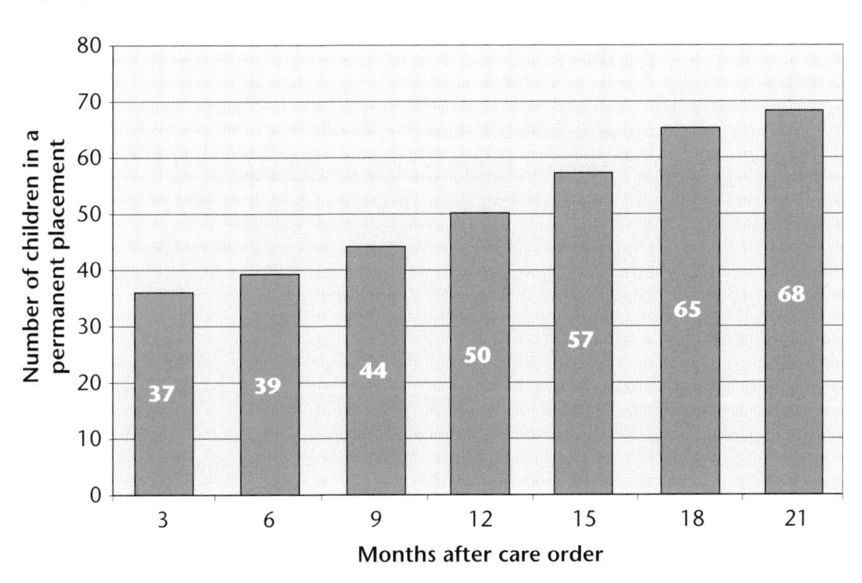

Nevertheless there was steady progress towards permanence during the course of the study, and the hope was that it would be achieved for all or most of the children in the course of time.

Discussion and conclusions

Sixty of the 100 children in the sample were living in the recommended placement at the close of the study, and these placements count as 'fulfilled'. Given the difficulty of placing some of these children successfully, this is a positive result. However, there is worrying evidence of delay in finding places for some of the children, and from the point of view of stability we must be concerned about the 32% of children who at the end of the study were still in temporary accommodation. The other 68% were in placements regarded as permanent, and they had found their way to these placements, on average, in less than a year; but in most cases permanency had not been officially confirmed, and because a number of children had 'stayed put' or been placed extremely quickly, the average figures for the time taken to reach a permanent placement are perhaps more optimistic than the situation deserves.

The message of the permanency ladder is clear; practitioners need to aim for a clear resolution of the child's placement status if stability is to be maximised. By so doing, drift and delay are also minimised. A broader message, however, is that naming the type of placement is not enough as a basis for planning. There are exit routes as well as entrances that need to be spelt out, and stages along the route to permanence, which sometimes could have time-scales attached. It is not only in adoption that these considerations are important, since residence orders and discharge from care can be important legal targets for children placed with relatives or remaining at home. Foster care is a useful umbrella option, which covers a range of different provisions – short-term and long-term, temporary and permanent. If the aims of the placement are not made clear there is a risk that children's specific interests will not be met, even when an apparent degree of stability is achieved.

The overall pattern suggests that there are wide differences between placement options – not simply in fulfilment rates and the type of care offered, but in terms of in their ability to accept children of different ages and to support children with problems. In the rest of this section, some of these crucial differences will be explored.

Summary

1 Six in ten children at the end point of the study were living in the placement type specified in the court plan. The rate of fulfilment was highest for kinship care (78%). It was lowest for children who had been living at home (41%). Sixty-eight per cent of fostering plans and three of the five residential care plans were implemented successfully.

2 There were two main reasons why plans were not implemented in the way the courts had been led to expect. Either the child never entered the placement (fifteen cases) or the placement broke down (25 cases). The circumstances varied with placement type.

3 Children's initial difficulties decreased the likelihood of the placement plan being fulfilled, especially if children had educational needs or developmental delay. Alcohol abuse was the only parental problem to have a noticeable effect on placement implementation – probably

because it was present in a number of families where children were placed at home.

4 The county courts were associated with higher odds of placement fulfilment than the family proceedings courts. The placement plans were also more likely to be fulfilled if the contact arrangements were implemented as scheduled.

5 Foster care was the main collecting ground for young children when placements broke down. Older children tended to move towards residential care or independent living. The group was fairly stable, however, and only eleven children moved three times or more.

6 Sixty-eight per cent of the children had reached a placement with some degree of permanence by the end of the follow-up period. There were delays in finding some long-term fostering placements as well as adoptive homes, and only 50% of the children were in a permanent placement at the twelve-month point.

---

[1] As in previous chapters, the categories used to classify the placement options are as follows. Adoption refers to the placement of a child with a view to adoption by strangers. Kinship care covers placement with relatives, including some previously estranged fathers with whom the child had never lived. Home placement refers to situations where children returned to or remained with the person who had looked after them prior to the order. Residential care includes special schools and therapeutic communities in addition to children's homes, and foster care refers to placements in ordinary or specialist foster homes.

[2] For details of this framework see Chapter 2.

[3] As indicated in Chapter 13, the fulfilment of contact plans was measured in two ways. First we tracked whether the contact plans that named specific individuals at the final hearing were carried through. Then we monitored whether contact arrangements lasted as long as indicated in the care plan or ran to the same frequency. At the end of the study 82% of the plans to terminate or maintain contact with named individuals had been carried through, but only 45% of the children had experienced contact of the expected duration and frequency.

[4] Permanence in this context means that a placement was intended to last at least until the child reached the age of 16. It is appreciated that adoption offers a degree of permanence not matched in any other placement option.

9 Adoption

Introduction

More than any other placement option, adoption has undergone a transformation during the last few decades. Out of a service whose main role used to be seen as finding homes for illegitimate babies and catering for the needs of infertile adults, it has achieved recognition as a viable option for children in the care system. In the new relationship between the state and the adoptive family there are elements of a 'public–private partnership'. Adoption is required to cope with a greater range of children than ever before, and its use is on the increase.

Adoption research has consistently pointed to good outcomes for children placed as infants. Disruption rates are low, averaging between 5% and 10%, and levels of satisfaction reported by young adult adoptees and their carers are very high – around 80% or higher (Maluccio et al. 2000). These results are impressive although it needs to be borne in mind that many of the findings relate to adoptions carried out at an earlier historical period when the reasons for placement were rather different from today. Recent research also suggests that overall breakdown rates in adoption are low compared with other placement options, although disruption rates increase with the age of the child and the complexity of needs.[1] Encouragingly research has suggested that even where adoptees encounter relationship difficulties with their adoptive families in their teens, by their early 20s these relationships have usually improved (Howe 1998; Thoburn 1999).

In spite of these findings, the proportion of looked-after children adopted from care was low in the years following the introduction of the Children Act 1989.[2] During most of the 1990s it comprised only about 4% of all those looked after, the majority of whom were under 5 years of age (Paton 2002). Inevitably these figures posed a central question: Is adoption under-used as a placement option? By the mid 1990s adoption issues were being actively explored in a number of research projects (DoH 1999a). At the same time the Social Services Inspectorate was scrutinising practice at the operational level, and by the time our research was under way in 1997, two SSI reports had highlighted some worrying concerns (SSI 1996a; 1997). They found that adoption tended to be somewhat marginalised in service planning, featuring only rarely in Children's Service Plans. Delays in processing adoption plans and monitoring their implementation were widespread, and the quality of services varied widely across the country.

Since our study began, strategies have been introduced to make adoption simpler, speedier and more accessible. The document *Modernising Social Services* (DoH 1998d), underwritten by a circular to local authorities (DoH 1998a), made clear the government's intention to bring adoption services into the mainstream of planning for looked-after children. The Quality Protects programme (DoH 1998e) prioritised adoption as a means to achieving its central objective of promoting stability for looked-after children and at the same time helping them to leave the care system permanently. This intention was set out forcefully in *The Prime Minister's Review of Adoption* (Cabinet Office 2000) and in the succeeding white paper *Adoption: A New Approach* (DoH 2000a), which was the forerunner to the Adoption and Children Act 2002.

Government aspirations for adoption are now more ambitious than at any previous time. It has set a public service agreement target to increase by 40% – and if possible by 50% – the numbers of all looked-after children adopted by the year 2004/05. The new Act puts the needs of the child at the centre of the adoption process by aligning adoption law with the Children Act 1989, making the child's welfare the paramount consideration in all decisions. The Act also contains measures to increase the supply of adopters, to speed up the process, to ensure that adopters are given access to support, and to assist both prospective adopters and children who wish to make a complaint.[3]

Underlying all these developments is a perceived need for adoption to be treated as an integral part of the care system, without destroying its essential character. The transformation of adoption into a placement option for looked-after children is well-nigh complete; but it would not be surprising if the system studied in our research still carried some of the hallmarks of its very different history and culture. The findings reported here need to be seen in this context.

This chapter, like the ones that follow it, is divided into three parts. The first part reports on the implementation of the plans – fulfilment rates, the circumstances of the children whose plans were not fulfilled, and the factors that helped or hindered placement. The second part looks back to the original plan and asks whether any lessons can be learned retrospectively. The third part looks in more detail at how the plans were actually carried out; it includes details of time-scales and the number of moves made by the children, as well as issues concerned with policy, law, management and social work practice.

The implementation of adoption plans

How many placement plans were fulfilled?

Figure 9.1 shows the progress made in the implementation of adoption plans for the children in the 21 months after the care order. Fifty-eight per cent of adoption plans were implemented successfully during the study period. Nineteen of the 33 children had been placed, and they came from seventeen of the original 23 families. For nine of these children full adoption orders had been made.

Figure 9.1 ***Implementation of plans for adoption: progress of children 21 months after care order***

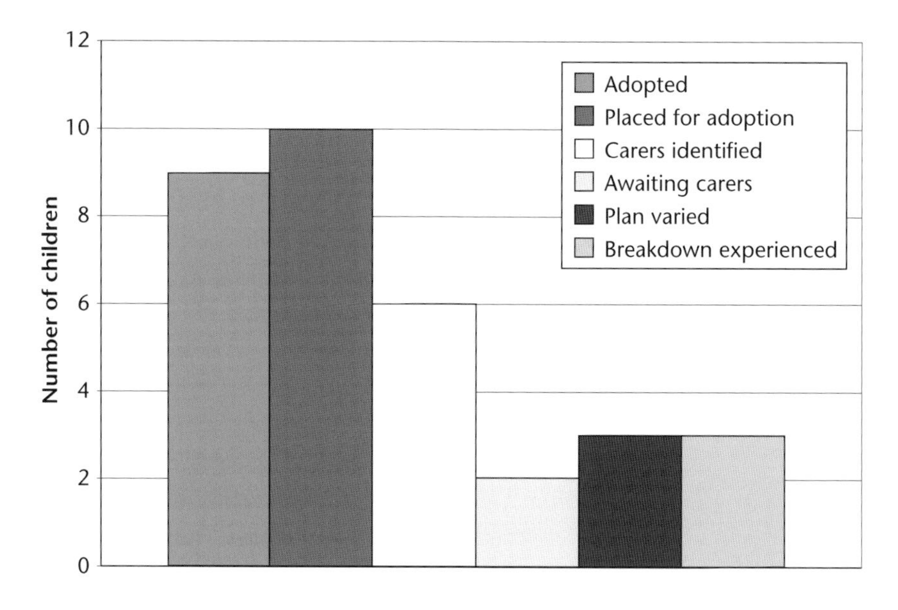

What happened to the children whose plans were not fulfilled?

Of the fourteen children who were not in adoptive placements at the end of the study:

- three had experienced breakdown of the proposed placement and were being reassessed;
- three had had their plans varied so that they could remain in foster care; and
- eight were still waiting for an adoptive placement.

In cases where adoption plans were not implemented successfully breakdown was less common than not finding a placement. Breakdown affected only three children for whom adoption was named in the care plan, and two of these experienced disruption of the arrangements during the introductory period. Some problems, if they existed, would not show up within the time-scale of our study – but it is encouraging to know that other research evidence suggests that most breakdowns occur before the adoption order is made (Murch et al. 1993), and from this point of view our research spans the most potentially unstable period of the placement. Nevertheless the breakdowns that did occur were extremely upsetting for the children, and also for the adults who were involved in them.

- Breakdown did not necessarily put an end to the adoption plan. It seemed likely that, for all these children, a second attempt would be made.

What happened to the children who failed to find a placement within our time-scale? For three of these children the adoption plan had been deliberately varied so that they could remain in foster care. For these children adopters had proved difficult to find, and permanence by means of residence orders was planned. Altogether there were five children who found permanent homes with a foster carer to whom they had become attached and in two of these cases the foster home had already become an adoptive placement.

- In all five cases where children with an adoption plan were allowed to remain in foster care, an attempt was made to secure some form of permanence. The intention was that the foster carers would apply for residence orders in three cases, and for adoption orders in the other two.

For another eight children who failed to find placements within our time-scale the adoption plan was still being actively pursued at the end of the study. It seemed virtually certain that these children would be placed.

- Six of the children whose adoptive placements were delayed were due to move to adoptive parents shortly after the period of data collection ended, and adopters were identified for the other two children a few months later.

However, the delays raised anxieties in children, sometimes resulting in a recurrence or exacerbation of difficult behaviour and emotional disturbance. They also gave parents and carers justifiable cause for concern. In two of the attempts at placement that disrupted, a contributory factor was that the children had formed strong attachments to their foster carers as a result of the length of time spent in temporary homes.

What helped or hindered placement?

When we consider the implementation of adoption plans in more detail, several factors stand out as having some importance:

- *Child factors* The older the child, the greater the difficulty in finding an adoptive placement. Fifteen of the nineteen children for whom adoption plans were fulfilled were aged 2 or less at the time of the final court hearing, but for the majority of those aged 3 and over the plan was not fulfilled. Children's special needs contributed to difficulties in placement-finding.
- *Family factors* Nine of the fourteen children who failed to find an adoptive placement within our time-scale came from just two families. There were considerable difficulties associated with placing several children from one family – especially if the plan was to place them together.
- *Organisational factors* Lack of adopters held back the implementation of placement plans for eleven children; but, as we have seen, the main issue was delay rather than total failure to find a placement. Breakdowns were also affected by delays, and by the way in which the transition to the adoptive home was managed.

Sibling group membership, developmental problems and shortage of adopters all affected the likelihood of children achieving a successful adoptive placement within the time period. Often these factors operated together. However, the factor that most clearly differentiated fulfilled from unfulfilled placements was the age of the children. As can be seen from Table 9.1, being just 3 years old at the final hearing severely constrained the likelihood of adoption. No child aged 5 or above was placed.

Table 9.1 ***Age of child and adoption plan fulfilment at 21 months***

Age in years at final hearing	Numbers of children with fulfilled plans	Numbers of children with unfulfilled plans
0	7	–
1	4	1
2	4	1
3	2	5
4	2	2
5	–	2
6	–	2
7	–	1

These findings chime closely with other research. For example the studies by Hunt et al. (1999) and by Lowe and Murch (2002) found that the same cluster of factors delayed adoptive placements.

The differential success rate of singleton and sibling group placement in our study is very marked, as can be seen from Table 9.2. While the majority of singletons were placed, the converse was true of plans to place siblings together. Worryingly, this applied even to plans for the joint placement of sibling pairs. More of these remained unfulfilled at the close of the study, when compared with those that were carried through. Yet research has suggested that placement with siblings can help stabilise the situation when a placement is actually made (Berridge and Cleaver 1987; Rushton et al. 2001).

Table 9.2 ***Placement fulfilment: children in terms of sibling groups***

	Planned placements	Actual placements
Singletons	17	13
Members of sibling groups:		
– to be placed singly	2	2
– to be placed as part of a sibling pair	10 (five pairs)	4
– to be placed as a group	4 (one group)	0
Total	**33**	**19**

It is worth noting that gender may also have played some small part. Ten of the fifteen boys were placed successfully, but only nine of the eighteen girls.[4]

All three placements of minority ethnic children were successfully implemented, and special efforts were made to ensure that these children were given culturally appropriate placements.

As well as the child's characteristics, the previous history of the case also discriminated between fulfilled and non-fulfilled adoption plans. There was an inverse relationship between the length of official involvement and plan fulfilment.

- By the time social services had been involved for just one year, the chances of fulfilment within our time-scale went down markedly.

In considering the meaning of these findings, it is important to bear in mind their link with the children's ages. Nevertheless, the results merit attention because they suggest that there might be some cut-off point where adoption plans start to look unrealistic – and unless there is a marked increase in resources, this cut-off point may be even more stringent than current practice would suggest.

However, the success of placement-finding did not depend solely on resources and the characteristics of the children. The results were materially affected by the way in which the placement was managed. Placements were most likely to remain stable if there was:

- careful preparation of carers and children, by social workers and family placement officers;
- sensitive timing of introductions; and
- a smooth transition from foster care to adoptive home.

The foster carers themselves were key actors in this process. In two of the three cases of placement breakdown there was a poor relationship between the foster carer and the adopters; but if there was a good relationship, the previous carers eased the child's passage before, during and sometimes after the adoptive placements.

In the light of implementation, how well-founded were the original decisions?

Once it was clear that rehabilitation could not be envisaged, and that no other family member could care for the child, the decisions to recommend adoption had been based on the children's ages, difficulties and contact needs – the most predominant consideration being age. At the stage of placement-finding the child's age, as expected, did have a very important influence on the fulfilment rates, although this was usually in conjunction with other factors.

The social workers had predicted fairly accurately which plans were likely to be implemented with ease. In the immediate aftermath of the care order they were all hopeful that the plans would be fulfilled – but they were sensitive to the presence of risks connected with the children's ages. The only exception to this pattern of accurate prediction was the last case mentioned here, where the social worker had taken on a particularly strong commitment to placing two children aged 3 and 4.

Social workers' predictions and the placement outcome

> I imagine that in two years time Sarah [a 1-year-old baby with an adoption plan] will be living permanently with her adoptive family, and that the adoption order will have been made.
>
> [Outcome: The child was placed and adopted.]
>
> Jason [a child with special needs] is not like a little baby that you move as quickly as possible. This is a special needs child and we have to do it properly. The adoption plan will succeed but it's going to take longer. I'm sad for him.
>
> [Outcome: The child was placed eighteen months after the care order.]
>
> With the twins and the girls [members of a sibling group of five, to be divided], I am fairly confident. I am very hopeful with them; but I have to be honest – I am a little less confident with Barry, because of his age.
>
> [Outcome: Carers were identified for the twins and the two girls. The plan for the eldest child Barry, who was 7 years old, was changed to foster care.]
>
> I think it's highly unlikely, but not impossible, that this sibling group will end up in long-term fostering.
>
> [Outcome: Adoptive carers were successfully identified for the sibling group – although at the close of the study the children were still in foster care.]

> If we haven't placed them in two years time I ought to be shot! If by this time next year they are not placed with an adoptive family, I think we've done them a disservice.
>
> [Outcome: Adoptive placements were not found. For these two children, the plan was varied so that they could remain in foster care.]

The accuracy of the social workers' predictions makes us wonder whether some of these judgements turned into self-fulfilling prophecies! It is perhaps more concerning that the risks that had been foreseen by the workers were not conveyed to the court and they were not always reflected in contingency plans. However, the factor that had been given least recognition in the court hearings proved to be children's difficulties, which came into prominence in the aftermath of the care order. Ongoing assessment of these difficulties was often necessary, particularly when there had been a last-minute change of plan and a swing away from rehabilitation in care proceedings.

Children's difficulties

Table 9.3 brings out forcefully the way in which initial difficulties, measured according to the LAC seven dimensions (see Chapter 2), were linked to the age of the child.

Table 9.3 ***Initial difficulties according to age in adoption cases***

Age of child (yrs)	Average number of LAC dimensions in which problems were experienced
<1	0.85
1	1.60
2	3.40
3	5.00
4	5.25
5–6	5.25
7	7.00

Some of these difficulties were minor, but they affected plan fulfilment in two ways:

- clarification and sometimes treatment were necessary, and this created delays – particularly when there had been a last-minute change of plan; and
- the presence of known difficulties could act as a deterrent to adopters.

Since most of the adopters who were interviewed reported that initial problems were quite surmountable once the children had been placed, and were generally fewer or less serious than they had been led to expect, it is possible that potential problems had been over-represented in preparatory sessions. (One new parent said that she had been presented with 'worst case scenarios' on her training course, and another spoke of the 'horror stories' she had received.) However, the discovery that things were easier than expected contributed to a feeling of relief and well-being once the child was placed.

Educational difficulties, and emotional and behavioural problems

Two kinds of difficulty in particular appeared to turn away adopters even if they were relatively minor: educational difficulties, and emotional and behavioural problems. Seventeen children (52% of the adoption sub-sample) fell into each of these groups. Only six plans were successfully implemented among children in the former group and five in the latter. Similar findings emerge from a study of children's difficulties cited in the court proceedings. Nevertheless children with these problems settled well in foster care, and were often experienced as rewarding by their carers.

Problems in the general area of 'education' were usually linked to learning difficulties – although sometimes they were merely the result of under-stimulation – and when they were present, they made adoptive placements more difficult to find. They did not appear to contribute to breakdowns, however, and the main reason for the association between learning difficulties and non-fulfilment of the plan (apart from the children's ages) appeared to be the shortage of adopters who were prepared to deal with these problems.

Family and social relationships, and health

As might be expected, a large proportion of the children heading for adoption (67%) had initial difficulties in the area of family and social relationships – but these did not usually prevent placement. Health difficulties (present in 64% of the children) were also fairly neutral in terms of plan fulfilment, although they did sometimes introduce delays. They included poor speech, asthma or eczema, defects of sight or hearing and a few more serious disorders. Not all health problems had been identified prior to the order. For example, one small baby was found to have a kidney complaint that could have been extremely serious. Another baby was monitored for over a year because of an obscure skin condition, which turned out to be no more than a form of dermatitis. Identification of adopters was postponed so that these assessments could be carried out.[5]

Emotional difficulties

Emotional difficulties were not allowed to hold up placement if adopters were available, since it was recognised that the children needed stability, but more specific knowledge might have helped to smooth the path. For example, one 4-year-old girl whose adoption arrangements failed had been sexually abused in a previous placement with relatives. This was not known at the time of the attempted placement, and the attempt failed because the prospective adopters could not tolerate her sexualised behaviour towards their son – a problem that has often been identified when sexually abused children are placed in substitute care (Farmer and Pollock 1998). In another case where two small children proved exceptionally difficult to handle, the social worker said:

> We did have a full assessment of the children before we went to court. I think the difference then was that there were lots of other things going on. What is being done now is actually focused on their behaviour, whereas before it was expected that it was just emotional [turmoil] because they had had all this disruption, and once they were settled we were hoping their behaviour was going to settle down.

Initial problems in emotional and behavioural development were often related to anxiety, because of the experiences children had been through. (For example, night-time disorders such as sleeplessness, rocking and moaning were reported in young children.) Thirty-nine per cent had poor social presentation at the start of the placement as a result of neglect. These difficulties were not usually permanent, but they were serious enough to be reckoned with.

Contact needs

During the initial decision-making, the presence of contact needs had made it less likely that an adoption plan would be chosen for the child. Whether or not this policy was justified, it simplified implementation, inasmuch as contact with the birth family could be phased out in accordance with the care plan. However, there were some cases where contact needs had to be reassessed during the follow-up period, for example because the original care plan had not included a back-up arrangement for family contact if the child remained in foster care. Another common disadvantage was that the care plans did not state whether the intention was to place children separately or together; yet in terms of plan fulfilment as well as children's welfare, these decisions merited more attention than they had received during care proceedings.

How were the plans carried out?

Timing and number of moves

In the care plans that had recommended adoption, the timing of the placement was referred to very briefly in fourteen cases (usually with a phrase such as 'as soon as possible') and it was omitted altogether in nine of them. Only ten care plans contained detailed information, stating the number of months that could be expected to elapse between care order and placement.

Where a time-scale was mentioned in the care plan it was almost always exceeded. The average time to adoption placement in fulfilled cases, based on the statements in the detailed care plans, was estimated as five months. In reality it was eight months in those cases where estimates were provided, and ten months across the sample of fulfilled adoption cases as a whole. There were only two cases where the estimated time-scale was actually shortened.[6]

Table 9.4 ***Link between time-scales in care plan and implementation of adoption placement***

Quality of information about adoption time-scales (number of cases)	Average time to placement in fulfilled plans	Number of plans not fulfilled
Mentioned with detail (10)	8 months	2
Mentioned briefly (14)	11 months	5
Omitted altogether (9)	15 months	7

In spite of the fact that the time periods quoted in the care plans were generally exceeded, the study does seem to underline the importance of including time-scales and making them specific wherever possible. Table 9.4 sets the ten plans described as 'detailed' in the larger context of all adoption plans. It can be seen that:

- as the quality of information about time-targets diminished in the care plan, the average time to placement increased during the implementation period – and more plans were left unfulfilled.

We cannot be certain that regular inclusion of time-scales would automatically produce an improvement, however, since the details may have been omitted or glossed over where it was known that children would be difficult to place.

The timing of stages in the adoption process

During the follow-up period children moved through a number of stages, and delays could occur at any one of them. These stages are summarised in Table 9.5, together with the time taken to reach them in fulfilled cases.

Table 9.5 ***Stages in the adoption process***

Event	Average time after care order
First approach to adoption panel	immediate
Identification of suitable adopters	6 months
Linking with prospective adopters	8.5 months
Entry to the placement	10 months
Application to the court	12 months
Adoption order	17 months

The National Adoption Standards for England state that when adoption is the plan for a child subject to care proceedings, a match with suitable adoptive parents should be identified and approved by the adoption panel within six months of the court's decision. Inasmuch as six months was the *average* time taken to identify adopters, and another two and a half months was required, on average, to complete the linking, this target would not have been met in our study – although there was a considerable degree of variation. The time between court decision and placement (ten months) could also be considered too long, and if the time spent in care proceedings is added, few children would have met the government's target of waiting no more than one year from becoming continuously looked after to being found a new family (DoH 2000a, section 5.18). Once again, however, there was a tremendous amount of variation, and children were affected materially by the whole process.[8]

Reasons for delays

The main reason for delays in the early stages of the adoption process was *lack of suitable adopters*. This problem affected eighteen children. In other words, for just over half the sample, no suitable adopters were found within six months of the care order. By comparison, other reasons for delay were situation-specific and usually confined to one or two cases only. Nevertheless they were important. From the results shown below it can be seen that the relevant 'actors', in addition to social workers and adoption panel members, included prospective adopters, foster carers, birth parents, lawyers and members of the judiciary.

The reasons for delays in the adoption process, apart from the lack of suitable adopters, were as follows.

Delays between care order and identification of adopters

- The child's medical needs were assessed and monitored over a longer period.
- There was uncertainty about whether the foster parents might adopt the child.
- Owing to sickness and resignations, the social work team was short of staff.

Delays between identification of the adopters and linking

- Further assessment of the adopters' skills was requested by the panel.
- Further assessment of the child's behaviour was requested.
- The linking was delayed because the birth parents were seeking discharge of the care order.

Delays between linking and placement

- There was a need for further preparation of the child – for example, by therapeutic input.
- There was a need for preparation of the environment – for example, by extension of the adopters' home.

Delays between placement and application to adopt

- The social worker felt that the adopters were not yet ready to assume control.

- The adopters feared that the adoption would be contested.

Delays between application and adoption order

- The birth mother could not be found.
- The hearing was contested.
- The case was dealt with by more than one judge.

Some of the delays recorded in the above list were 'planned and purposeful'. Others were less so. *Delays associated with legal proceedings* were seen as inevitable, though some examples of parental obstruction might have been avoided by more sensitive handling of the case. *Waiting long-term for medical assessments* was also accepted as inevitable; but a good case could have been made for proceeding with the placement as long as the prospective adopters considered themselves able and willing to cope with what might emerge.

Once adopters had actually been identified, extra time spent on the preparation of adults and children could be helpful as long as there was steady movement towards placement. However, prolonged inaction in the early stages between care order and the identification of adopters was always unproductive no matter how or why it was caused, and it seems clear that a determined search for adopters should be put in train as soon as the care order is made. Indeed the search should start before the care order, if the likely outcome of care proceedings is known.

Monitoring progress to prevent delays

During the course of the study there was a growing realisation that in-care reviews are not a good enough mechanism for preventing delays in adoption, because of the time lapse between one review and the next. One authority appointed an officer with special responsibility for monitoring adoption cases regularly. Members of the legal department who served on adoption panels also said that they kept an increasingly watchful eye on cases they had previously been involved in, although they had no formal oversight role. Most typically it was the family placement officer who picked up on delays if there was slippage in the social work teams – for example because of problems caused by reorganisation and shortage of staff – but it seems likely that the independent reviewing officers mentioned in the Adoption and Children Act 2002 will take over a large share of the work in this area.

Number of moves made by the children

Fifteen of the nineteen children whose adoption plans were fulfilled made only one move after the care order, and this took them into an adoptive placement. Another three children made two moves, because there had to be a change from home to foster care or from one foster carer to another prior to the adoptive placement. One child stayed in the same placement throughout the follow-up period because she was adopted by her foster carer.

Among the children whose plans were not fulfilled there was one child who moved twice and another who moved three times. (Both of these experienced adoption breakdown.) However, there were twelve who made no moves at all during the study period.

- In other placement options children suffered from moving too much; but one move is usually necessary in adoption, and lack of movement is one more indication of the fact that adoptive carers were in short supply.

Policy issues

In the matter of seeking adoptive carers and supporting adopters, some of the local authorities in the study were more proactive than others, but few would have met the rather stringent requirements now set out in the National Adoption Standards for England: 'Agencies will plan, implement and evaluate effective strategies to recruit sufficient adopters to meet the needs of children waiting for adoption locally and nationally, especially those from diverse ethnic and cultural backgrounds and disabled children.'

The National Adoption Register was not available at the time of the research, but those authorities that had strong pro-adoption policies or were determined to find carers for particular children were more generous with allowances and one-off payments, and they also made better use of advertising and agencies such as BAAFLink. Where opportunities for finding adoptive parents were limited by membership of a consortium, it was unusual for the trawl to be extended beyond the geographical area served by the consortium. The main reason was cost; interagency fees were high. But it was also argued, not unreasonably, that it was not in most children's interests to be placed a long way from the region in which they had been born, and that local placements would provide a better service through continuity of care. However, in view of the young age of most of the children and the lack of plans for face-to-face contact with birth families, opportunities to extend the trawl over a wider geographical area might have resulted in the interests of some children being better served.

Specialist adoption teams

A specialist team was available in one local authority, and within this team the approach to adoption procedures was understandably more streamlined – although the work of the team was still being developed at the time of our research. The results in terms of plan fulfilment were evenly spread.[9]

Most social workers believed that in the long run specialist adoption teams would produce a more efficient service – although this does not answer the wider question of how adoption can best be integrated in the range of options for children entering and leaving the care system. Some practitioners felt that there were already too many barriers to integration, because of the distinct way in which adoption services have developed, and adoption workers themselves expressed a desire to stay in touch with the situations affecting birth families and to remain appreciative of the alternatives available to them. Specialism offers opportunities for the development of professional skills, but this is of limited value if social workers are deskilled in the competences that should be part and parcel of the planning process.

Legal issues

At the time when the care order was made with a plan for adoption, the final hearing had been contested in the case of eleven children – all of them singletons in eleven different families – but there were comparatively few challenges made by parents after the order. Only two applications were lodged for increased contact and discharge of the order. There was only one case where the adoption hearing itself was contested, and it was not successful. There were, however, several cases where the birth mother withdrew and could not be reached, perhaps because she did not want to be seen as 'signing her children away' (DoH 1999a), and in these circumstances her consent was usually dispensed with.[10] In two cases where the court insisted that more effort should be made to find the birth mother and obtain her consent, the local authority felt that this was time-wasting and counterproductive. Nevertheless it does call into question the relationship between plans for adoption made at the care order stage and the making of the adoption order, which does not automatically follow.[11]

Freeing for adoption was used only on two occasions, both of which were similar; in both cases the agency was slow in identifying adoptive parents, and this encouraged the birth parents to apply for increased contact and discharge of the order – at the six-month point in one case, and at the nine-month point in the other. The social services department responded immediately with an application to have the children freed for adoption, which happened approximately six months later.

It took these 'freed' children some considerable time to enter their adoptive placements (fourteen months and seventeen months respectively). In view of the fact that other research has found an association between freeing and protracted proceedings (Murch et al. 1993), we have to ask whether the process of application and counter-application had slowed things up. In one case it seems as though the reverse happened – at least at the start. The parents' challenge may actually have stimulated the department to search for adopters more earnestly, so that they could tell the court that they had been identified. There was, however, some delay between the identification and the linking, because the agency was unwilling to commit the adopters and begin introductions while the outcome was uncertain. The stress and tension of the court hearings badly affected the children in one family, and the transition to the adoptive placement was far from ideal.

Management issues

In terms of *financial support* for adoption, there were variations not only between authorities but within them. A means test was usually operated in the allocation of allowances, because although the provision was introduced to facilitate the adoption of 'hard-to-place' children,[12] it was recognised that an adoption allowance is a form of income for the parents. Nevertheless the first criterion is based on the child's needs, and it follows that this judgement is discretionary. A young, black single parent who adopted a small baby in one local authority was found to be living on a very restricted income with no ongoing help from social services. If the social worker had been more experienced, or the mother more worldly wise, an allowance might have been obtained and it would have contributed greatly to the quality of life for mother and child (Hill et al. 1989; Owen 1999).

Owing to recent restructuring within the local authorities, social work managers often found themselves struggling with *staff shortages and administrative difficulties.*[13] It was anticipated that these difficulties would be reduced when the new system was established, but adoption work is time-consuming and it seemed likely that there would be ongoing problems with human resources. It was rare for two social workers to be allocated to one case at the same time. Birth parents probably suffered most in this regard, because agency action was focused on the child.[14]

Necessary discontinuities were accepted between the pre care-order and post care-order stages when a child had to be 'referred on', and in some cases these same discontinuities were seen as an advantage – for example because the new worker could collect information from the birth parents without being associated with the unpleasant events of care proceedings. However, it was generally recognised that there had to be continuity of worker for the child between care order and adoption. One family placement officer said:

> I think there needs to be one person who actually has an idea of the whole thing and the reasons behind it, and if you're going to be doing or arranging direct work with the child then you have to be the one with the knowledge ... There's an awful lot of knowledge that goes in that doesn't get written down but actually comes out in one way or another. It's amazing how much you soak up.

In addition to ensuring that the necessary 'knowledge' was available for report-writing, of course, adoption managers had to ensure that traumatised children and those around them were given emotional support throughout introductions – a task that might be shared but which could not afford to be neglected (Byrne 2000).

Issues of social work practice

The social workers involved in adoption clearly enjoyed their work, and where children were placed extremely quickly, an experienced social worker had usually found ways of short-circuiting the system. Those who were in close touch with adoption panels or involved in recruitment had some knowledge of the existing stock of adopters and also of those who were 'in the pipeline'. It was not unusual for prospective adopters to be approached about a child and 'snapped up' when they were on the verge of approval. This slightly competitive way of working seems to have emerged from the combined pressures of concern about delay and shortages of provision, and it undoubtedly benefited some children; but it worked best with children who were easy to place, and it did not allow for the careful matching and preparation that was necessary in the placement of sibling groups or older children with special needs. It could be argued, too, that there is inherent injustice in a system that depends heavily on the bargaining power of individual workers.

These strategies were necessary because the choice of adopters was limited. In many cases there was only one couple (or none) who would have been suitable. There was only one adopter in the study who was a single person, and this lends some support to the belief that social workers can be over-fussy about rejecting adopters – although our evidence in this study is confined to the placement-finding phase of the adoptive process, and we have no direct knowledge of the way in which the adopters had originally been approved.

With hindsight, some mistakes were made. In most cases of breakdown there was an unresolved issue concerned with an existing child in the prospective adopters' family – something that has been identified and explored as a risk factor in a number of research studies (Wedge and Mantle 1991; Quinton et al 1998; Rushton et al. 2001) and there was also a bad relationship between the adopter and the foster parent, which made the transition difficult. During the preparatory period inexperienced social workers sometimes allowed themselves to be bullied by adopters whom they felt to be 'pushy', and consequently they withdrew from sensitive areas of investigation or else allowed the placement to happen too hurriedly – perhaps as an attempt to compensate for delays in other parts of the system.

The adopters who slid most easily into the parenting role were described as having personal qualities such as warmth, honesty and flexibility, and crucially they had the ability to understand and sympathise with the child.[15] The evidence from interviews and file studies suggests that in many cases prospective adopters ruled themselves out, not just because of children's problems but because they could not accept the children's backgrounds – particularly where the birth parents had suffered from mental health or learning difficulties that were believed to be transmissible. There were also worries about the information from the past that would be held in store for the child. This difficulty was particularly acute where a previous child had died in suspicious circumstances or through proven injury. One couple who regarded themselves as experienced adopters were said to have great difficulty in accepting this situation because their first child, adopted several years ago, had been relinquished voluntarily by a young mother. In another case three or four sets of adopters were put off by the knowledge that the birth parents might appeal against the care order and that they might also oppose the adoption if an adoption order was pursued.[16]

Social workers tried their best to allay the adopters' fears, but better preparatory work – with a positive orientation – was needed as well as intensive recruitment of new parents.[17] In view of the fact that some adopters found it difficult to handle breakdowns without rejecting the child, it might have been useful for them to discuss the possibility of disruption and ways of dealing with it before it happened. However, in successful placements the social workers were able to be honest about children's difficulties and at the same time present them in their proper context – not as insuperable obstacles or necessarily permanent defects, but as factors related to the experiences the children had been through. All the prospective adopters had shown at the approval stage that they had potential parenting skills; but it was the development of empathy in the adoptive parent that ensured the attachment of the child and stabilised the placement.

What the adoptive parents said

> As a small child ... she deserves the best chance of life there is, and I think by adopting her and making her your own child, that's how she'll get the best deal really.

> I don't know if it could be speeded up. When you decide to adopt, sometimes you have to wait months before you can begin to be assessed, to get on the training course. I think there could be some improvement there – just so that children aren't in care for so long. It would make our life a lot easier once they came to us.

> The courses that social services run are all well and good, but when I did it they tended to want to talk about children from ethnic minority backgrounds and how it may affect them etc. They never told you how to look after a sick child, or what sort of equipment you might want to buy for your house. They didn't tell you anything you really wanted to know.

> Everybody else there [on the preparatory course] had infertility problems, and they didn't have the same agenda really; so it was quite hard for them as well. Somebody said to us: 'God, you got three children and you are still here?' It was like 'You are being greedy.' Yes, it was like 'Goodness me, what are you doing here? You have already had three of your own.'

> I think we were extremely lucky because we clicked with the foster parents very quickly, therefore they made the whole process very easy for us ... The house was designed so that their backroom on the visit was ours, and they

> would get involved or disappear as we wanted. The help was always there ... but because we got on so well with the foster parents, the whole process was painlessly easy. And that's what made it so easy – it was their input.
>
> To be honest, the theory of having post adoption groups if you like is very nice because you can chat to each other and whatever – but in practice once you've got your children and everything's OK you want to break away from the stigma of being in contact with social services. You want to get on with your life and be a normal family.

Discussion and conclusions

The rapidity of reform since the late 1990s has been striking and in some ways the context of adoption today is markedly different from when our study began. As we have noted already, the Adoption and Children Act 2002 has brought adoption law into line with the Children Act 1989, the paramount consideration now being the child's welfare, and National Adoption Standards have been drawn up to guide local authority practice. A nation-wide register is in place to extend local authorities' placement finding opportunities. Measures to support adopters include a new right to assessment for post adoption support, within a framework that is intended to assist adoptive parents looking after children with complex needs. Under the Adoption and Children Act courts will have to produce timetables to ensure adoption cases are handled without delay, and this is also one of the matters prioritised in the national standards.

These measures are excellent; but in the light of our findings, what more needs to be done for them to succeed? There is clearly a lot of inconsistency among local authorities. The most urgent need is to increase the supply of adopters who are prepared to deal with older children – particularly children who are more than 3 years old at the time of the final court hearing, who are members of sibling groups or who show signs of developmental delay. Extending the trawl by means of the national register will help; but in view of the fact that children over the age of 2 were regarded as 'hard to place' in our study, there is an ongoing need for public information and recruitment. There is also a need to advance on all fronts. Not all of the adopters in the study were prepared to accept a 'contract' model of adoption akin to foster care and, given the history of adoption, it seems likely that the mainstream of prospective adopters will continue to be composed of childless adults who want to parent children whom the world sees as normal. (In that respect, the adoptive parents' wishes and the wishes of the children probably coincide.) The adopters in the study needed to know how to understand and handle children's expressions of disturbance; but they also needed limits to be placed on their own fears – for example about the effects of learning difficulties or mental illness in the children's backgrounds – and they needed contact with adopters who would talk not just about problems but about the positive rewards of parenting.

The adoptive parents in this study were generally satisfied with the help they had received; but our follow-up period was restricted to 21 months, which is not long in the life of a child. What happens if problems arise at a later date? The right to be assessed for post-adoption support is valuable, but it does not necessarily imply that support will be given – and in order to be acceptable to those for whom it is intended, the service may need to be removed as far as possible from the stigmatisation of the care system. This means that attention has to be paid not only to the consumers' right of entry, but to the source and style of delivery.

The other main issue in this part of the research is delay, which has been a persistent theme of judicial and government comment. The research confirms that time-scales are an important ingredient of planning, and that the search for suitable adopters should be started as early as possible – ideally before the order. Nevertheless we need to make a distinction between planned or purposive delay and hold-ups that cannot be justified in terms of the child's welfare. An extended period in foster care prior to adoption, if this is really necessary, is certainly preferable to leaving children at home in damaging environments – and since the research also shows that breakdowns were more damaging than delays, a major priority of the social workers in adoption cases must be to get the placement right.

Summary

1. By the end of the study nineteen of the 33 children whose plan was adoption had been placed, and for nine of these children adoption orders had been made. Delay in finding suitable adopters was the main reason why some plans were not fulfilled. Breakdown occurred in only three cases, at a relatively early stage.

2. Cost factors as well as geographical considerations restricted the likelihood of adoption trawls being extended beyond the local area served by the consortium.

3 Homes were found most readily for children who were still babies at the time of the care order – especially if they did not have significant problems. The children who failed to find a placement were aged 3 or over, belonged to sibling groups and had some degree of developmental delay. Behaviour problems and learning difficulties were over-represented in children whose plans were not fulfilled.

4 Adoption plans did not always state whether siblings were to be placed together or separately, despite the importance of this information. Delays were increased when these decisions had to be made after the care order.

5 On average it took children ten months to reach placement. Plans with detailed time-scales took the least time, and those where time-scales were omitted altogether took the longest. However, there were positive reasons for delay as well as negative ones.

6 There was no difference in implementation rates between the authorities that used specialist adoption teams and those that did not, although most social workers thought that specialisation would in the long run lead to an improved service. Prospective adopters were keen to take on a parenting role and there was no marked enthusiasm for post-adoption support at this stage; but preparatory work was valuable in helping them to understand and sympathise with the children in their care.

---

[1] Disruption is of course only one measure of 'outcome' in adoption. Some researchers have focused on children's progress or the stability and security of the placements (DoH 1999a).

[2] The assumed or actual impact of the Children Act 1989 has been blamed for this, although there is no necessary tension between adoption and family support (SSI 1999, p. 51).

[3] The Act enables ministers to establish an independent review mechanism for prospective adopters who feel that their application has been unfairly turned down. It also provides a right of access to assistance and representation for all looked-after children in the context of complaints.

[4] This statement is made cautiously because the numbers are very small. Lowe and Murch (2002) report that it is usually more difficult to obtain adoptive placements for boys.

[5] In the study of disruption by Barth and Berry, disruptions were found to be significantly more likely among children with emotional problems, behavioural problems and 'mental retardation' – but not more likely among children with a physical disability or a medical condition (Barth and Berry 1988). If adopters are available and willing to face an element of risk, the emotional cost of delaying the placement for extensive medical assessment may be more than is justified.

[6] The first of these cases involves a baby girl who was less than 1 year old at the time of the care order. The guardian had been strongly critical of the local authority's timing, and since she had aired her dissatisfaction in court, it seems likely that this helped to speed up the process. In the other case, where a 2-year-old boy of mixed parentage was placed almost immediately after the care order, the social worker said that she had been 'extremely lucky' in finding two adopters with exactly the right ethnic match.

[7] The study by Ivaldi quotes seven months as being the average time to placement, although it varies with age (Ivaldi 2000).

[8] Councils are now required to monitor the time-scales that they are achieving for children with an adoption plan, and the Department of Health has developed an Integrated Children's System framework to support all aspects of the planning process for looked-after children.

[9] Among the children whose adoption plan was not fulfilled there were six children (from three families) who were being dealt with by the specialist team and eight (from four families) who were dealt with by non-specialists. This reflects the general distribution of adoption cases post care order, since placement-finding for sixteen of the 33 children whose care plan recommended adoption had been allocated to members of the specialist adoption team, whereas placement-finding for the other seventeen was done by social workers who did not consider themselves adoption specialists, although they were all specialists in work with children and families.

[10] To sign the consent form, birth parents had to confirm that they agreed to the adoption 'freely and unconditionally'. Since then the form giving consent to adoption has been amended to reflect the reality that the birth parents have agreed to the adoption 'on the basis that it is in the best interests of the child' (DoH 2000a, section 8.28). It is hoped that this will make it easier for parents to give consent.

[11] This issue has been extensively discussed in *The Prime Minister's Review of Adoption* (Cabinet Office 2000) and also in the run-up to the Adoption Act.

[12] The regulations state that an adoption allowance may be payable 'to help secure a suitable adoption where a child cannot be readily adopted because of a financial obstacle'.

[13] Much depended on the pace of change. Radical restructuring introduced too quickly was destabilising, and some social work managers found that they could only cope by means of an enormous influx of temporary, agency staff.

[14] The National Adoption Standards recommend that birth families should have a worker independent of the child's social worker from the time adoption is identified as the plan for the child. This very rarely happened in the study.

[15] The study by Quinton et al. (1998) explored new parents' sensitivity and responsiveness. They found that problems in parental responsiveness were strongly related to placement instability when linked with particular vulnerabilities in rejected children. (This interaction was important.)

[16] Interestingly, none of these reasons was related to the age of the child – although, as previously noted, older age and the presence of problems in the children did act as deterrents to adopters.

[17] The interviews with carers, too, suggest that preparatory work might have been more popular than post-adoption support – although the need for the latter might have emerged at a later stage.

10 Fostering and residential care

Introduction

Fostering and residential care together form the backbone of provision for children in the care system. In recent years fostering has been the more favoured option while the use of residential care has diminished; so it is not surprising to find that in this study plans for long-term foster care were made for 22 children and young people between the ages of 5 and 15. Residential care, on the other hand, was planned for only five adolescents, all of whom were over the age of 12 at the time of the final hearing.

This study confirms the extent of our dependency on foster care. Although planned for just over one-fifth of the children, almost double those numbers (n = 42) ended up in foster care at the end of the study. To this extent our findings are in line with national trends. At the time the study was undertaken, foster care accounted for the largest proportion of all looked-after children (65%), a rate that had risen steadily throughout the 1990s from 58% in 1992 and it continues to predominate today. Most of the increase is attributable to the decline in the use of residential care, largely owing to a shift in favour of family-based upbringing. By 1997 residential establishments catered for only 13% of all looked-after children.

Both residential care and foster care have faced their fair share of troubles. Residential care has been the subject of numerous inquiries where children have suffered abusive treatment (Wagner 1988; Local Government Management Board 1992; Utting et al. 1997) and there has also been much concern over the poor educational and employment rates of residential care leavers, together with levels of offending and absconding (Sinclair and Gibbs 1998; Wade et al. 1998; DoH 1998c). Foster care has been beset by persistent difficulties in recruiting suitable carers for all children, and particularly for children from ethnic minorities (SSI 1996b; SSI 1998; Sinclair et al. 2000). There have also been concerns over the adequacy of measures to safeguard children living in foster care, the extensive and persistent pattern of placement instability and the wide-ranging vulnerability of care leavers (HC Health Committee 1998).

To address the issues of supply and quality in foster care, the government has introduced a wide range of measures. These include the launch of a national recruitment campaign in 2000, the introduction of performance indicators to measure placement stability and, most recently and for the first time, external inspection of public, private and voluntary foster care services by the National Commission for Care Standards. Exchange of best practice has been encouraged by the creation of Beacon Councils. Specific strategies have also been put forward to raise standards in residential care as a result of the Children's Safeguard Review; but many of the measures apply equally to both groups. For example, as part of the Quality Protects initiative, targets have been set to increase the educational achievements of all looked-after children. The Leaving Care Act of 2000 extends the responsibilities of local authorities towards young people after the age of 18. Individual pathway plans, and the introduction of personal advisers to help manage the transition to adulthood, are intended to help reverse the trend of young people leaving care early and drifting thereafter.

Of particular relevance to this study is the role of long-term foster care and more particularly how it compares with other placement options such as adoption and residential care. The research evidence suggests that the gap between adoption and long-term foster care has narrowed in terms of placement stability and welfare outcomes in recent years, although higher rates of breakdown still occur for fostered children aged 5–12 (Triseliotis 2002). The main factor that seems to differentiate the two placement options is the adopted child's stronger sense of belonging and security. The findings on the comparative merits of foster and residential care do not always tally with popular perceptions either. The study by Rowe et al. (1989) found success rates to be comparable for placements ending in adolescence, as did Colton's comparison of child-outcomes in specialist foster care and residential care; but Triseliotis et al. (1995) found very high levels of breakdown in residential and foster placements for teenagers.

In this study care plans for fostering or residential care were made for approximately one-quarter of the children – but foster homes and residential institutions also absorbed three-quarters of the children who had suffered breakdowns of other placement options or failed to find a placement elsewhere. The need for ongoing planning and stability for these children is underlined.

The implementation of fostering plans

How many placement plans were fulfilled?

Figure 10.1 shows the progress made in the implementation of fostering plans for the children in the 21 months after the care order. Fifteen children and young people had their plans for foster care fulfilled, out of the total of 22 – a success rate of 68%. In terms of families, the success rate is 10 out of 15.

Fifteen plans count as fulfilled because the children were in foster care as recommended in the care plan; but *for the majority of these children the long-term status of the placements had not been officially confirmed.* The permanence panel had confirmed the status of the placement in only two cases, and three more were awaiting panel consideration. In six cases the placement was informally considered permanent and treated as such; but four of the children whose plans were fulfilled were still in temporary placements.

Figure 10.1 ***Implementation of plans for fostering: progress of children 21 months after care order***

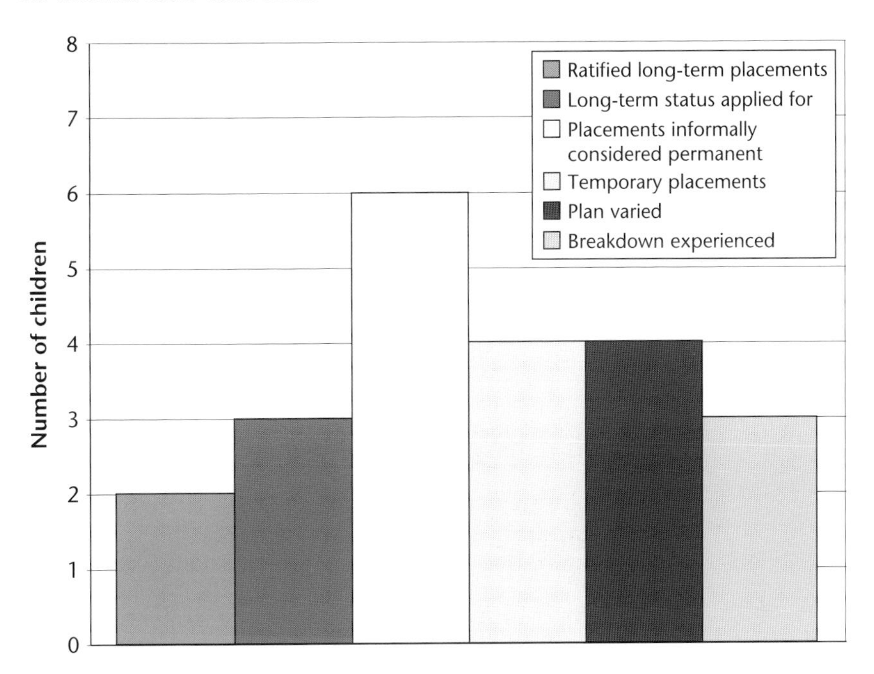

What happened to the children and young people whose plans were not fulfilled?

Seven young people were not in foster homes at the end of the study. Three of them had been moved to a different type of placement after the foster placement broke down, and plans for the other four were varied because they failed to enter a foster placement.

Of the three who did not remain in foster care:

- One boy who was 9 years old at the time of the final hearing was moved to residential care after he had absconded constantly from the foster home.
- One 12-year-old boy was looked after by a relative who arrived late on the scene, at a time when a move to another foster home was being considered.
- One 14-year-old girl returned to her parents, who arranged for her to spend part of her time at boarding school.

Of the four young people who never entered a foster placement:

- Two 13-year-old boys remained in residential care, although these placements had been planned as temporary.
- Two 15-year-old girls chose to live independently on reaching the age of 16.

In every case where the fostering plan did not succeed the plan had been varied by the end of the study, so that current plans reflected the status quo.

What helped or hindered placement?

Once again a number of recognisable factors appeared to contribute to fulfilment or non-fulfilment of the placement plan:

- *Child factors* All the young people whose fostering plan did not succeed were 9 years old or older, and the average age in non-fulfilled placements was 13. There was a high tolerance of problems in foster care, however, and bad behaviour did not necessarily prevent or disrupt placements unless it was extreme. The young person's wishes and feelings had a major impact.

- *Family factors* The quality of contact, including sibling contact, was very important in foster care. The families of children who failed to settle in foster homes were often opposed to this type of placement, and they were reported to be accidentally or deliberately undermining it. In the two cases where young people did not move on from residential care, this option was more acceptable to the parents as well as to the children themselves.
- *Organisational factors* Non-fulfilment tended to be related to a lack of specialist foster placements, compounded by difficulties in finding suitable and acceptable homes for young people over 12 years old. Fulfilment was more common in the non-specialist placements used by children between the ages of 5 and 11.

Nine of the twelve girls with fostering plans were in foster homes at the end of the study, while six of the ten boys were successfully placed. Thirteen of the eighteen white children, and two of the four children of mixed heritage, had their plans fulfilled. The two children of mixed heritage whose plans were varied both rejected foster placements, and problems of ethnic identity may well have been a factor in this rejection – although this was not apparent from the case details.

Where plans were made for the joint placement of siblings in foster care, these plans were followed through, although there was more fragmentation of sibling groups in this placement option than in adoption. The intention was usually to make placements easier to find, and also to increase placement stability by reducing conflict between warring siblings. Seven children who entered care as part of a sibling group were to be placed alone. These children were rather vulnerable. The plan was to preserve necessary links by sibling contact, although the arrangements were sometimes difficult to sustain. See Table 10.1.

Table 10.1 ***Placement fulfilment: children in terms of sibling groups***

	Planned placements	**Fulfilled placements**
Singletons	8	4
Members of sibling groups:		
– to be placed singly	7	4
– to be placed as part of a sibling pair	4 (two pairs)	4
– to be placed as a group	3 (one group)	3
Total	**22**	**15**

In the light of implementation, how well-founded were the original decisions?

In terms of overall placement fulfilment in our study, foster care was more successful than adoption in providing homes for older children and it also had another advantage; *children's difficulties did not necessarily place obstacles in the way of placement*. Foster care is a collecting ground for children with a great variety of problems, and it is interesting to note that:

- out of the seventeen children and young people who had initial problems in emotional and behavioural development, approximately two-thirds were successfully placed in foster care.

The problems affecting older children were of considerable severity. For example, health problems such as smoking and drinking, or promiscuity and refusal to accept medical care, affected teenagers' lifestyle and safety. Educational problems at the start of the placement included non-school attendance and school exclusion, and these difficulties extended into the workplace in the form of low motivation, lack of attention to careers advice and lack of career opportunities. These problems have been well documented elsewhere and are now regarded as almost stereotypical of adolescents in the care system (DoH 1996a; Butler and Payne 1997). However, there was an immense amount of variety in the cases we have been examining.[1] One 6-year-old girl who was extremely disabled was looked after by a foster carer with back-up support from special education, a respite carer and a raft of services. This seemed a particularly creative use of foster care, which in addition to being beneficial to the child and family, was undoubtedly less expensive than the residential alternative.

The wisdom of consulting young people

The results confirm the wisdom of consulting children and young people and incorporating their wishes wherever possible in decision-making. In fact, this seemed to be more important than any other consideration in ensuring placement fulfilment, whether non-fulfilment was related to breakdown or failure to enter the placement.

- In cases of breakdown, the young people had been somewhat ambivalent about the original fostering plan – although they had been willing to give it a trial.
- In cases of failure to enter a foster placement, the young people had never agreed to the fostering plan in the first place.

The two adolescents (both aged 13) who did not move into a foster home remained in residential care, which had been arranged as a bridging placement, although the hope and expectation was that they would move to a foster home at a later date. The other two (both aged 15) chose to live independently when they reached the age of 16 and they tried to refuse all help from social services with the exception of housing and finances.

It was recognised during care proceedings that the fulfilment of fostering plans would be very dependent on children's feelings. However, the 'sticking points' varied from one case to another. Children who had originally harboured doubts about foster care because of their attachment to their own families were more inclined to accept the provision when they realised that contact with home would continue and that their own parents' role would not be entirely usurped. More problems were experienced in placing children who did not want another family because they were disillusioned with family living altogether – although the social workers felt that they needed at least one satisfactory experience before moving into the outside world. The young people who were hardest to place were not only disillusioned with family life but had previously had bad experiences of fostering. Hostility was particularly acute when they did not accept the need for the care order, which in one case was made against the wishes of the social services department.

Availability of resources

In addition to the child's wishes and feelings, availability of resources had been one of the limiting factors in the original fostering decisions. Did this turn out to be a problem at the stage of implementation? Because of the determined efforts of social workers and family placement officers:

- foster placements had been identified for seventeen of the 22 young people by the time of the final hearing, and others were found soon after it.

However, only five of these placements were designated as long-term from the start. For most of the children long-term carers would be needed; but they were not always deliberately sought, since it was felt to be better for children to remain where they were if the placement was going well.

Without doubt, the greatest resource problems were in specialist provision. Specialist placements had been recommended in the care plans for all seven young people who were aged 13 or over, and only two of these plans were fulfilled. The wishes and feelings of the young people concerned were probably a more important influence in these cases than resource scarcity but the two considerations went hand in hand, since the agency was unwilling to make extra efforts to obtain a scarce fostering placement if it was clear that the adolescent did not want it. In the two cases of specialist fostering that were successfully implemented in this age group, the placements had been arranged and visits made prior to the order.

- Fulfilment of the plan was much easier when children had met the foster carers, visited the foster home and entered into an active commitment before the care order was made.

This of course meant that a suitable resource had to be identified and funding arranged at a fairly early stage in care proceedings. In cases where children failed to enter a foster home during the follow-up period, an individual placement had not usually been identified. The plans could still appear detailed, however, because the naming of a 'bridging placement' postponed the decision about long-term foster care to some time in the future.

Social workers' predictions and the placement outcome

Once again the social workers had usually been sensitive to weak points in the care plan and they were able to predict which placement plans would be difficult to implement, either on grounds of resources (as in the first of these quotations) or (as in the second) because the children had other views.

> Resources are going to be the big issue. We have a large number of children waiting for long-term foster carers and we have a shortage of resources. That's going to be the big problem.

[Outcome: Separate foster homes were identified for the three children in this case but only two of the placements survived, and one of these was short term.]

Paul is adamant that he will not go into foster care. I think it's his fear of the unknown – and maybe there's that deep-rooted fear that I'm going to give him a new mum and dad.

[Outcome: A specialist foster placement was found, offered and rejected. This boy remained in residential care.]

Were these self-fulfilling prophecies? Perhaps – but foreknowledge does not imply acceptance. When it was known at the time of the care order that plans would be difficult to fulfil, social workers were able to intensify their attempts to find foster placements and also develop contingencies (for example, by exploring the possibility that a residential placement might become long term). *What they found most difficult to predict, however, was the actions of parents.* Fears were often expressed that parents would destabilise the situation by appealing against the order or by applying at a later date for the order to be discharged – although no appeals were ever made, and there was only one instance of an application to discharge the order in a fostering case and it was unsuccessful. The social workers' anxieties in this area seemed to stem from the atmosphere of mistrust that had been generated during care proceedings, and in the aftermath of the care order it was heightened by a lack of accurate knowledge of what the parent was doing or feeling.

She'll either appeal or make an application to discharge the order. That hasn't happened so far, but she's probably rounding up solicitors to represent her ... I could see her doing that.

[Outcome: The foster placement survived and no application was made to the court.]

Contact is going to be a problem. And I think we're going to have some difficulty in identifying carers who can cope with the legal side, because Mother is not accepting that the children are going to be away from her and I think at some point she may well go back to court ...

[Outcome: Placements were found for the children, and the children's mother did not go back to court – although contact continued to be problematic.]

In the social workers' accounts there was not only doubt about what parents might do; there was doubt about *the parent's proper role* post care order – something that had not been set out in any detail in the care plans – and since the child's contact needs had featured highly in the original decision-making, contact became the main focus for debates about parental responsibility after the order. Proposals for *reunification* had been absent from the care plans, and this was another 'grey area'. Social workers found it difficult to predict whether reunification would happen within the context of the study or in fact at all.

Clearly this is an area where some uncertainty must be allowed, and the care plan must be capable of adjusting to it; but in the absence of targets that had been negotiated and agreed, predictions about the effect of family influences on the foster placement (as in the following examples) were frequently off key.

> In eighteen months or two years' time Andrew will be 16 and I would be very much surprised if he wasn't back with his mum ...
>
> [Outcome: This boy did not return to his mother. The placement continued.]
>
> My prediction for Elsa is that the relationship with her mother will not be patched. It's too damaged ... She will stay with the same foster carer.
>
> [Outcome: The foster placement broke down; but the relationship with her mother improved and the young person went home.]

In short, social workers in fostering cases were able to predict the likelihood of placement breakdown or non-entry to placement on the basis of resource constraints and children's feelings but, having no immediate targets for rehabilitation and being unsure of how relationships would develop, they were either over-optimistic or unduly pessimistic in their attitudes to return.

How were the plans carried out?

Timing and number of moves

Unlike adoption, foster care provided an environment where carers were readily sought during care proceedings, and in many case they had *had* to be identified either for ease of assessment or for the protection of the child. The result was that in seven cases (almost half the total number of successful foster placements) the children were living in foster homes where they remained after the order was made. (See Table 10.2). This does not mean, however, that they were necessarily in *long-term* foster homes. The boundary between short and long-term care was permeable. By this strategy the number of moves that had to be made by the child was kept to a minimum, although the status of some placements – especially in the early stages – was slightly unclear. There was also a time-lag before the need to move was identified, and this delayed the start of some final placements.

Table 10.2 ***Moves made by children whose fostering plans were fulfilled, and average time to final placement***

Number of moves	Number of children	Average time to final placement
None	7	–
One	6	11 months
Two	2	15 months

As in adoption, questions need to be asked about the delay in finding long-term placements for some children. Why did it take nearly a year to place six children and even longer for the other two? The six children who moved once had lingered in placements that, though not entirely suited to their needs, were not totally unsatisfactory, and attempts had been made to shore up these placements for as long as possible. The two children who moved twice experienced late breakdowns – at fourteen months in one case and seventeen months in the other – which required them to be moved immediately. The timing of the moves indicates that the social workers' actions had positive and negative aspects.

- The positive aspect of limiting movement was a striving for stability.
- The negative aspect was reactive planning – a reluctance to act except in an emergency.

Five of the six children who moved once experienced the highly structured placement-finding approach used in adoption, where application to an appropriate panel was made so that long-term carers could be selected to meet their needs. It was always known that these children would have to be moved, either because the existing placement was unsatisfactory or because it was definitely short term; but it took a long time to accomplish. (The average was thirteen months, and the range was from nine months to 21 months.) In the sub-sample of fostering cases as a whole, the average time taken to reach a placement that could be considered final was about six months.

Understandably, the children whose plans were not fulfilled made more moves than the others. Only one of them 'stayed put'. Four children whose plans were not fulfilled moved twice during the time period, and two particularly unsettled children moved between four and six times.

Policy issues

By contrast with adoption, foster care is a flexible, adaptable service with fairly fluid boundaries. Behind this apparent flexibility there is a lack of clarity about what 'long-term fostering' actually means. Some writers identify 'long-term or permanent fostering' as a single option (Triseliotis et al. 1995; Hill 1999). However, the Department of Health study *Patterns and Outcomes in Child Placement* made a distinction between permanent fostering and placements that were intended to be 'open-ended long term' (DoH 1991a, p. 68). At that time permanent fostering was said to be 'a relatively new development used mainly for older children' and it was clearly intended to offer a degree of permanence almost equivalent to that found in adoption.

- In the current study some foster placements – particularly those for teenagers – were intended to be permanent, but the majority would be better described as 'open-ended long term'.[2]

At the start of the care period, as we have noted, there were no actual plans to return any of the fostered children home, but in more than one case distress was experienced because the parents believed otherwise. There were also cases where children and their carers appeared to be uncertain about how long the placement would last. One foster carer who looked after two sisters described the start of the placement as follows:

> My understanding was that they were to be with us for a month, although off the record our social worker had said a month usually means a lot more – until they find somebody for them long term ... There was no plan for them to go back. It wasn't until a couple of months ago that I found out the girls believed they were going back. I understood that they knew they weren't going back – but they didn't.

Some carers were prepared to set their own targets. One couple who were fostering two children of primary school age said 'After they are 18 they can stay as long as they like. They are just like part of the family now.' It was more common, however, for carers to expect that the decisions would be made by social services. One foster carer who felt that it was important to have the status of the placement clarified complained about the length of time it had taken for the placement to be officially designated as permanent.

> What annoyed me was the fact that a long time ago they decided to go for a long-term placement, and they decided to go long term with me. But it took about a year to do the paperwork, so it left the girls not knowing where they were going to go and live for far longer than I thought was desirable.

Exploration of the social work interviews shows that in all of these cases there was official ambivalence, and a desire to keep options open. In one case, the social worker was harbouring a 'hidden agenda' that the children might return to their parents. In another, there was indecision about whether it was right to place two girls together rather than separately because there had been conflict between them in the past; and in a third case there was doubt about whether the foster carer herself had the qualities necessary to parent these children in the longer term. These cases raise fundamental issues concerned with social work ethics and pragmatism. Was it right to have so much lack of openness in the dealings with carers and children? Even on a practical level the strategy did not work, since the attempt to spare people distress resulted only in confusion and distress being increased.

From a policy point of view, the main issue is the need to clarify what is meant by 'long-term placements'. There was some difference between the perceived permanence of *ordinary and specialist* foster placements. Specialist placements, which were routinely recommended for young people of 13 and over, were more likely to be permanent because the adolescent was nearing the end of the care period. The 'ordinary' placements were treated more casually and sometimes perhaps undervalued (a finding that was reported by Berridge and Cleaver in 1987) although they coped quite successfully with a wide range of vulnerable and distressed children in middle childhood. Their status may have suffered from the fact that they were readily available, although not in sufficient numbers to offer a lot of choice. The matching was never easy, and many placement successes can be attributed to the resilience of children and their carers.

Legal issues

In fostering cases there were five families, containing six children, in which the care order had been contested. The children concerned were mostly adolescents, and in three cases the main challenge had come from the young person concerned. One girl was independently represented, though she failed to turn up for the final hearing.)

It is probably not coincidental that in these cases the grounds for care proceedings were not merely significant harm but '*beyond parental control*'. These grounds were actively resented – although they did not always impute blame to the child.

- The grounds of 'beyond parental control' were used in two cases of possible sexual abuse to protect the children from intensive questioning in court. The parents denied the accusations, and the hearings would have been contested strongly if the grounds for the order had depended on proof of abuse.

In both of these cases the use of the 'beyond parental control' label was criticised by medical practitioners, who felt that the children's allegations ought to have been treated with more respect even though they were not supported by evidence. In both cases the social workers were at pains to spare the young people unnecessary distress and to secure their safety by separating them from their parents. For these reasons it seemed advisable to have a care order made with parental agreement; but there remains a question mark over the use of the 'beyond parental control' grounds. In their interviews both of the young people reported an enduring sense of stigmatisation, and in both cases the care plans were unfulfilled.

> When they admitted me, it was like 'You're a failure. You can't get on at home ...'You look at other people and you think: they've got a mum and a dad and a house ... They get clothes, and Christmas presents and proper family things, and you think 'Well, that's not on.' And you are so hurt by things like that, you will go out and attack anyone who comes in your way.

> I would have agreed to anything to get out of there. I said 'Right; I'm beyond parental control.' But it seemed, and to a certain extent it still does seem, ridiculous. I always thought kids who were beyond parental control were ones that went out at night and never came home. Just very unlike me ... This seemed like something so completely different, but there was no allowance made for that.

In spite of their displeasure at the order, there were no young people who applied at a later date for discharge of the order. It is possible that some of them did not know their rights, or felt that the attempt would be fruitless; but the evidence from the social work interviews suggests that in most cases of dissatisfaction they were persuaded not to apply because the care order would be an advantage in the transition to independent living. In one of the sexual abuse cases, the girl concerned would definitely have liked the order to be discharged but felt that it would be painful to reopen the issues.[3]

More generally, there were problems for local authorities who wanted to bring the care order to an end in 'beyond parental control' cases if the plan was not working – especially if the child was frequently missing.

- For children who were genuinely out of control and remained so, the care order was clearly not fulfilling its function; but it was usually felt that in this situation the court would be unwilling to discharge the order and the application was not made.

Some solicitors said that problems associated with discharge often acted as a deterrent to seeking an order in the first place. (See Chapter 4.) Clearly someone had to be responsible for the young person's welfare, and there is no ready answer to this dilemma.

It was of course possible for parents to apply to have the order discharged; but this happened rather rarely and the attempts were unsuccessful. However, the approach to the court was certainly not fruitless. In view of the debates about post-order review, it is interesting to note that:

- when applications were made to the court during the implementation period (regardless of who was making the application), efforts to fulfil the plan were increased. There were fears that the guardian would be critical of the local authority if the care plan had not been fully implemented.

When parents made the application, it is arguable that non-fulfilment of the care plan strengthened their case – and when the application was made by the local authority, it was even more clearly in their interests to show that the plan had been fulfilled. At any rate, when the court was reinvolved for whatever reason, more determined efforts were made to find long-term placements for the children and the contact arrangements were also firmed up. The court hearings were stressful and time-consuming, but they were not entirely unproductive.

Management issues

A major issue for case managers was finding suitable placements for teenagers.[4] Foster carers were sought in the first instance from the local authority's list of approved carers, and identified with the help of the family placement officer. If no suitable carers were available, the trawl was extended to a larger geographical area. In accordance with local fostering policy, approaches could then be made to 'known voluntary agencies' that had been inspected and approved, and if this failed an approach could be made to an independent fostering agency – though this was regarded as a last resort because of the high cost involved.

Foster placements also had to be supported by *services*, and the quality of these services could make or mar the placement. In one case involving a seriously disabled child, as we have already noted, creative use of foster care with appropriate input from health and education, together with the services of a respite carer, proved a viable and less costly alternative to residential care.

It has been known for some time that the supply of foster parents in local authorities is often inadequate, and that lack of choice can compromise decision-making (SSI 1996b; SSI 1998; Sinclair et al. 2000). It is symptomatic of the difficulty experienced in finding specialised adolescent placements that:

- one social worker contacted eight different fostering agencies before finding a place for a youth who was in a secure unit at the time of care proceedings.

The placement that was found was a long way from home; but nevertheless funding was arranged, and agreements were drawn up with the young person's consent, and the move took place as soon as the care order was made.

At first sight the efficiency with which this placement was arranged and carried out suggests that more children could benefit from this type of provision if only more money was available. This may be true; but the later conduct of the case also reveals the considerable problems of working at long range. For the social worker and manager there were difficulties in retaining responsibility and control of the case. For the adolescent boy there were conflicts with other children in the foster home (which is not unusual, given that specialised foster homes almost by definition accommodate children with challenging behaviour) and although he made a successful move to another foster home within the same agency, he faced increasing anxieties about where he 'belonged' when he realised that discharge from care was imminent and his ties with the home area had been largely severed. This placement plan was fulfilled, but the cost of fulfilling it was very great.

Issues of social work practice

Apart from the identification of carers, the main issue faced by social workers in the implementation of fostering placements (as the above case illustrates) was the *management of transitions*. The same problem of course exists in adoption, but adoption is more readily conceived as a 'journey' to be undertaken by the child (Fahlberg 1994), and the actual transition is carefully structured. In foster care, social workers had to find their own ways of helping children cope with change, and this included managing the links with home and school as well as helping children to become part of the new family. It also included maintenance of contact with previous carers, who in some cases were just as important to the children as the parents themselves. This could pose problems for the current carer, as the following quotation from a foster carer's interview shows.

> She still has contact with her previous carer, roughly once a month. It was necessary because she had been with them so long – but at times it was hard, because if she was having a bad day, everything was thrown up about how she would like to go back there and how everything was rosy there. She used to get quite high before and after she went.

Transitions of a different sort occurred in *disruptions*, and much depended on how the disruptions were managed. In a few cases where the child had to move between carers, the reality of breakdown was disguised by emphasising subsidiary reasons for the move, such as the foster carers' accommodation problems or plans for an extended holiday. (There is no evidence that children were helped by this strategy, however.)

When the placement continued, there could still be problems concerned with *relationships within the foster home*. Several pieces of research, in recent years, have commented on the difficulties for young people entering placements where there are already other children – both looked-after children and birth children of the carers (Berridge and Cleaver 1987; Wedge and Mantle 1991; Quinton et al. 1998; Rushton et al. 2001). These difficulties were certainly present in the sample, and in one case problems of jealousy and hostility were largely responsible for the foster placement breaking down. Here is the young person's account of difficulties in his previous placement:

> It was this boy who lived with them. It was hell – it really was. I didn't like him at all, and after a couple of months I hated him, but I couldn't say anything ... The foster parents didn't listen to me. I said 'Alexander is annoying me' and

they didn't listen. They said 'David, stop lying.' I was thinking 'I am not lying', but they wouldn't listen.

Apart from the need to help carers with interactions between children (a need that is highlighted in the example above) social workers could avoid some problems by selecting an appropriate family structure for the child. Most social workers believed, without treating it as a 'rule of thumb', that in an ideal situation there would be an age gap of not less than three years between any existing children and the placed child. However, the impact of a new sibling-type relationship is not always negative. A study of adolescent fostering by Farmer et al. (2002) reported that in 53% of cases the fostered child had a positive or very positive impact on other children in the household, and that placements were less likely to disrupt when the foster carers had children of their own who were close in age to the young people. In the present study, the results emphasise the need to pay due attention to the requirements of *individual children*. One foster carer who found that the looked-after child did not get on well with her daughter said:

They didn't pre-empt that side of it at all. They just assumed she would be so pleased, where in fact if she had had a choice she probably wouldn't have chosen a family with a younger child. They thought it would be the ideal thing she needed. It is getting better now, but Jane found it very hard.

At the stage of placement-finding, the stability of foster placements could be increased by taking into account the existing family structure, including placed children; but it was also improved by limiting the number of new children who could be admitted to the placement, either short term or long term. Foster carers who were not designated as long-term carers could be under pressure to take additional children, and this occasionally resulted in a mixture of young people who not only had different ages and problems but different destinations in and out of the care system. Control of the placement arrangements was most effective when it had been officially designated as long term, and this provides yet another reason why long-term status should be sought.

What the foster carers said

The social worker has got her head screwed on. She's good. I first said to her 'What do you want me to do?' and she said 'What you normally do; just get them going.' She allows me to choose the pre-schools because I know them around here, and register them with a GP that I like ... Having done it before, I know what steps to take and she's just there to make sure that it's done...

Yesterday they had a meeting for John and Julie [the siblings of the child in foster care] and she phoned me up after the meeting to say what they had done. She doesn't have to – but she feels that we all need to know what's going on with the other children.

We got on very well with her [the social worker]. Unfortunately she left the children just at the time when they needed her. She left after two years. I'm sure the work was her creation, her doing, her input – but she left them and in came a new social worker.

In our profession, we wouldn't do that to them. They can leave the job just like that and carry on with their lives. They are changing people's lives only to walk out and start another job. We will always be in contact with the children. We will be the ones that, if anything untoward were to happen, will have to live with it. We wondered how much she ever felt that. I tried to explain it to her, that when those children walk out of the door, it doesn't stop. For us very often, children come back.

Some children think they will be dead by the time they're 16. Others think they will go to prison. They haven't got a lot of self-esteem, which is what you have to teach them as carers – that they can achieve and have a future. How do you tell a child who has had such a disruptive life to go forward?...

With most carers, the problems arise where they can only take the children for a short time. Every carer has a different attitude. In an ideal world children in care would go to one carer and stay with them all the time. Our own children don't have lots of different parents; they just have us!

The implementation of plans for residential care

How many placement plans were fulfilled?

The numbers in this category are small, since it was planned for only five children. However, the results are telling. In three cases the new placements found it difficult to contain the young people. One of these plans counts as 'fulfilled' inasmuch as the girl who was the subject of the plan was in residential accommodation at the end of the study; but this happened only because she was admitted to a secure unit after several weeks on the run. The two placements that proved stable – one in a residential home and one in a special school – were already 'home' to the children concerned at the time when the care order was made.

What happened to the children whose plans were not fulfilled?

- One girl who had been 15 years old at the time of the care order was living independently, having forfeited her chances of further education and employment.
- One 13-year-old boy had absconded in search of his mother, and social services did not know where he was for a substantial period of time.

What helped or hindered placement?

Child factors

Entering a strange community presented a considerable hurdle for adolescents with low self-esteem. If they didn't feel comfortable they absconded, especially if they had already acquired a feeling of rootlessness. If they were already settled in a residential establishment prior to the making of the order, it was more likely to continue.

Family factors

Contact with family and community was a stabilising influence – as long as it was beneficial. Two young people in the group were adamant about the fact that they did not want any contact with parents or siblings.

Organisational factors

In residential care, as with foster care, it was not the run-of-the-mill facility that was problematic – it was the specialist resource. Suitable placements in therapeutic communities with education were difficult to find and sometimes difficult to fund.

In the light of implementation, how well-founded were the original plans for residential care?

As before, social workers were asked for their predictions about placement fulfilment – but it seemed somewhat inappropriate in cases where young people had already absconded by the time the first social work interviews were held. Obviously the social workers were hopeful that the position could be recovered, but they were also expressing feelings of grief and exhaustion.

> I feel with Marion that we've lost it. It took over my life before, and I know that I came close to thinking 'I'm not going to go on doing this.' So I think those cases you can't hold as a social worker for ever and ever because it just takes too much out of you.

There was an exceptionally high level of problems among the five young people bound for residential care. In this placement option, as in foster care, all of them had initial deficits in the area of family and social relationships; but in addition, all of the young people for whom residential care was planned had severe problems in emotional and behavioural development. Four of them also rated poorly in education and identity, having been absent from mainstream school for long periods of time. Three had health problems resulting from their lifestyle, which included smoking, drinking and under-age sex. Two had deficiencies in social presentation and self-care skills. All had previous episodes in care or accommodation. Nevertheless there is no evidence that the number and extent of children's problems directly affected the achievement of the placement in the sense that they were unacceptable to carers.

- No one asked for the young people to be moved; they moved of their own free will. The effect of their problems was indirect.

For two of these young people – a boy aged 12 and a girl aged 15 – the placement decisions had been relatively easy to make because the young people were already accommodated in residential establishments and wanted to stay there. In the case of the other three young people who were given residential care plans the decisions were much more problematic – mainly because the young people's choice of where and how they wanted to live was unacceptable to the agency; but at the same time the young people found it equally unacceptable to be faced with a choice between a residential placement and a specialist foster home. Given the current policy initiatives, the social workers would usually have preferred the fostering option; but when it was clear that this was not going to work, a search was made for a place in a residential community. It was hoped that such a community would not only stabilise the adolescents but give them therapeutic and educational input, which was certainly something they needed.

In theory, the plans were excellent. The faults, if any, lay in implementation. The plans did not succeed in these three cases because they never had a chance to succeed.

- In cases of breakdown, young people absconded before they had been there long enough to build relationships or even to feel a sense of association with the environment.

In the case of one young man who later found a niche in specialist fostering, care proceedings had been initiated precisely because he kept absconding from accommodation in residential care – and as has been noted in other cases, the absconding started with a placement move.

> The main reason for seeking the care order was that he was moved, once he became 13 or 14. He was in a younger children's home, and he was bullying all the younger children – so we had to move him to a teenage children's home, unfortunately, because he was putting the other children at risk ... He really didn't settle – and then of course once he didn't settle he started to abscond.

The 13-year-old girl who was moved to secure accommodation settled there and was well liked by staff and peers, which suggests that she might have settled in the residential community that was planned for her if she had only been persuaded to stay there. When planning foster care, it was generally sufficient preparation if children were introduced to the new carers and had a chance to visit the foster home before the care order; but for adolescents facing untried residential placements in what seemed to them to be distant parts of the country, this did not seem to be enough.

How were the plans for residential care carried out?

Policy issues

Residential care as last resort

Considerable efforts were made to find places for the children who needed residential care, but because of the policy-based preference for fostering there was often a feeling that this was a second-best option and a last resort. This position is understandable, not just because residential care failed to offer care in a family setting but because some of the local authority homes in the study were accommodating children with severe behaviour problems, and the social services department was faced with a very high cost in seeking specialised therapeutic placements elsewhere. If this feeling of entering a 'last resort' was transmitted to the young people entering residential care for the first time it cannot have been helpful in securing placement. It should be noted, however, that:

- for some adolescents in the sample a residential institution had become their home and they were distressed at the prospect of removal from it –

> even to the extent that feelings of insecurity accompanied a move to another building when the existing building had to be repaired.

Permanence of the placement

In residential care, as in fostering, there were different views about the permanence of the placement. In two cases residential care was written into the care plan only as a bridging placement, but the children felt settled there and had no wish to move on to specialist fostering. The promises made to young people in these circumstances were remembered, and there could be repercussions if they were seen to be ignored. One residential carer made this comment, about a girl who regarded the placement as her home:

> I think we actually agreed that Tracy would not have to move on at 16 and could remain placed in a residential unit. One of the difficulties, if I am really honest here, was that a promise was made to her that she could remain at this particular home – but what we should have said was that she could remain in residential care. Now what we have to do with her is to firm up what the conditions of that are, because she is extremely violent and will throw fire extinguishers around.

Moving children from one home to another

It seemed to be a matter of policy in one of the local authorities that children should be moved from one home to another, as a way of managing resources and at the same time maintaining control in difficult situations – and sometimes such moves were unavoidable, for example because the court had imposed bail conditions on some of the residents which meant that they could not have contact with one another. However, considerable distress was caused by frequent movement, and the policy of transferring children from one home to another may need to be revised in view of the growing acknowledgement of the need for stability for all looked-after children.

A common reason for movement was that a child had reached the *age limit* for children in a particular home. In one very innovative plan for an immature young man with learning difficulties, provision was made for him to stay in a home with younger children at a time when his chronological age dictated that he should be moved elsewhere. (He related well to the younger children.) By this means he was protected from contact with offenders, which would have given rise to fears of possible 'contamination', and his placement was made secure; but the residential social workers had to go to some lengths to arrange contact with his own age group – for example by means of music events – and they acknowledged that it was difficult to prepare this young man adequately for leaving care.

Legal issues

Secure orders

For children who absconded frequently, either from residential care or from foster care, there was always a practical and legal issue about whether or not a secure order should be applied for. The grounds for obtaining a secure order are slightly different from those that apply to care orders under the Children Act 1989, and for some solicitors this was a live dilemma; but in terms of the child's best interests, secure orders were generally felt to be unhelpful. They were regarded as short-term, high-cost strategies, which did little to aid long-term planning or further the child's integration into the community.

Secure orders were more often talked about than sought, but one 13-year-old girl spent a total of fourteen months in secure accommodation during the course of the study. She did not enter the residential community that had been planned for her after the care order – partly because of a misunderstanding, which led her to think that funding had been withdrawn – and she was placed in a local children's home from which she ran away. She managed to avoid contact with social services for four months.

This case provides some evidence of the limited powers available to guardians who want to challenge the local authority's decisions. When the guardian was reappointed she threatened the local authority with judicial review, on the grounds that the care plan was not being implemented. However, the reality was that the guardian panel would have had to pay the solicitor's costs and the bill might have been prohibitive. Judicial review would still have been an option if the young person herself had wanted to pursue it, in which case she might have been granted legal aid; but she did not seek legal action. She did, however, receive an apology about the placement that was never implemented. Ironically, she also made progress during further spells in secure accommodation, which provided (at considerable cost) a stable environment with a structured, supportive regime and therapy and education on the premises. These were precisely the benefits that had been intended to come from residential care.

Management issues

Joint funding was always a major issue in arranging placements in residential communities. Understandably, there was a reluctance to undertake commitments until funding had been arranged, and although the necessary mechanisms were in place, there could be delays as well as misunderstandings such as the one reported above. Other agencies were unwilling to commit funds if it was suspected that the young person might abscond and 'waste' the place – so the child's lack of confidence was reflected in official lack of confidence in the plan; but social services managers did not want to take on the whole burden of expensive placements when a considerable input from health or education was required. (An annual fee of £70,000 had been requested for one boy to attend a special school, but this placement did not take place.)

The study does, however, highlight an interesting situation, which is the exact corollary to the one represented above. In the case of two placements, one of which was funded by health and the other by education, there were doubts about the extent to which children's needs were being met – but the fact that these placements were externally funded was a strong incentive not to reverse the decisions whenever they came up for review. In yet another case where funding had been provided, the placement (which was within the private sector) ended abruptly and without warning because the agency went bankrupt. There is clearly more than one way in which funding problems can interfere with the realisation of a child's best interests.

Issues of social work practice

In the document *People Like Us*, which reviews the safeguards for children living away from home, Sir William Utting makes the following penetrating statement: 'The key to a child or young person feeling safe in care is the quality and stability of the relationships they form with significant adults they can trust' (Utting 1997, p. 76).

In residential placements which worked (and it should be remembered that seven children were in residential care by the end of the study), the young person's primary attachments were respected and encouraged. It so happened that social workers wished to encourage them, because the links with parents and siblings in these cases were considered beneficial. In the three cases where young people failed to settle, on the other hand, the social workers wished to discourage links or even sever them altogether. In the first case a girl who had long ago fallen out with her family was attached to a community of prostitutes in the city where she lived. These were the people from whom she did not want to be separated, because they gave her friendship, food, shelter and a form of employment. In the second case a boy was considered to be unhealthily 'enmeshed' with his mother. As a result, contact in the new environment was to be strictly controlled, and geographical distance was seen as a way of controlling it – but this did not work. In the third case, somewhat unusually, an adolescent girl was strongly attached to two people who had treated her for emotional illnesses over a number of years, and in all attempts to move her on, she had learned to manipulate a return to the institution where they worked. These were difficult situations for social workers to deal with; but it is clear that no placements would be suitable for these young people unless the question of their attachments was sensitively addressed.

Obviously the young people also needed to feel wanted in their new environment. Besides being abused by adults, they had been scapegoated by their peers in the past, and even a therapeutic community could appear threatening in these circumstances. The 'tough cookie' image adopted by some of these adolescents was deceptive. They needed understanding and acceptance; but in the absence of parental support and clearly identifiable carers they also needed to feel that the agency was indeed taking on a parental role. In cases like this social workers found themselves trying – often without success – to enter a vicious circle. A stable placement was necessary to improve the young person's mental health; but the fulfilment of the placement plan was itself dependent on improvements in the individual's state of mind.

What the residential social workers said

> I don't truly believe that residential should be the first option. It should always be the absolute last, really. I mean there are some people who clearly can't cope in a family setting and they need to have a place of safety like a residential unit, but I don't really agree that most kids should be coming here before they go anywhere else.

> Matthew [a child removed from foster care to a residential home] feels safe here; but he cried to me the other day that he is fed up with it at the moment. He is fed up with everyone feeling sad. I think he probably picks up on staff being quite sad, because there have been four assaults in one week here. Another member of staff had a book thrown at her face and had stitches in her face. We had one member of staff pushed by the family of a particular lad, one member of staff bitten and myself smacked in the head.

> To me they are a very supportive staff group, excellent in picking up if someone has had a bad shift. Just recently I had a nasty experience with a young person here making accusations and yes, I was supported by my manager, but I felt the staff group did it from the heart.

> Gary [an adolescent in a residential EBD school] is happy about being here because his previous school was an academic-orientated place ... It was very reminiscent of the schools he must have been in at one time, and probably for some of the boys including him, there are memories he would rather not deal with ... It is much more relaxed here. The academic side of things is sort of sneaked in between much more practical life skill exercises. This morning he was going down with some staff to a supermarket to buy the ingredients for a menu that he had decided to attempt. At lunch time today, there he was – having cooked it, eating his stir fry.

> I would like someone somewhere to always check up on these young people and offer them support. I know that we do it through [statutory] reviews and things like that; but there are some young people that slip through the net, and they do need some help somewhere. There is a constant flow of young people. They can't go out there and not survive too well. They need to be picked up on, through the after-care.

Discussion and conclusions

Both foster care and residential care emerge as 'umbrella options' offering protection to some of the most damaged and vulnerable children in the sample. Unlike adoption, they readily accepted older children and children with problems – as long as resources permitted, which was by no means certain – and if the promised placements did not happen, it was often because children had rejected the placements rather than this happening the other way round.

The flexibility and availability of these placement options, relatively speaking, is an advantage in securing placement; but in both environments there were concerns about long-term planning. Stability was particularly problematic in residential care because of the pattern of absconding and frequent movement; but children who were settled in a particular institution usually wanted to remain there as long as they were allowed. In foster care, as other researchers have noted (Schofield et al. 2000; Lowe and Murch 2002), there are different meanings for 'long-term' or 'permanent' placements, which give rise to different expectations on the part of social workers, carers, parents and children.

These misunderstandings caused distress in our study and they could leave the arrangements for children ambiguous and uncertain. The position may now have changed, since the National Adoption Standards for England state that 'a plan for permanence must be produced for all looked-after children at the four-month statutory review'. However, it is disturbing to find that ambiguity was actually welcomed by social workers who wanted to keep the options open. Reactive planning meant that on the one hand the long-term status of placements was not officially confirmed, and on the other hand definite plans for reunification were not made. The solicitors' reluctance to apply for discharge of the order in cases where children were beyond parental control, or to encourage children to apply for discharge even when they were dissatisfied, meant that the care order was compelled to run its course.

The interviews give us a brief but disturbing snapshot of the difficult work undertaken by residential and foster carers, and they underline the importance of training and support for the task. The use of the 'beyond parental control' grounds in sexual abuse cases did not imply that the young people's behaviour was unmanageable; but when young people were genuinely 'beyond parental control' and had conduct disorders or more severe problems in emotional and behavioural development, carers were faced with a range of day-to-day problems, which could include theft, drug-taking and physical violence. It was crucial to get the relationship with family members right; but above all there had to be attachment between the child and an individual carer who could encapsulate the parenting role of the state and stabilise the placement. Placements survived in the face of conduct disorders, and sometimes they survived in the absence of strong attachment; but it was apparent that, without attachment, no placement could survive in a way that was meaningful to the child.

Summary

1. Fifteen plans for foster care were fulfilled, out of a total of 22. Three out of five residential placements were fulfilled.

2. Fulfilment was more common in relation to non-specialist foster placements for children between 5 and 11. In both fostering and residential care, specialist resources for teenagers were difficult to find and sometimes difficult to fund.

3. Four of the fifteen children placed in foster care were living in short-term accommodation at the end of the study. For all of these, a move

was imminent. The remainder were in placements regarded as permanent; but long-term status had been confirmed by the permanency panel in only half of these cases. Few children experienced the highly structured approach to placement-finding that was common in adoption.

4 The wishes and feelings of young people were probably a more important influence than resource scarcity. Their full agreement was needed for plans to succeed – and they did not want to move if they were happy in an existing placement.

5 Some children had severe difficulties; but the presence of initial difficulties did not discriminate clearly between fulfilled and non-fulfilled plans. By comparison with other placement options, fostering and residential care both provide environments that are tolerant of children with problems.

6 Residential and fostering placements were more likely to succeed if the young person was already living there prior to the order. The presence of a 'bridging placement' postponed the decision to some time in the future.

---

[1] Among children who were 11 years old at the time of the care order there were two children who were placed mainly for family reasons and they had no particular difficulties in other areas of welfare; but there were also two children with difficulties in five areas including emotional and behavioural development and self-care skills. These young people were all girls and they came from four separate families.

[2] The study by Schofield et al. (2000) also found that there was confusion over terminology, and that the different meanings ascribed to long-term foster care led carers to have different attitudes and expectations, which affected the way they delivered care to the children.

[3] The grounds for discharge of the order would not necessarily have 'reopened' the sexual abuse issues, but lack of clarity about the grounds for the care order put obstacles in the way of discharge because it made it harder to prove that harm no longer existed.

[4] This is one of the issues to be addressed in the government's Choice Protects programme.

11 Kinship care

Introduction

Prior to the Children Act several research studies of children in care had shown that placements with relatives, and sometimes 'significant others', could give children stability, continuity and a positive sense of identity (Rowe et al. 1984; Millham et al. 1986; Berridge and Cleaver 1987), and the Act itself recognised that if children could not return home, they could sometimes be placed satisfactorily with members of the wider family or friends.[1] Since then there have been further indications that 'kinship care', as it has come to be known, compares well with other placement options in a variety of care situations (Rowe et al 1989; Farmer and Parker 1991; Broad 1999; Marsh and Peel 1999).

At the same time there have been worries about the difficulties social services may experience in supervising kinship placements, particularly in managing the complex intra-family relationships involved in contact, and more fundamentally working at the interface of competing family loyalties. There have also been concerns about the amount of support and remuneration available to carers, who may be both old and poor. Kinship carers have sometimes found themselves to be the poor cousins of the foster care system – difficulties that reflect policy ambiguity over the role and expectations of family carers.[2] Since they are family members, is it right that allowances should be on a par with those of non-relatives, given that they are assuming a formal role for the state in taking on parental responsibility – or does it undermine family commitment? These questions go beyond the specifics of childcare policy to society's beliefs about the nature of family ties and obligations, but the answers have direct implications for the way in which kinship care is used for looked-after children.

Despite the legislative support for kinship care, there is general consensus that it remains an under-used option, although it may be increasing. Some sources suggest that the rates have risen from 8% of all looked-after children in 1997 to 10.5% in 1999, when they comprised 16% of those who were fostered

(Maluccio et al. 2000), but it is difficult to obtain accurate figures because the statistics combine placements with relatives and with friends. Nor has kinship care been evenly used. Studies here and in the United States have found that because of the perceived importance of community links, kinship care is the favoured choice for minority ethnic children (McFadden 1998; Hunt and Macleod 1999) – though it is possible that the persistent shortage of foster carers from ethnic minorities may be another factor.[3] In this study seven of the eighteen children selected for placement with relatives were Afro-Caribbean or of mixed white/Afro-Caribbean parentage. Placement with relatives has also been used extensively in cases of substance abuse, both in black families and in white families, and again this study is no exception. Ten of the eighteen children for whom kinship care was planned were considered to be at risk because at least one of their parents had misused drugs, and once again this seems to mirror what is happening in the USA (Hornby et al. 1995).

As mentioned in Chapter 4, a feature of the present study has been the number of children transferred from a mother's to a father's care. In all of these cases the child entered a different household and experienced a change of main carer. The common factor, and the crucial one, was a pre-existing connection between the carer and the child.

The implementation of plans for kinship care

How many placement plans were fulfilled?

Figure 11.1 shows the progress made in the implementation of kinship care plans for the children in the 21 months after the care order. They had a good rate of fulfilment. Out of eighteen children (from eleven families) there were only four (in three families) whose plans were not implemented successfully. There were no resource difficulties in terms of the availability of carers since carers had to be identified before any of these plans were made, and there were no children who failed to enter the proposed placement. All failures were therefore a result of breakdowns.

As can be seen from Figure 11.1, the results indicate a strong desire on the part of carers to achieve legal forms of permanence – especially residence orders, although in two cases adoption orders were sought. By the end of the follow-up period legal orders had been made or applications submitted on behalf of eleven of the fourteen children whose placement plans were fulfilled.

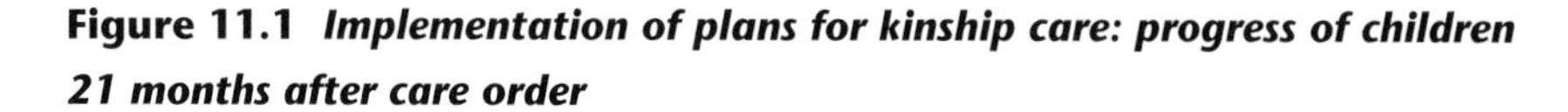

Figure 11.1 ***Implementation of plans for kinship care: progress of children 21 months after care order***

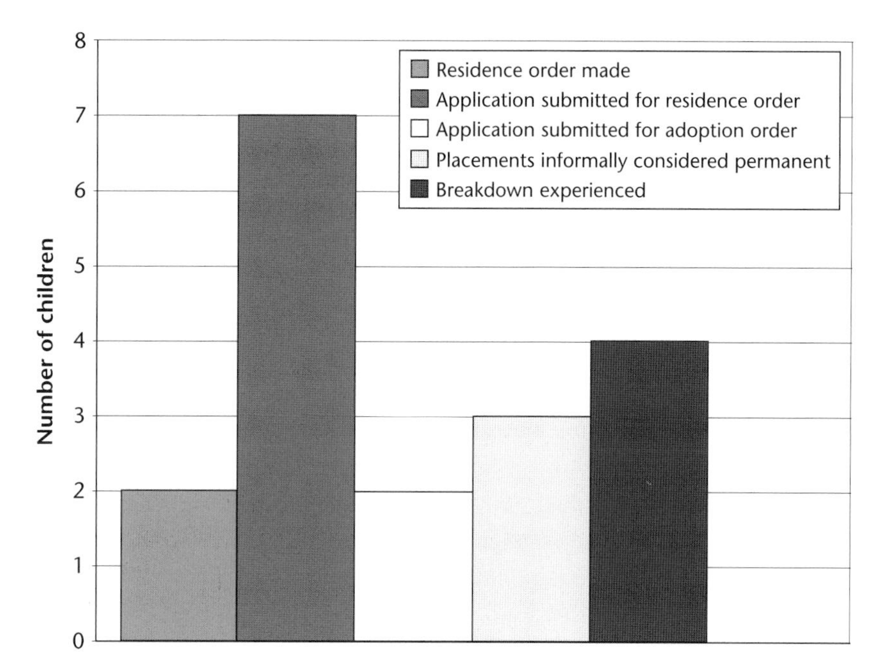

What happened to the children whose plans were not fulfilled?

Of the four children whose placements broke down:

- two children – a boy aged 6 and a girl aged 9 – were removed to foster care;
- one 14-year-old girl entered a residential home; and
- another adolescent (aged 15) disappeared for a time, and then lived independently with friends.

In three of the four placements that disrupted, the children had originally been placed with an aunt or an aunt and uncle. The placements succeeded at first, but broke down mainly because of difficulties concerned with family structure – partners and other children in the household. Here are the social workers' comments about these cases.

> The aunt had so many of her own children. She was a single mum at the time. She then met a new husband and got pregnant again, and I think it must have

> been him that was saying 'I'll take on these children but I'm not going to take on your sister's as well.'
>
> [Outcome: The 6-year-old boy was removed to join siblings in foster care.]
>
> A large part of this is that her auntie wants her freedom, and she's got a partner who's putting a lot of pressure on her, and the relationship is very difficult. She is finding Martha a very big responsibility – more than she thought it would be.
>
> [Outcome: This 14-year-old girl entered a residential home.]
>
> Jodie wanted to go off and do things that she wanted to do – dealing, breaking boundaries – and there was some friction within the family because this is a very large family as well.
>
> [Outcome: young person living independently.]

Contact with the mother was an issue contributing to breakdown where family relationships were problematic. In the case of the 9-year-old girl who was removed to foster care from her father's household, the social worker said that the main problem had been the child's feelings of divided loyalty; she had wanted more contact with her mother, who was believed to be undermining the placement.

> It broke down I think primarily because of Lindsey being caught in the middle between her feelings for her father and her feelings for her mother. She wanted contact with her mother but her father couldn't cope with it.
>
> [Outcome: The child was removed to foster care in order to stabilise the situation; but she was returned to her father shortly after the close of the study.]

The 6-year-old boy who was removed to foster care did not want contact with his mother, who had abused and maltreated him. The 15-year-old girl who ended up living independently had ambivalent relationships with her mother and avoided contact, which usually resulted in physical fights; but the 14-year-old girl who entered residential care had liked living with her mother, who had problems with alcohol and drug abuse as well as unstable mental health, and according to the social worker she wanted to resume living with her mother when she was 'cured'.

I think Martha has always resented our involvement because she liked the set-up when she was with mum. She had her own life and she didn't go to school at all and had her friends round all the time and her boyfriends were allowed to stay. Now she's being told 'no' and she doesn't like that word very much ...

She's very angry with her mum at the moment. She wants her mum to go back to the flat so that she can resume the life she was living. She did want to live with her auntie – but if mum got well again and came out of the treatment unit, she would want to live with mum again.

Breakdowns in kinship care were not necessarily permanent. In the above cases contact was maintained with the previous carers and efforts were made to heal the damaged relationships – except in the case of the adolescent who absconded and disappeared. She had been placed with a very distant relative and the placement lasted only a matter of days. The friends she chose to live with later gave her a measure of stability and companionship as well as a bridge to independent living, although her welfare outcome was extremely poor.

What helped or hindered placement?

All of the placements of *minority ethnic children* (seven children from four families) were fulfilled. As noted earlier, this means that half the successful placements with relatives involved non-white families, and out of the fourteen children in the total study who were black or of mixed heritage exactly half were placed in kinship care. The pattern was extremely regional, however. All the minority ethnic placements were in two inner cities, although the cities were in two different local authorities. Community structure, as well as family structure, was an important ingredient in these placements.

Apart from membership of an ethnic community, the following factors appeared to be related to plan fulfilment or non-fulfilment:

- *Child factors* Young children's problems did not readily lead to failure of the plan. In the majority of cases where children were placed with relatives the placement was made and continued in spite of problems – perhaps even *because* of them. However, most of the children placed in kinship care were below the age of 9. In this age group there was only one placement that did not continue for 21 months. Conversely, two of the four breakdowns involved teenagers.

- *Family factors* The most important quality offered by kinship carers was commitment. A sense of 'belonging' inspired many carers to persevere with children's difficulties in the face of considerable odds. Apart from this, the main criterion of success was a positive attitude towards the child's previous experience, and a willingness to preserve links with the child's previous carer who was usually the birth mother.

- *Organisational factors* In successful cases there was considerable input to the new carer in the form of emotional support and advice and also practical or material help. The need to work steadily towards a residence order or adoption order provided a focus and a target for intervention in many cases.

Gender was comparatively unimportant, although slightly more boys than girls had their placements fulfilled (eight out of nine as opposed to six out of nine).

The low rate of breakdown in kinship care is fairly remarkable when we consider that even quite young children had considerable emotional difficulties as a result of the instabilities they had suffered before and during care proceedings. All of the children who were aged 2 or over were exhibiting some form of disturbed behaviour at the time of the care order, and five were receiving psychiatric help; yet most of these plans succeeded. This was in marked contrast to adoption plans, where children's initial welfare difficulties were commonly linked to non-fulfilment of the plan. In adoption, children's problems had a tendency to turn away prospective carers, but in kinship care:

- children's problems did not readily prevent placement, because the plight of young children who were previously known to the carers attracted sympathy and stimulated a desire to help.

Here is how one carer described his previous experience of a child who was made subject to the care order on grounds of neglect.

> We used to give him a bath every night he stayed with us and there were never any unnatural bruises – in that respect we weren't concerned – but I would pick him up from school or from home in the holidays and he would be absolutely thrilled. He would run to us ... Then I'd take him home and as soon as he got through the door, he'd be so introverted. He would go in and just kneel down on the floor and pretend he was playing with something. He certainly wasn't happy. Things weren't right. That was the depressing side of it, rather than suspecting any serious abuse.

The pre-existing link with the child generated commitment on the part of carers; but it should be noted that *the main carers were not always blood relatives of the child.* The carer mentioned above had taken on a grandparent's role because he was married to the child's grandmother. In another case both the new carers were completely unrelated to the child. (They were parents of the mother's former partner, but they were acting as grandparents.) There was only one person who became involved because she was a 'friend' of the child, and this was a school welfare assistant who looked after an 8-year-old girl temporarily until a long-term foster carer was found; but five children were being looked after by birth fathers plus partners, and because of the traditional role of women in these families, the female partners undertook most of the parental duties.

Was the placement more stable in the cases where the carer had approached the department in the first instance and *volunteered* to look after the child? Clearly this was a demonstration of commitment but it very rarely happened, because potential carers had to obtain all the information about events surrounding the child and at the same time have the courage to come forward.

- There was a general expectation that the initiative would be taken by social services – and in two cases where relatives did volunteer, they complained that they had not been contacted earlier.

Carers who had been strongly persuaded to take on the task sometimes saw themselves as doing the local authority a favour (which was of course true); but the driving force in these decisions had been the desire of the child to live with this person, and it seems right that this should have been supported. Given the need for carers who were already known to the children and trusted by them, there seems to be scope for more active recruitment of kinship carers rather than less.

Table 11.1 ***Placement fulfilment: children in terms of sibling groups***

	Planned placements	Fulfilled placements
Singletons	6	4
Members of sibling groups		
– to be placed singly in kinship care	3	2
– to be placed as part of a sibling pair	6 (three pairs)	5
– to be placed as a group	3 (one group)	3
Total	**18**	**14**

Twelve of the eighteen children who entered kinship care were members of sibling groups, and eight were placed with at least one other sibling. (See Table 11.1.) This was a higher rate of success than was noted for joint placements in adoption, and the deciding factor was often the wish of the carer that children should remain together. In a case where three small boys were placed with their father, the local authority solicitor said:

> His great wish was to take all three and not split them. That's the ideal, that they shouldn't have been split. But the reality was that if he hadn't been able to take them, we'd have been in great difficulties trying to place those three little boys together elsewhere.

We know from other research that children's difficulties are not necessarily cumulative and that joint placement may be a protective factor (Rushton et al. 2001). However, our findings also confirm the disadvantages of sibling placements from the carers' point of view – the fact that young children who were placed together often fought with one another, creating difficulties for carers because of their noisy and aggressive interactions. More placements might have broken down if the siblings had been in substitute care placements without any sense of a family tie.

In the light of implementation, how well-founded were the original decisions?

Since the carers had always known the children before care proceedings were initiated, and sometimes there was more than one relative who might have been approached, it is interesting to speculate about the importance of previous roles. Birth fathers already had a parental role, and they were keen to exercise it. They had not always had formal parental responsibility until granted it by the court, but they would sometimes have taken more part in their children's lives at an earlier stage if they had not been prevented by conflicts within the family. When assessment had been carried out in tandem with the mothers during care proceedings, there had sometimes been an element of competition, which helped to carry them through; but the social workers were concerned to make sure that they could cope in the longer term.

For carers in the extended family, it was not strictly necessary to take on a parental role – especially with older children who had known them for some time. (For example, one child saw herself as living with her grandmother.) Aunts did experience more difficulties in exercising authority in the new situation than grandparents did; but some difficulties were caused by the attitudes of their male partners. More importantly, the numbers in our sub-sample are rather few, and the young people who were placed with aunts were older and had a greater number of initial problems. One placement of a 4-year-old girl with her aunt and uncle was extremely successful. Furthermore, as we have already noted, the main carers were often people who were not blood relatives at all. See Table 11.2.

Table 11.2 ***Relatives with whom children were placed, and the rate of breakdown***

Relative	Number of white children	Number of black children	Placements not fulfilled[a]
Father	4	5	1
Paternal grandparents	2	1	–
Paternal great-aunt and uncle	–	1	–
Paternal aunt and uncle	2	–	1
Maternal aunt	3	–	2

[a] All the children whose placements broke down were white children.

In placing children with relatives, one of the main considerations had been that children would experience a sense of continuity through family and community membership; but there were also child protection concerns, which usually focused on the mother. Predominantly, these concerns had been about substance abuse or mental ill health, or both. Because of the element of risk, the plan was commonly for the child to be moved not to a member of the mother's family but to a member of the father's family and, on the whole, the protection issues were satisfactorily dealt with by means of these cross-family placements. The fear that maternal relatives would have too much sympathy for the mother was not always borne out by reality, however – and in one case where the responsibility for injury to a child was uncertain, the social worker said that the two sides of the family ended up blaming one another: 'At one time the mother's family were saying it was Leonard – they were sure it was Leonard – and the other side were saying they were sure it was Marion. Unfortunately you never get to the bottom of it.'

Placement with paternal relatives

The children who were placed with paternal relatives were given protection from neglect and emotional abuse (and in one case physical abuse) resulting from the mother's problems; but there also had to be recognition of the bond between the children and the mother, and ability to maintain contact arrangements appropriately. There was often strong animosity between family members, and it is tempting to deduce that if the carers had been too much 'in league with the parent' they would not have been selected as carers because of the need to protect the child. This made contact more difficult, as the history of some of the breakdowns demonstrates. (See also Chapter 13 for more information on this issue.) In all kinship care placements arrangements for contact were a major source of concern for social workers, who often left the job of supervising contact to the carers themselves: 'The father lives quite close to where mum lives and was quite happy to drop the children off and to collect them at fixed times. He is quite good at making sure the boys are okay; so we left it to them and pulled out the supervision.'

Membership of a minority ethnic community

How important was membership of a minority ethnic community in securing placement? As we have already noted, all the breakdowns involved white children. The black children, who lived in urban areas, were younger and the social workers had rightly predicted that their families would be able to draw strength from community networks (Ahmed et al. 1986; Barn et al. 1997; Rashid 2000). In one case an anchor was provided by the grandmother's church, and in another case where some Afro-Caribbean children were being looked after by their father, they received support from a number of people including their mother's partner. However, the presence of a racial or family tie does not lessen the need for thorough assessment and monitoring. As we noted in Chapter 5, social workers and guardians sometimes admitted that the assessments had been less rigorous, even where foster-carer status was envisaged for the carers, because they were only being approved for one particular child. As the report on the death of Tyra Henry pointed out more than a decade ago (London Borough of Lambeth 1987), we must be wary of relying on positive stereotypes. There are perhaps two cases in the kinship care sub-sample that raise concerns about the rapidity of placement and the need for more thorough assessment – ideally before the care plan is presented to the court. This caveat applies in white families as well as black families, if there is a risk that difficulties have not been sufficiently well perceived.

The high fulfilment rate of kinship care

However, in spite of the problems, kinship care plans had the highest fulfilment rate out of all the placement options (78%). The social workers were usually cautious about making predictions in the early stages, and the results suggest that they could have approached some of the placements with more confidence.

Social workers' predictions and the placement outcome:

> When we actually moved her we were going around touching wood, saying, you know, 'If this fails, what are we going to do?' We knew that it could always break down, because of Debbie's capacity to disrupt things – but if that was going to happen it would have happened quite quickly. I'm more optimistic now ... I just think that the family has got to feel okay, and they have got to feel that this is what they want for themselves.
>
> [Outcome: The child settled, and the placement survived.]
>
> I don't think I predicted that Mrs R [the kinship carer] would have had as much problem with their behaviour as she has had. I would like to say to mum, 'Look, they are really settled and you don't have a hope in hell!' I actually can't say that with any confidence at the moment so I'm not saying it. What I am saying is 'This is our plan, and I hope it will succeed.'
>
> [Outcome: The placement of two little boys continued in spite of challenging behaviour, and a residence order was made.]
>
> The difficulty was that we couldn't predict when housing would become available – and that was such a pivotal thing with everything else. All we undertook was that we would support the application and expedite it as much as we could. Apart from that, I would like to see progress in three areas – home routine, school achievement and a settlement in the contact. If I saw those three happening, I'd feel we were well on the road.

[Outcome: Housing was provided approximately two months after the order. There were improvements in all the three areas mentioned.]

He is very proud that he is their dad and that he can look after them [twin girls, aged 2]. He feels really good about himself. I think it bodes well for the future ... What I am worried about is the mother's part and how that could interfere.

[Outcome: The children were transferred to their father's care and the placement proved stable, although the mother continued to 'interfere'.]

How were the plans carried out?

Timing and number of moves

Most children moved to live with the caring relative either shortly before or shortly after the time of the care order. The placement was sometimes slightly delayed because of preparations for the move, and the main need was for housing.

- In three cases the carers had to be rehoused, because their current accommodation was not suitable for the child.

In the city centres accommodation for families was in short supply and the social workers had very little control over council waiting lists or the allocation policies of housing associations. However, social workers were reluctant to hold up the placement for this reason, and in two cases the children were placed before housing had finally been arranged. The new accommodation, when it arrived, was not always ideal. (See Chapter 14). In spite of this, none of the single moves into placement took more than two months, and the average time to placement was about six weeks.

Table 11.3 ***Placement moves made after the care order by children whose kinship care plans were fulfilled***

Number of moves	Number of children
None	6
One	5
Two	1
Three	2

Overall, as can be seen from Table 11.3, the children did not experience many placement moves, largely because (unlike adopters and long-term foster carers) kinship carers had been identified before the time of the final hearing. Most children were able to continue living with their relatives after the order, or else they made one move from foster care into the placement; but, worryingly, two small children had to make three moves within a comparatively short space of time – in one case from one kinship carer to another, and in the other case from one foster placement to another until it was clear which relatives the children ought to live with. The families appeared to be in control of events in these situations, and the guardian who had been reinvolved in one case said that the child had been 'passed around like a little parcel'.

The longest time from care order to final placement was sixteen months. Moving the child was delayed because it had been planned that the father would take over the care of the child at a later date – but when events reached crisis proportions the date had to be brought forward.

How long would the care order last? In many of these cases the care order was a temporary measure. It was considered necessary because of children's difficulties, and the carers' lack of experience and the extent of family conflict, all of which gave rise to fears that the situation would never have been resolved without statutory control. The care order would have continued as long as necessary, but in most cases its main function was to enable the social services department to oversee the move to the new household and offer support to the carer. It was always intended that when stability was achieved, the carer would be encouraged to make application for a residence order or – as happened in two cases – an adoption order.[4] The biggest issue in the timing of these cases was not therefore the time of entry to placement but the exit point.

Policy issues

The local authorities varied in their use of kinship care and in their approach towards it. One inner-city authority with only fourteen cases in the total sample placed seven children including five black children with relatives, and this comprised 50% of the successful kinship care placements. Two authorities did not use kinship care at all during the period of our research – perhaps simply because the numbers of their children entering the care system were relatively low. The fourth made four successful placements, and the remaining authority attempted seven although four of these broke down.

There seemed to be two different orientations underlying attitudes towards kinship care in the local authorities. The main variant was individual circumstances in the families, but there was also a slight regional variation. The region that made greatest use of kinship care had a strong community-based philosophy, which made extensive use of services for families and children in need. One of the local authority solicitors described it in these terms.

> We've got a reputation of having good social work practices and although we are subject to cuts they haven't been as harsh ... It's easy because it's a smaller authority. It's not geographically very big, although the population is on a par I think with some of the others; but it's an authority that's got all kinds of mixes.

In the authority where several breakdowns occurred there was a more scattered population and a greater orientation towards professional fostering and adoption services. The sense of family was strong, but the sense of community was often weak. As a result, the kinship carers in this region were sometimes more isolated – especially if they were ostracised by other family members who felt disgust or guilt about the mother's problems. In this region they were usually regarded as substitute foster carers, and encouraged to look to social services for support. One of the local authority solicitors in this region said:

> In nine cases out of ten, you know, the relatives say: 'Well, we would welcome the local authority acting as a buffer. We wouldn't want to negotiate contact with the mother who might have mental health problems, for example, who isn't very easy to deal with.' They welcome that safety net and support.

Policies also varied with regard to the awarding of *allowances*. As reported in Chapter 14, the main criterion for the awarding of a fostering allowance appeared to be the relationship between child and carer, since allowances were not usually given to birth fathers with parental responsibility – but they were given to other relatives such as aunts and grandparents, though not in every case.[5] At the close of the study slightly less than half of the children in the kinship group (eight out of eighteen) were living in a household where there was an allowance of some kind, but it was usually a residence allowance rather than a fostering one. There were only three cases where a full fostering allowance was still being provided, and in one of these cases the child had been removed to ordinary local authority foster care.

Where a fostering allowance was paid, the importance of the task done by the carers was recognised and the extra funding enabled them to maintain an adequate standard of living for the child; but the kinship carers did not usually experience the other sources of help available to foster carers, such as group meetings and training sessions, nor did they have regular and frequent visits from the family placement officer, and in two cases the presence of the fostering allowance seemed to act as a deterrent when the change to a residence order was envisaged.

Whether or not allowances were provided, kinship care was heavily dependent on informal systems of support. (See also Sykes et al. 2002.) As in adoption, there must be concerns about how care by relatives and significant others can be integrated into the childcare system without sacrificing the unique benefits it offers.

Legal issues

The extent of legal activity post-order was considerable – more extensive than in any other placement option with the exception of adoption. One mother took a number of different actions through legal channels. First of all, with the help of a local law centre she threatened the social services department with judicial review, on the grounds that she was not receiving services to which she was entitled. When this did not succeed, she attempted to have the care order discharged. At the close of the study she had instructed a solicitor who was about to apply under the inherent jurisdiction of the High Court to prevent the local authority from immunising the children.

Residence orders

Needless to say, the above case was unusual. Most of the post-order activity in kinship care was concerned with residence orders. Nine were applied for during the course of the study, and out of this number four were granted.[6] Two were refused, two hearings were adjourned and one application was withdrawn.

Very few care plans had actually mentioned residence orders, and the timing of the application was never stated. In the two cases where children in kinship care had been made subject to residence orders by the end of the study, the application for the order was submitted after the first six months; but in several other cases the application had just been submitted prior to the end of our research.

- A common delaying factor in these cases was court action or the threat of court action on the part of the birth mother; but for some carers there would be a financial loss, because a fostering allowance would be given up or changed to a residence allowance at a lower rate.

On the part of social services there was a wish to support the carer through legal proceedings; but there was also a desire to ensure that the caring relative would be able to cope with children's behaviour and contact arrangements after the care order ended. This meant that when the local authority was considering discharge of the care order they often wanted it to be replaced by a supervision order, which would give them oversight of the placement for a longer time.

Some of the local authority solicitors who were interviewed expressed concerns about residence orders. These concerns usually centred on the lower level of financial support available to families and the withdrawal of other support services once the residence order was made, while the fact that residence orders only run till the young person's sixteenth birthday was seen to offer a lesser protection to the child than a care order. Many of these disadvantages have been addressed in the Adoption and Children Act 2002, which extends the powers of the court to make a residence order lasting until the child is 18. Furthermore, the new provision of the 'special guardianship order' carries with it an obligation on local authorities to provide support services in the form of counselling, advice and information and 'such other services as are prescribed'.

Within the time-scale of our study it is impossible to judge the effectiveness of residence orders over time; but in the short term the research suggests that the application for a residence order was often accompanied by problems.

- There was much more controversy surrounding the making of residence orders than adoption orders, and the local authority did not always have a smooth passage.
- The support of the social services department was a necessary but not a sufficient condition for family members to attain their ends. Poor contact arrangements and lack of services were destructive in terms of legal objectives as well as social work plans.
- The court was more inclined to favour a residence order which fulfilled the care plan than one which was made because the care plan was in default.

In a case involving two residence orders which were made within the period of the study, the local authority prepared the ground carefully . In addition to offering help and advice with the children's behaviour, they arranged for the children to be assessed and treated by a child psychiatrist. They obtained funding for an allowance. They also made sure that the couple's application for a residence order was accompanied by a request for a supervision order for one year, so that ongoing support to the family could be guaranteed. Most importantly, they made sure that the care plan was fulfilled.

Management issues

Planning and provision of services

The planning and provision of services was important to ensure that the needs of children and carers were met; but kinship carers were sometimes ambivalent about social services support – even in the form of financial help – because they wanted their integrity and independence to be recognised, as the following quotations show:

> I didn't go into it looking for pay because I am her grandmother first and foremost. I am her grandmother before her carer or whatever.

> I don't need their help. I can get on quite fine now. He's never without food in his mouth. But like I say, if it was on the other foot and his mother had him, she'd be at their door every five minutes asking for money.

> I'm not dependent on social services. I ring them if it's a last resort or if I need confirmation from them to give to someone else. Most of the time I just get on and do it, or buy it, or whatever I need to do.

Nevertheless allowances were badly needed by people on low incomes and, as one of the local authority solicitors had predicted, some carers also wanted the support of the Department in dealing with difficult contact and legal arrangements: 'I do want the local authority in there, because I know what the mother and the family is like – and it might mean we would have to go to court and things like that. I would have someone there to stand up for me.'

The incentive of allowances

Most social workers felt that allowances provided a powerful incentive to care for the child, in addition to making it easier for the carers to cope and for themselves to control the placement. Some fathers resented the fact that they did not qualify for an allowance since they were birth parents, although their partners were doing most of the work.

As reported in Chapter 14, one-off payments were made for essential items such as bedding and furniture. These payments were usually less than £500 in value and their main purpose was to get the placement off the ground. Nevertheless they were very welcome, and one father expressed appreciation of the set-up grant, which had provided him with necessary 'white goods' – although he said that it had taken some time to come through.

> The fridge freezer and the washing machine are life savers ... I was hand washing. I wouldn't go to the laundry – too many weirdos – and I'd have to bring the two kids with me. No way! I was hand washing for six months. There always seems to be these interim periods from them saying 'yes' to actually getting it.

This father received help with childcare and also transport costs, which saved his having to negotiate the difficult bus journey between his home and the nursery. Since he was coping on his own with two little girls, he was also offered the help of a female carer to get the children ready for bed at night – something he welcomed because he said that they 'played him up'. Carers always appreciated services that were responsive to individual needs, rather than simply being offered as a matter of routine.

Forward planning

When the intention was to seek residence orders it was necessary have good forward planning to ensure that services would be available and easily accessed at a time when the carer would be solely responsible for the child or children. (This was particularly important when carers were not used to dealing with professional agencies and could have difficulty in approaching them.) In a case where an Afro-Caribbean father was about to take on the care of a sibling group, he was helped to establish a good liaison with the school that the children attended, as they all had problems with low achievement and the eldest would truant occasionally. Since the local hospital had also been involved in therapeutic work with the children, it was arranged that this would continue after discharge of the care order and that consultancy would be available for the father if he required it at a later date.

Issues of social work practice

As a purveyor of services, the social worker was always welcome. More problems were experienced with *supervision and control* of the placement. Carers had their own views about disciplining children, for example, and they were not always agreeable to seeing things differently. Here are the views of two carers, one of whom was a grandmother and the other a father's partner.

> They said you shouldn't, you mustn't hit her – but a smack here and there doesn't hurt a child ... I was told not to. They don't like it. But I say she is my grandchild and I will discipline her in the way I see fit. If she does something I am not going to be cruel to her, but I smack her on the leg or on the hand ... unless they have got kids of their own they don't know what they are talking about. All they know is what they read out of books.

When carers really wanted help with controlling children, it was possible to give them advice about doing it; but another bone of contention for the social workers was *maintenance of contact*. As with discipline, it was virtually impossible to coerce the carers into doing things they were really unwilling to undertake, and they had to be persuaded of its value. In the majority of cases necessary contact was maintained and the placement was not destabilised; but in view of child protection concerns, some problems were also experienced with *limiting contact* in situations where it might have been harmful to the child. (See Chapter 13 for more information on this issue.)

Social workers often had worries about the *vulnerability of carers*; but since every placement was a one-off arrangement, the presence or absence of problems in the child could be balanced against the strengths and weaknesses of the carer. One birth father had been diagnosed as manic depressive, which seemed at first to rule him out (and perhaps would have ruled him out, as a prospective adopter or foster carer); but the placement of two children went ahead and survived because he was successfully maintained on lithium.

The effect of children's problems was not always predictable. On the whole it was easier for a relative to cope with the behaviour of young children, even in a boisterous sibling group, than the problems of a single, rebellious adolescent. However, kinship placements worked best when:

- the carers were encouraged to be as independent as possible and to take a gradually increasing amount of responsibility for the children.

The social workers hoped that the position of many of these children in the future would be no different from that of others who are living with family members as a result of bereavement – and where the care of the child was undertaken by a birth father, the situation was certainly not unlike that commonly experienced in divorce. In such cases, once the children had settled in the placement and a workable pattern of contact had been achieved, the input of social services was no longer necessary.

What the kinship carers said

> It's been much more difficult than anybody could have imagined. I think it is because he was emotionally secure when he came here ... He's felt secure enough to give vent to all his emotions. I hope that in the long run he'll be a lot better off for it, as opposed to children who are placed in homes where they feel unable to express their anger and grief. At least he is going to get it out.

> What made it much easier compared to foster carers was that Debbie [aged 4] wasn't going in somewhere with strangers. She knew me as her auntie, and she knew her uncle and she knew the children ... I remember one incident a long time ago – about a year ago. Her dad came to visit, and after he'd gone we took the dog up to the woods for a walk. Something happened – I can't remember what it was – but she turned round and said 'I hate you and I hate living with you.' We didn't take any notice of it. We just basically said 'Well, we're your family. You know, sometimes families do hate each other.' And that was it and no more was said. She just got on with her life.

> He'll always know his mum, you know, as long as she can keep up the contact. I'm happy for her to take him out – but if she comes here and she looks like she's been on something, then that's it ... I say 'No way. Off you go!' I wouldn't even let her take him, if she looked like she was out of control or something.

> Her mother would take her and wouldn't bring her back till very late at night, or didn't bring her back on the day when she should come back. That was the part I was very strict about, because her schooling for me was first and foremost. If they didn't get her back in time so that I could wash her hair and groom her for school the following day, I couldn't do it in the morning before ... So I used to have a problem there. But the welfare stepped in and said no, they can't have that, because I had other things to do.

> Liam [aged 3] is really disturbed. He is in a fight every day. Well, you have seen him; he is like that every day, from the time he gets up till the time he goes to bed. This is the second three-piece suite I have had since he has come here, because he used to just pull it to bits. Now he is getting to that age where he knows it is wrong – but he will still do it, he will still test you ... People say 'Oh

why don't you give them back?' and I say 'Well how can you give them back when you have known them since they were so young. They are just like my own now. I couldn't give them up. It would be just like giving one of mine away. I couldn't do it.

The only change will be when we apply for a residence order on him, which will take place some time in the future. We are not entirely comfortable with that at the moment for two reasons. First we get a bit of financial help now, and that will reduce somewhat under the residence order. With my employment circumstances, that would disadvantage Kevin for us to do that at the moment. Also his behaviour has been so difficult and his well-being so poor that we really do need the support and therapy ... As his life normalises and his behaviour problems hopefully diminish, then it won't be quite so time-consuming looking after him. Then I will be able to put all my energies back into work, and we'll be able to move forward with the residence order. That's the long-term plan.

Discussion and conclusions

As has been documented elsewhere (Broad 1999) the role of the kinship carer is ill-defined and there can be real tensions between the social worker, the local authority, the carer and the child about the relationship between the state and the family or individual. The special guardianship order introduced in the Adoption and Children Act 2002 may help to clarify these relationships since – unlike the residence order – it makes it possible for a kinship carer who becomes a special guardian to exercise parental responsibility 'to the exclusion of any other person with parental responsibility for the child' (CA89 amended: section 14C). Nevertheless on a human level, it seems likely that children will continue to experience divided loyalties unless the carer and the parent are capable of working in harmony.

In spite of obvious difficulties, the plans had an excellent rate of fulfilment (78%). The authority that placed most children successfully was generous in its material and financial support for the carers, and when the children were placed with inexperienced fathers the social services department provided a lot of advice as well as support – especially as far as contact with the mother was concerned; but the good results are surprising in view of the fact that the children often presented extremely difficult behaviour. The secret seemed to lie in the commitment of the carers and the child's sense of 'belonging', which in some cases was aided by a distinct sense of racial or cultural identity.

For social services there were problems both in maintaining contact and in limiting it. To protect the children from harm in these circumstances, and at the same time retain sympathy for the former carer, relatives needed to be well informed about topics such as substance abuse and mental illness, and their own attitudes to these problems needed to be made clear at the assessment stage. Most important of all, as the reasons for breakdown show, was the need for them to be able to provide the child with a secure place within the structure of their own households. However, the importance of the community and environment cannot be stressed enough. In many cases it offered continuity of friendships and schooling for children – black and white – as well as continuity of medical care. In the most satisfactory cases social services worked in partnership with the carers, helping them to take an increasing amount of responsibility for the children.

It seemed unlikely that many of these children would be rehabilitated to the former carer, and consequently the kinship placements that survived should be regarded as lasting for the duration of childhood. In spite of the solicitors' concerns and the complexity of some court hearings, the availability of the residence order – and now the special guardianship order – have increased the range of options and therefore the number of possible targets for children in kinship care. The court always made the final decision and the achievement of a residence order could not be guaranteed; but with the exception of adoption, no other placement option had such a well-defined exit route. If the transition is made successfully in other cases, and if necessary supports are not withdrawn, the social services departments will have helped these children to establish themselves in their own family and community by means of a care order whose purpose was positive and clear.

Summary

1. Fourteen of the eighteen plans for children to live with relatives were successfully implemented. Non-fulfilled plans were all a result of breakdown, which occurred only in white families where there were older children.

2. Kinship care was most often used where children belonged to minority ethnic groups, and where the mother had problems of mental ill health or substance abuse. Community structure as well as family structure had an impact on fulfilment.

3 The commitment of the carer crucial to the success of the placements. Many of the children were in sibling groups. Their initial difficulties, though often severe, did not necessarily delay or disrupt placements.

4 The care order was commonly intended only as a temporary measure to manage the transition to other legal orders. In the case of nine children residence orders had been made or applied for by the end of the study, and two adoption orders were sought.

5 Contact arrangements were sometimes problematic. The children needed protection; but where fathers and paternal relatives took over the care of children, it was essential to have good contact arrangements with the mother who was usually the previous carer.

6 Local authorities varied in the amount of material and financial support they were prepared to offer kinship carers. In order to launch the placements successfully, attention needed to be paid to the carers' housing needs and income levels as well as helping children with problems of divided loyalty.

---

[1] Section 23(2) states that the local authority may place the child with a family, a relative or any other suitable person.

[2] A recent change is that since the judicial review of Manchester City Council's policy on allowances (the Munby judgement) payments to friends and relatives must be on the same basis as payments to stranger carers.

[3] See *Fostering for the Future* (DoH 2002b). It should be noted, however, that kinship carers from ethnic minority groups were not over-represented in a recent study of support for foster carers (Sykes et al. 2002). Possible explanations are the poor response rate from non-white carers in this particular study, or the fact that some relatives may not be officially classified as foster carers.

[4] Since the introduction of the Adoption and Children Act 2002, the legal options available to kinship carers who want to remove the child from care and at the same time increase their own parental responsibility include the special guardianship order. (See 'Legal issues', below.)

[5] One of the aunts did not claim a fostering allowance, since she was intending to adopt the child and wanted her to have the same status as her own children.

[6] These numbers include two cases were residence orders were sought for children in foster care.

12 Home placements

Introduction

Theoretically, the placement of children at home is the most direct expression of the principle of shared parental responsibility when children are subject to care orders. In no other placement option is the sharing of parental responsibility so considerable, since parents have day to day responsibility for the child's welfare. It has always been recognised, however, that sharing parental responsibility in high-risk situations is 'a leap in the dark'. These placements raise fundamental questions about thresholds for significant harm and about professional capacity to predict risk in the shorter and longer term. Indeed, some writers have suggested that home placements are built on a central paradox; the carer's parenting is judged sufficiently worrying to warrant the need for a care order, yet good enough to enable the child to remain at home (Thoburn 1980; Pinkerton 1994).

Home placements for children on care orders have been increasing since 1994, and today they make up 12% of all children looked after – more than twice the proportions who are adopted from care. Yet this trend that has gone largely unnoticed and unexplained. Government statistics do not tell us whether this rise is because of more children being placed at home when a care order is made, or because there is an increase in the numbers of children formerly classified as 'home on trial' – that is, returning home as part of a planned reunification programme after a period in substitute care. In addition, the figures include some children placed at home while on remand.

Not only is there very little factual information on the usage of home placement, which actually represents different strategies in different contexts, but there is also a dearth of research into the viability of this placement option for children who are made subject to care orders. The studies that exist are mainly focused on returning children home from substitute care (Farmer and Parker 1991; Bullock et al. 1998; Pinkerton 1994). This gap makes it particularly interesting to track the 22 children in our study who were placed at home when the care order was made and, since the research into reunification has shown that most looked-after children will sooner or later end up back in the home environment, this is an added reason for asking why it was that some home placements succeeded when others foundered.

The implementation of plans for home placement

How many placement plans were fulfilled?

Figure 12.1 shows the progress made in the implementation of home placement plans for the children in the 21 months after the care order. Sadly, more placements of children at home failed than succeeded. Only 41% of the children – that is, nine out of 22 – were still at home at the end of the follow-up period. In terms of families, the success rate was five families out of ten. All the children were white British.

Figure 12.1 ***Implementation of plans for home placement: progress of children 21 months after care order***

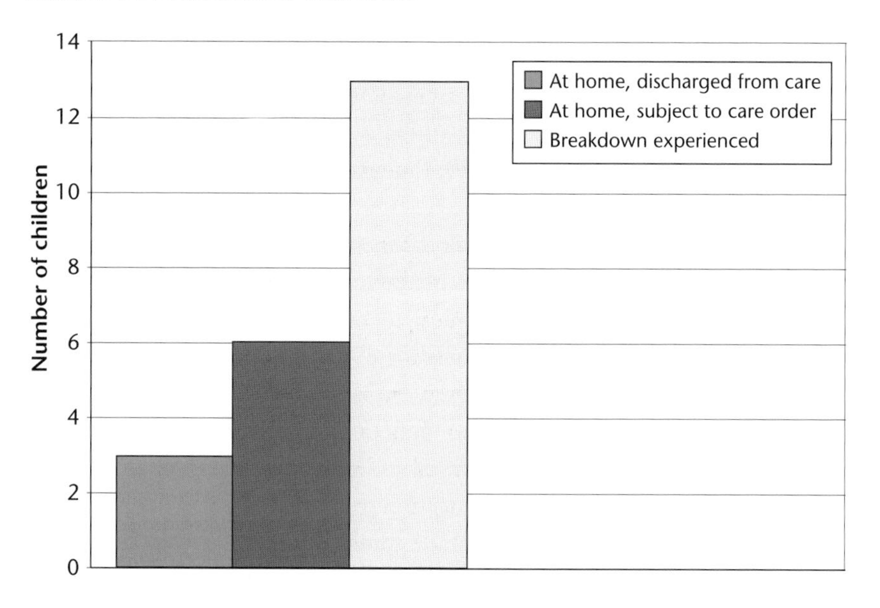

What happened to the children whose plans were not fulfilled?

Because the families were waiting to receive the children, all the placements were implemented either during care proceedings or immediately after the care order. Breakdown of the placement was therefore the only reason for the plan not working out.

What really differentiates breakdowns in home placement from those in adoption and other forms of substitute care is that:

- the disruptions were social-work led. They did not result from absconding or from demands by carers to have children removed.

Of the thirteen children who were not allowed to remain at home:

- one small child was moved from the mother's to the father's care;
- another child who had been less than a year old at the time of the care order was successfully placed for adoption;
- a 2-year-old child was placed for adoption unsuccessfully, and returned to foster care to wait for a new adoptive placement;
- six children between the ages of one and three were undergoing assessment in temporary foster homes at the end of the study; and
- four children between the ages of 7 and 9 were in long-term foster care.

Some attempts at rehabilitation broke down almost immediately; but if this hurdle was passed, the vulnerable placements tended to survive for sixteen to eighteen months. Most of the children who were undergoing assessment in temporary foster homes at the end of the study had only recently been removed from home. For those who suffered breakdown of the plan soon after the care order, on the other hand, alternative plans had been made and efforts had been made to implement these changed plans – in two cases by means of adoption placements (although one of these did not succeed) and in another four cases by means of long-term foster care.

What helped or hindered placement?

- *Child factors* When children were placed at home, the age pattern associated with disruption was different from that recorded in other placement options. The risk of breakdown was not greater with adolescents than with younger children. Those between the ages of 2 and 9 were most at risk of removal, but three children aged 10, 11 and 13 remained in placement and had the care order discharged.

- *Family factors* Sibling groups were commonly placed at home, and the thirteen children whose placement disrupted came from just five families. The children usually wanted to stay at home, but disruptions show the impact of unrelieved parental problems such as alcohol abuse.
- *Organisational factors* When plans failed, social work action had often been focused on the monitoring of child protection concerns and there had been little additional input. In plans which succeeded, there was more likelihood that the social services department and other agencies would have been seen as a source of help and support.

A very striking feature of these cases was that the children had *fewer initial problems* than those recorded in other placement options. This held true whether the placement continued or disrupted; but any behaviour problems that did exist were difficult for the parents to manage. The lack of success associated with children in the 2 to 9 age group (where only 22% of placements survived) reflects the fact that young children were perceived as more vulnerable than adolescents in a risk-laden home environment. They were therefore more likely to be removed when things appeared to go wrong. However, children aged 1 year or younger had a better success rate (40%, which is close to the average for the placement type). Some of these children were removed for their own protection, but babies undoubtedly presented fewer challenges than children who were growing out of babyhood and for that reason were easier for parents to manage.

Age of the children

Can any general messages be extracted from the pattern of breakdowns? The age of the children was important, but it had a different kind of significance in different contexts. First, there were young babies whose mothers had been described as 'deserving a chance' because there was no previous history of concerns focused on childcare. Three out of four of these placements survived. Second, in three families involving nine children who were placed at home, the history of the family suggested that the mother's care would be reasonably satisfactory in the early stages but there were increasing concerns about neglect and the risk of abuse from the mother or her partners as children got older. As a result, the risk of removal increased over time, and six of these nine children were removed at a fairly late stage in the follow-up period. The average age of these children at the time of the court hearing was 3.5 years.

Mother's misuse of alcohol

In another three families (again with nine children), the main concern was the mother's misuse of alcohol. Here the child's age was seen in an entirely different light; it was considered to be less risky for school-aged children to be placed at home because they could (within limits) seek help when needed, and the average age of these children at the time of placement was 7.5 years. Again, six of the nine children were removed; but the three adolescent children who remained at home and who also experienced discharge of the care order within the follow-up period belonged to one of these families. Much importance was placed on the children's understanding and resilience in the face of their mother's problems, which had to some extent been alleviated by work during the care period; but an additional factor was the children's attachment to their mother and their wish to remain with her.

Sibling groups

The fact that so many of the children were in sibling groups probably contributed to breakdown by placing a lot of stress on single mothers. They also placed considerable demands on the key worker and on the support services. As can be seen from Table 12.1, the plans for home placement included six groups of three children each; but only two of these groups were still at home at the end of the study.

The parents' wider social network

A mediating factor was access to support from the parents' wider social network, which appeared to function quite well in the fulfilled home placements. In one case a non-resident partner supported a vulnerable mother and got on very well with the children, and in another the extended family played a prominent role, which took pressure off the nuclear family unit and may have helped to reduce acrimonious conflicts – a factor associated with the collapse of reunification in the studies by Packman and Hall (1998) and Bullock et al. (1998). In two of the successful home placements involving a sibling group of three, the children were all doing well at school. This is another factor that has been found to be associated with a reduced risk of disruption.

Table 12.1 ***Placement fulfilment: children in terms of sibling groups***

	Planned placements	**Fulfilled placements**
Singletons	4	3
Members of sibling groups		
– to be placed singly at home	0	0
– to be placed at home as part of a sibling pair	0	0
– to be placed at home as a group	18 (six groups)	6 (two groups)
Total	**22**	**9**

In the light of implementation, how well-founded were the original decisions?

Accurate assessment of the degree of risk

Accurate assessment of the degree of risk was crucial in determining whether children continued to live at home or whether they should be placed in substitute care. It seems unlikely that a longer period of assessment during proceedings would have helped in most cases, since nine of the eighteen care plans made in cases that spent a year or more in care proceedings were for home placement, and it was only in this placement option that hearings lasted more than eighteen months.[1]

The fact that some home placements broke down should not be taken as evidence that social workers were ignorant of the risks.

- The parents' problems were usually known to the social workers at the time of the care order, and a deliberate decision was made to place the child at home in spite of them.

The social workers were taking what they believed to be a calculated risk, and in all except one case, the guardians agreed with the social workers' judgements. The decision to rehabilitate was accompanied by a risk assessment which suggested that harm, if it occurred, would be minimal, and that the situation would be recoverable. However, the follow-up information suggests that the degree of harm associated with neglect and eventual breakdown of the placement was sometimes underestimated.

Co-operation of the parent

An unknown quantity in the assessment, and one that was often misjudged, was the co-operation of the parent. The 'parent' was usually the mother – either because she was a single parent or because, in two-parent families, she saw childcare as her role.[2] In cases where rehabilitation remained on the agenda throughout care proceedings, the mothers were not actively hostile to social services. In fact they could appear compliant and willing to change. They accepted the fact that abusive partners should be banned from the household. (If this had not happened, the children would probably have been placed in substitute care.) The issue was how far they were able to improve their own parenting, in the face of persistent problems such as substance abuse and learning difficulties. The situations had originally appeared to be manageable, but in the aftermath of the order:

- a small amount of active hostility would in some cases have been more manageable than passive resistance, extremely low self-esteem and an inability to comprehend the concerns of the professionals.

In cases of breakdown, a low level of co-operation combined with uneven support and monitoring contributed to a continuation of parental problems.

The ability of the care order to produce improvements

The third consideration, and one which was often misjudged, was the ability of the care order to produce improvements. In spite of the fact that in home placements the level of initial problems was generally lower than that recorded in other placement options, there appears to be a clear link between children's problems and breakdown of the placement. The children whose plans did not reach fulfilment had more initial problems on every dimension of welfare than those whose plans were fulfilled. This mirrors the situation found in adoption, except that it is more extreme – that is, the children's difficulties, even if they were minor, appear to have had much more impact on plan fulfilment than happened in adoption. One way of interpreting this is to say that:

- the ability of the home environment to support children with problems was extremely low.

The problems were predominantly those associated with neglect and emotional abuse. All the families had a low standard of living and the children suffered the effects of socio-economic deprivation; but the neglectful mothers also lacked understanding of children's age-appropriate needs, had difficulty in empathising with the child's experience, and had many unrealistic and negative expectations. (See also Browne et al. 1988; O'Hagan 1993; Iwaniec 1995; Stevenson 1998.) Insecure attachment was indicated by the difficulties in family and social relationships, and in young children these difficulties were often accompanied by lack of educational progress (the result of lack of stimulation) and problems in emotional and behavioural development. The attempt to produce improvements by coercion – that is, by attempting to force the parent to do things differently – was not successful in the majority of cases where it was applied, and social workers continued to operate what Pinkerton (1994) calls 'a sustained watching brief'.

Social workers were not unsympathetic to the mother's problems but in the aftermath of the care order they were working in a somewhat adversarial climate, and they were often torn between supporting the mother's interests and those of her children.

Social workers' predictions and the placement outcome

> The only person that can make those children's lives better is their mother, so the work needs to be concentrated on her … I hope there will be a good outcome, but I can't say because I don't know. Some things change, don't they? There is going to be a different manager that will manage this case, and a lot will depend on what he or she is going to be like and what attitude they have towards her.
>
> [Outcome: The new manager took a strongly protective stance, and the children were removed after a minor incident of risk.]
>
> There has not been a huge success rate with mums and babies when there is drug use and sex work. I have got several colleagues and we talk about the comparisons, and this is one of the few that has actually got this far. You know, it feels on a knife edge, almost. I feel very much that it's in the balance, and you need to help.
>
> [Outcome: The baby was transferred from his mother's to his father's care.]
>
> It was a very finely balanced decision, and I think my personal opinion is that it probably won't work out for them – or it probably won't for Colin [the eldest]. It might for the younger two; we don't know. But I don't think we quite had the grounds to remove them.

[Outcome: Colin was abused during the follow-up period and all three children were removed at that stage.]

There are three children in this family very close in age. I think it's a tall order, actually, for the most capable parent. It would have to be looked at very carefully, but if breakdown happens, I would have thought that some sort of a split might have to be seriously considered.

[Outcome: The placement broke down and the sibling group was divided.]

This family will always require a worker. It's never going to be a family that's going to be able to be left to run on its own ... But I am more hopeful now, because mum is agreeing to respite care so that the children can go to other families at weekends and she's allowing the children to have a worker. She's being more open in allowing people into the family.

[Outcome: The placement of three children with their mother survived.]

I feel fairly confident about a good outcome now, because of the amount of time that has passed where the mother has remained abstinent from using alcohol – in spite of a high level of stress at times. I feel that she has managed to make effective use of those relapse strategies that she learnt. She has also shown that she can cope. For herself, she feels very proud that she's succeeded.

[Outcome: the placement survived.]

How were the plans carried out?

The timing of home placements

Fifteen children were already at home when the care order was made, either because they had never left home or because they had been returned before the care order. For the other seven, rehabilitation was planned almost immediately.

Since, as with kinship care, the placement resource was ready and waiting, the 'time-scale' heading in the care plan was occasionally used not to state the time between care order and placement but to give *a date by which the placement should be reviewed* or alternatively (rather rarely) a date when application might be made to discharge the order. However, these arrangements were not always kept. In the case of one of the families, the standard of welfare to be reached was very unclear and consequently there was conflict among the professionals about whether the level of improvement was good enough to justify discharging the order at the appropriate date. In another case the twelve-month point was passed without anyone apparently noticing that the planned review had not taken place.

It is useful to look at the *timing of breakdowns*. For six children in two families, breakdown happened very soon after the care order because the mother resumed her misuse of alcohol, and the children were removed within two months of the care order being made. Another child was admitted to foster care at nine months because it was clear that his mother could not cope; but for another six children in two families, the breakdown happened quite late in the study period – at sixteen months in one family and nineteen months in the other.

Where home placements broke down, there was usually *a sudden collapse of confidence*. There was, however, a difference between the early breakdowns and the late ones. In the cases where the mother had previously abused alcohol and breakdown happened within the first few weeks, the children were being moved back home from a foster care placement and a phased plan of rehabilitation was still being carried out. In other cases the breakdown happened after a longer period of intervention which put continuous pressure on the parent, and two of these placements ended in a 'crisis' involving allegations of physical or sexual abuse.

One social worker expressed a view that if breakdown was going to happen, it was best if it happened early.

> The children have just been through so much. I would rather it happened sooner rather than later if it was going to happen; let's get it over and done with for the children's sake! But I'm not rushing into anything simply because I think it might be a good idea.

In all cases of breakdown it was believed that sustained attempts at maintaining the children at home would be impossible. At least partly, however, it happened because the mother herself had started to believe that failure was inevitable. Similar patterns were observed during care proceedings when a plan for rehabilitation was abandoned.

Policy issues

Recognising parental responsibility

As noted in the introduction, the placement of children at home under a care order provides unique opportunities for the continuing exercise of parental responsibility as outlined in the Children Act. In theory, this placement option makes it possible for social services to work in partnership with parents. In practice, however, the social services agency is the dominant partner (Hunt and Macleod 1999).

The philosophy of family support sits uneasily in the compulsory framework of a court order. The *contract model of working* that had usually been adopted at the care plan stage assumed that parents were not only willing but able to fulfil the demands that were made on them; but in the presence of chronic substance abuse or learning difficulties this position was difficult to achieve. Moreover, the making of the care order meant that some contracts had been entered into by parents who were under duress. Some families might have benefited if there had been more input from adult services; but because of resource shortages as well as agency and policy boundaries, these services were not much involved in post care-order intervention, which fell within the ambit of child-care teams.

In one case the social worker tried to obtain the services of a community psychiatric nurse for a distressed mother; but this was refused since the parent could not formally be classified as mentally ill. The presence of a child or children in the household did not confer any priority as far as the allocation of adult services was concerned. As a result, the social worker was obliged to support both the adult and the child.

- When children were placed at home, there was a need for intensive input to the main carer who was usually the mother. With better arrangements for co-ordination and funding, some of this input might have been appropriately supplied by adult services.

Parents with learning difficulties

In one rather unusual case, a young woman with severe learning difficulties was placed with her baby in an adult care home. The plan, which was supported by a clinical psychologist, was that the mother would continue to take responsibility for her baby, who was regarded as being placed at home with her mother – but 'home' was an adult care placement with 24-hour supervision from the carers. The social worker who dealt with the case was clear about the benefit not only to the child but to the disabled mother, who had been described as performing at the level of a 12-year-old:

> She is a completely different person now, compared to what she was last year. She looks different, she acts differently ... Before, she looked and acted like a stroppy 13-year-old – head down, mumbling, would not co-operate, nobody would do anything for her, she didn't want to do anything for herself. Now she's actually thinking of going to college to study computers.

At the 21-month point this placement was still surviving and the child was doing well, although the adult carer was undertaking a lot of the childcare work. This creative solution to a common problem could conceivably provide a way forward in other cases. However, the specialist disability worker who had formerly supported the mother could not be retained indefinitely, and at the end of the study some questions – including the long-term funding of the placement – were still unresolved.

This raises the question of whether it is ever right to remove the children of learning-disabled adults at birth because of a cost-benefit analysis that suggests that the cost of maintaining the placement of mother and child together is untenable. The argument supporting removal in these cases is that failure of the resource would result in the child being put at risk; but the rights of disabled adults as well as their children are at stake. Furthermore, financial pressures acting in the other direction could result in more older children being left at home because of the high cost of maintaining them in substitute care. It seems important that issues such as these should be discussed at national level, if parity of provision between local authorities is to be obtained.

Legal issues

Discharge of the order

One of the issues raised by the implementation of home placements is the role of discharge of the order, and the value of including this in the care plan. Where discharge from care was mentioned it certainly provided an incentive and a target for parents to work towards, but social workers and solicitors were often reluctant to set definite targets. Some views expressed by the solicitors are listed below.

- Parents would be reluctant to share problems if they knew that the possibility of discharge would be affected, and this could result in unhelpful cover-up.

- As in the case of residence orders, the decision of the court could not be pre-empted and the application would not always be successful.
- Commitments made to parents in the initial care plan could become a source of conflict when things went wrong.

By the end of the study only three children – all members of the same sibling group – were living at home after having been discharged from care. There were frequent debates about discharge of the order, both in meetings with parents and within the local authorities themselves. In addition to the lack of pre-arranged targets, the trouble was that:

- social workers found it difficult to decide at what point the care order could be abandoned with safety.

This is a natural corollary to the difficulties that had surrounded the decision to seek a care order in the first place. The assessment of risk was ongoing. It might help to speed up the movement of cases – and at the same time to keep parents involved – if the criteria for discharge were openly discussed and clarified at an earlier stage.

The role of the contingency plan

The second contentious issue in home placements was the role of the contingency plan and its effect on contact arrangements – especially when adoption was the placement of second choice.

Two very small children whose plans collapsed in the early stages were removed from home and placed for adoption during the course of the study. In both of these cases it was seen as problematic that the contingency plan did not spell out the changes that had to be made to contact arrangements if adoption were to be the outcome. In the first case the local authority applied to the court for reduction of contact, and the birth family's visits were curtailed with the sanction of the court. In the second case the local authority did not return to court but set about reducing contact on the strength of the care plan, which had named adoption as the contingency; but the social worker and the prospective adopters were concerned about the lack of clarity and feared that there might be a legal challenge at the time when the adoption order was being sought. The conclusion seems to be that:

- possible changes to contact should always be made clear in the care plan, and when a contingency plan for adoption is brought into play, the permission of the court to reduce or terminate contact should be sought.

In keeping with Articles 6 and 8 of the Human Rights Act, it seems best that a court should always be asked to adjudicate on the termination of contact, and the contingency element in the care plan should not be asked to carry too heavy a burden in this regard.

Management issues

Because of their aetiology and the fact that they reflected the agency's concerns about risk, the care plans made for children at home bore a strong resemblance to the *protection plans* produced at child protection conferences. It could be argued that the care order performed a similar function to registration, although of course it provided a much stronger sanction. It was clear that in some cases the child protection review would continue to have an active role in reviewing progress, and the plans for support indicated that the same personnel would be involved – for example, the social worker and health visitor would continue to visit and monitor the placement.

- The first challenge for managers was to disassociate these cases from routine child protection work and see that they were given the priority they deserved.
- The second was to ensure that the care order was more than a 'sanction' to improve the parent's performance.

Some problems in case management can be traced to the care plan itself. In plans for the provision of services, family centres and the development of parenting skills were often mentioned, and treatment was recommended in cases of alcohol abuse; but it was not always clear that any new input would be provided, or that meaningful and achievable targets were being set. The 'detailed tasks' referred to above were usually concerned with tangible activities such as keeping appointments or making sure that children attended playgroup; but the preconditions for the mother remaining in a parenting role were not limited to activities of this kind, since the hurdles which had to be overcome (not unreasonably) included assessments of the child's welfare which were usually open-ended. In one such case, the two conditions for terminating the placement were stated in the care plan as follows: 'Should she [the mother] not adhere to the plan we suggest, or should it be clear that she is unable to provide better care, stimulation and protection, we would remove him [the child] from home, and seek an adoptive placement for him.'

Were some of these mothers set up to fail? In the above case the mother fulfilled the requirements by adhering to the plan, but she was still unable to provide 'better care, stimulation and protection' because of her own difficulties.

Some of the dilemmas experienced in these cases echo the research on children 'home on trial' (Thoburn 1980; Farmer and Parker 1991; Pinkerton 1994). For example, Farmer and Parker reported that:

> The very fact of a child's return home on trial is tantamount to an official endorsement of the placement. It may then be difficult to decide to withdraw that endorsement, particularly in the absence of a major crisis such as serious abuse to the child. Continuing low standards of care may not be seen as a sufficient reason for taking such a step.

For similar reasons, it was difficult to identify the point at which children should be removed from home when the placement had survived for a year or more, unless there was a definite 'trigger' of physical or sexual abuse. At the same time, as we have said, it was difficult to decide when the care order had to end. Because proof of improvement seemed to be necessary to discharge the order, there was a real danger that some care orders would continue long after the planned intervention had run its course.

Issues of social work practice

Supporting children at home under a care order is labour-intensive

Eighteen of the 22 children placed at home belonged to sibling groups, and resource shortages might have played a part in the decision not to place them elsewhere. However, any savings in placement resources were cancelled out by the demands made on social work time.

It was unusual to have two social workers allocated to the same family but it did happen in three cases where the sibling group was divided and children being looked after by social services outside as well as inside the home. These families benefited from having two workers who were able to share ideas and support each other. The fact that in a few cases older children had been removed to foster care also made it easier for the mother to look after the younger ones in her care, although the effect on the separated child was not always beneficial.[3]

In three of the five fulfilled home placements, the social worker was changed after the order – or else responsibility was deliberately delegated to another member of staff whom the client trusted and who was able to keep open the channels of communication. This strategy seemed to help increase co-operation by distancing the social worker and client from the adversarial care proceedings.

Workers' relationship with families

The importance of the workers' relationship with families (mothers as well as children) is indicated by the fact that two families collapsed when the key social worker was on annual leave. This might have happened anyway; but a contributory factor was that no one who knew and understood the family was available at that time to deal with a crisis. In some cases where the decision was finely balanced, the removal of the children might actually have been prevented by the presence of a social worker who was prepared to act as an intermediary as well as advocate for the family.

> You can look at the information both ways. You can say 'This is an appalling case history and what are we doing?' – or you can turn around and say 'This is an appalling case history; lets get some work done and see if that work is actually achievable, and look to keep moving on.'

The social workers rightly understood that for home placements to succeed, there had to support for the main carer who was usually the mother. They also felt that they were walking a tightrope in some cases, since they could easily be criticised for sympathising with the mother at the expense of the children.

Emotional neglect and 'failure to protect'

When breakdown occurred, the main source of worry was usually not physical neglect but emotional neglect, coupled with 'failure to protect'. These were concerns that had been present in care proceedings, and they were the problems that proved most difficult to shift; but at the same time there could be improvements in some aspects of parenting while progress in others remained 'stuck', and the challenge was to maintain a sense of priority – a difficult task when the faults being addressed were acts of omission rather than commission. In the following example the mother of three children had learning difficulties. At the 21-month point her key social worker said:

> In a lot of respects Tracy has changed. The physical care of the children has been very, very good – the feeding of the children, keeping them clean, appropriately dressed – so she has been able to learn that this has got to be done.

> Where our concerns remain and always will remain without the right help for Tracy is her ability to emotionally stimulate these children and to keep them safe. She can see that if there is broken glass you clear it away and don't let the children near it. She knows that if the children are in the street you keep control over them because they may run under a car. What she doesn't see is that if she lets them out to play in the complex they may go into other people's flats. She doesn't somehow comprehend the danger and is therefore unable to deal with it.

In cases where one or more parents abused alcohol, neglect was once again an issue; but there were other interrelated problems which needed to be addressed, and in one family the decision to abandon rehabilitation was taken when there was an escalation of domestic violence.

> *Interviewer:* What was it that actually led to the abandoning of the plan to rehabilitate?
>
> *Social worker:* There was a series of events that were happening over the summer and it was mostly around these instances of violence between the two [the mother and her partner] – the break-ups, the running to me with bruised faces and asking to be taken off to hospital ...

The need for multi-dimensional support

In cases where plans were implemented successfully much was a result of the parents' determination to keep their children; but there was often very intensive input from the social workers and also other agencies. Where health visitors and school staff were sympathetic and engaged, this was always helpful. *Respite care* had mixed results because, although it was popular with parents, it could be misused to the point where there was little interaction between parents and children and the children's ability to attach was diminished. The provision of *housing*, which was extremely helpful in kinship care because of accommodation problems, was also useful to parents who had children at home but for different reasons. Some house moves were necessary because children were bullied, or because the family was victimised by neighbours. These problems stemmed from the fact that the parents had poor social skills and were easily scapegoated in their neighbourhoods; but they were also indicative of the fact that the families lived in poor, deprived areas and when a transfer was arranged, the situation might be little better. In one case the children were physically and perhaps also sexually abused by one of their new neighbours. In another case where the family was rehoused with the help of social services because a mentally ill neighbour had thrown a block of concrete through the front window, the children were safer as a result of rehousing, but they lost contact with the neighbourhood school staff who had given them emotional as well as educational support, and the mother was also more isolated from her friends.

In a few cases insufficient attention was paid to the mother's difficulties – particularly problems with partnerships, which were instrumental in provoking drinking bouts and domestic violence, and poor physical or mental health. In one case where the children were removed towards the end of the follow-up period, cognitive therapy had been recommended by one of the specialists who saw the mother during care proceedings, but this had never been carried out. The children also had health difficulties which were not discovered until the children entered foster care.

In home placements, perhaps more than in any other placement option, multi-dimensional support was necessary to help some of the more fragile placements to survive.

Discussion and conclusions

Over twenty years ago Kempe memorably concluded in the inquiry into the death of Jasmine Beckford that 'if a child is not safe at home, he cannot be protected by casework' (Brent Borough Council 1985). It is not known what would have happened if the placements in this study had been allowed to continue, and it is possible that the decision to remove the child or children was not always well founded. However, the low rate of placement fulfilment suggests that there is a need to improve initial assessments – particularly when children are living in sibling groups. The concerns in these cases focused on neglect, which was usually associated with parental alcohol misuse or learning difficulties. Partly because of their frequency and chronicity, the damaging impact of these problems was less likely to be recognised and taken seriously by professionals than child abuse or misuse of drugs. Other research by one of the authors into parental substance misuse in social services has noted this same pattern (Harwin and Forrester 2002).

The findings expose the difficulties of achieving shared parental responsibility when trying to secure stability for children placed at home.[4] Parental co-operation was a key plank to fulfilment. Where co-operation was lacking, the plans proved to be over-optimistic, and in particular they overestimated the capacity of coercion by means of the care order to bring about positive sustained change. As will be shown in Chapter 14, parents in home placements were the least likely of all current carers to make use of services offered in the post-order period and, even in cases where plans were fulfilled, parents were more likely to take up services for their children rather than for themselves. Some parents were reluctant to continue in alcohol abuse treatment – a finding that sadly is consistent with American research showing that court-ordered treatments in substance misuse cases do not work well – and this reluctance was exacerbated by a shortage of locally based treatment services. Reliance on the resilience of older children to manage their parents' alcohol misuse could leave these young people in the role of young carers, and in some cases the plans for discharge of the order seemed to set up parents and social services to fail by committing them to targets that proved hard to achieve.

What constitutes good practice when working with children at home, and is it possible to achieve it when parents may have reason to keep their difficulties hidden from the professionals?

- First, parents need a social worker they can trust, and to this end it may be a good idea to change the social worker after the order.
- Second, the order must offer more than control; it must provide assistance and services that are perceived to be relevant.[5]
- Third, it is important to ensure that services do not wither away over time.[6]

Home placement should only be chosen for positive reasons. As discussed in Chapter 5, this was not always the case. Sometimes home placements were seen as a halfway house that avoided the need for removal. Greater awareness of risk factors may improve the chances of stability, but only if the lessons from other studies are also taken into account. Although many of these apply to children returning home after a period in substitute care, there are some clear commonalities. For example, the importance of active help from social services directed towards improving the quality of parent–child relationships emerges again and again. In Packman and Hall's study of section 20 accommodation, tensions between siblings also emerged as one of five key risk factors predicting the need for children to be looked after again after a return home (Packman and Hall 1998) and children of primary school age were the most vulnerable – probably because of the greater demands they place on parents. Yet frequently, as in our study, the social work task was focused on the monitoring of 'captive clients' who had little choice in what was offered to them and sometimes received very little.

Undoubtedly far fewer children would be placed at home if all the risk factors were taken on board, leaving perhaps only a minority where it would be judged appropriate and likely to succeed – and in these situations a supervision order might suffice. By the end of the study at least one authority was seriously questioning the justification for using care orders to place children at home, and this is a question to which we shall return in our conclusions. It is unfair to single out faults of implementation if the plan should have recommended a different placement – or if the plan should never have been based on a care order at all.

Summary

1 Only nine out of 22 children were successfully maintained in the home environment. This means that the implementation rate for home placements is 41%. Some attempts at rehabilitation broke down almost immediately but, if this hurdle was passed, the vulnerable placements tended to last for sixteen to eighteen months.

2 Children placed at home had fewer initial problems than in any other placement option. However, the ability of the parents to tolerate problems was low and the presence of any initial difficulties contributed to the likelihood of disruption.

3 Since placements were usually made or continued immediately after the order, there was no need to state the time to placement in the care plan. Instead, time targets were sometimes set for review of the case; but they were usually exceeded.

4 If the contingency plan was adoption, new contact arrangements had to be made when the home placement broke down. Legal problems could arise if the court had not been informed of these arrangements at the time of the care order, and in cases of breakdown it seems advisable to go back to court for a no-contact order, if this is required, before the adoption plan is pursued.

5 The work was labour-intensive and demanded sustained input to the families, both from social services and from other agencies. Health visitors and school teachers had important contributions to make. Good services were essential to the success of home placements, and it was less than satisfactory if post-order intervention was focused on monitoring only.

6 Discharge of the order provided exit from the care system and it sometimes acted as an incentive for parents to work towards. Failure to achieve discharge at the promised time could exacerbate tensions, however, and there were occasional worries that difficulties such as renewed alcohol abuse were being covered up. There is a great need to improve assessments, both at the start of home placements and when it seems appropriate to end them.

---

[1] The recent House of Lords judgement *Re S* (2002) HL has argued in favour of extended interim care orders, but only in cases where the uncertainty can be resolved prior to the final hearing and is not either 'chronic or inevitable'.

[2] 'Mother-blaming' is an unhealthy and largely unjustifiable aspect of the child protection system (Farmer and Owen 1995, 1998). Nevertheless, Stevenson has pointed out that although social workers need to remain sensitive to the gender issues, the fact that mothers are the main caretakers in cases of neglect makes them the natural focus of day-to-day work (Stevenson 1998).

[3] The study by Quinton et al. (1998) reports on the vulnerability of children placed alone in established families – especially in circumstances where they feel rejected by their birth families.

[4] Hunt and Macleod's study (1999) of care plans also found high rates of breakdown in home placements, including those involving a small sub-sample of children on care orders.

[5] There was a tendency for follow-up to be organised around reviews, which at least one set of parents found routine and unhelpful. This echoes the work of Grimshaw and Sinclair (1997) who have emphasised the importance of seeing the review as part of a much more active and flexible process.

[6] Guardians had sometimes supported the need for the order on the grounds that it would generate particular services, but the uptake proved complicated because of parents' own fluctuating commitments as well as variable investment on the part of the SSD.

Part

IV Contact and services

13 The implementation of contact plans

Introduction

The Children Act 1989 recognised the importance of keeping looked-after children in touch with their families, and it is now assumed that social workers will strive to promote contact for children in the care system unless there is clear evidence that this is not in the child's interests. The term 'contact' can encompass a number of different options, ranging from complete openness at one end of the scale to very limited 'indirect' contact (where messages are exchanged via a third party) at the other. In the current study indirect contact has been excluded from the analysis since it was only used in adoption cases. Contact therefore refers to face-to-face contact and it comprises all those family members who were in regular touch with the child – including those who were in shared placements.

Research has shown that the maintenance of links between separated children and their families increases the likelihood of reunification (Millham et al. 1986; Berridge and Cleaver 1987; Bullock et al. 1998); but there is also evidence that contact can have psychological value for children whether or not they return home, and in recent years this has helped to fuel the argument that more adopted children could have ongoing contact with their birth families (Mullender 1991; Fratter 1996; Lowe et al. 1999). No large-scale study of post-adoption contact has yet been undertaken; but there is evidence that contact in foster care is positively associated with children's behaviour and well-being (Thoburn 1994; Cleaver 2000). A research finding of major importance is that it has constantly been requested by children themselves, both in our own study (see Chapter 16) and in other people's (Shaw 1998; Masson and Oakley 1999; Masson et al. 1999). In the right circumstances it can be supportive of placements, defusing anxiety and making children feel more settled, while it may also contribute to children's sense of identity by giving them direct knowledge of their origins. It offers children the option of maintaining contact in the future with birth family members including brothers and sisters. Moreover, ongoing involvement with parents honours the principle of partnership that is enshrined in the Children Act, putting flesh on the bones of parental responsibility.

In spite of these benefits, there have been reports that contact is not always beneficial and it may in fact create problems for children, family members and carers (Quinton et al. 1998; Schofield et al. 2000). Foster carers may be ambivalent or even hostile towards the birth parents and if they have negative attitudes, the meetings between children and parents are impoverished (Triseliotis et al. 2000). More seriously, there is the risk that children will be rejected or abused during contact sessions, or that they will be caught up in domestic violence (Hester and Radford 1996; Sturge and Glaser 2000). A recent study of the fostering task with adolescents (Farmer et al. 2002) reported that while 69% of the young people had at least one contact that could be regarded as beneficial, 63% had some contact that had a detrimental effect on them.

Contact plans cannot be written in stone; but when contact arrangements have been presented to the court as part of the care plan, it is important to know how realistic these plans were. What is crucial is the quality of interaction – not the number of visits – but regular contact is clearly essential if relationships are to be maintained. Furthermore contact has a special place in the legal system, because if contact plans are likely to remain unfulfilled, the court has the option of making a contact order simultaneously with the care order – and this gives the court greater powers of intervention here than in any other aspect of the care plan. For this reason alone, the subject is of interest to courts and social services alike.

This chapter starts by explaining how contact plans have been evaluated, then moves on to document fulfilment rates. The second half of the chapter explores difficulties in fulfilling contact plans in relation to the individual placement options.

Evaluating the fulfilment of contact plans

In order to evaluate the progress made in fulfilling contact plans presented to the court, two key dimensions were selected from those represented in the care plans, and on this basis two criteria were drawn up. Plans were deemed to be successfully implemented when:

- contact had been terminated or continued with named individuals as stated in the care plan; and
- the arrangements for contact reflected what had been said in the care plan about frequency and duration.

Plan fulfilment

Contact with named individuals

Eighty-two per cent of the children had their original plans fulfilled inasmuch as contact was continued or terminated with named individuals. This may be considered a good result – especially as our criteria were rather tight. However, if the plans changed there was a tendency for contact to be axed rather than reinstated. Of the eighteen children who experienced changes to plans naming specific individuals:

- fifteen children did not experience continuation of contact as recommended in the care plan; and
- there were only three children for whom contact was unexpectedly continued when it was due to be terminated.

It should be noted that no child was re-abused as a result of plans for the termination of contact not being fulfilled. For two of the children whose contact was unexpectedly continued, the plan to terminate contact had been abandoned when the placement plan changed from adoption to long-term fostering. In the remaining case the placement choice was kinship care; the birth father managed to continue visiting because the carer was his sister, and contact was officially reinstated when the arrangement turned out to be satisfactory from everyone's point of view.

The reasons why plans for the continuation of contact were not fulfilled are more complex, and they will be explored later in the chapter.

Patterns of contact with particular family members

As can be seen from Table 13.1, the highest rate of contact plan fulfilment with named carers (100%) was actually experienced by grandparents, although they were mentioned in only twenty care plans. However, the person most frequently mentioned in all plans was the birth mother, and she was also the person who attracted the second highest rate of contact plan fulfilment (95%). The next most numerically important group is siblings. If the categories of siblings and half-siblings are combined, to include children both in and out of the care system, the total number of plans giving information about contact between brothers and sisters is 79, out of which 66 were successfully implemented (a success rate of 84%). This is similar to the fulfilment rate associated with birth fathers, who featured in 61 contact plans of which 51 were carried out.

Table 13.1 ***Implementation of plans for contact (or no contact) with named individuals***

	Plans to continue contact with named individual		**Plans to terminate contact with named individual**		**Total**	
	Initiated	Fulfilled	Initiated	Fulfilled	Initiated	Fulfilled
Birth mother	68	65	24	22	92	87
Birth father	42	35	19	16	61	51
Stepmother or female partner	5	5	–	–	5	5
Stepfather or male partner	8	4	9	9	17	13
Siblings in care	36	33	3	1	39	34
Siblings out of care	8	7	–	–	8	7
Half-siblings in care	18	14	2	2	20	16
Half-siblings out of care	12	9	–	–	12	9
Aunt or uncle	8	7	–	–	8	7
Grandparent	15	15	5	5	20	20

It should be remembered that the plans for continuation of contact include plans for joint placement. Without this, the number of proposed contacts with birth mothers, fathers and siblings would have been fewer[1] although there is a similar rate of fulfilment.

Here is one social worker's account of her difficulties in establishing contact for a sibling group of five children, spread over three placements. Four of them had adoption plans while the fifth was to remain in foster care.

> When I first took over the case it was left to the foster carers to do it themselves, and they are really good foster carers, but contact was in their own home and it just wasn't working. I mean, it was a lot to ask ... By the time the case came to this team the final contact with the birth parents had been organised, but the contact between the siblings wasn't always happening. It took me a little while to fathom this out. They are all in different foster homes and it takes some time, you know, before the foster carers really open up to you ...
>
> We've got a key to a playgroup now and they all go there. It's a purpose-built room so there is lots of space and lots of equipment. There is tea and coffee-

> making and things. They go there for two hours on the first Saturday of every month.

Not all of the plans were for continuation of contact, of course. As can be seen from Table 13.1, plans to terminate contact accounted for:

- 6% of the plans involving siblings (5 out of 79);
- 25% of the plans involving grandparents (5 out of 20);
- 26% of the plans involving birth mothers (24 out of 92);
- 31% of the plans involving birth fathers (19 out of 61); and
- 52% of the plans involving stepfathers (9 out of 17).

Many of these plans to terminate contact with birth relatives (especially siblings, grandparents and birth parents) had been made in association with adoption plans, and the assumption was that this would make placement easier. Nevertheless the higher incidence of plans to terminate contact with certain relatives, and particularly fathers and stepfathers, indicates that in more of these cases there was believed to be risk of actual harm to the child. There were no striking differences in the implementation rates, depending on whether contact was to be continued or terminated, except in the case of stepfathers. The numbers here are too small to permit generalisations; but plans for contact with a stepfather were allowed to disappear in four cases where they should have continued and, conversely, all nine plans to terminate contact with a stepfather were fulfilled.

The case details suggest that males, and particularly birth fathers, were more persistent and also more successful in pursuing contact where they had a mind to do this – although at the same time contact with birth fathers could wither if they were not actually designated carers. Contact with the birth mother was cut back when there were irresolvable difficulties in foster care or kinship care, or when home placements broke down; but contact between siblings seemed to be the most problematic as far as frequency is concerned, and this no doubt reflects the difficulties of bringing children together if they were not in joint placements.

Court orders

Most of the contact arrangements outlined in the care plans were not independently supported by a court order, but in certain cases contact orders under section 34(4) of the Children Act were made. The greatest number of section 34(4) orders were made in adoption cases, where there were orders in six cases authorising termination of contact with eleven individuals – six with the birth mother, four with the birth father and one with a stepfather.

For children in long-term fostering or kinship care, there was an order to terminate contact only with one stepfather who was considered an abuser, although several children were affected by this order. There was a total absence of contact orders in residential care or home placement, and kinship care was the only placement option in which the court was anxious to ensure that contact would be preserved. For six of the eighteen children (in two families), the court made an order that contact with the birth mother was to continue.

All of the contact orders were carried out, except in the adoption cases where there was a change of plan.

Frequency and duration of contact

When we consider the plans for frequency and duration, there is a similar tendency for contact to be diminished rather than increased at the implementation stage, but the differences are even more marked.

- Fifty-five children did not experience contact of the planned duration and/or frequency.
- The changes involved reduction of contact for all but four of these children.

Table 13.2 ***Implementation of plans for frequency and duration of contact***

Placement recommended	Frequency and duration of contact fulfilled	Frequency and duration of contact not fulfilled
Adoption (n=33)	14	19
Foster care (n=22)	11	11
Placement at home (n=22)	9	13
Kinship placement (n=18)	9	9
Residential (n=5)	2	3
Total (n=100)	**45**	**55**

As can be seen from Table 13.2, the situations that chimed best with the original plans were found in kinship care and fostering cases, although plans for frequency and duration were still only fulfilled for 50% of the children. In other placement options, contact arrangements were out of line with the original plans for more than half the children.

- In the few cases where the amount of contact was unexpectedly increased, it was increased through the initiatives of family members themselves.

There is of course a difference between *duration* and *frequency*. Most deficiencies in duration can be traced to the early cessation of contact with the birth mother prior to adoption. Changes in the frequency of contact, however, occurred in every placement option and they affected contact with the full range of family members.

Reasons why contact was reduced

The main reasons for reduction are shown below. It should be noted that these are overlapping considerations. The numbers in parentheses indicate the approximate numbers of children whose experience of contact was affected by these difficulties – and it is interesting to note that the most prominent reason for contact variation was a change of placement plan.

Parents withdrew:

- being too upset to continue (5);
- wanting contact to be on their own terms (10); or
- rejecting the child, or using non-contact as a punishment (3).

Children withdrew:

- having become distanced from the parent, and forming attachments elsewhere (4);
- being angry about previous treatment (6); or
- feeling embarrassed or distressed by parents' problems (8).

The local authority cut back contact:

- when it was considered to be upsetting for the child (12);
- when it had ceased to serve any useful purpose (7);
- when the parent was seen as a bad influence, for instance undermining the placement (16);

- when the arrangements were too difficult to sustain (14); or
- when there was a change of placement plan (20).

The overall picture is that contact with named individuals had a good rate of fulfilment, but it was *less frequent than had been planned for*:

- one in ten children who had contact with the birth father;
- one in three who had contact with the birth mother; and
- more than half of those who had contact with other siblings.

These differences were not apparent when we considered only the criterion of whether or not contact had been continued or terminated, and they confirm that a fall-off in the frequency of arrangements was more common than total non-fulfilment of the contact plan.

Contact variations in different placement options

The above reasons apply across the board; but we need to consider the situation in relation to placement options in order to understand the nature and extent of the changes. The purposes of contact usually went beyond the simple right of parents and children to see each other.

Contact in adoption cases

Because there were so few plans for post-adoption contact, most of the contact plans in adoption cases were concerned with the time prior to the child's placement. The main purposes of contact with the birth family during this time were:

- to help the grieving process in parents and children;
- to enable the child to relinquish important attachments gradually; and
- to assist the child to move on.

Reasons why the duration of contact was not according to plan

In adoption cases the usual plan was for the child's contact with birth family members to be decreased gradually after the care order, and the care plan stated that it would be ended with a 'goodbye visit' at the point when adopters were identified or introductions begun. In approximately half of all cases this period of contact was shortened.[2] One of the reasons offered was that the birth mother was too distressed to continue, although it was equally true that the social worker would encourage the parent to withdraw if the child was being upset by the visits. In some cases it was also claimed that once-a-month contact had become meaningless, because the child no longer had any significant attachment to the birth parent.

Here is what one social worker said about contact visits prior to the adoption of a 2-year-old girl:

> There was a tenuous bond between mother and daughter, perhaps because Lucy had been looked after by so many different people. Sandy [her mother] was only 15 when she was born ...
>
> When her mum was there during contact, she would be quite challenging towards her and Sandy found this very wearing. The contact was two hours at a time; but Sandy would quite often be finished after an hour and a quarter, because she just could not cope with Lucy. She didn't know how to play with her. She didn't know how to talk to her. She didn't know how to interact in any way.

These difficulties might have been eased by better structuring of the contact arrangements, but a more potent argument was that the child was distressed by contact. One of the birth mothers who was interviewed said that access had been arranged at a level of one hour per week between care order and adoptive placement, but she stopped visiting her small son after the first month because of the distress it caused him.

> He got used to me being there and he'd be all happy, and then when I had to go he'd think he were coming with me and he wasn't, and he'd cry his eyes out; so each time he saw me he got more and more resentful towards me because he knew I would be leaving him. It was tearing him apart.

The effect of delays in placement finding

One factor that had a strong impact on the arrangements for pre-adoption contact was the delay in finding placements. As we mentioned in Chapter 9, the average time taken to identify adopters was six months, and an average of 8.5 months elapsed between the care order and the linking. This was considerably more than had been bargained for. It is understandable that some parents should give up in the meantime; but when the parents' contact was foreshortened and the time to placement was lengthened, there was for some children a considerable period when neither birth parents nor adopters were available, In fact these children were living in foster care without family contact of any kind.

The argument usually advanced in defence of this situation was that, for these particular children, birth family contact was unhelpful and it would not be resurrected even if the adoption plan were to fall through. There were, however, a number of points that give rise to anxieties. First, the reduction of contact was not always done at a pace that suited children's interests (although if parents wished to withdraw, it was clearly difficult to stop them). Second, the visits by parents could be regarded as a form of monitoring. Independent visitors, though sometimes mentioned at reviews, were never provided. Third, the decisions to end parental contact in the run-up to adoption did not always have proper legal support. In the absence of a section 34 order giving the local authority leave to terminate contact, or a statement by the court that contact would be at the discretion of the local authority, decisions to shorten the period of contact without full parental agreement appeared to rest on the fact that the care plan had named adoption without face-to-face contact as the ultimate aim, and the making of the care order appeared to sanction both the means and the end. This is an interesting off-shoot of the importance given to the care plan in the court setting – that at the implementation stage, far from being ignored, it could be elevated to the rank of a quasi-legal document. However, in the light of the Human Rights Act more of these decisions may now be open to legal challenge.

Post-adoption contact

As mentioned in Chapter 5 the plans for face-to-face contact after adoption were very few. There was only one family in which contact was to continue with the birth mother and the birth father, for a sibling group of four, and most of the plans for continuation of sibling contact can be attributed to joint placement. The social workers had sometimes formulated tentative plans for contact with other siblings who had been adopted, but these were not written into the care plan since the social workers felt that it would be wrong to bind the adopters to commitments they might not be able or willing to undertake. They were, however, discussed with prospective adopters and possible problems were identified, as this quotation from one of the adoptive carers shows.

> The only post-adoption contact we discussed with the social worker was seeing one of the elder children ... We haven't pursued it at the moment, simply because it has been quite busy for us and also it's not going to be the easiest

> thing. The elder lad must be about 6 now; he is white, with blond hair and blue eyes. Suddenly he is going to see these brothers, you know – a little black brother and a little half-black brother. It might come as a bit of a shock to him.

Face-to-face contact with siblings who were not adopted had usually been ruled out, whether they were at home or in foster care, on the grounds that ongoing contact was not in the adopted child's interests – although it might well be in the interests of the other siblings. In a case where a 2-year-old child was awaiting adoption and two older children were to remain in foster care, the social worker said:

> We have been having a very long debate about future contact between Carla and her sisters – but this would be for the sisters' sake and not for Carla's sake. For her as an individual child we feel that on-going sibling contact, face to face, at this stage wouldn't be helpful. For the two older girls I think it would help them a lot; but we have had to come up with a decision that we will just go for post-box contact, because it is Carla you have got to look at.

Because of the reluctance to recommend post-adoption contact (apart from indirect or 'post-box' contact, which was widely used), radical changes to contact arrangements were necessary after there had been a variation of the placement plan from adoption to fostering, or from placement at home to adoption. In moves between placement options not involving adoption, it was more likely that the direction of the original contact plans could be maintained.

Altogether face-to-face contact was continued or terminated with named individuals as had been intended in 94% of adoption cases, but because of the combined effects of the foreshortening of pre-adoption contact and the lengthening of the time to placement, plans for frequency and duration were met in less than half the cases.

Contact in long-term fostering and residential care

The main purposes of family contact in fostering and residential care were:

- to provide continuity and a sense of identity through the maintenance of family links;
- to reassure children about the well-being of parents and siblings; and

- to help children develop a realistic understanding of the reasons why the care order was necessary.

In cases bound for fostering or residential care, there was an assumption that birth family contact would continue unless it was not in the children's interests. Where there were plans to terminate contact, for example with an abusing stepfather, there was clear evidence of risk to the children if contact was pursued. In this respect plans to terminate contact in fostering cases are quite different from those made in adoption. When the care plan named adoption as the placement choice the main concern of the court and the social services department was to help the child to move on – and, as a result, contact was to be discontinued with fairly 'harmless' family members such as grandparents who had expressed an interest in looking after the child. Plans for termination of contact were less common in other placement options, but at the same time the concerns were more serious.

Actions taken by parents and children

Contact issues were always taken seriously in fostering and residential care, but when the plans for contact were being implemented parents and children had a considerable share of the action. This was partly because the children were older. In three cases the parents rejected an adolescent child, who was blamed for the making of the care order, and non-contact was used as a punishment. However, it is interesting to note that:

- there was an even greater number of cases in which parents were rejected by children themselves – perhaps encouraged by social workers or carers who felt that contact was unhelpful or even damaging.

Here is how one social worker described the views of an 11-year-old girl:

> She decided that she didn't want to live at home and that she wanted contact to be supervised. I think she felt there was some pressure from mum to assist her to parent the boys and take on quite an adult role. Mum was treating her as an ally rather than a person who needed parenting herself. Tina, in my opinion, just opted out of that.

This girl's 9-year-old brother is also said to have rejected contact with the parent, but for different reasons:

> We've just been through a very difficult period where mum was saying that she wanted contact with Jeremy; but he was saying he did not want contact with her, because he thought that she'd been using drugs, despite promises

> that she had made to him that she had stopped that, and that she was turning over another new leaf and everything was hunky dory. But he is quite sharp and picked up on things.[3]

Six adolescent girls refused to see their parents either totally or for long periods of time because of their anger at previous treatment, which included, in three separate cases, a refusal to believe allegations of sexual abuse. (The girls' anger was further inflamed in these cases by the fact that their mother appeared to side with the alleged abuser.) However, another eight children wanted to withdraw from contact or at least to have it reduced in scope because they were simply embarrassed or distressed by their parents' problems. These feelings were respected by social workers, who felt that the care order had set children free from unhealthy pressures. The children's views were relayed to the parents and contact was not pursued.[4]

Should contact have been promoted more?

One of the mothers who wanted to see more of her daughters in foster care said:

> Every review I go to, I bring this up. I just get told: 'Well, they're teenagers!' Yesterday I arranged to meet them in town as I normally do, and June the eldest one had brought her two friends along so I only saw them for half an hour and then they were gone, doing their own thing. I'm not at all happy.

Another mother complained that when she visited the placement, her daughter was never there.

Was there enough support for contact in these cases? There is general agreement among practitioners that it is quality of contact that matters rather than frequency of visits (Barker et al. 1999) and some requests for contact may be in the parents' interests rather than the child's. However, there was perhaps rather little attention given to helping the children cope with anger and ambivalence, as an aid to developing their own sense of identity and self-esteem. Foster carers were not always very active in supporting birth family contact, and when we examine residential placements that remained intact we are reminded that at least one research study (Bilson and Barker 1995) reported that contact was often better maintained for children in residential care. However, these results are not universal. In the study *Remember My Messages* (Shaw 1998), which explored the views of 2,000 looked-after children (not all of whom were on care orders), young people in children's homes and secure units were less satisfied with the extent of contact than children in foster care. The younger children in the Shaw study were also less satisfied than the older ones – perhaps because they were consulted less.

Some of the blame for poor contact must be laid at the door of parents' unreliability, as this quotation from a foster carer shows.

> If it is raining, the likelihood of the mother turning up is that she fails to turn up. So we just stay there for half an hour and then get on our way. On a good day, she's never on time. You can guarantee that she'll turn up a good quarter of an hour, twenty minutes late, half an hour – if she turns up.

The consumer interviews show that parents often felt uncomfortable meeting their children in day centres, feeling that they were being watched and judged. Who knows what difficulties this mother was experiencing? Nevertheless, from the children's point of view, the only relevant consideration was whether or not the contact actually happened.

Reduction of contact by social services

Court orders authorising termination of contact were complied with; but in addition, there were several cases where a large amount of contact was deemed to be harmful and consequently it was strictly controlled by social services. This happened most often in the case of children admitted to foster care as a result of emotional abuse and neglect in middle childhood.

Supervision of contact was rarely undertaken after the first few weeks, except for sibling reunions or meetings with 'risky' adult relatives at the family centre. The preference of family members and practitioners was for contact to take place in the family home,[5] and the main reasons for restricting this contact were usually found in association with one another. They were first that the parent was likely to undermine the placement and second that the home environment was unsuitable for children, either because the parent was destructively cold and critical or because the home was very unhygienic (an allegation that was common when the parents had learning difficulties), or because the home was believed to provide a refuge for criminals and/or drug-users. There were also some concerns that children might be physically, sexually or emotionally abused during contact, and other research has drawn attention to this risk (Hester and Radford 1996; Sturge and Glaser 2000).

In spite of its psychological importance, *sibling contact* was in some cases sadly neglected. Schofield (2003) points out that the loss of sibling contact often means the loss of a normal childhood, since biological ties have social as well as psychological importance. Yet parental contact generally took precedence over sibling contact, unless it was possible for siblings to see one another in the presence of parents. Alternatively informal arrangements were made between foster carers who knew one another – but these arrangements were easily disrupted when they became too difficult to manage, or when the placement changed. Some siblings fought with one another and were difficult to control, but one of the main reasons for cutting back on sibling contact, unfortunately, was that the arrangements were too difficult to sustain.

Contact with named individuals was continued or terminated as planned in 82% of fostering cases and 60% of residential ones, but by the end of the study a very much lower proportion of children were experiencing contact of the requisite frequency and duration. We have to remember, however, that most of these contact plans had been marked 'subject to review'.

Contact in kinship care

The main purposes of contact in kinship care were:

- to provide continuity and preserve important attachments;
- to defuse children's anxieties about the previous carer's welfare; and
- to stabilise the child's position within the extended family and community.

In kinship care the key relationship was obviously the one between the child and the carer, but it was also an advantage if the child and the carer could share visits to other relatives whom they had in common. If relationships were difficult, the relative looking after the child could not easily be coerced into contact, as this quotation from one of the kinship carers shows: 'They used to go to see their great granny, where I used to take them, and every time I took them down there I used to get a load of abuse. I said to social services "I'm not doing that."'

On the other hand a woman who planned to adopt her small niece and bring her up along with her own children said: 'My mum is my children's grandmother – but she's Debbie's grandmother as well. That made a big difference. When she was in foster care it was somebody else's grandmother – it wasn't really her grandmother. So we knew it was going to work from Day One.'

Race, culture and ethnicity

How important were considerations of race and culture as determinants of contact in kinship care? As a source of continuity they were enormously important, as long as the placement choice reflected real relationships and the children's sense of where they belonged. The woman in the case mentioned above was Irish, and the child saw her family roots as being in Ireland. One paternal grandmother who described herself simply as 'a black woman' said that her grand-daughter, who was of dual heritage, 'had known the black side from when she was born'. Now that she was being looked after by her grandmother, nothing had really changed. 'It's something that just flows.' This woman did not particularly want to talk about her ethnic group. She said:

> Not that I am ashamed of my ethnic group or anything, but it seems in everything that you do today that ethnic group crawls into it like something from under stone ... I have lived here over 40 years and although I am a black person I know my whatever it is [identity] and I know how to link with the white, with the black, with the Jews, with the Irish, with the Greeks. I have worked with them all ... and I can always fit myself in.

The 8-year-old girl who had been placed with her grandmother in the above case was similarly confident about her identity. She said that she had 'both white and black in her' and she did not want to be categorised as belonging to one side or the other; but this meant that contact with her mother's family was essential to her peace of mind, and the arrangements were complex and difficult to sustain.

In the case of three black children who were to be looked after by their father, the sheer numbers of friends and relatives and the complexity of contact arrangements had contributed to the choice of kinship care in the first place. Here is the social worker's description of the original decision-making.

> What kind of contact arrangements [should there be] and how would that work? It was an incredibly messy sort of concept to work with. These children had such complicated networks within the community. And they were so embedded – you know, they are deeply rooted here. The idea of removing them from it just seemed abhorrent.

Relationships with separated parents

Community links were important; but when children were to be looked after by other relatives and particularly by fathers, the relationship with the original parent (who was usually the child's mother) was an important one to maintain. If the new carer was seen as having too close an alliance with the parent, there were worries that contact might be extended without limit and that difficulties or risks would be covered up. The reverse situation was that family conflicts could escalate because the new carer was seen as having an alliance with social services. Knowing that in most cases a residence order would be the ultimate goal, the social workers concentrated on helping the carer to establish a workable pattern of contact which could be part of the children's lives without undermining the stability of the placement.

This was not an easy task. The situation could and did quite frequently result in a battle of wills. In the first few months after the care order it was not unusual for the mother to withdraw entirely because she wanted contact to be under her own control; but since she did not usually want to stay uninvolved for long, she might continue to request contact but act erratically, refusing to accept the boundaries of time and place that had been set. There are reports of attempts at manipulation by the previous carer – for example when children were told (falsely) that they would soon be returning to their original homes, and sometimes they were bribed or threatened. (In one case the child's mother said that she was redecorating his room. In another, she threatened to sell his bed if he did not return.) In a case of substance abuse where children cared deeply about the parent they were distressed to find that she was constantly complaining of being ill or having no food in the fridge, and they returned to the kinship carer with demands for money or help. Attempts to reduce contact could result in the child absconding from one parent to see the other and, as we have seen, this provoked breakdown in one case where the child was removed to foster care.

Contact arrangements tended to become less formal as time went on, and when there were difficulties the net result was usually that contact was reduced in frequency, either because the mother defaulted on the arrangements or because the children withdrew from her. Where the contact arrangements worked well, the carer was usually convinced of the advantages of contact – if only for the somewhat negative reason that it gave children direct experience of the parent's failings. Carers easily saw the value of preventing children from fantasising about their absent parents.

> We were on about the contact with Kate's mother and saying 'Why should she have it?' The social worker said 'Well, if you take the mother away from Kate, Kate will idolise her and make her out to be someone she is not. All the time you have contact there, Kate is seeing her mother for what she is.'

Another variation on this theme was that, in the absence of face-to-face contact, children would learn about their parents from other people in the vicinity. One father whose ex-wife was still part of the community in which he lived said: 'I believe that children – no matter how ill or demented their parents might be – they should still go on to see them, because then they'll discover who their parent is by themselves and not by gossip.'

Necessary contacts were usually maintained when the child was in kinship care; but in view of child protection concerns, some problems were experienced with attempts to limit contact in situations where it might have been harmful to the child. If contact plans were not adhered to, there was little that the agency could do about it short of returning the case to court. In one case the local authority solicitor was asked to send a letter to the child's mother – but he admitted that his powers were rather limited.

- The ultimate danger was that if contact had spun out of control it could have destabilised the placement – and by renewing contact with substance-abusing family members, older children could put themselves at risk.

In spite of problems concerned with family loyalties and the constant risk of deception, the arrangements for ongoing contact were never discontinued completely. Maintenance of the family network was seen as crucial to the success of kinship care. Once again frequency and duration were lower than the court might have been led to expect; but contact was continued or terminated with named individuals as had been planned in 94% of cases, and this record was not matched in any other placement option with the exception of adoption.

Home placement

The main purposes of contact when children were placed at home were:

- to encourage bonding through regular interaction with parents and siblings;
- to build on children's existing sense of identity and family membership; and
- to stabilise the placement in the nuclear family.

When children were placed at home, contact was not generally considered a problem since parents and siblings were close at hand – and it was presumed that parents would give access to the extended family, or at any rate to those members of it who were regularly in touch with the nuclear family. In view of this, it is surprising to find that the fulfilment rate for contact with named individuals was only 59% in home placements, and the success rate for frequency and duration of contact was 42%. Both these results are worse than those in other placement options.

Reasons for contact plans being unfulfilled

In a situation where parents and children are in regular touch with each other, why were so many contact plans unfulfilled?

Children living at home sometimes had poor contact with siblings elsewhere in the care system; but these arrangements had not usually been written into the care plans in the first place. It was predicted that the most important contacts would take place within the home environment, and consequently the main reason for contact being reduced and plans not being fulfilled was that there were breakdowns leading to placement changes during the course of the study.

Sibling contact was particularly badly affected. According to the care plan eighteen children were to be placed in six groups of three; but at the end of the follow-up period only two of these joint placements survived. In the other four cases sibling groups were divided, and in two families younger members were syphoned off for adoption. Even if this did not happen, however, the changes experienced by the children were considerable because contact with parents and siblings had previously been continuous and it was clearly less extensive once the children had been admitted to foster care.

As in adoption cases, radical variation of contact usually followed a change of placement plan. When children were placed at home, disruption of the placement brought disruption of contact in its tow.

Discussion and conclusions

Contact plans had a good rate of fulfilment – but they were not always implemented in ways the court would have envisaged. The good fulfilment rate in plans for contact to be continued or terminated with named individuals is offset by the fact that in every placement option there was a tendency for the frequency of contact to decrease over time. The study has shown that each placement option had its own characteristic difficulties that needed to be faced if plans were to be realistic and achievable. Some examples are:

- the tendency for birth family contact to be ended prematurely in adoption cases, leaving small children without family contact if the adoption is delayed;
- the need to make complex arrangements for supervision in fostering and residential care, to facilitate contact between siblings in different placements;
- the difficulty of maintaining harmonious contact between the child and other relatives in kinship care, in the face of family conflict and distrust; and finally, in every placement,
- the need to protect the child.

Social workers were aware that the successful maintenance of contact always required more than administrative arrangements; it required sensitive negotiation with family members and direct input to the child from social workers, carers and sometimes therapists. The dwindling of sibling contact is particularly worrying, in view of the importance now given to this issue, and so is the priority given to organisational imperatives; but one point which emerges forcibly from the study is that social workers did not have strong powers to ensure that the contact plans were adhered to. They were very dependent on the goodwill of carers – especially foster carers, kinship carers and parents in home placement. A lot of initiatives were taken informally by family members themselves, and formal variation of the plan was often tantamount to recognition of the status quo.

As reported in Chapter 8, the fulfilment of the contact plans presented to the court was accompanied by greater likelihood that the placement plan itself would be implemented. The reverse side of the same coin, of course, is that the fulfilment of the contact plan depended to a large extent on the fulfilment of the placement. This was particularly true when children experienced breakdown of plans for adoption or home placement, since this provoked very radical changes, but it was true to a greater or lesser extent in every placement option. It underlines the need to make sure that important contact needs are documented in the care plan for future reference and that, to ensure stability of contact as well as stability of accommodation, the placement plans are met.

Summary

1. Plans to continue or terminate contact with named individuals were carried through in 82% of cases, but only 45% of the children experienced contact of the expected duration and frequency. Contact was reduced when parents or children withdrew from it because they found it impossible to continue, or when the local authority cut back on the arrangements because they were seen to be unhelpful or positively damaging to the child.

2. Section 34(4) orders authorising termination of contact had been made by the court in six adoption cases and one case of long-term fostering. Kinship care was the only placement option where the court had made orders to ensure that contact would continue. All the court orders were carried out.

3. In approximately half of all adoption cases, the period of contact prior to the adoptive placement was shortened and the good-bye visit was brought forward. Because of delays in finding placements, this meant that some children were in foster homes for a considerable period without family contact of any kind. (It is a source of concern that in these situations independent visitors were not provided.)

4. When children were in long-term foster care, supervision of contact was time-consuming and difficult to arrange, and it was rarely undertaken after the first few weeks unless it was absolutely necessary. There was a tendency for contact to become more informal and to take place in the family home; but parental contact generally took precedence over sibling contact, and siblings could lose out if it was not possible for them to see one another in foster homes or in the presence of their parents.

5. In kinship care, relationships with other relatives were usually well maintained; but it was most important to establish a workable pattern of contact with the previous carer, who was usually the child's mother.

6. Radical variation of contact usually followed a change of placement plan. The general view of practitioners was that placement stability was essential and therefore the placement must take priority over contact – although it is clear that the two are intertwined.

[1] When joint placements are excluded, the plans for contact involved 46 birth mothers, 31 birth fathers and 29 siblings.

[2] In *Berkshire County Council* v. *B* [1997] 1 FLR 171 the local authority wanted to reduce a child's contact with his birth mother to two meetings a year, since he was to be placed for adoption. Having received evidence that the child would be hard to place, the court made an order that contact should continue at its current rate of two hours a week. This decision was upheld on appeal. However, Hale LJ described the decision about the level of contact in such situations as a 'balancing act', balancing a number of different factors in the welfare of the child.

[3] In his own interview, this boy said that he smoked marijuana once a week and that he had learned this from his parents; but he also said he would not take other drugs because 'they're not worth it'.

[4] Masson and Harrison (1999) argue convincingly that the significance of contact and its loss is often underestimated by social workers, since there is a need to view children's identity from a lifetime perspective rather than one that is focused on childhood.

[5] Cleaver (2000) also reports that home visits are the preferred choice of parents and children. The parents in her study were less satisfied with contact in the foster home, feeling that their role had been usurped, and social services venues were not popular meeting places because they offered little privacy and restricted everyday interactions.

14 The implementation of services

Introduction

Careful attention to the plans for and delivery of services for children, parents and carers is every bit as integral to the care plan as the decision over placement. Indeed the failure to provide services which had been committed in the plan was the core issue in one of the test cases that went to the House of Lords. (See Chapter 1).

Yet the plans for services to be provided after the care order are bound to be multi-faceted and they may not be easy to implement. Some may not be within the control of the local authority, while the choice may be limited by resource constraints as well as barriers to interagency funding, and it stands to reason that services that are not acceptable to the recipients will not be taken up.

To what extent were children and adults provided with services that matched their needs? The first part of this chapter looks at the fulfilment rates for services mentioned in the care plan, and asks why some services were not taken up or were provided later. Then follows an outline and an assessment of the help made available to children, birth parents and carers in addition to 'placement-finding' or 'social work support'. What did we count as a service? Roughly speaking it was any input from an organisation or from an individual acting in a formal capacity that was calculated to increase the welfare of the child and/or family. (For example the provision of an adult 'befriender' was regarded as a service, but not the encouragement of friendship, although the latter might be subsumed under 'social work support'.)

The fulfilment of plans for services

The overall take-up of services listed for children was around 86%, whether the recommendations were made in the care plan or at a subsequent review. The take-up of services recommended for birth parents, on the other hand, was only 43% in the aftermath of the care order. It actually improved slightly when services were offered at a later date – either because the unpleasant events of care proceedings had been left behind, allowing the need for services such as counselling to emerge, or because the parents' needs were now better known and recognised. However, the take-up of services by birth parents was only 52% overall (see Table 14.2), and it was not appreciably better when the parents had children living at home with them. Services were provided on an *ad hoc* basis for foster carers, kinship carers and adopters, but it was difficult to calculate the fulfilment rate in services for carers because the initial plans were so patchy.

Why were some services not taken up?

When plans for services did not materialise, we are justified in asking whether this was because of lack of a suitable resource being available, or whether the proposed recipients did not want it. In practice there was an interaction between these factors, because low availability sometimes led to loss of interest through delays;[1] but much depended on the way in which the service was offered. In some cases the recipients had not been asked about their consent to services prior to the care order, and the care plan simply set out what was on offer – so it is hardly surprising that in many of these cases the plans were not implemented.

The criteria that most readily ensured take-up of a service were:

- popularity (with all parties including children, carers, family members and social workers);
- availability, in a choice of forms or settings;
- ease of access;
- low cost; and
- absence of stigma.

An example is to be found in the provision of nursery or playgroup experience for young children. This service, which was highest on the list of fulfilled services and was enjoyed by more than one in four children in the sample, had 100% take-up. The reasons are partly but not solely to do with the number of young children in the sample. Pre-school provision was extremely popular; it was thought valuable by social workers (as an aid to child development) and welcomed by parents, carers and children for different reasons. Second, it was locally based and easily available in a number of forms that offered consumer choice. Third, access was not usually problematic since the approach by a carer could be made direct and, fourth, the cost was reasonably low. Finally, it was a universal service, which could be claimed on behalf of any child irrespective of background and legal status.

Why were some services provided later?

Some services named in the care plan were not provided immediately but were offered and taken up at a later date. There were two main reasons for this. First, in a few cases a judgement was made that the timing was wrong. (For example, therapy might be postponed if there was too much going on in the family, or if the child was not yet in a stable placement.) Second, there were delays in gaining access to some facilities within the health service, such as Child and Family Guidance or hospital consultancy, because of the length of their waiting lists.

The subsequent recommendations and provision of services did not usually result from delays, however, but from changed circumstances. Examples are:

- children grew older, necessitating different inputs;
- children and parents changed their views on the acceptability of services;
- fresh assessments were required for court hearings; and
- placement breakdown produced a need for different facilities.

These events confirm the need for ongoing planning and review – not only to ensure that services named in the care plan have been offered, but to provide services in line with people's changing requirements.

Services for the children

Table 14.1 lists all the services recommended and provided for the children during the period of the study, whether the recommendation was made in the care plan or at a subsequent review. It can be seen that the services cover a wide spectrum; but how well do these services relate to the 'baseline problems' identified in Chapter 3?

Table 14.1 ***Provision of services for children***

	Services recommended in care plan		**Services recommended subsequent to care plan**		**Total**	
	Recom-mended	Provided	Recom-mended	Provided	Recom-mended	Provided
Psychotherapy	9	5	2	2	11	6
Art or play therapy	27	22	5	4	32	26
Counselling	12	9	8	7	20	16
Life story work	19	16	6	5	25	21
Speech therapy	10	10	12	10	22	20
Assessment and treatment of behavioural difficulties	5	5	16	16	21	21
Assessment and treatment of physical illness or defect	12	11	8	8	20	19
Monitoring by paediatrician	8	8	2	2	10	10
Nursery or playgroup	21	21	7	7	28	28
Help with schooling	17	16	8	7	25	23
Youth justice	–	–	2	0	2	0
Leisure activities	10	6	5	4	15	10
Adult friend or helper	3	2	3	1	6	3
Housing or Finance	–	–	4	4	4	4
Preparation for independent living	1	1	2	2	3	3
Total	**154**	**132**	**90**	**78**	**244**	**210**

n=100

The main question to be asked here is whether the right services were identified and offered; but questions of provision and take-up must inevitably enter into this equation, as services named in the care plan would be of little use unless implemented. We must also take into consideration the fact that 40 children were not in fulfilled placements at the end of the study, and their need for services may have changed as a result.

Therapeutic input

The largest proportion of services recommended for children in the care plan were concerned with therapeutic input. This was usually aimed at minimising the effect of the traumatic events suffered both during and prior to care proceedings, and so the welfare dimension most likely to be affected by it was family and social relationships; but it also related to emotional and behavioural difficulties (EBD) and identity.

- Almost half the sample had received some form of therapy by the end of the study, although it took a number of different forms.

Seventy-eight per cent of the children had problems in family and social relationships at the start of the study and 69% in EBD – although not all of these problems would have required formal therapeutic input. Unfortunately it seems that the serious problems were less well served than the others. *Psychotherapy*, obtainable only through medical channels, was recommended for disturbed adolescents; but it was often refused because the young people tended to associate it with the stigma of mental illness. It was not always available, either (for example, if the young person was living out of the county), and the cost to the agency of engaging a private psychotherapist could be very high. *Art or play therapy* could be provided by hospitals or independent specialists, but it was most commonly made available for young children at the local family centre. It had a good rate of take-up (81%) and it was well liked, although some children had no more than two or three sessions. *Counselling services* (for example, those organised by the NSPCC) were regarded as more specialised and the recipients were mainly abused or rejected children in middle childhood. It is noticeable that seven of the sixteen children who received counselling were referred at a later date, mostly as a result of placement breakdown.

Where adoption services were detailed in the care plan, *life story work* was usually recommended for children over the age of 3. It was also recommended for older children who had suffered disruption or multiple moves. In all the work that was undertaken there was a common core, which involved helping children to understand and come to terms with their own history, as an aid to developing a stable sense of identity. This was very much needed. There was a wide range of styles and approaches, however.

- What counted as life-story work varied from a simple compiling of information at one end of the scale to a complete series of counselling sessions at the other.

It should be noted that life-story work was not always beneficial – at least in the short term. There were suggestions in some of the carer interviews that it was upsetting for very young children, who responded to it with bed-wetting or nightmares. In one agency life-story work was regularly given to students, as a way of acquainting them with the problems of children in the care system. Nevertheless skilled work was done by many workers including adoption specialists and it was particularly valuable when carers as well as children were able to participate in it.

Assessment and treatment

Health problems

It will be recalled from Chapter 3 that health problems affected just under half the sample. As can be seen from Table 14.1, the numbers of children and young people who were to receive a health-related service fell far short of those indentified with a health problem. Yet research shows the high incidence of health difficulties for children in public care (Butler and Payne 1997; DoH 1999).

Swift action was taken to remedy such problems as were identified. Speech difficulties were common in young children, and the number of referrals for speech therapy which were made subsequent to the care order indicates that more problems were identified as babies and toddlers grew older. Some of these problems were found not to need treatment, but where necessary, they were dealt with. There were also some physical illnesses which required monitoring or treatment over a long period, including a serious metabolic disorder. Most other conditions identified as needing treatment were minor by comparison with this. The ones most frequently mentioned were defects in children's sight or hearing. It was not unusual for health needs to be identified in the first instance by carers, who were also actively involved in making appointments and escorting children to and from hospitals or surgeries.

- Many physical defects were identified and treated at the point when children left home to enter the foster care system. This highlights the difficulty of carrying out adequate health monitoring and treatment when children are in unsatisfactory environments.

Some of the adolescents in the study had significant health problems. One adolescent girl with a heart condition refused to have medical checks or treatment, and this was worrying, but treatment was never imposed on young people against their will.

Emotional and behavioural difficulties

Assessment and treatment of emotional and behavioural difficulties was carried out during the follow-up period in the case of 21 children. Surprisingly, in view of the high incidence of initial problems in EBD (69% of the sample), there were only five children for whom this service had been recommended in the care plan. They were bound for kinship care, and the concern was to make sure that the children's behaviour could be managed by the person who was about to take on the main parental role. For the majority of the children who received official help with emotional or behavioural development (sixteen out of 21) there was no recommendation for this service in the care plan. Referral to a psychologist or psychiatrist was made subsequent to the care order.

- Ten of the sixteen children referred at a later date had experienced placement breakdown, two of which were adoption breakdowns, and the assessments were needed to contribute to decision-making about their future.

It seemed that new referrals always had to fulfill some *official function*. In one case further assessment was requested by an adoption panel, and once again the concern was that the child might be too difficult for the prospective carer to manage. In another case involving several children the mother had applied to the court for extension of contact and discharge of the order, and fresh assessment was commissioned from the psychologist who had acted as expert witness during care proceedings. Other requests for behavioural assessments were made in situations where residence orders would soon be applied for. The conclusion is that:

- assessment and treatment of EBD were predominantly linked to decision-making in a formal and legal context.

The positive outcome was that some carers were given help with managing children's hyperactive behaviour and, since hyperactivity is known to be a high-risk factor in placement maintenance (Quinton et al. 1998; Rushton et al. 2001), the placement was probably more stable as a result.

Help with education

Special help seems to be required with educational difficulties because of the close association between educational needs and lack of fulfilment of the care plan. In particular, as can be seen from Chapters 8 and 9, educational needs tended to make it difficult for small children to find an adoptive placement – and these needs were strongly associated with learning difficulties or developmental delay. The main provision for these children was playgroup funding, which provided social experience and also encouraged skill-development. Nursery places (in day nurseries rather than nursery schools) were usually provided for reasons of childcare rather than education, and in most cases there was no specific educational input except what was provided by the carer.

Once children were of school age, 'help with schooling' took a number of forms. The children who were most in need of educational input were those who required special schooling. One boy with learning difficulties was already in a residential school, and all that was required of the social services department was liaison work; but in another twelve cases application was made for '*statementing*' so that children's needs could be met either by special schooling or more probably by welfare assistance in the classroom. The motivating force behind 'statementing' was often the fact that children were disruptive in school, and extra staff were needed to manage the child's behaviour. Some of these applications were ongoing at the close of the study.

- Private tuition was provided only for three children who were in foster care and awaiting adoption. The aim was apparently to make the children more easily adoptable.

For some older children special efforts were needed to ensure that they attended school, and social workers and carers (including residential carers) were occasionally involved in negotiations to prevent school exclusion or to release alternative provision when this was necessary. However, most of the tasks done by carers and social workers in connection with education were fairly routine although they were none the less important. They involved:

- attendance at school meetings and open days;
- liaising with teachers who had posts of special responsibility; and
- selecting the most suitable school when children had to move from one placement to another.

Some children experienced a change of school as beneficial, but it was usually thought important to ensure continuity if this was possible – especially in cases where the child felt supported by the school and was well integrated with staff and peers. The social experience of school was considered important, and certainly it was a vital element in peer relationships. A service greatly appreciated by carers and some older children was the provision of *transport*, although this should not be regarded as an exclusively educational service as it was available for medical appointments, contact visits and other purposes as well. All these inputs had the possibility of contributing indirectly to children's achievements; but it is noticeable that:

- very little additional input, in terms of education, was actually concerned with cognitive skills.

This could conceivably have spin-offs in adolescence, as some of the young people who were excluded from school at a later stage appeared to be bored and under-achieving, and without suitable qualifications they had little prospect of finding satisfying employment in the adult world. (See also Biehal et al. 1995; Jackson 2001.)

Other activities

Youth Justice was suggested at reviews in two cases where children had become involved in absconding and offending, but the opportunities were not taken up. A number of suggestions were also made for children's leisure activities including attendance at clubs or special projects. Understandably, perhaps, one young man refused to join a 'multi-agency group for children with challenging behaviour'. Some activities did find favour with the young people, however, and particular favourites were:

- sports clubs – especially swimming or football;
- computer activities;
- a cadet troop;
- a support group for looked-after children;
- a car-mending project; and
- for younger children, holiday playschemes.

These were activities that fostered identity and self-esteem, and they were extremely valuable to the young people. Two children were given short-term help from an adult befriender, who gave them confidence as well as introducing them to new interests, and in another case two sisters were given an adult helper to assist them with making a complaint.

Three adolescent girls – all of them aged 15 at the time of the care order – were given some fairly basic *preparation for independent living*. In one case this had been written into the care plan, but for the other two young people it became necessary when it was clear that they could not stay where they were or return to live with their families. More preparation might have been appropriate, but the young people wanted to move into independent accommodation as soon as possible after reaching the age of 16, and consequently the preparation was rather brief. One girl was already pregnant. In all, there were four young women who were still subject to care orders and living independently at the close of the study – and one other who was in a semi-independent unit attached to a residential home.

- Once the young people were actually living on their own in the community or with friends, the contribution of the agency was usually limited to help with housing and financial support.

Attempts to make financial payments conditional, for example by requiring young people to adopt certain standards of self-care, did not usually succeed because the support could not reasonably be withdrawn. The help of trusted people was valued, however, and some social workers or residential carers managed to stay involved in a counselling role; but if a long-standing relationship had not been established there was little opportunity for social workers or carers to offer anything but material assistance at this stage. In all except legal terms, the care order had run its course.

Services for birth parents

Table 14.2 documents the services planned and provided for birth parents. Understandably, the parents who were expected to be looking after children at home had more recommendations for services at the time of the care order than parents who would be living apart from their children, and in fact those who had children living with them were offered nearly four times as many services as the others. In spite of this:

- the take-up of services by parents was only slightly better when children were placed at home than it was when children were in other placement options (52% as opposed to 50% elsewhere).

Table 14.2 ***Provision of services for birth parents****

	Services recommended in care plan[a]		Services recommended subsequent to care plan[b]		Total[c]	
	Recom-mended	Provided	Recom-mended	Provided	Recom-mended	Provided
Family work	6	0	1	0	7	0
Treatment project, child protection	2	0	–	–	2	0
Treatment project, alcohol or drugs	2	1	2	2	4	3
Alcohol or relationships counselling	5	2	4	3	9	5
Support group	6	3	1	1	7	4
Adoption counselling	9	5	6	5	15	10
Individual adult worker	9	4	–	–	9	4
Respite care	4	2	2	1	6	3
Help with housing	3	2	1	1	4	3
Financial help[d]	1	1	–	–	1	1
Total	**47**	**20**	**17**	**13**	**64**	**33**

* n=57

[a] Take up rate was 43%. [b] Take up rate was 76%.
[c] Take up rate was 52%. [d] Apart from playgroup fees and transport.

Since the focus was still on children's interests, the services for parents sometimes included work or treatment that had to be undertaken; but since there were usually no plans for family reunification after the care order, there was little incentive to embark on this task. An added disadvantage was that the agencies that were responsible for providing 'treatment', such as the NSPCC, Child and Family Guidance, residential projects, family centres and even hospital departments, had often been used in an assessment role during care proceedings. The fact that the outcome of the assessment had been negative made it less likely that the parent would see them or social services as a source of advice or assistance. As research on child protection has shown (Farmer and Owen 1995), many parents in these circumstances prefer to turn to their GPs for help.

Family work and treatment projects

As can be seen from Table 14.2, there was very poor take-up in the case of family work. In the care plans this applied most often to family therapy, but it also included specific pieces of work on parenting skills or contact.

- In some cases family work was not undertaken because the option had already been explored, or else the parents saw little point in exploring it. In others, there was difficulty in getting the whole family together or obtaining a slot at the local child and family guidance clinic.

There were two attempts to persuade parents to continue work on child protection issues. In both cases there were allegations of sexual abuse within the family or extended family, and fears that other children might be put at risk because the professionals' concerns were not understood or accepted by the birth parents. Since the existing children in both cases were to be adopted, the work was purely preventive; but once again there was no incentive for parents to continue working on the issues. Referrals to alcohol and drug treatment projects had a slightly better response. Out of the three mothers who accepted treatment, two were alcohol-abusing and had children placed at home with them. One other mother accepted treatment for drug misuse for a short period subsequent to the care order because she realised that this was in her interests, although she knew by that time that her child was to be adopted.

Counselling and support

Alcohol counselling

Alcohol counselling, as distinct from special treatment projects, was not readily available; this reflects the general lack of community-based provision for parents with alcohol-related difficulties. In one case where it was recommended in the care plan as a follow-up to intensive treatment there proved to be no local resource. One mother in another area was given counselling about her use of alcohol as well as other problems, but in general there was more demand for counselling which dealt with feelings or relationships. Two of the support groups that were attended did have an alcohol focus, but the others were purely social or else they were mainly concerned with parenting.

Support groups

The invitation to join support groups had a mixed response. Many birth parents were socially isolated and they also needed to experience the skill-sharing that support groups could provide; but they could not always identify with the people who formed the core of the group. One middle-class mother who abused alcohol refused to join a group because, in the estimation of her social worker, she could not identify with people she regarded as 'down-and-outs'. Family centre groups involving other mothers were popular with parents who had children at home; but a young woman with learning difficulties felt ill-at-ease in a group of ordinary mothers discussing parenting skills. She would perhaps have been more at home in a group for people with learning difficulties; but the object was to help her with childcare.

Relationship counselling

For parents who had had children removed, the most important service was relationship counselling. This was often seen as purely palliative by social workers; but in fact it was very much needed.

- Eight mothers gave birth to another child during the follow-up period, and in six of these cases the timing suggests that the child was conceived during care proceedings – probably around the time when it became clear that the child who was subject to interim care orders would not be allowed to return.

Immediate action was taken to protect the new children when they were born, and in most cases care proceedings were initiated once more; but the fact that the situation was now different meant that the case was dealt with by different social work personnel and sometimes in a different court (especially when the mother had moved from one region to another). This may have been in the interests of justice, and certainly there were indications that in at least two cases the mothers would be allowed to keep the new children; but the lack of support to them during care proceedings and the lack of therapeutic input afterwards may carry some of the blame for their initial distress.

Adoption counselling

The take-up of adoption counselling showed a similar pattern to the one recorded for relationship counselling, except that it was more pronounced. Out of nine cases in which it had been written into the care plan there were five cases in which the birth parents (usually the mother) made use of the service soon after the care order; but in five out of six cases where it was offered at a later stage there was immediate acceptance.

- The offer of adoption counselling was most acceptable at the point when the child was being placed with new carers, or when the application for the adoption order was being submitted to the court.

These were of course occasions that brought the agency into contact with the birth parent, perhaps for the first time since the care order or the 'goodbye visit', because there was a need to give or receive information about the child. For the birth parent, these events provoked an upsurge of grief. Whether or not they engaged in adoption counselling, there is some evidence that they derived consolation from social workers who were sensitive to these issues.

Support from an adult worker

There were nine cases in which social services wished to see the birth parent given help from an adult worker, either because of precarious mental health (seven cases) or learning difficulties (two cases). Only four of these nine recommendations were fulfilled.

- Support from an adult worker such as a community psychiatric nurse was considered justifiable only if a parent could be classed as mentally ill or with severe learning difficulties, but most birth parents who fitted this description were already receiving help from an adult worker before the order.

Other services

Parents with children at home were provided with three services that were not usually available to the others, namely respite care, help with housing and financial support. Surprisingly, the offer of respite care was not always taken up. Nursery or playgroup performed a similar function, and at other times the parents wanted their children to be with them or else they mistrusted the provision, seeing it as part of the apparatus of social services.

- Respite care was welcomed by the birth parents who used it, but it was not always well monitored by social services, and consequently there were reports that birth parents misused it and that children found it rejecting.

Help with *housing and finances* was valued by birth parents who were looking after children, although opportunities to help in this area were limited by budgetary and other restrictions. With the exception of playgroup fees and transport costs, there was only one care plan which specifically mentioned financial help as a service for the birth parent, although the files indicate that a string of small payments was often necessary because many parents were operating on or below the poverty line. The agency did not manage to share these aspects of parental responsibility and, not wishing to undermine the parent's responsibility, they did not choose to do so; yet when children had been removed from home, the cost of their upkeep was considerable.

Services for birth parents: the consumer view

The main criticism of the services offered was that they did not provide enough support, or else that they offered support of the wrong sort. Some were seen as making demands and imposing further burdens, when parents felt that they had reached 'the end of the line'.

> I know that their main priority is the child, and to me that is the way it should be; but it is always the child, if you know what I mean. They see this road that they want to go down and they won't come off it for anyone ... When I sought their help, they said that they couldn't help me, that they didn't have the power to help.

Some of the parents who were interviewed in the aftermath of the order showed extreme levels of stress. In the analysis of the General Health Questionnaire (see Appendix 2), the highest stress scores and the greatest number of high scores were found in the forms completed by birth parents. (The adopters had the least number, and foster carers proved to be an intermediate group.) This is hardly surprising since the birth parents interviewed had suffered the loss of their children, and some were worried about patterns of absconding or changes to the care plan; but parents themselves mentioned additional sources of stress unconnected with their children, such as divorce, illness or social isolation. There was a high rate of physical illness in the group.

The birth parents' take-up of relationship counselling was better than that recorded for any other service with the exception of adoption counselling, but it was offered to fewer than one parent in five and taken up by one parent in ten. Parents were not limited to the facilities provided by social services, of course. Two parents obtained counselling by way of their GPs, and another through friends at work; but several parents who needed it were receiving no service at all.

Mothers, who were often single parents, were the main recipients of counselling. However, it should be noted from the interviews that a number of *fathers* were seriously distressed and receiving no input. The mother of a disabled child said that her estranged husband had never fully recovered from the shock of the child's birth, and the remarks of two other birth fathers indicate the particular problems of men seeking help and support when they were separated from their children:

> I could do with it [counselling], I think. I don't know where I am going and I feel that every road that I am taking seems to be the wrong turning. I get so far down and I have to turn back and find another route.

> I never had anyone to talk to. Being a bloke, it is more awkward. You can't go with a mate and sit in the pub and tell them all about it.

When GPs were approached for help they sometimes responded by prescribing antidepressants or other drugs, which were capable of being misunderstood and misused. A father who had clearly been depressed for some time complained that the medication did nothing but put him to sleep.

> I have rejected a lot of medication off the doctor or I have taken it off him. I have got it home and I have tried one tablet and if it has not worked – if it hasn't done anything for me – I have left the packet in the cupboard and eventually thrown them out.

A mother who was a drug-user revealed another down-side of treatment by prescription: 'There's always loads of people quite ready and willing and able to buy medication from you, which enables you to go and buy stuff on the street.'

The people who complained most often about lack of services were parents whose children had been removed. As a group, they tended to be alienated and dissatisfied. However, they did need therapeutic input and they also needed practical assistance when children visited them. For example, one mother found her scarce resources depleted when her children returned from foster care to stay with her, and she also needed help in getting the boys to school. The mother whose child was badly disabled refused counselling or membership of a support group, but she would have liked help with installing a ramp for the child's wheel chair and more taxi fares to visit friends, in order to avoid having to carry the heavy 6-year-old child on the bus.

The fact that no financial support was given to parents who were not current carers was a source of grief to some. When they were living on social security benefits, they felt that it was difficult for them to match the standards set by foster carers, and the situation was potentially invidious. At the same time they did not always know what services the children were receiving in foster homes or residential units. Some parents would not have been able to complain about the standard of care if it had been inadequate, because they were content to take it on trust that the children were receiving all that was necessary.

Services for carers

Services for carers were not well documented in the care plans, but in spite of this they were offered and received during the follow-up period. They can be divided into two categories. First, there were those that were short term and designed to get the placement started. Second, there were ongoing services to help the carers cope with newly arising problems.

Services to get the placement 'off the ground'

Most of the services offered to kinship carers and adopters in the initial stages, and some of those available for foster carers, were essentially short term. The carers were encouraged to seek access to community facilities in their own right. For example birth fathers taking over the care of children for the first time were helped to liaise with the school and with medical authorities. Visits by the health visitor were established. Hospital appointments were set up. In the long term it was expected that social work input would become less and in some cases the care order itself would be discharged.

Help with housing

Help with housing was an important short-term input, particularly for kinship carers who were living in rented accommodation and had low incomes.

- The social worker acted as advocate with the local council in cases where carers needed more rooms to accommodate the children; but the choice of accommodation was limited and not always very suitable.

One birth father and his partner were offered a flat on the thirteenth floor of a block of flats in an area frequented by drug addicts – a very unsuitable choice in view of the fact that the mother's substance abuse was the main reason for the care order. Another birth father with two small children had to accept a top floor flat on a main road site because it had the requisite number of bedrooms and no alternatives were available. The need for extra accommodation was not confined to council tenants, of course. Assistance with home extension (for example by means of loft conversion) was requested by foster carers in two cases so that more children could be fostered. In the first case financial assistance was offered in the form of a loan which would have to be paid back, and in the second case the local authority agreed to help with the costs of dividing a room to prevent two children having to share. All other costs had to be met from the carers' capital or from allowances.

Equipment grants and financial help

Most kinship carers, adopters and some of the foster carers received an equipment grant of less than £500 for furniture, bedding and essential items when the child moved in. In addition, an allowance was paid where appropriate (see below).

- Financial help for adopters included provision for legal costs where the adoption was likely to be contested. This was greatly valued, partly because it guaranteed the support of social services during the adoption hearing.

A mileage allowance was also paid for adopters to visit foster homes or attend meetings at the social work office and, rather exceptionally, a motor vehicle was provided for a couple who were intending to adopt a large sibling group.

Family support workers

Short-term family support workers were offered in two cases where kinship carers had financial or relationship problems. In a few other cases where it was felt that the carers might have trouble with children's behaviour, a short period of consultancy was provided by hospital-based psychologists or psychiatrists. As already reported, the main aim was to facilitate decision-making and stabilise the placement; but where assessment was combined with therapeutic input for the children this did seem to be effective, and a valuable feature was that it could be reinstated at a later stage if this was necessary.

Ongoing services

Respite care

As was common in the case of birth parents, respite care was regularly available but not always taken up by carers. They sometimes felt that it was in the children's interests to limit the number of carers, at least temporarily, to create a greater feeling of stability. The offer of respite care was not unwelcome, however. Apart from anything else, they were glad to know that there was a back-stop in case of illness. Foster carers were often the people who could benefit most from respite care, since it helped to ease the pressure, and the effect could be one of 'shared care'. This was successfully used in the case of a disabled child, and it could provide a model for use in other cases.

Visits to carers by social workers

During the period of the study, most carers including adopters received regular visits from the family placement officer, but the social workers who visited the placements most regularly were the children's social workers, who were primarily concerned to ensure that the environment was right from the point of view of the child's welfare.[2] This did not mean that they were unsympathetic to the new parents, however. Adopters reported that much of the advice that was given was concerned with the welfare of other children in the family, because it was realised that if an existing child felt displaced or rejected, the placement would be less stable.

Support groups and training

Most adopters had information about support groups such as those run by Parent to Parent Information Adoption on Services, although they did not often use them. They valued the help given during initial training, but they wanted to move on from it to what they considered 'normal parenting'. Support groups were also available for foster carers, and although some attended regularly, others found it difficult to attend because the group meetings took place in evenings and the carers had baby-sitting problems. There were informal links between foster carers, which often seemed to serve a similar purpose. Being employees of social services, foster carers also had the opportunity to attend training sessions on particular topics – and of course they received a regular allowance, which was a benefit not available to all carers, although the financial demands made by caring for difficult children frequently left them out of pocket.

The provision of allowances

Allowances of all sorts – that is, fostering, adoption and residence allowances – were not always mentioned in the care plan, but we have details of them from the file studies and from carers' interviews. They were clearly an important form of input to the placement, but there were considerable inconsistencies both in the amounts offered and in the methods of allocation.

Payment for childcare has always been kept at a low level, because of the fear that people would undertake the work for the wrong reasons (Hill et al. 1989; Rhodes 1993). According to the carers, the standard rates for foster care and residence allowances were scarcely adequate to pay for the child's keep and a few 'basic' extras. Adoption allowances were means-tested, but their main function was not to increase the adopters' income. According to Vol. 9 of *The Children Act 1989: Guidance and Regulations:* 'An adoption allowance may be payable to help secure a suitable adoption where a child cannot be readily adopted because of a financial obstacle' (DoH 1991b).

'Financial obstacles' included the cost of bringing up a difficult child. A small baby who was considered to be without problems and easy to place attracted no adoption allowance, even if the adopter's income was rather small. In foster care too, where the carers were paid regularly, specialist fostering or 'project care' for hard-to-place adolescents was funded at a higher rate. One county authority had a scale of increments for foster carers based on experience, and this meant that extra money could sometimes be found to upgrade and stabilise a difficult placement.

The overt aim of all allowance-giving was to facilitate placements for the most needy children; but there were built-in rewards for competence and also a strong element of compensatory justice. Some of the payments made in our study were compensation for real costs incurred by the carer, in financial and in emotional terms.

Allowances for kinship carers

At the close of the study slightly less than half of the children looked after by members of the extended family and friends (eight out of eighteen) were living in households where the carer had an allowance, but it was usually a residence allowance rather than a fostering one. The carers for the other ten children paid for all expenses out of their income.[3]

On what grounds were fostering allowances given to kinship carers? The first criterion appeared to be the nature of the relationship between the child and the carer, since birth fathers were not usually given allowances – presumably because they had parental responsibility and were expected to exercise it. Aunts and grandmothers were usually made foster carers, but not in every case. For example there was no allowance in one case where a 4-year-old child was joining her aunt's family, probably because the child wanted to be the same as the other children in the family and the intention of the carer was to adopt her. In another case where two children had moved into their father's household, the social worker managed to obtain permission for the carers to receive a residence allowance at the point where they were applying for a residence order. This was certainly unusual, given that the designated carer was the children's father; but it was recognised that the day-to-day care of the children would be done by his partner, who was unrelated to the children, and the two boys were exhibiting very difficult behaviour, which would have made them hard to place in foster care.

In cases like the one above, the social worker had to negotiate strongly with senior management on the carers' behalf. In a very similar case in a different local authority, the birth father who, with his partner, took over the care of his 9-year-old daughter, said that 'it took them six months to sort out financial help'. (The reason was apparently that the child's mother was still claiming child benefit.) When an allowance was given, the carers found it less than generous: 'They eventually started giving me £50 a week, and then when they decided that I didn't need £50 they knocked it down to £30. Once we had the residence order, they knocked it on the head altogether.'

Fostering allowances

The standard fostering allowance varied according to the age of the child. Among the foster carers interviewed the rates varied from £57 a week to over £100, but the average was between £70 and £80 per week unless the allowance was enhanced. There were special additions for clothing such as school uniforms, or holidays, or the purchase of a bicycle, but most foster carers found that there were times when they contributed money from their own income – especially when the child was growing quickly, which meant that more had to be spent on items such as winter clothes and shoes. Most foster carers were happy to do this, since they regarded the child as a member of their family even if the period of stay was only temporary, and one couple said that they did not 'keep a balance sheet'. On the whole, periods of high expenditure such as the start of a school term were balanced by periods when less was needed; but some children were destructive, with the result that household items were constantly having to be replaced: 'You don't make anything out of it. You just keep your head above water.' In addition, some foster carers worried about the possibility of redundancy or serious illness, because they knew that the social services department had no contingencies to help out.

Adoption allowances

During the period of the research adoption allowances were awarded in only two cases, one of which involved a sibling pair and the other a small child with behavioural difficulties. In two other cases the allowances were declared payable in principle, which meant that if the adopters were to suffer a drop in income (for example by reason of redundancy) an adoption allowance would then become payable.

All the children in these particular cases were more than 2 years old at the time of the court hearing, and they were aged between 3 and 5 when placed for adoption. The age of the child was clearly an important factor in the awarding of allowances. As we have seen, increasing age tended to be accompanied by an increased number of problems in adoptees, and children over the age of 3 were regarded as hard to place. More allowances would probably have been awarded, at least in principle, when the remaining children were found placements, as the children who were still waiting at the end of our study were all older children and some of them were in sibling groups.

The adopters tended to be middle-class people, many of whom had good incomes, and not all of them were interested in receiving financial help from social services. It is probably significant that the only adopter who was interviewed and who really felt the lack of an allowance was a single woman. She had to arrange childcare at a private nursery because she lived outside the district covered by the agency. It is clear that she felt inadequately supported in emotional as well as financial terms, and her experience reinforces the view that single adopters are not always given the support they need and deserve (Owen 1999). For married adopters, and especially those who had professional backgrounds, it was easier to campaign for whatever help was required.

Services for carers: the consumer view

Stress levels of carers and their need for emotional support

The interviews with carers of all types suggest that some of them were working with high levels of stress, even though it was less than the birth parents experienced. According to the General Health Questionnaires, which were completed during the interviews, two of the eleven adopters, six of the eighteen foster carers and three of the ten kinship carers had levels of stress that were over the lowest threshold. (For details of the test see Appendix 2.)

Seven of the people with high stress scores (one adopter and six foster carers) were looking after particularly difficult children. In three of these foster homes the children were being cared for short term, and in another two households there had recently been an upsetting change of plan. It is interesting to notice that in five of these cases the children themselves made poor welfare progress according to our measurements of outcome. However, the carers did not always attribute stress directly to children's behaviour. Physical illness was a factor; for example, the adopter with a high stress score had recently discovered that she had cancer. One foster carer said that she had 'always been nervy and lacked confidence' and another said 'I get too attached to these children and then they go; so why I do pre-adoption placements I don't know'.

In spite of the stress attached to their job the carers seemed to have fewer unmet needs for emotional support than the birth parents had. They had been admitted to a relationship of partnership with social services. In fact, the overall impression is that social services were now working with the carers rather than with the birth parents, and it was in this worker–carer relationship that the ideals of partnership in the Children Act were most clearly fulfilled.

One foster carer put things in a nutshell when she said: 'They [the birth parents] haven't had any say in things to do with Derek. It has been social services and us.'

The need for advice on children's behaviour

Carers varied in the amount of advice they wanted about children's behaviour. Kinship carers and adopters tended to see themselves as autonomous and they generally wanted to be left alone to 'get on with the job'; but most foster carers welcomed official support – although they could be quite hesitant about seeking it, as this quotation from a recently approved foster carer shows.

> Some things aren't actually explained very well about the system. You are left to find out yourself. And my wife will hardly ever phone up because she thinks she mustn't interrupt, or social workers are very busy – they haven't got time. The emphasis has always been on social services, how busy they are, you know, how much they are stretched – which is great, but you can't afford to become one of the people that everything is stretched for. You have to if necessary keep phoning up to get answers or put time limits on things.

Valuing prompt attention to difficulties

What people most valued was prompt attention to difficulties. There was praise for the workers who responded quickly to reports of problems or requests for help, and conversely the social workers who attracted most criticism were dilatory or unreliable about making contact and keeping appointments. Carers of all types disliked having to leave messages on voicemail and finding that the messages were unanswered. They liked to feel that there was 'someone on the other end of the phone'.

There was a lot of praise for family placement officers in this respect. They were experienced as friendly, sympathetic and helpful. One foster carer said that her placement officer often rang from her home in the evening if she had not had time to answer a call for help during the day, and some workers gave carers their home number because they were willing to be contacted out of hours. The carers felt that they were on duty 24 hours a day, and they were also aware that a difficult situation could escalate quickly to the point where it was out of control.

One foster mother spoke of previous attempts to control teenage violence by calling in the police:

> I have had kids here that have literally smashed their fists through the wall, taken every single thing out of their drawers and wardrobe and barricaded themselves in, and I have actually had to ring the police. I have had two big policemen come down here and one will talk to me maybe because I am a bit upset. The other would force his way in and talk to the boy ...

She called in the police because she felt that she needed someone to take her part, although she also realised that this was only a temporary measure: 'As soon as the situation is calm they go, and you have got the kid saying: "Ha. I told you they wouldn't do anything." Then you are back to square one.'

Consultancy: the need for specialised information

Formal consultancy was useful if it helped carers to understand the roots of children's problems, but if actual strategies were suggested they had to be realistic and effective. Consultancy worked best if it was hospital-based, if it was available on demand and over a period of time rather than short term or 'one-off', and especially if it was combined with therapeutic input for the children.

Like several other carers, a young woman who adopted a baby less than 1 year old had a need for specialised information. She said that as far as the normal process of bringing up a child is concerned 'you just lean back on stuff that you have learnt throughout your life'. However, she knew that the child's mother had used crack cocaine during her pregnancy and she worried about possible damage to the child. When asked what information she would have liked from the social worker, she said:

> I think stuff about the type of drugs the mother was using, what the possibilities could be and what signs you could look for. All the information I got about crack cocaine and its effects in children I have found for myself. I took the time to go on the internet to find out information, to satisfy myself that if anything did come up I would be able to deal with it.

She was reassured to discover that drug problems in later life were not necessarily linked to heredity, but she still worried about the possibility of the child having educational needs or even mental health difficulties. She wanted to be told about 'things that you should look for in behavioural problems – whether it was to do with drugs or other things'.

The problem of sexual abuse

Another problem that carers wanted to know more about was sexual abuse. The after-effects of this problem affected foster parents, adopters and residential carers alike. What they most needed, apart from an understanding of sexual abuse and its after-effects, was information about the children's backgrounds, and this had not always been given to them. (See also Farmer and Pollock 1998.) However, the carers felt that they had usually been given all the information that was available *at the time*. Disclosures of sexual abuse happened after the placement in five cases, three of which involved sibling groups. There were many more cases in which other forms of maltreatment were described, but foster carers were particularly disturbed by revelations of sexual abuse if they were inexperienced carers.

> I think the biggest thing was the sexual abuse. It didn't occur to me at all. I just assumed that because he [the father] had abused an older boy that boys would have been his preference and girls would have been well out of it ... which obviously wasn't the case and it was a real shock when I found them practising on each other ... I don't think I dealt with it very well in the beginning, but you get more confident as you go on.

In situations such as this, the children were helped by counselling and 'keep safe' work at the family centre, in addition to further training offered to the carer. Consideration also had to be given to the impact on the carers' own children, who were shocked and dismayed by the revelations of abuse. It seems likely that similar problems would have to be dealt with by the adopters of older children, perhaps with the aid of post-adoption support (Lowe et al. 1999).

Carers' hopes for the future

Given the narrow boundaries within which they had to work and the day-to-day events with which they had to become preoccupied, it is praiseworthy that so many carers managed to retain a perspective that was realistic and cautious without being totally despairing. Being service-givers as well as service-users, they were also capable of taking modest pleasure in their own achievements.

Here is how one foster carer expressed his hopes and fears for a disturbed 3-year-old boy whose home placement had recently broken down.

> Without being arrogant, we believe that we've given that lad six months that he's never had. Hopefully it'll be a valuable resource for him in the future. I'm not that confident that he'll get what he really needs ... I've got this dread that he is going to be lost in the system and the system will fail him for reasons that aren't his fault – and he's got so much to offer. I've got concerns that as a society we won't quite do what we need to do at each stage. I hope I'm wrong.

Discussion and conclusions

The 86% take-up of services for children is encouraging, although it was not matched by the take-up of services for birth parents (52% overall). Quite understandably, many of the birth parents felt alienated from social services as a result of care proceedings; but they had an unmet need for therapeutic input (as demonstrated, for example, by the number of mothers who became pregnant again in an attempt to replace lost children) and it is also of concern to find that the rate of parental take-up of services was little better when the parents had children placed at home with them. The fact that some services were offered and taken up at a later date, however, indicates the value of involving parents as well as children in ongoing reviews. The high stress levels recorded in the General Health Questionnaires indicate a need for support, not only for parents but for carers as well.

Were there any areas in which the provision of services could be improved? For birth parents without children at home, the main need was for supportive counselling and help with relationship problems. Carers, too, needed emotional support, but they also required access to specific information and help in dealing with challenging behaviour – especially when sexual abuse or violence was involved – and the research uncovered a need for a more consistent and generous system of allowances than was currently afforded them. For children, the main needs were in the areas of education and EBD. As was noted in Chapter 3, more than half the children had difficulties in these areas at the start of the care order and, as recorded in Chapter 8, these problems were also significantly related to failure to implement the placements. In both areas multi-agency support was required, since health and education services were involved. In theory the necessary co-operation existed – but the actual provision of services was hampered by delays, by budgetary restrictions, and by a focus on assessment rather than treatment.

Services, like contact arrangements, were often geared to supporting placements or finding and consolidating new ones. For example, private tuition was given to make children more adoptable, and assessment of children's behaviour was justified as part of decision-making and legal processes. Important as these aims may be, we must ask whether more services could have been provided as an appropriate response to the needs of children – and whether the children's welfare outcomes might have been better in some cases if this had been done.

Summary

1 The overall take-up of services for children was fairly constant – around 86% – whether they were offered at the time of the care order or subsequently. The use of services by birth parents was less good (an average of 52%). The parents who had children living with them were offered four times as many services as the others, but the take-up of services for birth parents was only slightly better when children were placed at home than when they were placed elsewhere.

2 Almost half the children in the sample received some form of therapy. Psychotherapy was offered to a few adolescents but it was expensive, difficult to obtain and associated with the stigma of mental illness. Counselling, life-story work and art or play therapy were more readily available and had a good rate of take-up, although the quality was variable and some children had no more than two or three sessions at the family centre.

3 Educational services were mainly delivered via 'statementing' – the gateway to special schooling or welfare assistance in the classroom. For pre-school children, the provision of nursery or playgroup experience had 100% take-up; but adolescents had the most serious problems and they often needed help to attend school. Holiday playschemes and some special projects were popular with children in middle childhood.

4 Assessment or treatment of children's behavioural difficulties was usually undertaken for some official purpose – for example because a court hearing was imminent or because it had been requested by the adoption panel.

5 In the analysis of General Health Questionnaires, the highest stress scores and the greatest number of high scores were found in the forms

completed by birth parents. The adopters had the least number, and foster carers proved to be an intermediate group.

6 There was a relationship of partnership between social services and the carers. In spite of the fact that some carers showed considerable levels of stress, they generally felt trusted and valued. Stress was associated with physical illness, with looking after children whose behaviour was very difficult, or with difficult situations such as those engendered by changes in the care plan. It is noticeable that in these cases the children's welfare outcome scores were also poor.

---

[1] On one social services file there was a letter from a clinic offering an appointment for a foster carer and her children, but by the time this letter arrived the placement had broken down several months previously and the children had moved on.

[2] In the case of adoption placements, this support would end when the adoption order was made, but there was no indication that it would be followed by post-adoption support unless this was specifically requested by the carer.

[3] Under the terms of the Adoption and Children Act 2002, kinship carers may now apply for a special guardianship order. If this is granted, local authorities will then be under a duty to make arrangements for support services, which may include financial support. Another recent change is that since the judicial review of Manchester City Council's policy on allowances (the Munby judgement) payments to friends and relatives must be on the same basis as payments to stranger carers.

Part

V Welfare outcomes

15 How the children fared at the end of the study

Introduction

Safeguarding and helping to bring about improvements in child welfare are two of the most important and challenging tasks for those with responsibility for children on care orders. The challenge derives from many different sources. First is the sharp rise in public expectations and ambitions for children who are looked after by the state. Second is the research evidence showing the complexity of the task. Any effort to bring about change and maintain progress needs to take account of a range of factors as well as their interaction and inter-dependency. Yet our knowledge often allows us only to chart the links between different facets of welfare without fully understanding the causal and non-causal relationships involved.

Despite these difficulties, the importance of rising to the various challenges cannot be overstated. For although there is good evidence of the dramatic impact of 'turning points' in life that can overcome childhood adversity and set up a 'virtuous circle', so too is there much work showing the worrying continuities between childhood and adult disadvantage, especially for children in public care (Quinton and Rutter 1988; Stein 1989; Biehal et al. 1995; Jackson 2001; Rutter 2001).

In this chapter we explore the extent to which children were able to maintain or improve their psychosocial functioning over the 21 months following the care order. As outlined in Chapter 1 (see Figure 1.1), both implementation and outcome may be influenced by a range of circumstances, which include child factors, family factors and organisational factors – and a key factor contributing to the children's outcome may be the implementation of the care plan itself, which is considered separately in Chapter 17. In this chapter we address the two aspects of welfare outcome described in Chapter 2. The first part of the chapter deals with welfare progress, and the second with welfare status. Information in both these areas is needed to help make the care order act as a positive turning point in both the short and longer term.

Outcome measure 1: welfare progress

Children's progress over time

As described in Chapter 2, the Looking After Children framework provided a basis for our two measures of welfare outcome. First, we studied the direction of change in the child's welfare over the 21 months of the follow-up period (*welfare progress.*) Second, we studied the child's standard of welfare at the end point and asked what deficits or unmet needs still persisted on each of the seven dimensions (*welfare status.*)

The changes in children's welfare progress during the period of the study allowed for four possibilities:

- normal progress;
- improvement;
- persistence of problems; and
- deterioration.

Normal progress and improvement were both positive outcomes, the first being enjoyed by children who did not have initial problems while the second meant that children with pre-existing problems had improved. Persistence of problems meant that there had been no improvement in children's initial difficulties. Deterioration was recorded when existing problems worsened or new ones developed.

When we combined the above categories in order to make more global judgements, normal progress and improvement were both treated as good outcomes but persistence of problems and deterioration were considered to be poor outcomes. By counting the number of dimensions on which each individual child had made good progress, we arrived at a score out of 7. A child who had maintained normal progress or made improvements on at least six of the seven dimensions had clearly done well; but a researcher judgement was made that those with scores of 4 out of 7 or less had done badly, and scrutiny of the cases confirmed that areas central to the child's welfare had been affected. Those who scored five out of seven constituted an intermediate group with a mixture of positives and negatives.

When these overall scores for welfare progress were considered, the children in the sample fell into three divisions, as shown in Table 15.1.

Table 15.1 ***Children's overall welfare progress***

Degree of progress	Number of children
Good	55
Mixed	12
Poor	33
Total	**100**

These results are encouraging inasmuch as a higher proportion of children made good progress than poor progress over the 21 months, but to understand the nature of the changes over time, we need to look at the scores for individual dimensions of welfare.

Welfare progress by dimension

Table 15.2 gives the more detailed findings from which the overall scores were derived, showing the number and percentage of children who made different types of welfare progress.

Table 15.2 ***Children's welfare progress by LAC areas of welfare***

Area of welfare[a]	Number making normal progress	Number showing improvement	Number where problems persisted	Number showing deterioration
Health	54	28	15	3
Education	48	27	19	6
Identity	50	21	18	10
Family and social relationships	22	45	22	11
Social presentation	64	24	10	1
EBD	31	28	33	8
Self-care	70	14	15	0

n=100

[a] In the case of one extremely disabled child it was impossible to make realistic judgements about her sense of identity, social presentation or self-care skills, and consequently the rating for this particular child was 'not applicable' on these dimensions.

Table 15.2 distinguishes good from poor progress, but it also makes it possible to identify whether good outcomes were achieved by 'normal progress' or by 'improvement'. For example, normal progress accounted for most of the good results in social presentation and self-care skills since comparatively few children started with deficits in these areas. By contrast:

- although 22 children were able to progress well in family and social relationships through 'normal progress', more than twice this number owed their good outcome to 'improvement'.

Similarly, it is useful to separate the proportions of children who made poor progress because of enduring problems from those whose welfare actually deteriorated. Some initial difficulties proved difficult to shift. For example:

- there were 33 children (one-third of the sample) who made poor progress in emotional and behavioural development because initial difficulties persisted, and in another eight cases the problems got worse.

It is perhaps encouraging to note that where the outcome in terms of change was poor, 'persistence of problems' was much more common than 'deterioration'. Nevertheless, it is of concern that 10% of the sample had a deteriorating sense of identity, while 11% showed deterioration in their family and social relationships during the 21 months after the care order was made.

Statistical analysis of factors associated with welfare progress

As was reported in Chapter 8, statistical analysis formed part of our study of placement implementation. At a later stage, statistical analysis was carried out to identify the main factors associated with outcome. Demonstrating an association does not of course prove any causal linkage but it still provides valuable information, for it highlights patterns that are potentially important for policy-makers and practitioners as well as providing a basis for further studies.

Ordinal logistic regression was used to investigate the relationship between a number of 'inputs' or explanatory variables and welfare progress.[1] Statistically significant factors were:

- the number of moves made by the child;
- the permanence of the placement;

- the child's age at final hearing; and
- the number and type of the child's initial problems.

Somewhat unexpectedly, the time between the making of the care order and the final placement move was not significantly related to overall welfare progress ($p = 0.51$). However, a longer time spent between the care order and the last move was associated with worse progress in family and social relationships (odds ratio = 0.92, $p = 0.011$, 95% CI from 0.87 to 0.98). This suggests that there is some justification for the concerns that have been expressed about delays in placement-finding.

The number of moves made by the children

The odds of poor overall welfare progress increased with the number of moves made by the children. Indeed this held true for each extra move (odds ratio 1.53, $p = 0.001$, 95% CI from 1.19 to 1.98).[2] However, as can be seen from the detailed results in Table 15.3, a great many children who made one move had good outcomes because it was necessary for them to make a single move into the promised placement. The relationship between the number of moves and welfare outcome emerges more strongly when we consider two moves or more.

Table 15.3 ***Moves and children's welfare progress***

Outcome	**Number of moves**					
	0	**1**	**2**	**3**	**4**	**6**
Poor	12	7	7	1	1	5
Mixed	6	3	1	2	–	–
Good	19	25	9	2	–	–

The permanence of the placement

The permanence of the placement was associated with good welfare progress. When placements were divided into two umbrella categories – temporary and permanent – it was found that children living in temporary placements were significantly less likely to make good progress than those in placements classified as permanent ($p < 0.001$, odds ratio = 11.14, 95% CI from 4.43 to 28.01).[3] More sensitive results were obtained by using the permanency scale described in Chapter 8. Each drop in the level of permanency represented by points on this scale was associated with poorer progress ($p < 0.001$, odds ratio = 2.19, 95% CI from 1.76 to 2.72).

The child's age at final hearing

As predicted, the child's age at final hearing was extremely important. Increased age was associated with reduced odds of good welfare progress ($p = 0.004$, odds ratio = 0.87, 95% CI from 0.79 to 0.95). Similar results were found for the length of social services involvement, which was closely related to age. Gender, on the other hand, seemed to have no significant effect ($p = 0.22$). There were insufficient non-white children to assess whether there were any statistically significant differences related to ethnicity.

Whether the child was listed on the child protection register

Whether or not the child was previously listed on the child protection register was not significantly related to welfare progress ($p = 0.47$), although sexual abuse previously suffered by the child did have an association with poor progress that fell just short of statistical significance ($p = 0.07$). There was no significant relationship between welfare progress and time spent on the child protection register prior to proceedings ($p = 0.59$), or the number of periods looked after prior to the final hearing ($p = 0.19$), or the time from first application to final hearing ($p = 0.92$).

The number and type of children's initial problems

The number of children's initial problems proved to be an important predictor of progress. As these increased, so the prospects of good progress diminished ($p < 0.001$, odds ratio = 0.58, 95% CI from 0.45 to 0.74). It is hardly surprising that statistical analysis should find an association between the *number* of initial problems and poor welfare progress (Kendall's tau-b = 0.44). However, there was also a relationship between most *individual baseline problems* and global welfare progress. Using ordinal logistic regression, it was found that the odds of poor overall progress increased if there were initial problems in the following areas:

- education (odds ratio = 5.95, $p < 0.001$);
- identity (odds ratio = 4.52, $p = 0.002$);
- family and social relationships (odds ratio = 5.31, $p = 0.001$);
- emotional and behavioural development (odds ratio = 38.38, $p < 0.001$); and
- self-care skills (odds ratio = 2.78, $p = 0.03$).

Other factors associated with poor overall progress

Interestingly, there was no significant relationship between global welfare progress and health ($p = 0.15$) or social presentation ($p = 0.14$); but it can be seen that initial difficulties in education, family relationships and identity – and, most importantly, emotional and behavioural development – were all associated with poor overall progress. These results remind us that we need to look beyond the incidence of improvement or lack of improvement on individual dimensions if we are to understand children's welfare progress as a whole. Initial difficulties have a differential impact on children's functioning – and the positive corollary to this is that amelioration, even in one of these key dimensions, carries with it the possibility that children's total welfare will be improved.

The extent to which children with problems improved

Normal progress was enjoyed by children who had not developed problems; but while the carers deserve credit for the fact that the children remained relatively problem-free, the task they undertook was different from the task of those who cared for 'troubled and troublesome' children. To understand the progress of the most vulnerable children under the care order, we need to consider the extent to which children had improved in the face of pre-existing difficulties.

Chapter 3 contained details of the children's baseline problems by dimension. Figure 15.1 presents the same information, but superimposed on it are the numbers of cases in which these problems improved during the course of the study.

The problems that showed the greatest rate of improvement were in *social presentation* (69% improved). Deficits in children's appearance and social behaviour, stemming from neglect prior to the care order, were probably relatively easy to address; but nevertheless social presentation can have an impact on other aspects of welfare such as relationships and self-esteem, and for individual children small changes in this area could be important. *Health problems* also showed a good rate of improvement (61%), and although some of these were relatively minor (for example, defects in sight or speech or hearing), their treatment made a distinct contribution to children's welfare.

Figure 15.1 ***Children with initial difficulties and improvement in each LAC area of welfare at 21 months***

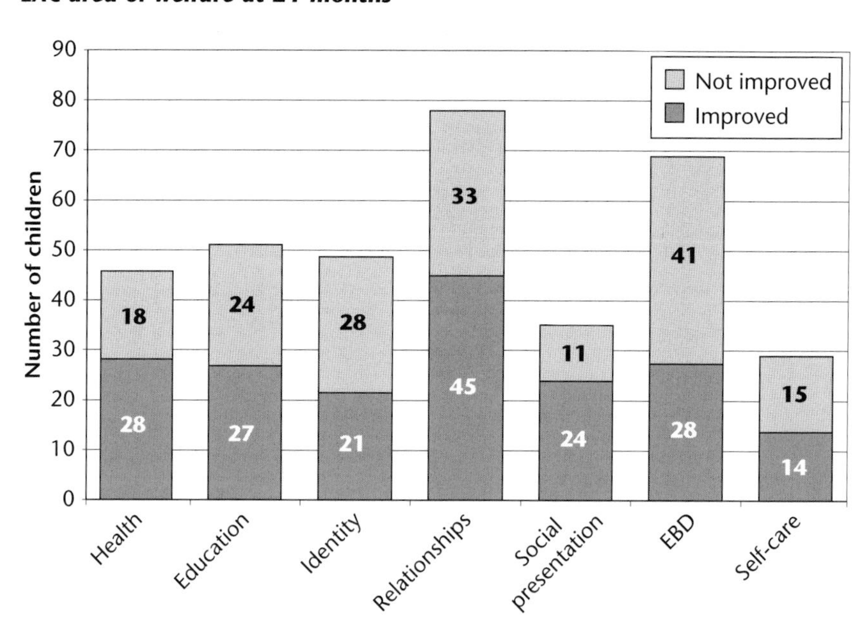

Educational problems improved in 53% of cases and *self-care skills* in 48%. (These two were related, since many deficiencies in children's self-care skills could be traced to learning difficulties.) Children's *sense of identity* was improved in only 43% of cases and, while in many cases this reflected children's lack of understanding and acceptance of the changes to which they had been subject, poor progress in this area can often be attributed to low self-esteem. (See the analysis of 'deficits' later in this chapter.)

The overall importance of initial problems of course depends on their incidence in the sample. It is interesting to note that:

- the problems that were numerically the largest at the time of the care order – that is, problems in family and social relationships, which had been identified as present in 78% of the sample – were subject to amelioration in 58% of cases; and
- the problems most resistant to change were emotional and behavioural difficulties, which had also been very numerous (present in 69% of the sample) but showed an improvement rate of only 41%.[4]

Outcome measure 2: welfare status

The progress data reported above indicate whether children had maintained their course, improved or deteriorated during the follow-up period, but they say little about the point that children had reached. As outlined in Chapter 2, a judgement about welfare status was necessary in order to establish how far children met or fell short of the welfare standards implicit in the LAC schedules.

There was a clear link between welfare progress and welfare status. We found that at the end point of the study the children with the best welfare progress scores had the fewest welfare 'deficits' or unmet needs, and the converse was also true. However:

- the well-being of many children had improved since the time of the care order and yet they still fell short of an adequate standard of welfare.

Table 15.4 shows that at the end of the study 40% of children had moderate to severe deficits in family and social relationships or emotional and behavioural development, and 30% in education.

When we look back to the list of initial problems in Chapter 3 and compare this with final deficits, it is possible to see how far children's difficulties remain or have been eradicated during the post-order period. Placement choice was one of the intervening variables. On key dimensions such as identity, family and social relationships and EBD, the children with adoption plans reached a better standard of welfare than those with fostering plans and their welfare was considerably better than those whose placement choice was residential care; but it should be remembered that there is a significant increase in total deficit score with the age of the children (regression coefficient = 0.48, $p < 0.001$). As with welfare progress, all the welfare status results need to be seen in the context of age as well as other factors connected with the starting-points of the children.

Table 15.4 ***Final welfare deficits by LAC areas of welfare***

Area of welfare	Number and percentage of children with deficits and degree of deficit at the close of study			
	No deficit	Mild deficit	Moderate deficit	Severe deficit
Health	67	15	10	8
Education	54	16	15	15
Identity	60	15	15	9
Family and social relationships	41	19	21	19
Social presentation	80	12	6	2
EBD	41	19	19	21
Self-care	78	14	5	3

n=100

What were the final deficits?

Health

The health deficits of children in the 0–9 age group were focused in the areas of illness and physical disability, with the addition of safety for children living at home.

- Most of the children who were less than 9 years old at the time of the care order made good progress in health, and if they had deficits at the end of the study these tended to be mild rather than moderate or severe (except in the case of disability).

In young children such as those placed for adoption, defects of sight and hearing had usually been addressed, but minor speech difficulties continued in spite of some improvement and there was one report of poor co-ordination and delay in the development of motor skills. Three children (one adopted, one fostered and one in kinship care) had unusual medical conditions that were not readily amenable to treatment and in two of these cases the children were rated as having severe problems. However, it seemed that in these cases whatever could be done was being done.

In the group of children placed at home, health problems were more insidious. One small child had feeding problems, was overweight and had constant colds and chest infections. Another had problems in locomotion that were not identified or treated until she was removed to foster care. A third child had been injured by his mother.

When we consider the health problems affecting those over 10 and in particular those over 13, a very different picture emerges. In this age group deficits in health were mainly a result of lifestyle risks – smoking, drinking, drug-taking, under-age sex and refusal of medical care. Where these difficulties existed they were not new, but they had not improved and in a few cases they had got worse.

- Health deficits as a result of lifestyle risks were recorded for ten of the 24 children in the over-13 age group, and of these deficits two were mild, three moderate and five severe.

The children with moderate or severe ratings usually had a combination of problems.[5] For example, one boy in residential care smoked heavily although he suffered from asthma, and he was also overweight and under-exercised. A young woman living on her own after placement breakdown suffered from a mixture of drug-taking and poor diet with no medical care. There was one pregnancy during the course of the study; but the saddest case was undoubtedly that of the 13-year-old girl who absconded and worked as a prostitute, during which she contracted syphilis. The health of some adolescents improved, especially when they were in secure placements; but none of the teenagers with severe health deficits were living in the intended placement at the 21-month point.

Education

There were some examples of exclusion and attendance problems in the younger age groups. Among pre-school children there was one toddler who was excluded from playgroup as a result of bad behaviour. In the 5–9 age group two children were excluded from school, one of them permanently, during the course of the study, while a third was hovering on the verge of exclusion and clearly having trouble with attendance. These examples are of concern because they reflect the spread of exclusion to a younger age group. However:

- in children below the age of 9 the main educational deficits were in the area of achievement, and low achievement was often linked to a diagnosis of learning difficulties.[6]

For school-age children 'statementing' acted not only as a gateway to resources but as a bench-mark against which children's needs could be judged. Eleven of the 26 children in the 5–9 age group were considered by social workers to have educational needs at the close of the study, although statementing had not always been applied for. Three children below the age of 9 were receiving special schooling and another two had been given welfare assistance in the classroom, while others on the borderline were said to be 'slow but struggling'. Once again, however, the plight of the adolescents was greater than that of the younger children. In the education of the 24 children who were aged 10 years or over, fourteen final deficits were recorded. None of these deficits were mild; two were moderate and the other twelve were severe. Learning difficulties were thought to have contributed to low achievement in the case of five adolescents, but non-attendance and school exclusion were the main reasons for deficits in this age group.

- Ten of the 24 children over the age of 10 had completed only partial attendance, or been banned or opted out of school altogether during the period of the study.

What happened to the seven adolescents who were recorded as having been excluded from school prior to the court order? (See Chapter 3.) With the help of a specialist foster placement, one was assisted into mainstream school. Three others were excluded again, but for two of these young people alternative provision was made by means of a mixture of pupil referral units and work experience and (within limits) it proved to be satisfactory. At the close of the study one girl who had previously been excluded was receiving education in a secure unit. The remaining three young people opted out of education altogether and were living independently.

The anxieties that prompted the Quality Protects initiative are confirmed, since none of the adolescents who were approaching school leaving age at the time of the final hearing had achieved any formal qualifications by the end of the study and none had any hopes of regular or satisfying employment. Other studies have reported in detail on the lack of educational and work opportunities for young people in the care system and the supports that seem to be needed (Biehal et al. 1995; Marsh and Peel 1999; Jackson 1989; Jackson 2001). The results of this study suggest that help should be provided at a much earlier stage than has usually been considered necessary.

Identity

Several of the small children for whom adoption was planned showed signs of confusion stemming from a poor understanding of their situation. The most vulnerable children were aged between 2 and 4 at the time of the final court hearing, and they came with a backlog of experience which they clearly found it difficult to process.

- The behaviour of eleven children (one-third of the adoption group) showed that they were confused and anxious about where they belonged.

These deficits may have been temporary, but they were rated as mild in five cases (in four of which the adoption plan had been fulfilled) and moderate to severe in another six (in five of which the plan was unfulfilled.) However, the results in terms of identity were worse when the plan was foster care, since only ten of these 22 children were free of identity problems at the end of the study. There were fewer deficits in kinship care. Predictably, the children in home placements had the lowest proportion of deficits in identity, and seventeen of the 22 children placed at home were judged to have no deficit.

Older children generally had a better understanding of what had happened, but this did not automatically bring emotional acceptance. Lack of acceptance revealed itself in a number of ways, chief of which was a refusal to talk about the past; so children who had been deeply hurt cut themselves off from the help that might have been offered through counselling or life-story work, and they also blamed or cut themselves off from individuals who reminded them of previous pain. These problems were not confined to adoption: they spanned all the substitute care options and were particularly common in fostering. They also spanned all age groups, since adolescents brought their own brand of identity problems to the care context. One boy fantasised about a relationship with his father whom he scarcely knew. Another denied one half of his ethnic inheritance by rejecting his black father and choosing to be regarded as white.

By far the greatest problem affecting children's sense of themselves was low self-esteem, which showed itself to some extent in almost all the 39 children who were rated as having deficits in identity at the close of the study.

- Low self-esteem on its own, reflected in a readiness to become frustrated or discouraged, was reckoned to be a mild deficit; but it became moderate to severe when it interfered substantially with children's progress or when it was combined with feelings of confusion and lack of acceptance of events.

Examples of severe deficits can be found in a 4-year-old child who said that she 'did not belong anywhere', in a 9-year-old boy who absconded and then oscillated continually between home and foster care, and in a 15-year-old who persisted in seeing herself as a victim even though she had been protected from the abuse that provoked the care order. In terms of children's total welfare, identity problems do not form the largest category; but the findings on amelioration show that where these problems existed they could be among the most difficult to eradicate.

Family and social relationships

There was a good rate of improvement in family and social relationships, probably because this area of welfare was targeted more than the others; but for 59 children there were some deficits at the close of the study and in 40 cases these deficits were moderate or severe.

The sub-themes for this section are continuity, attachments, relationships with the birth family and friendships. It was not unusual for children to have a mild deficit in one of these areas, and for children in substitute care the vulnerable area was usually relationships with the birth family. Seventeen of the nineteen mild deficits fell under this heading, and they took a number of forms, which included:

- children's anxiety at being separated from parents or siblings;
- worries about the welfare of other family members (sometimes with a continuing sense of responsibility on the part of the child);
- intermittent feelings of rejection;
- susceptibility to manipulation by birth parents; and
- difficulty in coping with the distress of poor quality contact.

For children placed at home there were additional problems associated with living in an atmosphere of constant tension and conflict.

Birth family problems were recorded more frequently in cases where contact continued, but only because these situations were more common than those where contact had been terminated. When contact was ended and the pain of loss badly affected the life of the child, it had to be rated as a deficit that was at best moderate and at worst severe. However, there were no problems associated with terminating birth family contact for small babies in adoption cases where there were no pre-existing relationships of importance to the child.

Difficulties in forming attachments to the current carer sometimes went hand in hand with problems concerned with the birth family. (Some children were described as clingy and demanding. Others 'would go with anyone'.) Once again it should be noted that these problems, though common, had usually diminished in frequency during the course of the study, and what is being noted here are residual deficits.

- Where there were attachment difficulties in the age groups 0–4 and 5–9, anxious and insecure attachments tended to dominate. Adolescents were most likely to show ambivalence.

Any pronounced difficulties in attachment were usually rated as moderate to severe deficits because of their effect on the key relationship between child and carer. However, sibling relationships that worked well could be a source of strength. Some children also managed to establish good peer relationships in spite of deficits elsewhere. The percentage of relationship deficits in the over-10s is not greater than that found among 5 to 9-year-olds, although the deficits of older children are worse in terms of severity, and this reminds us that work on relationships is still central to the social work task with children of all ages.

Social presentation

Though regarded by some social workers as relatively unimportant, children's social presentation was one of the keys to forming relationships with other children and adults and it was also a useful barometer of self-esteem. The sub-themes in this section were appearance and behaviour; but it seems that problems in children's behaviour were more off-putting than defects in appearance.[7] Of the twenty recorded deficits, eight were concerned with appearance and twelve with behaviour.

The children with poor appearance were said to be scruffy or dirty (a mild deficit), and a few children had more serious problems with personal hygiene. Children living at home were sometimes reported to be tired, unkempt and inappropriately dressed when they attended school – a sign that neglect was continuing. As far as behaviour was concerned, some young children were attention-seeking and demanding in a social setting, or alternatively uncommunicative. Adolescents were more likely to be described as lacking in social skills – for example because they avoided eye contact, or behaved inappropriately towards adults or their peers. Some problems were easy to improve with good care, but the very positive rate of improvement (69%) indicates that there would probably have been many more deficits in social presentation if the care order had not been made.

Emotional and behavioural development (EBD)

It is generally agreed that children in the care system have a much higher rate of mental health problems than children in the general population, although estimates of prevalence vary. A recent publication, *The Mental Health Needs of Looked After Children* by the Royal College of Psychiatrists (Richardson and Joughin 2000), quotes two studies, one of which (Phillips 1997) found that in the estimation of social workers 80% of the children in foster care required treatment from a mental health professional, while the other (McCann et al. 1996) showed that two-thirds of the children looked after by an Oxfordshire local authority had significant psychiatric disorders. This puts our findings into perspective – although it would be inappropriate for us to make clinical judgements.

The main problem which in this study led to the identification of a deficit in EBD was aggression in children. In the evidence leading to 50 of the 59 deficits, there were reports that the child was in some measure aggressive or withdrawn.

- Out of 50 cases in which final deficits were recorded, 22 were concerned with reports that the child was frequently aggressive, while another sixteen reported that the child was frequently withdrawn. In another twelve cases the child's behaviour apparently alternated from one to the other.
- The deficits were considered severe in one-quarter of the cases where children were said to be 'withdrawn', in one-third of those where the child was predominantly aggressive, and in one half of those where behaviour apparently alternated from one extreme to the other.

In addition to the above categories, and often alongside them, there were reports of specific behaviours that gave cause for concern. For example, sexualised behaviour was noted in three small girls and one older boy. A disabled child was said to be head-banging. Six children between the ages of 10 and 15 were reported to be 'immature' and this seemed to imply that they were exhibiting behaviour that, although not wildly problematic, would be considered more normal at a younger age. All of these reports indicate deficits in children's emotional and behavioural development, but for the sake of simplicity here it makes sense to concentrate on the main categories of children who were aggressive or withdrawn.

The children who were described as aggressive (n=22) were said to be 'bossy', 'stubborn' or 'difficult' at the pre-school stage. They were also described more positively as 'confident', 'disinhibited' and 'lively'.[8] They asserted their own wishes or bullied their peers, and adults found them difficult to control. This was not always seen as a disadvantage, because social workers connected bossiness with resilience in children who had suffered damaging life experiences prior to the care order, and carers were usually prepared to tolerate a certain amount of this behaviour during the settling-in period – especially if the child was of an age when tantrums would normally be expected to occur. In more than one adoption case the social worker became involved in lending support to other children in the family when the new adoptee was behaving aggressively towards them. Assessments by mental health professionals were rarely considered necessary, but in one case where a small child was found by her foster parents to be 'insistent and commanding', help was sought from a psychologist who said that the child was 'investing effort in maintaining sameness and control'. It seems likely that the same explanation could be applied to many other children in substitute care. However, some of the young children described as aggressive appeared to be hyperactive – a condition that has been shown to be particularly wearing for their carers (Quinton et al. 1998) – and there were only two cases where this was formally identified and treated.

In the 5–9 age group the children who were said to be 'aggressive' had a clearer affinity with what is usually recognised as conduct disorder. Their behaviour was often antisocial. When the deficit was mild, they were simply cheeky and challenging. When it was severe, they engaged in lying, swearing or hurting other people and animals. One boy who was only 9 years old at the time of the care order absconded during the course of the study and committed an offence of assault and criminal damage.

Antisocial behaviour was even more visible in the over-10s, and particularly in the over-13s.

- Seven adolescents committed offences that resulted in court appearances during the 21 months of the study.

The offences that resulted in court involvement were often minor incidents of shoplifting or receiving stolen goods (five examples) as opposed to the more serious crime of physical violence. No court action was taken against a teenage boy who assaulted another within the placement, and another youth was given a conditional discharge after assaulting a fellow pupil in school. The most damaging effects of these incidents were placement breakdown in the first case and school exclusion in the second.

It is interesting to note that the number of teenage offenders placed before the courts was the same as that recorded at the time of the care order – seven – but only three of these young people were repeat offenders. The three young people who reoffended had progressed to more serious crimes, which included drug offences on the part of two girls and car theft and glue-sniffing on the part of a 14-year-old boy. However, it is encouraging to note that four of the original group had not reoffended, to our knowledge. They were all living independently at the close of the study and it seemed that in this respect at least, their experience had stabilised.

Children who were described as withdrawn (n=16) were anxious and uncommunicative, and they were seen to be processing events within their own heads. They tended to be bullied by others and they were also prone to depression, which could be debilitating. Since their behaviour was more injurious to the self than to others, the deficits could easily be overlooked by social workers and carers. At the same time their anxiety often expressed itself in sleep disturbance, crying or enuresis, which some carers found more difficult to cope with than outright aggression.

- In the pre-school age group there were seven children who were said to be withdrawn. There were also five children in the 5–9 group and four in the over-10s. Two adolescent girls attempted self-harm during the course of the study.

In the youngest age group, and also in the 5 to 9s, the source of children's anxiety can often be traced to placement changes which were either pending or had recently happened. None of these children had been the subject of assessment by a mental health specialist, but since placements had not yet stabilised and the children were still young, it was hoped that the situation would improve with time.

One feature of these cases that cannot be ignored is the interaction between siblings, that could be harmful if not controlled.

- In total, thirteen of the sixteen children who were described as withdrawn were members of sibling groups in which they were overshadowed by a dominant member.

It seemed that the pattern of withdrawal had built up over time – either because the timid child had been constantly bullied or because the dominant and vociferous child (who was often the eldest) had received more attention from the parent, and other siblings had been neglected as a result.

Needless to say, children's behaviour was not constant over time, and there were twelve children who were said to be *alternately aggressive and withdrawn*. Some children had phases of anxious or unruly behaviour – usually in response to an upsetting event – which settled quickly, but the children whose behaviour oscillated from one extreme to another appeared to be in a different category. They had outbursts of aggression or phases of withdrawal, sometimes for no reason that was apparent to their carers. Because of this they were described as 'moody' or 'volatile'. The element of unpredictability made it more difficult for people to understand or cope with the child's behaviour, and this had an unfortunate feedback, which made the child's welfare worse.

The twelve children and young people in this category spanned all the age groups – though more than half of them were adolescents. They appeared to be more disturbed than the others, and the deficits were rated moderate to severe; but again there was a cumulative effect, with some of these young people displaying a mixture of conduct and emotional problems which the care order had done little to alleviate.

Self-care skills

Out of the 21 children who had deficits in self-care skills, eleven – that is, approximately half – had mild to moderate learning difficulties, which resulted in their being more dependent than might have been expected at their age. In most cases the deficits were slight, though one teenager in a special school had difficulty in handling money, and another in a residential home had to be helped to undertake journeys by public transport in order to see his family. Both of these children were deemed to have severe deficits in self-care skills.

Five young children had some difficulty in performing ordinary tasks such as washing regularly, tying shoelaces or using a knife and fork – not because they were cognitively impaired but because they had been neglected in the home environment and had never been taught the necessary skills. Most of these children were removed to foster care shortly before the end of the study.

Third, there were five young people who did not take good care of themselves for emotional reasons. They refused to wash or dress properly, and they refused to recognise that they lacked basic skills such as cooking and budgeting, which would be necessary in independent living. Not all of the rebellious adolescents were lacking in self-care skills, however. Some of them were 'streetwise' in a way that ensured that they made progress and survived, even if their final welfare was less good than might have been desired.

Statistical analysis of factors associated with welfare status

In the statistical calculation of welfare status, final deficits were weighted according to severity. This meant that 'no deficit' was represented by a score of 0, 'mild deficit' by 1, 'moderate deficit' by 2 and 'severe deficit' by 3. This gave a better distribution of scores for individual children, and it also ensured that the statistical calculations would take into account the varying degrees of influence that deficits were likely to exert in terms of the overall outcome.

The results were broadly similar to welfare progress. The time between the making of the care order and the last placement move was not significantly related to the standard of welfare reached ($p = 0.20$). However, the odds of a poor welfare status increased with the *number of moves*. Each extra move was associated with an odds ratio of 1.51 ($p = 0.002$, 95% CI from 1.17 to 1.95).

Permanence was once again important. The odds of poor welfare status was seen to be greater if the placement was temporary than if it was permanent ($p < 0.001$, odds ratio = 5.13, 95% CI from 2.12 to 12.38), and similar results were found for each decrease in permanency on the continuous measure (the 'permanency scale'). The greater the child's *age at final hearing*, the lower the chances of achieving good welfare status ($p = < 0.001$, odds ratio = 0.83, 95% CI from 0.75 to 0.92). The same was true of the length of social services involvement, which was closely related to age. Gender seemed to have no significant effect ($p = 0.10$), and once again the numbers of minority ethnic children were too small for analysis of their outcomes.

As was found in welfare progress, the question of whether or not the child was previously registered on the child protection register was not significantly related to welfare status ($p = 0.47$); but there was a difference inasmuch as a pre-history of physical abuse reduced the chances of achieving good welfare status ($p = 0.009$, odds ratio = 0.36, 95% CI from 0.16 to 0.78) and the same was true of sexual abuse ($p = 0.04$, odds ratio = 0.35, 95% CI from 0.13 to 0.93). It is interesting to note that these life-events were associated with a lower standard of welfare although they did not apparently prevent children from making progress during the period of the study. There was no significant relationship between welfare status and time spent on the child protection register ($p = 0.37$), or the number of periods looked after prior to care proceedings ($p = 0.28$), or the time from first application to final hearing ($p = 0.82$).

The number of *children's initial problems* was significantly associated with welfare status ($p < 0.001$, odds ratio = 0.32, 95% CI from 0.22 to 0.46). As their number rose, so the chances of a good outcome fell. This link between the presence of initial problems and final welfare status is similar to the one noted in welfare progress; but the association between initial problems and welfare status was considerably greater. There was a strong correlation between the number of initial problems and the standard of welfare reached (Kendall's tau-b = 0.67).

- These findings confirm that children's initial problems can be predictors of poor welfare outcomes, even when progress is made in the aftermath of the care order.
- The strongest predictors of poor welfare status, in terms of initial problems, are to be found in the areas of education and EBD.

About 30 years ago, Kellmer Pringle drew attention to the way in which child functioning in one area of life (such as school) could be affected by another (for example, well-being at home) (Pringle 1974). To test whether there was a link between the dimensions in the present study, further statistical analysis was carried out to measure correlations between deficits. Kendall's tau-b was used as a measure of correlation for the deficits on seven dimensions, and the Kendall's tau coefficients are given in Table 15.5. A value of 0.2 of more can be considered a small to moderate correlation. A value of over 0.5 is moderate to strong.

Table 15.5 ***Correlation between welfare deficits***

	Health	Education	Identity	Family	Social presentation	EBD	Self-care
Health		0.48	0.21	*0.15*	0.08	0.21	0.39
Education			0.42	0.40	0.31	0.50	0.47
Identity				0.66	0.30	0.57	0.35
Family					*0.17*	0.65	0.32
Social presentation						0.29	*0.17*
EBD							0.31

In Table 15.5 it seems most important to note:

- the link between family relationships and identity, and between both of these and EBD; and
- the link between education and EBD, between education and health, and between education and self-care skills.

This does not indicate the direction of any possible effect; but it seems likely that a major improvement on any one of these linked dimensions might stimulate improvement in the others.

Discussion and conclusions

One of the main objectives of the Quality Protects initiative is 'to ensure that children are securely attached to carers capable of providing safe and effective care for the duration of childhood'; another is 'to ensure that children looked after gain maximum life chance benefits from educational opportunities, health care and social care'. In view of the poor welfare status of many of the children at the end of the study, these concerns do not seem to be misplaced. Although 55% of the children made good progress, and the well-being of many had improved since the time of the care order, 40% still had moderate or severe deficits in family and social relationships or emotional and behavioural development, and 30% in education.

Not all faults can be laid at the door of the care system, of course. In some cases (such as those involving physical disability) all that could be done was being done. The close association between initial problems and welfare status shows that many of the problems that made life difficult for children and their carers 21 months after the care order had originated before the order was made, and even in cases of poor progress the low incidence of 'deterioration' indicates that many problems had been prevented from getting worse. Nevertheless the improvement rate is less than 50%, on average, and this rate clearly needs to be increased.

What would have aided improvement? First, the clear connection between age and welfare outcome suggests that some children might have been helped more readily by intervention at an earlier stage. Second, a multi-agency approach to children's difficulties was needed – especially where children suffered from learning difficulties or poor mental health. (Too often referral was postponed because it was hoped that problems would clear up on their own, or because social workers were afraid of stigmatising the child by the introduction of discriminatory treatment.) Third, the interaction between the dimensions of welfare needs to be noted and worked with. Does high self-esteem result in improved relationships and educational performance, or does success in these areas lead to high self-esteem? The direction of the effect may be difficult to determine in practice; but in view of the relationships we have noted between individual dimensions of welfare, in addition to the relationship between each of these dimensions and children's welfare as a whole, there seem to be many points of entry to the circle that could be identified and used.

Finally, we need to see problems from the child's point of view. With the exception of the cases where children were interviewed, the evidence for the deficits recorded in this study came largely from adult sources, and while we felt it right to give pride of place to professional judgements (including our own) we realise that there is another perspective to be examined. When power is an issue, the question of interests is never far below the surface.[9] We need to understand the importance of welfare dimensions to children themselves, and to admit that there may be conflicts about goals as well as the extent to which they are achieved.

Summary

1. In the calculation of welfare progress, which was a measure of change over time, normal progress and amelioration of problems were both considered to represent good outcomes. Persistence of problems and deterioration characterised poor outcomes. In terms of overall scores, 55 children made good progress and 33 children made poor progress, while the scores of the other twelve children were mixed.

2. When the results were considered by dimension, it was found that most children made good progress in social presentation and self-care skills, but since few children started with problems in this area, the results are mainly a result of 'normal progress'. Fewer children actually improved on dimensions where there were pre-existing difficulties. Nevertheless health was improved in 61% of the cases where there had been problems previously, and family and social relationships improved in 58% of cases. Emotional and behavioural difficulties showed an improvement rate of 41%.

3. As might be expected, there was a statistical relationship between the number of initial problems and welfare progress scores but there was also an association between individual baseline problems and global welfare progress. The odds of making poor overall progress increased very significantly when there were initial problems in EBD. The second most influential area, in terms of the global impact on welfare progress, was education.

4 In addition to measuring welfare progress, the study looked at the standard of welfare that children had reached. At the end point of the study the children with the best welfare progress had the fewest welfare deficits or unmet needs, and the converse was also true. The well-being of many children had improved since the time of the care order and yet they fell short of an adequate standard of welfare.

5 When the results were analysed in terms of placement choice, it appeared that on key dimensions such as identity, family and social relationships and EBD, an adoption plan (whether fulfilled or not) led to better welfare scores than a plan for fostering or residential care. However, it has to be remembered that there is a significant increase in the total deficit score in relation to the age of the children.

6 Correlations between the deficits on the seven dimensions show that there is a strong link between family and social relationships and identity, and between both of these and EBD. There is also a link between education and health, and between education and self-care skills. These links, together with the number and range of the final deficits, seem to lend support to the Quality Protects initiative, which aims to raise the overall standard of welfare for children in the care system.

---

[1] Here the standard errors were based on the sandwich estimator to take into account the fact that outcomes for children from the same family are likely to be correlated. When the explanatory variable was dichotomous, the odds ratio for good welfare status or welfare progress was estimated comparing the two groups. When the explanatory variable was categorical with ordered categories (for instance, number of moves), the odds ratio for good welfare status or welfare progress associated with a unit increase in the explanatory variable was estimated.

[2] This result was obtained by using a statistical model which assumed that each move had the same effect (an 'average' effect).

[3] This test used a dichotomous measure.

[4] A recent report on data collected for management purposes (Ward and Skuse 2001a) also found high rates of problems in family and social relationships (74%) and emotional and behavioural development (51%), although the sample is not directly comparable because it included children not on care orders.

[5] Ward and Skuse (2001a) also report that many looked-after children have more than one health condition. In their sample, 27% of the children had two conditions and 14% had three or more.

[6] In the sample studied by Ward and Skuse (2001a), 18% of the children were said to have a 'learning disability', but the authors comment on the high rate of variation between local authorities and the likelihood that the term is used inconsistently. It is also debatable whether 'learning disability' is best classified as a problem of health or education.

[7] This is almost certainly an adult view. Among young people, especially those in early adolescence, it is said that satisfaction with physical appearance contributes most to overall self-esteem (Harter 1990).

[8] These adjectives remind us of the 'open book' children described in *Growing Up in Foster Care* (Schofield et al. 2000). Alternatively they could be regarded as children who 'externalise' if the internalising–externalising classification is used (Quinton and Murray 2002).

[9] Some questions that could be asked are: Is it right that children who are aggressive should get most attention and treatment? Were social workers and carers preoccupied with the management of behaviour in order to meet the carers' needs and stabilise placement?

16 Welfare outcomes: the views of the children

Introduction

The views of the children provide a valuable complement to the statistical measures of welfare outcome and the views of others. The children interviewed were the older children, and there were none in adoptive homes or successfully implemented home placements (though two of the children interviewed had returned to their parents' care by the time of the interview despite this not being the original plan). Furthermore, while the information on welfare outcomes all relates to 21 months after the final hearing the interviews with children took place between 22 and 28 months after the full care order. Nonetheless the views of the children are not only important in their own right. They also provide important insights into the impact of care on these children (Grimshaw and Sinclair 1997; Shaw 1998; Thomas and Beckford 1999; Alderson 2000).

This chapter presents the children's views on how they were doing. The LAC framework was used to structure the interview and the material has been organised around the seven dimensions. As might be expected the children had a lot more to say about some areas than they did about others, and the balance of the chapter reflects this. It is also important to bear in mind that the views expressed are those of the children. There are issues – such as getting pregnant at 16 – that young people talk very positively about but that might be considered as negative developments by others.

Family and social relationships

Children in care have more complicated relationships than most other children. This was particularly true among the older children in the sample (and therefore among the children who were interviewed). They often maintained relationships from before the care order as well as developing sets of relationships with new carers, with children they lived with, and also often in new schools or areas. Furthermore the relationships from before the care order were generally mediated through contact arrangements that might be complex, while some children had been through several placements and maintained links with carers and children met in these. For ease of understanding this section therefore looks at relationships with parents and others from before the care order and then at relationship issues within various types of placement.

Maintenance of previous relationships: (1) Parents

Relationships with parents were very important for almost all the children.

- There were only two who did not identify their mothers as among the most important people in their lives. This was true whether children were in regular contact with their mothers or not, and for children of all ages.

The picture varied more in relation to fathers – three children who had been sexually abused either did not mention their fathers or mentioned them as people they actively did not want to see. For some of the others, fathers whom they had not seen for some time – or ever – were not particularly important.

Younger children tended to be either very positive or, less commonly, very negative about their birth parents. For instance, one 11-year-old girl described her mum, in the following way: 'She is brilliant, she is the best a mum can be ... She is really nice and she is kind, she is loving, sharing and she is caring, I am going to write a book about her, she is the best mum in the world.'

It was not uncommon for children to emphasise the importance of parents even if they had not seen them for some time. This appeared particularly true in relation to some of the boys who would talk very positively about the importance of their fathers even if they had little contact with them or had not seen them for years – or in one case where a 17-year-old had never met his father. Several of the younger children still appeared to harbour hopes that they would be returning to live with their parents, even when this was clearly not the plan for them. This was sometimes the case even when the parental care for them had been inadequate by any standards. For instance, the mother in the quotation above had chaotically misused drugs and neglected the care of her daughter for several years, yet her daughter idolised her. This idolisation appeared undiminished by the inconsistent contact that her mother kept with her.

There were two younger children who had very negative views about their parents. One 8-year-old, who had not lived at home for two years, said the following about his mum: 'She is not important … She is horrible; she used to twist my hand and that … and she used to make me watch all these scary things and put scary things on my wall.'

Another young boy described his dad sexually abusing him and said that he never wanted to see either his mother or father again.

Older children tended to have a more complex picture of their parents, which often recognised the negative sides of their parents' behaviour while valuing the positive aspects of their relationship. This more balanced attitude toward parents was a particular feature of successful placements and outcomes for older children. For instance one 15-year-old girl who made excellent progress in a long-term foster placement said of her mum: 'Yes, well it is just something you have got to accept that they are your parents really and you can't really sort of change the way they are.'

A 14-year-old boy who made very good progress in a kinship placement described his relationship with his mother in the following way: 'My birth mum … she is quite annoying at the moment, she like makes loads of lies up, but you can't just say I don't love my mum any more, I do. She is an important part of my life.'

It is not possible from our research to say whether the successful placements enabled these young people to have more balanced views of their parents or whether their rounded view contributed to the success of their placements. It was however noteworthy that:

- most of these young people said they were able to talk to their carers about issues that arose in relation to their parents and they appreciated being able to do this informally as the need arose.

It therefore seems likely that living in families in which they felt 'at home' and able to talk about issues had helped them to reach a rounded view of their often complex relationships with their birth parents.

Parental contact

The frequency and nature of contact between children and their parents was a key issue in children's ability to maintain their relationships. For many of the older children the plan for contact seemed irrelevant, as they were able to make their own arrangements with members of their families. As this 17-year-old girl put it:

> All I know is that there was no rules for me when I could see my family. When I was in foster care I was only allowed to see my mum once a week at a certain time. As soon as I moved into [the unit] I think they realised that my mum didn't care when I go over there and I could go over there whenever I wanted and she wouldn't mind.

This appeared to be universal for children aged over 14, and for most of them this flexibility had started some years previously.

For a lot of children – but particularly younger ones – there were complex and sometimes powerful emotions associated with contact. These were not helped by the difficulties associated with organising it. There were a number of drawbacks when it was supervised or held at social services' venues. The most obvious of these was that it effectively reduced the amount of contact that children had with parents. The comments of this 13-year-old girl were typical:

> *Interviewer:* Are you happy with the amount you see your mum?
>
> *Girl:* No.
>
> *Interviewer:* You would like to see her more?
>
> *Girl:* Yes.
>
> *Interviewer:* Have you ever had the chance to talk to anyone about that?
>
> *Girl:* Sometimes I say to Alison [my social worker] can I see her once a week or something like that and she says no because she can't work [it] out. Because it has got to be supervised and she hasn't got time.

All the children who complained about inadequate amounts of contact were meant to have supervised contact.

- All too often 'supervised' contact meant 'very little' contact. Lack of resources appeared to contribute to the limited amount of contact that was organised.

As other researchers have noted (Cleaver 2000; Farmer et al. 2002), supervised contact was also often held at venues that were experienced by the children as 'not natural' and apparently not child friendly. One 10-year-old girl commented: 'It was all right sometimes but nothing to do there or nothing – it was boring, you were always stuck in a small room like about half the size of this room.'

There were one or two positive examples of supervision by relatives or carers that allowed contact to remain regular and informal; however the danger was that children would not be adequately supervised and might be at risk of emotional abuse. For instance, one 7 year-old-boy had had very bad experiences as a result of his mum trying to disrupt his current care during contact that was meant to have been supervised by his maternal grandmother:

> *Interviewer:* Do you remember what it used to be like when you saw her?
>
> *Boy:* Yes every time she would say things and I always use to think they wouldn't happen, and they didn't, and once she said that I would be going home soon, but I didn't know that – and she gave me her phone number and I gave it to [my foster mum] and she gave it to [my social worker].

Whatever the frequency of contact and the arrangements surrounding it, it remained an emotional experience for almost all the children. They often talked about feeling upset afterwards, because they would miss their parent(s). One 13-year-old girl described it in the following way:

> *Interviewer:* How do you feel after you see them?
>
> *Girl:* Sometimes I go up in my bedroom for half an hour just to sort of think over what has happened that day and that, then I just come back down. It is normally dinner time then. Afterwards I just sort of either watch telly or go out with my friend or help out around the house.

Though other children described it more positively:

> *Interviewer:* And how do you feel afterwards?
>
> *Child:* Feel more happy because I know mum's okay. Because I'm worried in case she's upset or something.

No child complained that by the time of the interview they had too much contact (though one or two had cut down contact themselves as time went by). Several children said that they preferred a longer session where they could relax and it felt more 'natural' than more frequent but shorter sessions. This was because there was usually a 'settling down' period at the beginning of contact before they felt at ease with their parents.

Only two children – both 7-year-old boys – had had contact stopped with both parents, and both were glad of this. For the rest of the children contact remained an important part of their lives, though one that was often emotionally charged and full of high expectations and complex feelings of anxiety, disappointment and loss.

Maintenance of previous relationships: (2) Siblings

With the exception of some of the children in one large sibling group,

- children listed their brothers and sisters among the people who were most important to them. This was true even when social workers and other professionals had expressed concern about constant rivalries or arguments between siblings.

In general, children identified their siblings as very important but had little else to say about them. As one 11-year-old boy said, '[They're] very important. I don't admit it though!' However, when they were asked to give a reason they sometimes said that siblings were important because they had been through similar experiences and understood what they were going through.

The importance of siblings to children appeared not to be diminished by lack of contact – though lack of contact with siblings was among the most upsetting issues that the children talked about. In two families contact was stopped because a decision had been taken to place a younger sibling for adoption while older children remained in foster care. A typical quotation in relation to this is one from this 10-year-old girl:

> *Interviewer:* How do you feel about not seeing her?
>
> *Girl:* Awful, it is like it is my fault that I am not allowed to see her, because it seems like my fault when I haven't done nothing wrong and everything that I am in foster care, because I am not allowed to see her and I don't know why.

In two other families contact was infrequent because the child and carers felt that the social worker was not organising it as often as she should. This could be almost as upsetting for children. As one 11-year-old said, it made him feel: 'Upset, angry, annoyed. All of them.'

Maintenance of previous relationships: (3) Friends

For a number of children their closest friends were very important. This was particularly true for teenage girls, several of whom described very close long-term friendships. The children particularly valued the support and understanding that these friends had provided during and since coming into care. As one 11-year-old said: 'My real real best friend is Mera, and Nicky, because I have known Mera since all of my life and Nicky she is really good because she knows the situation and she understands.'

These girls valued the fact that their current carers had enabled the relationships to continue, in one case by making a big effort to keep the child at the same school and in another by encouraging regular contact.

Current carers: (1) Foster placements

Although not necessarily representative of others, the fourteen children in foster care at the time of the interview were all happy with where they were living and most actively went out of their way to praise their carers. Typical quotations include the following, from an 11-year-old girl: 'They help you … they're caring … They treat you like it's your own house. They treat you like we're in the family.'

- Foster carers were mentioned positively throughout the interviews, and not just when the questions focused on current care. They were consistently identified as the people children felt closest to, the people they could have a laugh with, the people who would be significant in years to come and in many other ways.

When children talked about previous foster carers there was a considerably more varied picture. Many children still had positive things to say about previous carers. Descriptions would commonly include words such as 'kind', 'fun' and 'patient'. However, there were also far more negative comments made.

- A few children had suffered serious emotional, physical and/or sexual abuse at the hands of previous carers.

One child said:

> [The foster dad] just used to pick on us. Me and Amy had an argument once, but I didn't hit her or anything and then [he] came upstairs behind me and grabbed me round the neck and threw me on the floor. He used to be really

> horrible to Amy. When she used to go up to the bathroom she had a nightie on, he used to hang her upside down [pause] so her nightie went up [pause] and when she used to sit with a skirt on he used to always try and look up her skirt [pause] and I told Amy she should put shorts on or something. Get a pair of shorts.

The current carers said that the bruises on this child's neck were still visible three weeks later. 'Amy' had also made allegations of inappropriate touching by this foster father.

For most of the children the negative experiences in foster care were not as extreme as this, but they could nonetheless be just as emotionally upsetting.

The most common complaint about previous carers was that children felt that the carers did not care and that the children were not treated as members of the family.

- ♦ The importance for the children of living with people who cared for them and treated them as a member of the family cannot be overstated. Indeed, it was perhaps the issue most consistently stressed by the children.

Typical examples include the following comments:

> When social services gave [them] the money for my bike they didn't get me a bike they got [their own child] one instead.
>
> [The next foster carers were] not very nice either. Well we wasn't allowed, they didn't make you feel at home because you wasn't allowed up the stairs, only her own children were allowed up stairs.
>
> It was just the environment you lived in. It wasn't a normal family household sort of and we would always argue with each other. I didn't really like it there.

At the end of the interview children were asked what advice they would like to give to the professionals responsible for children in the care system. More than one child expressed sentiments similar to those of this 12-year-old boy:

> *Boy:* Treat us the same.
>
> *Interviewer:* Treat you the same? Say a bit more.

Boy: Treat us the same as anyone else – like your grandchildren.

Another event that upset a lot of children was when foster carers had ended placements. Some children appeared not to understand why they had moved from a carer. Several children said that their carer had gone on holiday and had not been able to take them so they had had to move placement. For other children the reasons why a carer had said that they could not look after them remained mysterious (and upsetting) months later: 'I can honestly say that I never dreamt that she would chuck me out, so there was no way that I drove her to anything because I know that it wasn't me that made her. I don't know what happened. She just suddenly flipped.'

Current carers: (2) Kinship care

Four of the children interviewed were living in kinship placements while one had been placed with an aunt but this relationship had broken down. One of the successful placements was with the child's father, a second was with the paternal grandmother, a third was with an older brother's ex-partner while a fourth was with an uncle and his family. All four of these children were happy with their placements. One 11-year-old boy said: 'I get treated really good and there is lots of things to do like there are friends next door and [family] down the road.'

Kinship carers were mentioned positively throughout the interviews in answer to questions as wide-ranging as who was most reliable in their lives, who had the best sense of humour, who would they celebrate something good with and so on. Children in kinship placements also valued being able to keep comparatively informal contact with their mothers and other members of their families.

- They generally felt that kinship care was similar to foster care, but with the advantage that you knew the people before you moved in.

One 14-year-old who had experienced both fostering and kinship care, and who was currently living with a relative, said:

Young person: It is just the same, isn't it? But you know the person you are living with.

Interviewer: And you think that is important?

> *Young person:* Yes because if you are living with a complete stranger you worry about it, whereas if you live with someone you know, you are all right. You know what they are going to be like and everything.

Current carers: (3) Residential care

In total four of the children interviewed were in residential units and five had previously been in units. Three of the children who were no longer in residential care had moved out of a unit within the last few weeks and ongoing outreach was still a feature – so seven children were able to talk about current or very recent experiences of residential care.

The children currently in residential placements generally spoke positively about their experiences in the units. They particularly valued the commitment and personal touch of the staff. Typical comments include:

> I like everything about this place ... The staff are fine... I wouldn't change anything. It's perfect.

> You can tell that they are listening, and they don't laugh at you. They just try their best to sort out what you want. They try to feel what you feel. If I'm upset then they'll be upset. If I'm happy then they will be happy.

Problems with residential care were mainly in connection with bullying or violence.

- The main difficulty with residential care, mentioned by most of the children who had lived in residential units, was bullying or violence from other children.

While the bullying and difficult behaviour of other young people should not eclipse the fact that many of them spoke very positively about their experience of residential care, it does provide a more mixed picture than that which children gave of their foster placements.

The children were noticeably less positive about previous residential placements than they were about the ones that they were currently in. They generally considered them as chaotic and sometimes quite dangerous places. One 17-year-old described a unit she had been in thus:

> Can you imagine people taking drugs in their rooms all night? Loud music. Throwing cutlery down the stairs. Throwing fire extinguishers. Hitting members of staff. Smuggling stolen goods in. Smoking and drinking in the house. Not going to school. Barricading yourselves in someone's room and generally causing trouble. Throwing things at people. Beating other residents up. Bullying. Then you've got a good grip on Maybury Road.

The problems of violence and bullying were described as worse in previous placements and there were few, if any, references to positive relationships with staff in these placements. Possibly these were among the reasons why the children had been moved. Alternatively the difference may be related to the fact that most of the previous episodes in residential units had been comparatively short, while the children currently living in residential care (or having recently left it) had lived there for some time and had therefore had the opportunity to develop better relationships with staff and other children.

Attempted returns home

Of the 26 children interviewed, placement at home had been the plan for four of the children (none of whom were still at home). For a further four children attempts at return home had been tried even though it was not part of the care plan. (One of these had been successful, when combined with residential boarding school during term time, and one had happened the week of the interview so was at a very early stage.) Several of the children talked at length about these experiences, as they were obviously central to their understanding of their care experience and the plan for their care.

When one listens to the heart-felt love that many of the children expressed for their parents, it is easy to see why social workers tried very hard and repeatedly to return a number of children to their parents. One 12-year-old girl spoke about running away from her placement again and again to go back to her mother. Others clearly missed their mothers acutely and wanted nothing more than to return home to them.

- ♦ The issue of whether or not return was attempted appeared to be particularly difficult for children and social workers where parents – or, to be more exact, mothers – misused drugs or alcohol. In these cases there was often a very positive side to the care of the parents.

This meant that there was often a strong bond and it seemed to make the assessment process more difficult for social workers. Certainly in these cases it was more likely that there would be multiple attempts to return children to their parents. However, listening to the children it was clear that failed attempts to return children home could be very emotionally damaging for them. One 10-year-old girl, who spoke movingly about her love for her mum and had had three unsuccessful attempts at returning home, described an attempt at rehabilitation:

> *Interviewer:* How did things work out when they tried to get you back with your mum?
>
> *Girl:* Not very well … It was just bad. I couldn't talk to her then, when I was there, I would just talk to her and it would keep going through my mind. I would pretend like friends … I would talk to my teddy bears or something [about] why I was down and everything and what had been going on. So I use to just talk to them. [And to] my brother; but he didn't listen. He was too upset; because we use to cry and that when she was drinking.

Furthermore, while most of the children where rehabilitation was tried had expressed a clear desire to return home, one 7-year-old boy said that his views had not been listened to and that he had not wanted to be returned to his mother. (His carers supported this, saying that he had appeared 'scared' of his mother and that they did not think he should have been returned.) The resultant failed attempt to return him to a mother that he did not wish to live with had been traumatic and abusive:

> *Interviewer:* After they got that plan they then decided that you could go home after all; do you think that was a good idea?
>
> *Boy:* If I went back home my … [pause] she would only smack us and sometimes she would hit us with a stick or she would twist our ankles and our wrists.
>
> *Interviewer:* Do you remember if anybody talked to you about whether you wanted to go home?
>
> *Boy:* Yes.
>
> *Interviewer:* Do you remember what you said?
>
> *Boy:* I said no.

In addition to the pain of the failed return home, more than two years after the care order this young boy was still in a temporary placement and was clearly deeply upset about the prospect of having to move on.

In Chapter 8 the association between failed rehabilitation and children being in temporary placements at the follow-up point was identified. Interviewing the children made clear the real emotional consequences for a small group of four children. All four were still in temporary placements, though for two of them their current foster carers looked likely to care for them long term. The remaining two would have to move on.

- The children in temporary placements were the only children who appeared really upset when talking about the plans for their future.

One maintained that the plan was still for him to return to his mother, although in fact this was no longer the plan, and at the time of the interview his residential key-worker reported that there was no plan for him. The other child appeared on the verge of tears while he explained why he could not stay with his current foster carers:

> *Young person:* I want to stay here.
>
> *Interviewer:* Has your social worker talked to you about the reasons you can't?
>
> *Young person:* Yes, because if I stay here then there wouldn't be that much people fostered and [my foster mum] wouldn't be able to foster again. If she would still carry on there would be loads of people left to sleep in my bedroom and [pause]. On the one side is a bad life, in the middle it gets good and then on the other side is your new home and if I stayed there would be a blockage.

The dilemma for social workers is exceptionally difficult. On the one hand they want to give children every opportunity to live with their parents – as most of the children themselves wish. On the other hand, when such attempts fail, children can suffer emotional harm (whether deliberate or not) from their parents and are also far more likely to be left in the limbo of temporary placements some years after the care order has been granted.

Education

The attitude of the children towards school and further education varied greatly. On the whole younger children were quite positive about school. Where they were able to make a judgement about whether school had changed for the better or for the worse since the care order they generally found that it had got better.

- An unexpected finding was that where children had changed school they often saw this as positive. The move to a new school was seen as an opportunity to make a new start.

It was often when children appeared to be under-performing in school that they were moved – or else they were being bullied by their peers. They were moved either to a special school or to one that was closer to their foster carers. The children perceived this to be a positive development.

When support for children was discussed, the children in fostering and kinship placements generally spoke about carers helping them – or at least trying to. For instance, one foster mother who felt unable to provide help with maths homework ensured that her adult son provided regular help. In residential care, on the other hand, the children did not report getting much help with homework.

In the sample of children interviewed there were a number of examples of children significantly under-performing in school. However, talking to the children highlighted the complex underlying reasons for the educational under-performance of children looked after.

- More than one child suggested that they did not find the academic work that they had been given challenging enough. As a result they said that they would complete the work given to them very quickly and then misbehave as they had time on their hands.

Several children were considered to have special needs owing to their behaviour, even though they might be academically able to take on more challenging work. One 17-year-old young man said of his time in a special school:

> I have always been called the class clown. I finish my work before anyone else and I would sit there and get bored and mess around, because I have got nothing else to do. Everyone else still writing and I was done and finished. I ask for some more work; sorry we haven't got any, so I have to sit there looking like a pleb for another hour just doing nothing. I have always had that since I was younger.

It is interesting to note that at 11 years old this boy had been assessed as having learning difficulties and placed in a special school, but that subsequent assessment at age 15 had found he had no learning difficulties.

It was common for children with behavioural difficulties to say that they did not find the work that they were being given stretched them: 'I went to a behaviour unit for about half a year and … it was still a bit rubbish. You hardly do any work, you just go swimming and to the sports centre and cooking and stuff like that; it was like being at play school again.'

There can be little doubt that this young woman had very poor educational outcomes (she gained no qualifications), but it is instructive to consider what she thought the reasons for this were:

> I don't think it has got anything to do with where you live. It is the reasons why you are in care sort of screw you up a bit when you are doing school work … If everybody knows as well, they automatically presume that you are just going to be really naughty and then you kind of have to be really.

This was echoed by other young people, such as one apparently bright 17-year-old girl who detailed at length the support that she had received from social workers and residential staff but who said that by the time she had come into care it was 'too late' because she had 'got out of the habit of school'. A number of other children mentioned feeling upset or finding it difficult to concentrate at school before coming into care.

The overall performance of children at school appeared to be closely linked to their emotional and behavioural difficulties. These – whether they were the result of difficulties at home or the experience of coming into the care system – inhibited children's ability to perform on a level with their ability in school. They would then complain that they were given work that was too easy and that they therefore got bored. The exceptions to this pattern were a couple of teenage girls, both of whom were of high academic ability and came from middle-class backgrounds, who found school and academic work a refuge from the many other issues in their lives.

Health

Most of the younger children reported no concerns in relation to their health and, except for one or two normal childhood accidents among the youngest children, they had little to say about their health and development.

The picture was rather different as children became older, and in particular in relation to behaviours that might put health at risk – such as substance misuse and unprotected sex. Of the eight young people aged 15 or over, five spoke of smoking and drinking regularly and of taking drugs. Of particular concern was the fact that three of these adolescents described themselves as having been 'addicted' to Class A drugs (crack cocaine or amphetamine) during the period that they were in care.

Smoking, drinking and taking drugs

Table 16.1 shows the main concerns affecting health that were relevant to the children interviewed. While the numbers of children using drugs or alcohol was small overall they represented a very high proportion of the children aged 15 or over. Furthermore, the comments that they made were interesting and there was a great deal of consistency in what they had to say. For most of the children their use of substances had started with smoking, then progressed to alcohol and cannabis and they had then tried other drugs.

- Of the seven children who smoked, all but one of them appeared to have started prior to coming into care. However, once they were in care these children found that there was a culture of smoking, drinking and taking drugs, particularly in the residential units, that made it difficult to avoid increasing their substance use.

One 16-year-old was introduced to the interviewer while she was smoking with a number of younger children and members of staff outside the back door of the unit. She felt that giving up had been impossible in residential care because smoking was such a key part of the social side of things.

Table 16.1 ***Lifestyle issues among children interviewed***

	Total	Smoke regularly	Drink regularly	Take/ took drugs regularly	Caution or conviction	Pregnant/ had baby
Aged 7–11	8	0	0	0	–	0
Aged 12–15	12	2	1	1	1	0
Aged 16 +	6	5	4	5	5	2

Three of the young people described serious drug misuse. This misuse had contributed to problems in placements, educationally and in other ways. For one girl her misuse of amphetamine had contributed to her anorexia and put her health at risk. For a second girl, her amphetamine misuse had been implicated in a wide range of anti-social behaviours and non-school attendance. For a third girl her misuse of crack cocaine had almost led her into prostitution at the age of 15, and had resulted in her being severely injured and going missing for some weeks.

Sex, pregnancies and births

Of the five girls aged 16 or over, one had recently had a baby and a second had just discovered that she was pregnant (she had also had two previous miscarriages). For both these girls the babies were planned and wanted:

> *Interviewer:* So this time you very much want to have the child?
>
> *Young woman:* Oh yeah definitely. It is not like I want to make up for the child that I have lost it is just the feeling I have lost two. Since then I have longed for a child, but it has been like I am not settled, it is not right, it is not the right time. But with Dave it has just almost come natural ... But up until [last night] I think he was really nervous and really kind of like I am too young, whereas I don't feel like I am, but like I say I feel about 25–30 years old. I really don't feel like I am young at all.

Both young women, who had had extremely challenging behaviour in their mid-teens, saw having a baby with a boyfriend whom they loved as a chance to settle down and leave some of their wilder behaviour behind. They had both recently obtained their own tenancies and were living with their boyfriends.

Information and education

In the light of the high level of substance misuse and pregnancies, and their well-documented associated risks to young people, it is useful to consider the nature and sources of information for the children in relation to 'lifestyle' issues.

- Almost all the children and young people said that school was their major source of information on sex education and on drugs. However, children who lived in family settings appeared able to talk comparatively easily about such issues with their current carers.

In contrast with these more 'normal' interchanges about such things as drugs and sex, the opportunities to discuss such issues informally with staff members in residential units were much more limited. The 17-year-old who had had a child made the following observation:

> I don't think any teenage girls or boys for that matter will discuss sex with children's home staff. I think sometimes drugs and drink they might do, but I don't think sex education. I think they already know, they think they know everything. I think they might think they look a bit stupid if they talked to the staff about it.

The girl who had had a serious crack cocaine and alcohol misuse problem by the age of 15 made the following comment: 'I actually was involved in a youth awareness project. I was probably, out of everyone I know, I probably knew more about the risks and everything than all of them.'

What appeared to be lacking for these young people was an adult or adults whom they trusted and felt able to talk to informally about issues in their lives. In contrast, young people in family-style placements (such as foster care and kinship care) said that they were able to talk over issues in conversations with carers and older children in the household.

It appears clear that educating young people in the area of drugs, alcohol and sex is about much more than the provision of information. It is also about the quality of the caring relationships that these young people have. Where young people have carers whom they can trust and talk to about issues such as drugs and sex, in a context where feelings and relationships are also discussed, they appear to be less likely to misuse substances or become pregnant.

Emotional and behavioural development (EBD)

Emotional and behavioural development is a wide-ranging category. The children talked about their emotional responses to a wide variety of issues throughout the interviews. These are often detailed in other sections, as seems appropriate (for instance, feelings about contact or parents under family and social relationships and feelings about living independently under self-care skills). In this section the children and young people's emotional and behavioural development is related to their scores on the SDQ.

Strengths and Difficulties Questionnaire

Twenty-two of the children completed an SDQ. (See Appendix 2.) This test provides a brief and well-validated measure of children's emotional and behavioural development, which has been widely used for research purposes and has been linked with the LAC schedules and the 'Children in Need' assessment framework. The SDQ has five sub-scales – emotional, conduct, hyperactivity, peer relationships and prosocial behaviour. A child can be abnormal on any one of these and/or on the overall score, thus giving an indication not only of the extent of any difficulties but also of the areas that are most affected. Table 16.2 lists the number of children whose scores were normal, borderline or abnormal on each dimension.

Table 16.2 ***Children with normal, borderline and abnormal scores on the Strengths and Difficulties Questionnaire***

Sub-scale	Normal	Borderline	Abnormal
Emotional behaviour	18	3	1
Conduct	14	3	5
Hyperactivity	18	1	3
Peer relationships	16	3	3
Prosocial behaviour	18	2	2
Total score	**14**	**5**	**3**

As a comparison we should note that approximately 80% of 11–16-year-olds in the community have 'normal' total scores, while 10% of the scores are borderline and 10% abnormal (Goodman et al. 1998). In contrast, the proportion of 'normal' scores in our sub-sample was lower (64%) and, although the numbers are very small, the proportion of borderline or abnormal scores seems to be considerably higher.

Overall the scores of the self-administered SDQs were similar to the scores from the SDQs completed by carers. There were a couple of exceptions. One 10-year-old girl with no obvious behavioural difficulties gave herself very negative marks while one 11-year-old boy with extremely disturbed behaviour gave himself positive marks. Interestingly, for these children the 'prosocial' sub-scale appeared to provide a better indication of their behaviour as described by carers and social workers.

- There was a very strong relationship between high problem ratings in the SDQ scores and young people living independently or semi-independently. Of the eight young people with overall scores that were borderline or above, four were living in their own flats and talked about feeling unsupported and lonely.

Of course, many of the young people's emotional and behavioural difficulties would have preceded the care order. However, given their pre-existing difficulties it seems all the more important that these young people are offered appropriate support once they move towards independence. It is noteworthy that the one young person who was happy with the support she was receiving in her flat scored as 'normal', despite a history of extremely challenging behaviour in the past.

- Two of the other children with a high number of problems (in fact both scored in the 'abnormal' range) had been sexually abused and their extremely disturbed behaviour was clearly related to this.

For both of these children the abuse had led to their acting in a sexualised way with other children and adults, and this was causing them (and their carers) a great deal of concern. The remaining two children who scored highly were both girls (one aged 10 and the other 12) who had been through failed rehabilitation attempts. They both had strong relationships with mothers who had substance misuse problems. Interestingly, neither scored very highly on the carer's ratings (indeed one of them had one of the lowest overall scores) and both gave themselves favourable ratings on the prosocial scale. However, they both scored highly on the emotional and the hyperactivity scales, suggesting that the effect of no longer living with a mother whom they missed persisted. One was receiving counselling about this but the other was receiving no input. She said a number of times how much she enjoyed talking about things during and after the interview and it is difficult to avoid the conclusion that some sort of therapeutic input might have been appropriate.

At the other extreme, there were some clear patterns among the nine children who gave themselves the lowest problem scores. First, all these children were living in placements that they and the carers considered permanent, though some had not been officially sanctioned by panels or courts. Second, all of the children were living in either foster families or kinship placements. (Indeed, all three of the children in kinship placements, who were interviewed, were in this group of happier children.) Third, most of these placements had a positive and flexible approach to continuing contact between the children and their parents. In the one case where there were some difficulties arranging contact, the foster carer was actively advocating increased contact for the children. The specific comments that children made in relation to these areas can be found earlier in the chapter, but the link between their satisfaction with their placements and contact arrangements and their apparent lack of emotional or behavioural difficulties is clear.

Identity

At the beginning of the interview the children were asked for a few words that best described them, and they were also asked about the activities that they enjoyed and felt they were good at. The children gave a wide range of answers, and only a couple of children found the questions difficult. Most children were quite positive in describing themselves.

- When itemising things that they were good at, most of the boys and a number of the girls picked sports or similar activities (such as dancing).

For some of these children achievements in these areas appear to have provided boosts to their sense of self-worth; for example sisters aged 9 and 11 showed the interviewer with pride their awards for disco dancing. These children identified support and encouragement from foster carers and staff as important in the development of these interests.

For some children aspects of the care experience had dented their self-confidence. In particular, children talked about how difficult it was to move between carers and the difficulties of settling into a new placement where you did not know the 'unwritten rules' of the place.

Only two of the children interviewed belonged to a minority ethnic group, and they were both of mixed heritage.

- For the children of mixed heritage, it was important to have both halves of their racial identity recognised.

One 17-year-old boy had been considered white until recently, when his mother had told him his father might be of Asian origin. He had the following to say about this: 'It has given me a peace of mind to know what he is, where he comes from, basically my origins.'

For the other child of mixed heritage, it was important to have the link with her white mother recognised. This 8-year-old girl had been removed from her mother and was happily placed with her black paternal grandmother. However she felt that it was important to hold on to both identities:

Interviewer: You said your race is important; how would you describe your race?

Girl: Mixed race, because my dad says I am black, but I am not, because if I was black then I would be like him and grandma. I am not. I am mixed race because I have got white and black in me.

Self-care

Few of the children who were interviewed identified any particular difficulties in relation to self-care – probably because they were older children who were not disabled and they did not experience the younger children's difficulties with eating, washing, toileting, and so on. However, for one young person things had improved considerably in this area. He had a severe incontinence problem, which had previously troubled him at school, in the gymnasium and in other social environments, and he had had considerable medical and practical help with this problem since being made subject to the care order. Other children in residential care had been encouraged to use public transport for contact visits if this was appropriate, and they had learned how to cook themselves simple meals.

- The exceptions to this generally positive picture were the five young people who had now left residential care and were either living independently or in one case with parents. Several of these young people talked about difficulties in managing their lives.

Some of them found coping with bills and budgeting on a limited income difficult, and they were also unhappy that as soon as they moved out of the residential care home – even if they were under the age of 18 – the level of support offered to them fell dramatically. One 17-year-old's comments were typical:

> If they are too busy why don't they allocate a new social worker? ... I haven't heard from her since I moved in [three months] ... I feel basically that when you move out the contacts and everything shouldn't just stop if you are still on a care order ... basically I think this is going to be probably the hardest time of my life anyway ... it is not like the money side of things, it is not anything like that. It is just if I need to see somebody, or if I need advice about anything at all really then I should be able to speak to my social worker.

A particularly worrying aspect of the lack of support that these young people were getting when they left care was that it seemed likely to undo a broadly positive experience. Often they had been made subject to the care order with multiple emotional, educational and behavioural difficulties and after some time they had found a placement that supported them and in which they made relationships that they valued. They felt disillusioned that as soon as they left their placements the support of social workers and residential staff seemed to stop very quickly.

Social presentation

The children did not generally express concerns in relation to their own social presentation, either in terms of appearance or behaviour, but they did not like being presented to the outside world as 'children in care'. A couple mentioned group outings from children's homes as being potentially embarrassing and stigmatising in front of other young people.

> At the moment it is a hell of a lot of a stigma. When we went to the cinema I remember it being (whispering) 'Oh, they're from the children's home. They get in free.' When you are with your mates you don't want that sort of thing. It is not what you want at all.

One 10-year-old girl discussed the difficulty of not knowing how to describe her foster mum to her friends. Her difficulty in doing this meant that she rarely invited friends home. However, most of the children did not have significant concerns in this area as long as the placement was happy and secure.

Discussion and conclusions

One notable feature of the children's views is their *individuality*. On some issues, such as contact with parents, siblings and friends, there was a large degree of consensus, but there were still some children whose wishes were different from those of the majority (for example, because they had been abused or manipulated by parents), and attempts to impose a blanket policy without consulting these children would have resulted in grave injustice.

Second, the interviews give us an insight into the *needs of children in the care system* – needs that can be corroborated from other sources. Apart from the need for contact, and for counselling or therapy where the sense of loss was severe, there was a clear need for an ongoing relationship with at least one trusted adult in the new environment. Kinship carers seemed to have an advantage over foster carers inasmuch as they were known when the care order was made. However, foster carers who were seen as caring and concerned were important sources of support and guidance for many of the children and their encouragement boosted self-esteem. Residential care seemed to offer less support, less guidance and less protection – although one teenage girl from a middle-class background said that she had profited greatly from her boarding school. Family living was something that most of the children liked and welcomed, as long as they could be admitted to the family circle and not made to feel on the outside.

A third important element in these interviews is *children's explanations for events and circumstances that might be defined by the professionals in different terms*. It is useful to know, for example, that some of the children with emotional and behavioural difficulties were simply bored by their education and wanted more interesting things to do with their time. It is sad but not surprising to learn that babies were wanted and actively sought by young women who were little more than children themselves; but the expression of their views reminds us that for these young people, as for most mothers, the birth was looked forward to as a positive and joyful event. When faced with the need to move on from the placement, on the other hand, they explained this in terms of resource issues and the need not to 'block a bed' – which suggests that they saw planning as being service-led rather than focused on their own needs and interests. The young people also had opinions about the effect that the care system had had on their behaviour, because of the expectations it created in others, and in spite of some fantasising they were remarkably accurate in their self-assessment by means of the SDQs. Some children should clearly be credited with more awareness than was usually attributed to them.

However, the interviews also give us a disturbing snapshot of the *risks that surround children in the care system*. Carers are not always benign, and the risk of physical or sexual abuse and neglect emerges strongly from children's accounts of previous care episodes. (They apparently found it easier to talk of past problems. Was anything wrong in their current environments – and, if so, did they feel they needed to conceal it?) Other risks that children reported being exposed to included the insecurity of temporary placements, failed attempts at return home, bullying in residential homes, lack of sexual counselling, and problems of social isolation on leaving care. A major concern for all carers must be the damage done to the health of teenagers by smoking, drinking and drug-taking, since in these interviews five out of six young people over the age of 16 said that they smoked or had taken drugs regularly, and four out of six admitted to regular drinking. Research has indicated that long-term problems are also likely to result from poor educational performance and having babies at a young age. One of the most important tasks undertaken by carers and social workers must be to help young people avoid or minimise the harm associated with these risks.

Final thoughts

At the end of the interview children were asked 'If you could tell the people responsible for children under care orders in Britain one thing about the way we should look after them, what would it be?' All the available answers are reproduced here.

> I think basically they should always find out whether they are happy in their placements on their own. Don't ever ask them in front of anybody.
>
> Place them with foster carers closer to where they came from.
>
> If [children] feel like they want to run away, they should think about it first.
>
> To listen to what children say.
>
> Treat us the same as anyone else – like your grandchildren.
>
> Probably to change the whole welfare state to provide more facilities ... You can make all these elaborate care plans but the reality is not that you don't want to give this child that but that you do not have the facilities to give to the child.
>
> They should listen to what the complaint forms say and not just write back to you and say they are sorry; they should do more. Because if they were in care and that is happening to them, they would not be very happy getting the same letters back.
>
> As long as they treat them with respect – I know they do, but I mean like more. As long as they treat them like they would a normal child who is with their mum and dad.
>
> Not really. I don't think having a care order on you really makes a lot of difference actually.

> I would say that I believe on the whole foster care does not work because foster carers are not as they seem.

> Reasonable explanation why people say you can't do things. Not like 'you can't do it'. Why? Speak to you about it.

> You should stay in school because you need an education.

> Should let the children see their mums more.

> Basically give us love and affection and we'll love you ... All kids in here just want to get on ... Basically all they want is to have a little bit of fun, a little bit of love and a little bit of affection. That is all they want so that is what they should get.

Summary

1. Overall, the children were positive about their current placements. By the follow-up period every child interviewed and still in care felt that they had found a placement in which they had good and enduring relationships with carers or staff.

2. The exceptions to this positive picture were the five young people who had left care. Three of these young people talked of feeling lonely and unsupported.

3. Many of the children described negative experiences in previous placements. In residential care, complaints tended to be related to bullying and violence from other children. In foster care there were a couple of examples of physical or sexual abuse by carers; however, the most common complaint was that children felt they were not treated as part of the family.

4. Contact with parents – particularly mothers – remained important to almost all the children even when it was upsetting. Children also highlighted the significance of siblings, whether or not they were still in contact with them, and for some children maintaining links with close friends was also important. Contact was particularly satisfying where it was fairly frequent and held in informal surroundings.

5 Most of the children enjoyed school and talked positively about it. Children attributed any under-performance to their own emotional or behavioural difficulties, and also to lack of stimulation in the work that they were being given.

6 The children who were most satisfied with their placements, among those who were interviewed, were living in families (foster care or kinship care), in placements considered permanent, and they all maintained regular contact with their parents and significant others. The children with most difficulties were children who had been sexually abused and young people who were living independently.

17 The links between children's welfare and implementation of the care plans

Introduction

We are now in a position to address one of the central issues of the research – the relationship between plan implementation and welfare. It seems best to begin with the largest question of whether or not care plan implementation was associated with better outcomes. As part of this theme, we shall examine the relationship between plan implementation and outcome when children's initial difficulties and other factors are taken into account, and ask to what extent fulfilment of the plan offered opportunities for the amelioration of problems. Finally we shall look at the progress of children who do not fit the general patterns of our research, since this is one of the keys to understanding risk and protective factors in care planning.

Did children tend to have better welfare outcomes when the care plan was implemented successfully?

Statistical analysis was used to test the relationship between plan fulfilment and the two measures of welfare outcome. In brief, we found that:

- successful implementation of the placement plan had a significant association with *welfare progress* and with *welfare status;* children with the best welfare scores on either measure were more likely to be living in the placement type specified in the court care plan, and *vice versa.*

The details of the statistical analysis are as follows. Ordinal logistic regression was used to investigate the effect of placement plan implementation on children's progress. Fulfilment of the placement plan significantly increased the odds of good welfare progress and, conversely, non-fulfilment increased the odds of poor progress (odds ratio = 3.01, $p = 0.003$, 95% CI from 1.44 to 6.31). The same method was used to test the relationship between placement plan implementation and welfare status. Children whose placement plan was fulfilled were likely to have fewer welfare deficits at the end point of the study, and their final welfare status score was likely to be better than those whose plan remained unfulfilled (odds ratio = 4.01, p = 0.001, 95% CI from 1.82 to 8.82). There was a significant negative correlation between the number and severity of endpoint deficits and welfare progress (Kendall's tau-b = -0.72).

A study was also made of the relationship between good progress and placement type. The results are interesting, although the links between welfare progress and placement choice are many and complex and, as outlined in Chapter 15, a key factor is obviously the age of the children.

- All placement types were represented in cases where children had their plans implemented and made or maintained good progress, but successfully implemented adoption plans accounted for the highest proportion with kinship care in second place.

Did fulfilment of the placement plan still have an impact when other factors were taken into account?

The analysis reported above suggests that implementing care plans matters, and successful implementation makes a difference to children's welfare; but is it possible that the implementation of the placement plan itself, and the good outcomes that accompanied it, were determined largely by factors such as the number and complexity of children's initial difficulties?

Hardly surprisingly, children with a high number of initial problems were less likely to have their placement plan implemented successfully than those with a low number (odds ratio = 0.66, p = 0.004, 95% CI from 0.50 to 0.88). Initial problems on certain specific dimensions were also associated with placement implementation. In particular, the odds of placement fulfilment were less when the child had initial problems in family and social relationships, emotional and behavioural development, education and self-care skills.

As we have already noted, these problems were also related to poor welfare progress and a high number of final deficits – and so were two other factors that were universally present at the start point, namely the age of the children and the length of social services involvement. However:

- the statistical relationship between placement plan implementation and welfare progress was still significant when these factors were taken into account.

This is an important result – although we need to note that the statistical findings were slightly different for our two measures of outcome. In the case of welfare progress, after controlling for the number of initial problems, age and previous involvement, plan implementation remained significant ($p = 0.03$) and the adjusted odds ratio for good welfare progress if the plan was implemented was 2.99 with a 95% CI from 1.11 to 8.07. In the case of welfare status, plan implementation became non-significant at the 5% level; but there was a 'trend' towards significance ($p = 0.074$) and the adjusted odds ratio for achieving good welfare status if the plan was implemented was 2.54 with a 95% CI from 0.91 to 7.08.

- The implications of these findings are that, even when other major factors are controlled for, plan fulfilment remains a dominant factor associated with children making good progress. There is also a connection – but a slightly less strong connection – between fulfilment of the plan and the standard of welfare reached.

The difference between the findings probably reflects the fact that the second measure of welfare outcome is more closely linked to the level of initial problems.

Contact fulfilment

It should be noted that the most important consideration was the implementation of the placement plan. Although the fulfilment of the contact plan was closely related to placement fulfilment (see Chapter 8) there was less evidence of a direct relationship between contact and welfare outcome. Services also tended to support the placement, and as we have seen they were provided *ad hoc*.

Implementing the contact elements of the care plan, both by continuing or terminating contact with named individuals and by arranging contact of the requisite frequency and duration, was not significantly related to overall welfare progress ($p = 0.26$ and $p = 0.09$, respectively). However, analysis of the final deficits on fulfilment of the contact plan did show a trend, inasmuch as the mean welfare status score of children whose contact plan was fulfilled was lower by 2.86 points than the score of children whose contact plan was not fulfilled ($p = 0.087$). Moreover:

- carrying out contact arrangements in agreement with the original plan was significantly associated with good progress in family and social relationships (odds ratio = 3.5, $p = 0.014$, 95% CI 1.28 to 9.54) and in identity (odds ratio = 3.62, $p = 0.027$, 95% CI 1.16 to 11.33).

We should remember that fulfilment of contact plans often meant termination rather than continuation of contact with parents. In adoption cases this probably enabled young children to establish themselves in their new families; but the beneficial relationship between contact, family and social relationships and identity also held good where contact continued. This highlights the importance of getting contact arrangements right.

Did children with initial problems have a better chance of improvement if the placement plan was implemented successfully?

This question was explored by analysis of the welfare progress scores – although the results have to be treated with caution since the numbers are very small. See Table 17.1.

Table 17.1 ***Improvement of problems according to placement fulfilment and non-fulfilment***

Area in which a problem was identified	Percentage improvement when plan fulfilled	Percentage improvement when plan not fulfilled
Health (n=46)	68% of 22	54% of 24
Education (n=51)	61% of 23	46% of 28
Identity (n=49)	56% of 25	29% of 24
Family and social relationships (n=78)	68% of 41	46% of 37
Social presentation (n=35)	61% of 18	76% of 17
EBD (n=69)	31% of 35	50% of 34
Self-care (n=29)	70% of 10	37% of 19

In the above table, the percentage of children who started with initial problems on each dimension and experienced improvement was examined according to whether or not the placement plan was fully implemented.

- The percentage of children who showed improvement tended to be greater among those whose plan was fulfilled – but an exception was found where the child had problems in EBD.

Paradoxically, the chances of experiencing improvement in emotional and behavioural difficulties actually decreased when the placement was fulfilled. (The reality is that when these problems were present they tended to persist in any environment and, since the problems of children in failed placements were more severe, there was more room for improvement.) However, the general trend in favour of an association between placement fulfilment and amelioration is positive, and there are patterns that would profit from exploration in a larger sample.

Why did a minority of children make poor progress when the plan was implemented successfully, or good progress when the plan was not fulfilled?

Figure 17.1 charts the progress made by the children over the 21 months whether or not their plan was fulfilled.

Figure 17.1 ***Children's welfare progress and implementation of care plan***

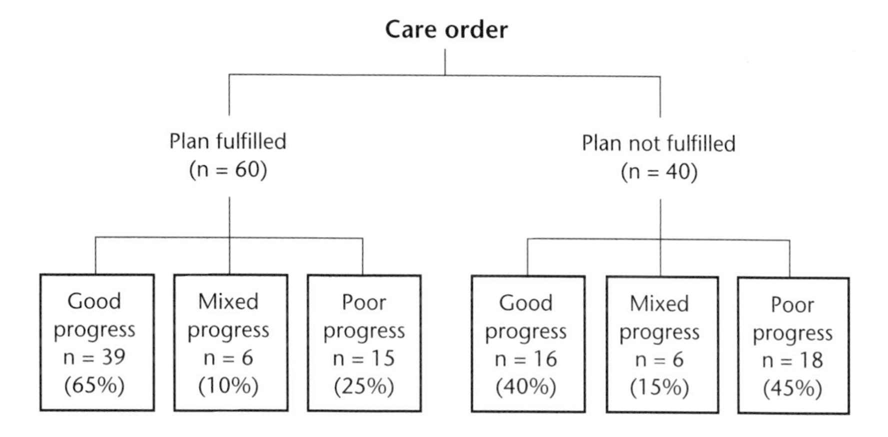

The chart shows that when care plans were fulfilled, the number of children who made good progress (39) far exceeded those who made poor progress (15), and the group of children who enjoyed good outcomes were still in the ascendancy even when poor and mixed outcomes were combined. When plans were not fulfilled, as one might expect, the picture was to some extent reversed. Poor outcomes predominated in these circumstances; but there were still sixteen children in this group who did well, and this is only slightly fewer than the number who did badly (18). This leads us to ask: Why did some children whose plans were implemented successfully have poor outcomes, while others whose plans remained unfulfilled made good progress? To put this another way, what are the risk and protective factors in implementation?

Reasons for the difference between good and bad progress when the plan was successfully implemented

As we have seen, there was a connection between good or bad progress and *placement choice*. Of the 39 children who were in their recommended placements and made good progress, eighteen – that is, almost half the number – had been placed for adoption. Another eleven had been placed in kinship care, six were fostered and four placed at home. Of the fifteen children who made poor progress in spite of the fact that their placement plans had been fulfilled, eight were fostered and three were in residential care. Two others were in kinship care, one was adopted, and another one placed at home.

This reflects what we know of the success rates of various placement options in our study, together with the tendency of agencies to place *younger children* with adopters or members of the extended family – although these children were not necessarily problem-free. There is also a slight *gender bias*, which did not show up in the total sample. In the first group (the fulfilled and good progress group) 23 were girls and sixteen were boys. In the second group (the fulfilled but poor progress group) four were girls and eleven were boys, while the intermediate group was equally divided. It appears that younger girls may be more resilient than boys, or were found to be more rewarding by their carers,[1] and consequently they made good progress; but this is certainly not true of the teenage years, since the study includes six girls with severe problems who were aged 14 or 15 at the time of the care order, and none of them did well.

Table 17.2 shows the figures for welfare progress by ethnic origin. *Ethnicity* was closely associated with placements in kinship care, which had a good rate of fulfilment as well as progress. Of the eight children from ethnic minority groups who made good progress (four Afro-Caribbean and four of mixed heritage) all were in fulfilled placements – six in kinship care and two placed for adoption. One child with mixed progress was also in a fulfilled kinship placement.

Table 17.2 ***Welfare progress by ethnic origin***

Progress	White	Afro-Caribbean	Mixed heritage
Good	47	4	4
Mixed	12	1	–
Poor	27	–	5
Total	**86**	**5**	**9**

However, among the five children from ethnic minority groups who made poor progress, three were in placements that had been fully implemented. (One of these children was in a kinship placement and two were in foster homes.) They tended to be older than the others and had a greater number of difficulties at the start point; but all the non-white children who made poor progress were of mixed heritage, and four of them were of Asian/white parentage. (No firm conclusions can be drawn from this as the numbers are so small.)

Apart from the obvious factors of placement choice, age, gender and ethnicity, there were a number of factors in the case details which help us discriminate between the children who made good progress and those who made poor progress when their placement plans were fulfilled.

The suitability of the individual placement

In the group which made poor progress although the placement plan was fulfilled, the individual placement chosen for the child did not completely meet his or her needs. Most often, the descriptions from social workers and carers suggest that:

- although the placement survived, the relationship did not 'gel'. The child had pre-existing difficulties and the carers were tolerant of these difficulties but found the child unrewarding.

When interviewed, the carers had a tendency to complain about the child. In almost all these cases there seemed to be a lack of secure *attachment* between child and carer.[2]

Interestingly, resource difficulties in terms of placement provision did not play a prominent part here. The placements were relatively stable and the social workers were usually convinced that the choice of placement was a good one. Some of the children had complex needs, which could not easily be met in *any* placement and there was no suggestion that another placement would provide anything better.

There were, however, shortages in terms of the provision of services such as therapy and educational help, and in some cases there were contact problems, which intruded on the quality of life within the placement. All these factors conspired to limit the amount of progress made by the children in the fulfilled but poor progress group.

Stability and permanence

Among the children whose plans were fulfilled and who made good progress, there was a high degree of permanence at the close of study. Thirty-one of these 39 children had reached Category 1 or 2 on our permanency scale (see Chapter 8), which meant that the placement had been officially ratified as permanent (for example by an adoption or residence order) or that long-term status had been applied for. In the group that made rather less good progress although their plans had been fulfilled, only three children had reached Category 1 or 2 on the permanency scale. The majority (eight children) were rated as belonging to Category 3 – that is, the placement was considered permanent and treated as such, but permanence had never been officially confirmed. Another four children were in placements that were definitely temporary and short term.

Statistical analysis confirms that in the sample as a whole the odds of poor welfare progress were greater if the placement was temporary rather than permanent ($p < 0.001$, odds ratio = 11.14, 95% CI from 4.43 to 28.01). It could be argued that lack of permanence was a response to poor progress rather than the other way round; but for at least three children the reason for their placements being temporary had nothing to do with their difficulties or the unwillingness of carers to look after them.

- In three cases there had been a lack of clarity about the initial planning, which had resulted in foster care being used as a placement of convenience.

There had certainly been an assumption that if necessary the placements could become permanent; but it was seen as equally possible that the children might return home, and at the end of the study neither of these options was being pursued because the plan had changed to adoption. Throughout all these planning shifts, the children never moved from their original placement.

One issue this raises is concerned with the decisiveness of initial planning and the *viability of the care plan*. Another is concerned with the relative merits of permanence and stability and the priority given by agencies to one or the other of these. Stability was keenly sought, and there was an understandable reluctance to move children unnecessarily but, as we have already indicated, the children who made less good progress sometimes moved less often than the others. In fact ten of the fifteen children who made poor progress in fulfilled placements – including the three mentioned above – made no moves at all during the study period and remained in the placements they had occupied prior to the care order. By contrast, 24 of the 39 children who made good progress during the course of the study made one move into a permanent placement.

However, none of the children in fulfilled placements matched the number of moves made by children whose plans were not implemented successfully and who, as a result, took off into the unknown.

Arrangements for siblings

Twenty of the 39 children in fulfilled placements who made good progress, and eleven of the fifteen who made poor progress, were members of sibling groups. The arrangements for placement of the siblings appeared to be closely related to outcome.

- In the good-progress group only four of the siblings were placed alone, the other sixteen being placed with one other sibling or more. In the poor-progress group six of the eleven siblings were placed alone.

Other research has reported on the difficulties of children placed separately from their siblings, their sense of isolation or rejection and the impact on other children in the carers' families (Quinton et al. 1998; Rushton et al. 2001). It should however be noted that most of these children were happy to be placed alone and they were certainly not asking to be reunited with their brothers and sisters.

- The progress of siblings placed alone appeared to be hampered by the poor quality of pre-existing relationships, by variable contact arrangements and by knowledge of other events within the family.

When these events were upsetting (as in one case where the child's siblings were removed from home after an incident of abuse) the fact of not being involved could heighten the feeling of exclusion as well as anxiety. Separate placement was not protective, because siblings worried about each other.

Needless to say, the issue is not that siblings should never be separated but that the best possible arrangements should be made for their welfare. In one case where a teenage girl made poor progress, there were continuing worries that she should have been placed separately from her sister instead of being obliged to live in this girl's shadow. Like so many decisions, this choice needed to be made in the initial stages of the care order. Twenty-one months down the line, the situation could not be changed without a major upheaval and disruption of the placement.

Reasons for the difference between good and bad progress when there was failure to implement the plan

When the placement plan was not fulfilled, what distinguished the children who made good progress from those who did less well?

Not surprisingly, we find the same factors operating here as distinguished good from poor progress when the placement plan was fulfilled. The most obvious pre-condition of good progress was the *suitability of the individual placement*, and especially the quality of the relationship between child and carer. The presence of good attachment was one reason why plans were deliberately varied for three children when adoptive placements proved hard to find. All of them did reasonably well in long-term fostering placements with the possibility of residence orders being sought at a later date.

Variation of the plan could of course mean loss of permanence, and *permanence and stability were once again powerful factors*. Among the sixteen children who had good outcomes in the non-implemented group, eleven were in placements considered to be permanent, although only three of these had reached Category 1 or 2 on the permanency scale. In the group of eighteen children with less good outcomes, only two children were in situations that could be considered permanent – and both of them would soon be leaving care. A total of fourteen children were on level 6 of the permanency scale, which meant that there was no possibility of permanence in the present placement and consequently they would definitely have to move on. Six of these children had already moved three or more times during the course of the study.

The splitting up of sibling groups was less important as a factor in unfulfilled placements than in fulfilled ones because more attempt had been made to keep siblings together (perhaps at the expense of placement, in one case), and only six children were placed alone. Two of these solitary children made good progress – though one was a new-born baby who was later placed for adoption. The impact of separation and loss in this and in other similar cases fell not on the young child but on her siblings. The four separated siblings who made poor progress were all older – at least 9 years old at the time of the care order – and they all belonged to families in which there was ambivalence and conflict as well as a sense of belonging. They had unsatisfactory relationships with birth parents as well as siblings, and some incidents of absconding stemmed from the belief that brothers or sisters were receiving more or better contact than they were.

The information recorded above confirms the picture of positives and negatives already built up in fulfilled placements. However, in the groups now being scrutinised there were additional factors connected with the non-fulfilment of the placement plans.

The difference between breakdown and failing to enter the placement

When compared with children whose placement plan was implemented successfully, the odds of making good progress decreased non-significantly for children who failed to enter the planned placement; but the odds of good progress decreased significantly when the placement was entered and later broke down (odds ratio = 0.22, p = 0.01, 95% CI from 0.07 to 0.7). In other words:

- breakdown was more damaging than failing to enter the placement.

In the good-outcome group, the number of children who failed to enter the recommended placement (nine children) just exceeded the number of those whose placement broke down (seven children). In the poor-outcome group this situation was reversed, with thirteen children having experienced breakdown and only five failing to enter the chosen placement. Once again the 'mixed' group provided an intermediate position, with four placements that broke down and two that were never entered.

The reasons why breakdown was more damaging than non-entry may seem obvious, but they justify exploration because none of them are inevitable. On the face of it *the children whose placements broke down* had a better start, because they had fewer and less serious initial problems than the others. (See Chapter 8 for more information on this issue.) Very few of them had health problems or learning difficulties. The children were not passive; they were bright and energetic – but they could present challenging behaviour, and when things went wrong they were active in disrupting their placements. They were placed in environments that were not tolerant of children with problems; but contingency plans had seldom been made in any detail, because everyone involved in the case had a commitment to fulfilling the plan and there was an underlying belief that commitment on its own would make it work.

Breakdowns were particularly damaging in adoption cases. Even if the arrangements were at an introductory stage and the child had not actually entered the placement, the effect of disruption on a child who had been prepared to receive a 'new mum and dad' or a 'forever family' could be devastating. However, the risk of breakdown, though serious, should not be overestimated. The ratio of three breakdowns to nineteen children successfully placed in adoption means that the breakdown rate is not excessive, although the period of our study spanned the most vulnerable period of the child's career. (The greater risk in adoption was that a placement would not be found within the time-scale.)

In most environments, and not simply in adoption, there was a lack of preparation for disruption.

- Unlike foster carers, neither adoptive parents, kinship carers nor birth parents appeared to have had any advice about handling this situation if it should arise.

The result was that in many cases of disruption children felt rejected by their carers. Even children who were removed from home by social services were sometimes blamed by birth parents for the events leading to their removal, and earlier experiences of rejection were damagingly reinforced.

The experiences of *children who failed to enter the recommended placement* within our time-scale were clearly different from the experiences of those whose placements disrupted. They were either waiting to move or had had their plans varied so that they could remain where they were. (The numbers in each of these categories are approximately equal.) The children who were still waiting for a placement at the close of our study were anxious, and since many of them were already suffering from developmental delay and lack of educational opportunities, they were in great need of a stable placement and a start to remedial work. (In one case difficulty in finding a special school actually delayed the start of the placement.) However, some children had a more positive experience than this.

- When plans were varied so that children could remain in an existing placement, the option that had been selected as being in their best interests was abandoned; but this happened at least partly for positive reasons, such as attention to the child's wishes and feelings or attachment to the existing carer.

It may be argued that in some cases action should have been taken more swiftly and profound attachment should never have been allowed to develop. It may also be argued, with some justification, that where the fulfilment of the plan ran counter to the child's wishes and feelings the original care plan was at fault; but once the situation had changed there was no point in denying it, and in most cases where the plan was deliberately varied there would be little point in insisting that the original plan should be carried through, because the care plan presented to the court was unfortunately out of date.

The timing of any breakdown

When we compare the cases of breakdown where children made good or poor progress, it appears that there is another factor in addition to those already mentioned – the time when the breakdown happened.

- If the placement broke down fairly soon after the care order, the children tended to make better progress than if this occurred at a later date.[3]

Table 17.3 gives the numbers of children with good, mixed or poor outcomes in cases of placement breakdown. Although the numbers are rather small, it can be seen that good outcomes were much more common in the group experiencing early breakdown (that is, in the first half of the study period, and especially in the first few months) than in the group of twelve children experiencing late breakdown (in the second half of the period). Conversely, poor progress was more common in cases of late breakdown.

Table 17.3 ***Children's welfare progress in cases of early and late placement breakdown***

Outcome	Early breakdown	Late breakdown
Good	7	3
Mixed	2	–
Poor	4	9
Total	**13**	**12**

There appear to be several reasons for the link between poor progress and late breakdown. First, it may be a feature of the timing of our study; when disruption occurred towards the end of the follow-up period, there was obviously less time for children to become settled in a new placement and show a measurable recovery. Second, there were some placements that had always been somewhat unsatisfactory, but in the interests of stability the social worker had been 'nursing them along' until the situation became untenable. In such cases the child had made poor progress throughout the 21 months, and the result cannot be attributed solely to the ill-effects of the breakdown itself. The children had been left for too long in damaging environments.

In cases of very early breakdown, the plan never really had a chance to get off the ground. One 12-year-old boy left foster care very quickly when he did not get on with the family, and he was subsequently looked after by his older brother, which proved to be a better option. In two families where children were placed at home with an alcohol-abusing mother, the parent rapidly abandoned her attempts to remain sober and alternative plans had to be made for the children very soon after the care order; but the disruption merged with the distressing events of care proceedings, and the experiences of these children were not dissimilar from those of others who had brief periods of attempted rehabilitation followed by a change of plan at a late stage in care proceedings.

Breakdowns were always traumatic for the children involved, regardless of when they occurred. Nevertheless the list of children making good progress in cases where the plan was not fulfilled includes ten of the 25 children whose placement broke down. This reminds us that children are resilient, and given good care and encouragement they can overcome obstacles that land in their path before and after the care order is made.

In cases where the children made good progress outside the recommended placements, did the non-fulfilment of the care plan make any difference?

Figure 17.1 suggests that there are two groups of children with good outcomes, and that they are comparable except for the fact that 39 children (the greater number) were in the placements recommended in the care plan while sixteen others managed to make good progress in spite of the fact that the placement plan had not been fulfilled. For those on the left of the chart it might be construed that the fulfilment of the care plan had an impact, but for those who made good progress on the right of the chart, it looks as though the failure to implement the care plan simply did not make any difference.

At first sight our ratings of welfare progress seem to support this view, or at least they do not contradict it; but since we have two measures of welfare outcome, it seems appropriate to check the findings about welfare progress against those for welfare status. This second measure helps to discriminate between the two groups of children who made good progress. It shows that there are differences in the standard of welfare children had reached, depending on whether the plan was implemented or not. They did not all have an equally good welfare outcome.

Table 17.4 ***Comparison of welfare progress with final deficits and welfare status scores in fulfilled and unfulfilled placements***

Welfare progress	**Mean number of final deficits**		**Mean welfare status score**	
	Children with fulfilled placement plans	Children with unfulfilled placement plans	Children with fulfilled placement plans	Children with unfulfilled placement plans
Good	1.12	2.62	1.64	4.00
Mixed	2.50	3.16	4.33	4.66
Poor	4.28	5.16	9.07	11.20

Table 17.4 compares welfare progress with the standard of welfare reached at the end of the study. (It should be noted that these numbers indicate the presence of problems, and therefore a lower score denotes a better standard of welfare.) In the calculation based on the mean number of final deficits per child, the maximum number is 7 (that is, one for each dimension); but the welfare status score is more sensitive because it is weighted to take into account the severity of the deficits. (1 = mild deficit, 2 = moderate deficit, 3 = severe deficit) and the maximum score is 21. The findings offer further confirmation of the fact that the children whose placement plans were not fulfilled had more deficits and poorer welfare status at the end of the study than those whose placements were fulfilled. However, the point to notice in both these tables is how the data relate to welfare progress, and particularly to *good* welfare progress.

- Both in a simple count of the deficits and in the slightly more sophisticated calculation that involves weighting of the scores, the results for children whose placement was unfulfilled do not match the results in the fulfilled group.

In fact the best results in the unfulfilled group are nearer to 'mixed progress' than to 'good'. The two groups of children have made progress, but they have not reached an equally good standard of welfare.

Discussion and conclusions

The statistical findings show that when the placement plan was fulfilled, children tended to make better progress and they also enjoyed a better standard of welfare at the end of the study. The percentage of children who showed improvement on individual dimensions of welfare (health, education, and so on) was also greater among those whose plan was fulfilled – except in the case of emotional and behavioural development – and although implementation of the contact arrangements was not significantly related to overall progress, it was associated with good family and social relationships and a positive sense of identity. Furthermore, the statistical relationship between placement plan implementation and welfare progress was still significant when other factors such as age and the level of children's initial problems were taken into account.

The conclusion must be that implementation of the care plan matters. Good outcomes do not automatically follow; but research has shown that children's outcomes in the widest sense are influenced by risk and protective factors derived from the child's own characteristics, the family and the wider social environment, as well as from the services and supports that are available to address vulnerability and build on strengths (Ward 1995; Utting et al. 1997; Quinton et al. 1998; Cleaver et al. 1999; Rutter 2001). Similarly in the implementation of care plans there are protective factors that can mitigate the effects when things go wrong. We have seen that children can thrive as long as they have some degree of stability and permanence, attachment to the existing carer and ideally the support of one or more siblings in the placement. Conversely the absence of these factors increases the risk of poor progress even where the placement is fulfilled. But in a number of different ways it has been shown that successful implementation of the placement plan is associated with good welfare outcomes, and this strengthens the need for regular monitoring and review to ensure that targets are kept in view. This task will be undertaken by the special reviewing officer whose appointment is laid down in the Adoption and Children Act 2002 (section 118).

Children have multifarious needs and different starting-points, and fulfilment of the placement plan on its own will not guarantee a successful result; but it is clearly a vital ingredient in the achievement of good welfare outcomes for children, and no one involved in decision-making for children can afford to ignore its importance.

Summary

1. At the end of the study, children with the best welfare outcomes on both measures were more likely to be living in the placement type specified in the court care plan and vice versa.

2. All placement types were represented in cases where children had their plans fulfilled and made or maintained good progress. The highest proportion were in adoptive placements, followed by kinship care.

3. If children had a large number of pre-existing problems, this was related to poor welfare progress and a high number of final deficits. However, the statistical relationship between placement plan implementation and welfare progress is still significant even when initial difficulties, age and the length of previous involvement are taken into account.

4. Permanence was strongly associated with good welfare progress and also with fulfilment of the care plan. So was the stability of the placement. The more children moved, the worse the outcome was. However, the children who were successfully adopted – and also some of those in foster care – made a single satisfactory move into a permanent placement.

5. In terms of the reasons for non-fulfilment of the care plan, breakdown was more damaging than failing to enter the placement; but early breakdowns were less damaging than late ones. Some children went on to make a good recovery.

6. A minority of children made good progress even though their care plans were not fulfilled, and vice versa. In these cases the outcome appeared to be influenced by factors such as age, gender and placement choice, the quality of the child's attachments, contact and services, the degree of permanence and stability offered, and the presence or absence of other siblings in the placement. However, the children who made good progress when their plans were fulfilled had fewer endpoint deficits than those who made good progress outside the recommended placement. In other words, they reached a better standard of welfare.

[1] Lowe and Murch (2002) found that girls were more adoptable than boys. It may also be that little girls' difficulties are less likely to be of the antisocial type.

[2] Drawing on Ainsworth et al. (1978), Bowlby (1988) and others, Howe (1995; 1998) has identified four types of attachment experience – secure, insecure/ambivalent, insecure/avoidant and disorganised. All of these were represented in the study, although the main attachment-related complaint made by carers was that the child was simply unresponsive.

[3] There is some evidence in fostering research that later breakdowns may be associated with 'bad patches', but the findings reported here are specific to care order children and they cover all the placement options.

18 Conclusions

Childcare decisions require an interdisciplinary approach, and they have to be made in a constantly changing context. Inevitably, a project such as the one we have undertaken raises as many questions as it answers; but in this final chapter we discuss the main themes that formed the basis of the research objectives identified in Chapter 1 and try to draw out the main messages for policy-makers and practitioners. We begin by summarising briefly the key findings of the study as a basis for the ensuing discussion.

Brief summary of the findings

The study set out to answer three main questions:

- To what extent are care plans implemented according to the agreed plan?
- What factors influence fulfilment or non-fulfilment?
- What is the relationship between plan implementation and welfare outcome?

The implementation of the plan

By the end of the study 60 of the 100 children were living in the placement type specified in the court plan. The highest fulfilment rate was in kinship care where children were living with relatives (78%), followed by foster care (68%). Adoption plans were fulfilled for 58% of the children for whom they had been selected, but placements at home achieved only a 41% success rate. Foster care was the main collecting ground when placement plans were not fulfilled, and at the end of the study the number of children in foster homes was nearly twice as great as had been planned.

Children whose plans were fulfilled were more likely to be living in placements judged as permanent (that is, expected to last until the young person was at least 16 years old if this was needed). By contrast, two out of every three children whose plans were not fulfilled at the end of the study were still living in temporary accommodation. For a few of these children permanent placements had been identified, or else it was hoped that the current placement would become permanent; but a total of 21 children would definitely have to move on. Seventy-one children stayed where they were or made only one move during the course of the study. Eighteen children moved twice, and a minority of eleven very unsettled young people moved three times or more.

The reasons for non-fulfilment

In fifteen cases where the care plan presented to the court had not been fulfilled, children failed to enter the recommended placement within our time-scale. In the remaining 25 cases the placement broke down. The reasons for plans not being implemented successfully varied with the placement type but in all cases there was a complex interplay of factors. A lack of suitable adopters accounted for the majority of non-implemented adoption plans, especially for children from large sibling groups, those aged 3 or over at the time of the final hearing and those with developmental delay. Age was important in explaining breakdowns in foster care or kinship care, but this usually went hand in hand with higher rates of emotional disturbance and educational needs. Plans that ran counter to the wishes and feelings of the young person also helped explain non-fulfilment of foster care as well as residential placements.

The presence of a sibling group always complicated placement, as did the presence of initial difficulties among the children. However, some environments were more tolerant of children's problems than others. Foster care provided a tolerant environment. The children placed at home had few initial difficulties, but social services sought to remove young children when the placements were deemed unsafe.

The relationship between plan implementation and welfare outcome

The study found a clear relationship between plan fulfilment and welfare outcome. Among the children whose plans were fulfilled, 65% (n=39) made or maintained good progress, compared with only 40% (n=16) of the children whose plans were not fulfilled. Conversely, children who made poor progress were more likely to have had their plans not carried through.

Placement implementation had a statistically significant association with welfare progress, as did the level of permanency provided by the placement; but fulfilment of the contact plan was also important as it had a positive effect on children's family and social relationships and their sense of identity. The impact of services was impossible to measure statistically.

The importance of the relationship between placement plan implementation and welfare progress still held true, though less strongly, when the child's initial difficulties were taken into account. The same was true of welfare status. At the end of the study the children who were living in fulfilled placements, when compared with those whose placement plans had been varied, were likely to have fewer 'welfare deficits' across the seven dimensions of child well-being in the Looking After Children schedules. However, 40% of the sample continued to show moderate to severe deficits in family and social relationships and/or emotional and behavioural development, and 30% in education. Statistically significant factors associated with standards of welfare were children's age and initial difficulties at the point when the care order was made; but placement implementation still made a difference and mediated the welfare status outcome – for better or worse depending on whether the plan was implemented successfully or not.

Discussion of the main themes

In Chapter 1 several important themes were identified, all of them related to the Children Act 1989 and its underlying philosophy. These themes provided the basis for six research objectives, which were outlined as follows:

1. Monitoring the effectiveness of the care planning framework laid down in the Children Act 1989, with specific reference to the role of the care plan presented to the court for children on care orders.
2. Helping to clarify the status and quality of care plans.
3. Offering feedback to courts, children's guardians and social work personnel on the results of their decisions.
4. Tracking social workers' ongoing support for parents, carers and children.
5. Making a contribution to outcome-focused research for children.
6. Providing evidence to inform debates on the boundaries between judicial and social work decision-making.

We are now in a position to report on these themes.

1 The effectiveness of the care planning framework

Under the Children Act 1989 it was envisaged that the care plan presented to the court would have two main roles. First, it would provide the court with information that could influence the likelihood of an order being made or not made. Second, it would set out a framework for social services case management after the care order. Both of these roles were performed by the care plan in the sample cases.

Did the plan make a positive contribution to the court process?

The care plan was not always given overt scrutiny in court, and some practitioners would have welcomed more open discussion of the plan at the time of the final hearing. Nevertheless orders were made on the strength of the plans, and knowledge of the agency's intentions helped to shape parents' attitude to the order as well as giving the parties foreknowledge of the case they had to meet. Some of the parents who were interviewed could not remember the plan or were unsure of its contents; but others felt that the plan dealt with issues that were really important to them – especially arrangements for contact or rehabilitation. (See also Masson and Oakley 1999.) In one-third of the cases the final hearing was contested; but in approximately half of the cases where it was not contested, practitioners felt that positive agreement had been reached on the strength of arrangements in the care plan.

The small number of judges who were interviewed at the start of the study said that it was rare for them to be faced with a plan that was considered deeply flawed, although several could cite examples of plans that had caused considerable misgivings. If the plan appeared to be hazy or incomplete the judges said that they would make an interim care order and adjourn for further consideration of the plan – which suggests that the extended use of interim care orders legitimised in the House of Lords judgement *Re S* (2002) was a clarification and reaffirmation of existing practice. As has been pointed out elsewhere (*Re S and D* [1995] 2 FLR 464), the 'No Order' option was not considered realistic because in most cases it would leave the child at risk. However, it seems unlikely that greater certainty would have been achieved by extending interim care orders in most of the cases where plans were not fulfilled. The only possible exception was a case where the placement broke down because the medical problems of the carer had not been fully assessed.

Consultation during proceedings was sometimes extensive. Nevertheless the Children Act and subsequent case law have made it clear that the care plan is *the local authority's plan for the child.* The local authority did indeed 'own' the plan and took responsibility for it (an essential step towards implementation); but the research showed that important inputs in the early stages often came from children's guardians and local authority solicitors as well as key social workers. The extent of the activity during care proceedings is shown by the fact that although 15% of plans were complete at the time of application to the court and did not change, 25% of the care plans altered radically during proceedings and another 60% were 'firmed up'. (See Chapter 5.) As the numbers of plans for home placement dropped, the plans for adoption increased. The influence of the children's guardians on changes to initial plans for rehabilitation was strong; but the guardians also helped to identify substitute carers and accompanied young people on pre-placement visits. Local authority solicitors helped to check the ingredients of the plan and supported social workers in court. In short, the court process exerted an influence and it helped to improve the quality of the final plans.

Did the framework promote a proactive approach to case management after the order?

The plans were always treated as a blueprint for action, although the scarcity of resources was a constant and serious problem. The government set out to improve provision for children in the Adoption and Children Act 2002, in addition to the Quality Protects and Choice Protects initiatives, and these efforts are clearly justified since the study showed that placement choice was often restricted because carers were in short supply. There was a particular shortage of specialist foster carers and people willing to adopt older children. (It is worrying to find that children who were only 3 years old at the final hearing were not placed for adoption within the time-scales of the study.) In addition, difficulties were sometimes encountered with corporate planning, for example when financial commitments had to be obtained from health or education services. Resource difficulties in the widest sense included a shortage of qualified social workers and a high turnover of younger staff, accentuated by problems of reorganisation (Balloch et al. 1999). An increase in resources across the board would help speed up the planning process and increase the chances of children finding a permanent placement, which has been linked in this study to the likelihood of good outcomes.

Enhancing the effectiveness of the care planning framework: messages for policy and practice

- Accomplish as much as possible before the order.
- In cases where the plan is liable to be contentious, arrange a pre-court meeting with relevant professionals to discuss the plan.
- Ensure that parents and children understand the plan and note their views on it, since lack of support may influence likelihood of fulfilment.
- If possible, ensure that children and young people have visited the placement and given their consent to it before the final hearing.
- Use the skills of solicitors in checking plans, without actually giving them a case management role.
- Work to ensure a continuing supply of well-qualified social workers, and also children's guardians who will act as second opinions.
- In the recruitment of carers, target particular issues – for example, the need for specialist foster carers and adopters who will take older children.
- Make better use of the existing supply. (More cases might benefit from the involvement of kinship carers and 'significant others'.)
- Check that there is a databank of placement resources inside and outside the local authority, to help with the construction of both first choice and 'fall-back plans'.
- Consider the need for a feed-back loop to the courts.

2 The status and quality of court care plans

The status of the care plans presented to the court was generally high in the cases studied, even though the provision of a care plan was not made mandatory until the passing of the Adoption and Children Act 2002. There was no evidence of a lack of commitment on the part of social services, and in fact the majority of the people interviewed, including children's guardians, local authority solicitors, parents and judges, felt that there was a moral obligation to implement the plan. Most people also agreed that some flexibility was necessary to allow for changed circumstances. Paradoxically, an over-rigid belief that the care plan should be capable of being implemented in every detail may have led to the exclusion of some long-term targets – such as plans for family reunification or discharge from care – if there was an element of uncertainty about whether or not they could be achieved. The question of exit from the care system needed to be addressed as well as the child's entry to the system, and from the point of view of future planning it would have been an advantage to have these long-term targets included, even as statements of intent.

Ways in which the plans could have been made more effective

The study confirms other evidence that the presentation of care plans has become more streamlined in recent years (DoH 1998b; Hunt and Macleod 1999). There were, however, some ways in which the presentation of the local authority's intentions could have been made more effective. First, more evidence could have been produced in support of the plan – not simply evidence of feasibility, which has been requested in case law (*Re J* [1994] 1 FLR 253), but evidence that the plan was in the child's best interests. (This information was often missing from the social workers' reports, which concentrated on bringing forward evidence of significant harm.) Second, more attention could have been paid to ancillary arrangements to support the placement, and particularly to the integration of parts of the plan. Third, more consideration might have been given to vulnerable groups such as out-of-control teenagers, children with special needs, and young people leaving care. The first two of these groups sometimes attracted attention because they were regarded as hard to place, but in the light of research involving young adults (Stein 1989; Biehal et al. 1995; Stein and Wade 2000) and with obligations in place in the Children (Leaving Care) Act 2000, it is important that young people leaving the care system altogether should know what plans are being made for their housing, education and social support. Children from minority ethnic groups did not always have their cultural needs outlined – and if birth parents have not been given a role in the plans for their children, as other research has shown (Millham et al. 1986; Bullock et al. 1998), it will be difficult for any of the children to return home.

Plans for sibling groups and pairs

Section 23(7) of the Children Act acknowledges the need for siblings to be placed together 'so far as this is reasonably practicable and consistent with the child's welfare'. Specification of the plans for sibling groups and pairs, with details of whether or not the group or pair is to be divided, seems an essential part of care planning; yet sometimes the decisions about whether placements would be joint or separate were left until after the order, when the court and the children's guardian were no longer involved. These issues need to be set out in the care plan, along with a statement of the child's wishes and feelings about the proposed arrangements. Separation of brothers and sisters also means that careful attention has to be paid to contact arrangements, both to keep siblings in touch with each other and to preserve their links with parents and other family members (Mullender 1999; Rushton et al. 2001). Where section 34 orders to terminate contact were sought in order to underwrite an adoption plan, it would have been an advantage to have a clear account of the default contact arrangements if the adoption plan should founder, with information on the timing of when the default plans would come into play.

Time-scales and contingency plans

Time-scales and contingency plans were missing or too briefly recorded in more than two-thirds of the sample cases, but their absence seems more deliberate than might have been thought initially. As mentioned above, the solicitors were reluctant to bind social services to arrangements that could not be guaranteed, and this applied to time-scales and contingencies as well as long-term plans; but research and guidance have repeatedly underlined the importance of avoiding delay and drift (Booth 1996; DoH 1996b; Hunt and Macleod 1999) – especially in the placement of young children. There may be a mismatch here between court and local authority expectations, and simply urging greater attention to these matters may prove unsuccessful. Indeed, with the introduction of the Human Rights Act reluctance may have increased, for fear of attempts at litigation by parents and children.

This is a tension that needs to be resolved. From the point of view of the child and parent, knowing when a plan will come into being and what the alternative will be if it collapses seems a very basic entitlement. In this study the contingency plan should have become the main plan for the 40 children whose initial placements did not materialise; but in eleven of these cases the contingency plans were missing and for another 22 children they were found to be inappropriate or unhelpful. Stating the time-frames for planning is also important as a means of ensuring accountability. Without it, it is hard to judge the efficacy of social services' actions. Furthermore, the study has shown that in the few adoption cases where detailed time-scales were included, the case progressed faster than in the cases where this information was missing

All these points deal with ways of strengthening the care plan by providing fuller information, as a result of more forward planning, on existing categories. The corollary is that reviewing officers must monitor these elements of the plan as rigorously as the implementation of the placement.

Improving the quality of care plans: messages for policy and practice

- List all plans that are important for the child, including some that may be provisional (with a statement why this is so).
- Deal with long-term as well as short-term issues.
- Plan for exit strategies as well as entry to the care system.
- Address ethnicity and cultural needs.
- Identify a clear role for birth parents apart from contact.
- Document the help available to care leavers.
- Include details of time-scales to keep the implementation on target.
- Make contingency plans realistic and usable.
- Specify the arrangements for maintaining or dividing sibling groups and pairs.
- Ensure that after reading the plan, the court will have a good picture of *all* children in the family and their welfare needs.

3 Feedback to courts, children's guardians and social work personnel on the results of their decisions

Chapter 4 gives information about placement decisions, and it includes a suggested model of placement planning – a chart (Figure 4.1) that shows the commonly used method of selecting placements for individual children. In the cases studied, this model proved helpful and effective inasmuch as it identified relevant issues and helped to structure decision-making; but the conclusions to Chapter 4 record some of the perceived disadvantages of the model – the fact that it encouraged sequential rather than parallel planning, that the choice of criteria could be criticised, that it depended heavily on negative reasons for ruling out placements, and that some considerations were not addressed carefully enough at certain stages. All these arguments are true; but there is a difficult balance to be achieved. When viewed in the light of the combined philosophies of the Children Act and the Human Rights Act it can be seen that this chart, and the thinking it represents, is only partly concerned with empirical realities. It also, quite rightly, incorporates considerations of justice. By addressing placement choices in this order practitioners were prioritising care by the birth family and, if the birth family was unable to care, the choice of an adoptive placement would still prioritise the right to family life.

Which placements performed best?

Can we say which placements actually performed best in terms of plan implementation and outcome? These benefits did not always coincide, because placements differed in their capacity to accept children with problems and to respond effectively to their needs. Adoption placements tended to operate a hidden age threshold by screening out children aged over 3 as well as those with initial difficulties, but the welfare outcomes in adoption were very favourable – at least partly because of this selective process. Foster care and residential care accepted children with multiple, severe and long-standing difficulties but found it difficult to bring about improvement. The children placed at home had few initial difficulties, but in spite of this the breakdown rates were high, and even when placements lasted for 21 months the welfare outcomes of the children were no better than those noted in foster care. The average number of initial problems found in kinship placements was higher than for all other options bar residential care – yet the rate of plan fulfilment in kinship care was better than in other placement options, and it was also the second most successful option with regard to welfare progress. All of these results would merit testing with larger samples.

The differences in placement capacity, *to tolerate children's difficulties* on the one hand and *to bring about improvements* on the other, give us indications about how best to use existing options. They also indicate where pressure has to be applied if the standard of provision is to increase. For example, tolerance of problems needs to be increased in adoption, by means of better preparatory information as well as support services, if enough new carers are to be recruited and the government's target of 40% increase in adoptive placements is to be achieved. On the other hand improvement of welfare is the major challenge faced in fostering and residential care, and these are issues that the Quality Protects initiative has set out to address. In view of the fact that kinship care gave good results on both dimensions, it seems to be under-used.

How far had social workers predicted the outcome of their decisions?

The interviews conducted at the start of the follow-up period show that practitioners were often aware of weak points in the plans (although these had not always been shared with the court) and some plans were given no more than a 50/50 chance of success. The age of the children was often quoted as a reason why plans would be difficult to fulfil; but we need to note that in the overall results there was no statistically significant association between age and placement implementation. There was, however, a statistically significant relationship between the child's age and welfare outcome, older age being associated with reduced odds of good welfare progress. (See Chapter 15.) Among children's difficulties, we need to highlight the importance of education and the services it requires, since educational needs were associated both with poor rates of plan fulfilment and with poor welfare outcomes. The importance of parental alcohol abuse was also underestimated in assessments. (As a factor contributing to low implementation rates, this fell just short of statistical significance.) Both alcohol and drug abuse were major factors leading to care proceedings; but alcohol abuse in particular needed better assessments of the adults' problems and the impact of these problems on children, better facilities for treatment and better management of risk.

Was the care order justified?

One of the thorniest questions faced by courts and practitioners was the question of whether the care order was justified or not. Cases involving 'troubled and troublesome' teenagers often raised the issue of whether it was right to initiate care proceedings, since the window of opportunity seemed to have closed for some of these young people before the application was made. Should the case have come to court earlier – and if a care order had not been made at an earlier stage, was there any virtue in making it now?

Again, questions of justice had an impact on these decisions. Vulnerable teenagers at risk of significant harm (which could include drug misuse and prostitution) cannot simply be abandoned by the state because the prospects of achieving improvements under a care order are not good. Nevertheless the study does confirm that the care order was a rather weak mechanism of control. The options available to social workers trying to address the needs of delinquent and persistently absconding young people were rather limited. If the young person did not endorse the plan it was unlikely to be fulfilled, and specialist placements, whether in residential care or in fostering, were in short supply. It is difficult not to draw the conclusion that more might have been accomplished by community services at an earlier stage. Nevertheless some young people with behaviour problems did benefit from the care order when they were aged 13 or above. The key elements in the plan that made a difference were, first, ensuring that the young person's views had been fully taken into account and whenever possible acted upon; second, providing imaginative placements, including the use of residential schools; and third, identifying support services that were perceived to be of value. Where young people were extremely disoriented, short-term and well-targeted use of secure accommodation seemed to help them to regain direction, at least for a time.

The placement of children at home

Cases of home placement raise a different sort of concern. Did the case require a care order at all if it was judged safe to leave the child with the parent or return the child home immediately after the order? The results of home placements are disappointing and suggest that partnership in high-risk situations is more difficult to achieve than was envisaged when the Act was passed. (See also Farmer and Parker 1991; Pinkerton 1994; Hunt and Macleod 1999.) They raise the question of whether it is ever appropriate to make a care order with a plan for the child to remain at home. If the situation has been judged serious enough to require a care order, how can monitoring by social services provide sufficient safeguards to secure the child's well-being without a 24-hour presence? As Greenland (1987) argued, monitoring can never make a child safe. An alternative view would be to say that the cases chosen were simply unsuitable. They underestimated the risks of alcohol misuse and the effects of learning difficulties on parenting, while overestimating the input and support that could be made available by social services and other agencies. They also underestimated the pressures on single parents looking after sibling groups.

Assessments for placements at home need to be extremely cautious and well evidenced. As outlined in the Department of Health framework (DoH 1999c) *they need to consider the interaction of factors* in relation to the child, the family and wider community in order to reduce multiple risks. However, there is an argument for saying that the practice of placing children at home should cease altogether if a care order is needed, and that care orders should be limited to situations where children need to be removed. This means that a supervision order would be used in 'lighter cases' and, if it proved unsuccessful, care proceedings would be initiated. The advantages of this option are threefold. First, it would provide a clearer differentiation between supervision and care orders, and courts alone would have the power to remove the child. This may be more compatible with the Human Rights Act than present law because it increases parents' procedural protection where a major change of plan is envisaged (*W v UK* [1987] 10 EHRR 29). Second, it would not involve any change in law – only in practice. Third, it could also enhance planning at the assessment stage by requiring better evidence before the making of an order. The main drawback is that the unpopularity of supervision orders could result in a higher number of children on care orders overall.

Another option would be to consider *new ways of monitoring and supporting placements at home after a care order*. The model of intervention used in the study resembled work with families who are listed on the child protection register; but this is not ideally suited to situations where the local authority is the parent. A long period of intensive, anxiety-ridden work led to a sense of exhaustion in social workers and parents alike. Home placement cases will require careful tracking by the reviewing officers, to decide whether the supports being committed by social services at the time of the order have been provided and whether parents are complying with the arrangements set out in the plan. If the review identifies difficulties, a re-evaluation of progress with the help of a CAFCASS officer might result in the case being returned to court; but in cases that are going well it may be possible to apply for discharge the order, returning the children to a more normal form of family life.

Decision-making during care proceedings: messages for policy and practice

- Ask the purpose of the care order. Is it being sought mainly to gain control? If so, will control be effective?
- If home placement is planned, would a supervision order suffice?
- Is it advisable for children to have a period of assessment away from home?
- Consider whether the care order is being sought at a suitable time in the child's development.
- Concentrate on improving assessment skills in relation to the impacts of alcohol abuse, learning difficulties and emotional neglect.
- Identify the strengths and weaknesses of different placement options for particular children, and ask whether there is a case for 'parallel planning'.
- Try to increase tolerance of children's problems on the one hand and improvement of their welfare on the other.
- Ensure that kinship care has always been carefully considered.
- Identify and acknowledge risk factors or weak points in plans, so that appropriate actions can be taken at an early stage to ensure implementation.
- Put the care plans on file and make sure that they are available as reference points for further action.

4 Support for parents, carers and children

One of the more worrying findings of the study was the confusion revealed by some parents and children over the purpose of the care plan and their lack of knowledge of its contents. (See Chapter 6.) The anxiety experienced during care proceedings may have weakened their recall, for the plan would normally have been discussed in detail. However, there is a good argument for saying that children and parents should have a right to keep a copy of the document. The plan provides a bench-mark for shaping the child's future, even though children, parents and carers were not always able to see it in that light.

Sharing responsibility with the birth parents

Was there evidence of the continuation of parental responsibility after the order, in keeping with section 2(6) of the Children Act 1989? Except in cases where children were to be placed at home, the tasks identified for parents in the care plan were rather few. The role of the parent in day-to-day arrangements was usually to be 'advised of progress' or 'informed and consulted'. In practice, therefore, the involvement of parents in the post-order period was limited to contact visits and attendance at reviews. If they disagreed with the local authority they had little apparent power to change things. Only 25% of the care plans had mentioned arrangements for notifying disagreements, and if parents applied directly to the court for extension of contact or discharge of the order their wishes were not usually upheld.

The take-up of services for birth parents was poor, although one reason was that parents were not always in touch with social workers after the order. More community services were needed to support parents who had difficulties with alcohol misuse – especially in view of the frequency of this problem in society and the high cost to children and families as well as social services (Harwin and Forrester 2002). For alcohol-abusing parents as well as for others with learning difficulties or problems of mental health, it would have been useful to have had easier access to help from adult services. Among birth parents there was a strong need for emotional support and counselling. During the follow-up period one in seven mothers gave birth to further children, sometimes conceived during care proceedings, and it is possible that some of these mothers had not been able to cope with the loss of their previous children. We need to note that services such as adoption counselling were more acceptable some time after the order, when the request for consent to adoption provoked an upsurge of distress and a need for therapy which had earlier been refused.

What the children wanted

The supports that were welcomed by children themselves are outlined in the children's views. (See Chapters 6 and 16.) Children's descriptions of their feelings during care proceedings indicate a tension between wanting to participate actively and the fear of getting hurt – a tension that needed careful handling. However, the children made clear statements about the qualities that they valued in social workers, guardians and carers, such as honesty, reliability and the ability to listen carefully to concerns. These statements are mirrored in other studies (DoH 2001a). When living in substitute care they said that they wanted to feel a member of the family, whether they were living with relatives or with foster carers, and they disliked anything that made them feel stigmatised or 'different'. Their interviews also bear witness to the importance of contact with mother and siblings, and in view of the fact that birth family contact tended to be reduced over time (Chapter 13) active steps needed to be taken to safeguard important relationships. At the same time the emotional turbulence generated by contact was not always acknowledged, and children were not always able to cope with the trauma of failed attempts at return.

The need for supporting carers as a means to ensuring children's welfare

The children's reports of unfair and occasionally abusive treatment in previous placements remind us that support and monitoring need to be carefully combined. (See Chapter 16.) Nevertheless the study confirms the need for supporting carers as a means to ensuring children's welfare.

There were some exceptionally imaginative schemes. For example, one very disabled child was looked after by a foster carer who also received regular respite care and had breaks when the child was looked after by the mother and family, while social club outings were provided by a voluntary society and funded by the local authority. This type of multi-level support might have benefited other people looking after difficult children, especially as the responsibilities of caring for a particularly needy child often told on the physical health and mental state of the carers.

For support to be effective, attention had to be paid to the carers' expressed needs. With very few exceptions, prospective adopters and kinship carers wanted help with initial problems and introductions to community resources; but foster carers and residential carers wanted ongoing support and training and the promise of a continuing relationship with social services. In particular they needed *help to liaise with schools*, especially where statementing was an issue. Many carers had problems with illness and redundancies in their own families – problems that needed understanding and support as they increased the stress caused by caring for difficult children. At the same time it was necessary for all carers to understand the children's difficulties, without being made to feel patronised or incompetent. Among the adopters interviewed there was very little interest in the idea of post-adoption support, although other research has highlighted this need (DoH 1999a; Lowe et al. 1999; Rushton and Dance 2002) and the demand for it might well have arisen at a later date. *Legal help and advice* was always welcomed, especially in the run-up to adoption or residence orders, and this service may be increasingly necessary now that the range of options has widened to include special guardianship. Apart from this, all carers needed access to a social worker who understood their concerns, who provided useful and accurate information and responded quickly to requests for help. When children were placed at home and birth parents were the carers, the same conditions applied.

Financial and material help

For all carers, it was important to have access to financial and material help. This need has been acknowledged by government, and it may well be key to increasing the supply of carers – including single adopters and foster carers, who were not well represented or well supported in the study. The findings point up a need for greater consistency across local authorities in the payment of allowances for adopters, kinship and foster carers (and also special guardians, for whom the support systems are still uncertain). During the course of the study at least one authority introduced parity between kinship care payments and fostering allowances in recognition of the similarity of tasks, but others retained a two-tiered system. The approach to one-off payments also varied within as well as across authorities. In short, the whole approach to payment reflected different financial policies and different approaches to professional decision-making. It was not systematically related to child needs-led principles. Sometimes the probability of an allowance being withdrawn acted as a disincentive to carers who would otherwise have been willing to consider discharge of the care order. It is important to ensure that the opportunity to end supervision of the case does not lead to premature closure, which would leave children facing an uncertain future.

Supporting parents, carers and children: messages for policy and practice

- Develop ways of intervening in cases of substance abuse.

- Check that counselling is always available for parents, carers and children at times when they need it.
- Listen to children's views and let them inform policy and practice.
- Give carers information about children's backgrounds, with due regard for children's privacy.
- Help foster carers and adopters to liaise with schools and medical facilities.
- Make manageable arrangements for contact that safeguard children's important relationships.
- Make sure that all carers know how to manage placement disruptions.
- Recognise the effects of stress.
- Provide respite care for the carers.
- Ensure that there is a coherent and defensible policy for the provision of material supports.

5 Children's welfare outcomes

Ultimately the true value of the court care plan lies in its capacity to help safeguard and enhance children's welfare outcomes. The Children Act 1989 places this notion centre stage in the paramountcy principle, and it also assumes that the state will act as a 'reasonable parent' in the exercise of its duties, which implies that looked-after children should enjoy a standard of welfare comparable to that of their peers. This notion underlies the choice of our two measures of welfare outcome: *welfare progress*, which measured change over time, and *welfare status*, which was concerned with the standard reached.

Tracking children's welfare

Increasing children's life chances is now a central priority of government (DoH 1998e), and the emphasis on tracking children's welfare can only be welcomed. The assessment and action records from the Looking After Children scheme are intended to play a major role by enabling information to be collected systematically across the seven dimensions of welfare. (See Chapter 2.) Sadly, this study confirms other evidence that the completion of the records in social services departments is often patchy (Scott 1999; Ward and Skuse 2001), and if they had been used on their own in the research study they would not have provided a way of monitoring the children's progress over time. Since the most frequently mentioned problem was the sheer amount of information that needed to be collected and recorded, it might help to have a simplified and shortened schedule, which would make fewer demands on social workers' time. Practitioners certainly found the underlying ideas of the LAC scheme valuable and they drew readily on the research framework to conceptualise outcome, although they did not always have a clear sense of strategy about how to use the information to bring about change.

The link between plans that were fulfilled and the likelihood of good outcomes

The most important finding of the study is that a clear link existed between plans that were fulfilled and the likelihood of good outcomes. The fact that fulfilment of the plan was still associated with good outcomes when children's initial problems were taken into account is encouraging, since it suggests that the care system can produce good results even in the face of problems, although we need to note that the strength of the statistical link weakened when there were large numbers of initial difficulties. (See Chapter 15.) The child's age at final hearing was significantly related to welfare progress and to welfare status, and this finding reinforces the need to act promptly and decisively when a care order is needed, avoiding unnecessary delay during and after care proceedings.

The stability of placements

The first of the Quality Protects objectives is 'to ensure that children are securely attached to carers capable of providing safe and effective care for the duration of childhood' and this directs our attention to the stability of the placements. As a proxy measure of stability, this objective uses a count of the number of moves children make, instability being represented by three moves or more within a year. Lack of movement is not necessarily synonymous with attachment, and there were examples of cases in the study where the placement survived in spite of an apparent lack of attachment between child and carer. Nevertheless children cannot put down lasting attachments if they are constantly on the move (Howe 1995; Jackson and Thomas 1999), and friendship patterns, schooling and health care are also likely to be affected in these circumstances.

Our results confirm that there is a relationship between the number of moves and welfare outcome. However, as can be seen from Chapter 15, the detailed results were not evenly balanced. More of the children who made one move experienced good outcomes when compared with those who did not move at all, because it was often necessary for children to make a single move into a permanent placement. These and other moves made for positive reasons belong to Ward's category of 'planned transitions' (Ward and Skuse 2001b), which need to be distinguished from disruptions. We also need to draw attention to the issue of 'perverse incentives', which as other studies have noted can result from performance targets. For half the children with fulfilled long-term foster care plans, the wish to keep them in the same placement led to delays in looking for a long-term carer, and this meant that it took an average of eleven to fifteen months before these children entered the final placement. Nevertheless the detailed results do show that all the children who experienced four moves or more had poor outcomes. It would be useful to explore further through a large-scale survey whether there is any relationship between the number of moves and welfare outcome, and to see if it is possible to establish any clear threshold of risk.

The first Quality Protects objective also states that care should be capable of lasting 'for the duration of childhood'. This highlights another aspect of stability, which is *permanence*. As described in Chapter 8, a six-point scale was developed to measure the permanence of the placements, and this classification did seem to provide a helpful indicator of children's progress. First, it provided a way of looking across the full range of placement options within a common framework. Second, it proved a more sensitive measure of the need for action on the part of the social worker than did the number of moves and, third, it correlated well with both measures of welfare outcome. In the light of the findings, concern must be felt about the numbers of children in temporary placements.

Should long-term and permanent foster care be regarded as a single option?

The use of the permanency scale highlighted another important issue. Should long-term and permanent foster care be regarded as a single option? No one wants children to be tied to a placement regardless of change and progress; but the failure to clarify that placements would be available in the longer term had a number of negative consequences for fostered children in the study. First, despite the fact that there were no plans to return any of the children to their birth parents, some parents believed otherwise, and this confusion was shared also by some of the children and carers. Second, it may have contributed to drift and delay; the interviews showed that social workers sometimes wished to keep their options open and the strategy to keep placements undefined was therefore deliberate. Third, this open-ended approach may have complicated contact arrangements for, as other studies have shown, the status of the placement affects the attitudes of carers towards birth parents (Schofield et al.

2000; Triseliotis et al. 2000). Finally, it must be asked whether greater attention to the permanence of the placement might have helped to bring about better welfare outcomes in the children who were fostered long term. The importance of permanence and stability strengthens the case for 'maximising the contribution of adoption' (one of the sub-objectives of Quality Protects objective 1, and also a government target) although the difficulties in finding adoptive carers in this study suggest that the target may be difficult to meet and that long-term foster care will still have a significant role to play – particularly in providing homes for older children.

Individual dimensions of welfare

When we look at individual dimensions of welfare, can any conclusions be drawn from the link between these results and welfare outcomes? This takes us into the area of Quality Protects objective 4, which is 'to ensure that children looked after gain maximum life chance benefits from educational opportunities, health care and social care'. Good progress was made by more than half of the sample children on the separate dimensions, the largest percentage of satisfactory progress being recorded in health (82%). The problems most resistant to change were emotional and behavioural difficulties, which were very numerous but showed an improvement rate of only 41%, and identity problems – particularly those connected with low self-esteem – where improvements were made in only 43% of cases. These are both areas of welfare that may need therapeutic input (Harter 1990; McCann et al. 1996; Farmer and Pollock 1998) if children in the care system are to make better progress.

In spite of the progress made, there were many children who did not reach a good standard of welfare at the end of the study. In the light of Quality Protects objective 4, it is of particular concern to note that 40% of the children had moderate to severe deficits in family and social relationships and/or emotional and behavioural development, and 30% in education. (See Chapter 15 for a description of these deficits.) Once again the best results were associated with placement fulfilment although – as in the case of welfare progress – it is difficult to determine the direction of the effect. Good progress may have contributed to plan fulfilment, as well as this happening the other way round. We must remember, too, that the correlation was not complete. There were some children who did well in unfulfilled placements, with the help of factors such as permanence, sibling support and a good relationship with carers. Conversely, when these factors were missing, the fulfilment of the plan on its own was not sufficient to ensure good progress.

There is a great need for research into longer-term outcomes, both to discover what happens to children who have spent several years in the care system and to clarify the relationship between the welfare dimensions themselves.

Targeting children's welfare: messages for policy and practice

- Don't expect low standards.
- Consider using a range of data collection tools, including the Strengths and Difficulties Questionnaire.
- In professional practice and supervision, focus on the relationships between interventions and outcomes.
- Identify the aims of work and then monitor its effectiveness.
- Be aware of the effects of age on children's outcomes, and avoid unnecessary delays in implementing or reviewing plans.
- Make sure that children have access to therapeutic input where this is needed.
- In terms of welfare status, concentrate on improving outcomes in education, family and social relationships and EBD.
- Note and use the interaction between dimensions – for example by planning and providing activities that will raise children's self-esteem.
- Develop policies that will increase the permanence and stability of placements.
- Respect the complexity of social work, and remember that plan fulfilment on its own does not guarantee a good outcome.

6 The boundaries between judicial and social work decision-making: the question of post-order review

In 1994–95 the Children Act Advisory Committee Annual Report argued that there would need to be 'substantive evidence of difficulties occurring' before it would be appropriate for changes in the court's powers to be considered. The findings of this study do indeed suggest that there were difficulties in fulfilling some of the care plans, although there was no deliberate flouting of the plan; nor was there a lack of serious effort to put the plan into operation. Had either or both of these problems emerged, there would have been a strong case for supporting the introduction of a regular system of court review.

An outline for the possible remit of a post-order review was put forward in 1997 at the President of the Family Division's Inter-disciplinary Conference at Highgate House. (See Chapter 1.) It was envisaged at that time that a review power, if introduced, could be set in motion in the year following the making of the order if a guardian reached the view that this was justified in relation to certain specific criteria. However, with the advent of the Human Rights Act in 1998 the focus of the debate shifted, and a view was taken that the main justification for returning a case to court should be a breach of human rights.

As reported in Chapter 1, the passing of the Human Rights Act in 1998 appeared to open up more opportunities for the courts to exercise extended powers in care order cases; but the House of Lords decision in *Re S* (2002) upheld the boundaries between the judiciary and the executive that were laid down in the Children Act. Nevertheless the Adoption and Children Act of 2002 set out to remedy some of the problems that had been identified. Under the terms of this Act, reviews of looked-after children are to be chaired by independent reviewing officers, and a route back into court has been created through their powers to reinvolve a CAFCASS officer in disputed cases. However, a question mark still hangs over the identification of cases that should be a matter for the court's concern.

Which cases might lend themselves to review by the court?

The most vulnerable children in the study were very small children with no one to speak for them, such as the children waiting for an adoptive placement after family visiting had ceased. It was a matter of concern in the study that independent visitors were never appointed, although they were occasionally mentioned at reviews. An increase in the use of independent visitors, and also the provision of advocates for older children, would give more opportunities for independent scrutiny; but there is an argument for saying that if an adoptive placement is delayed beyond a reasonable period of time the court should be reinvolved on the grounds that the child's right to family life has been breached. Deliberate variation of the plan is of course possible, and this did occur in the study when a plan for adoption was reconsidered and changed to one for long-term foster care; but the plan may lose direction, and it would clearly be damaging for small children to linger for too long in temporary foster care without family contact of any kind. Second, the group of out-of-control teenagers might also qualify for review by the court, if acceptable placements have not been found and the young people are effectively living on the streets. Again, the right to family life is infringed – although the court might take into consideration the extent to which young people themselves are responsible for this state of affairs. Third, and perhaps most importantly, the CAFCASS officer and the court could have a role in appraising the direction of the care plan in rehabilitation cases. In some of these cases social services might welcome court backing for the child's removal, if this is necessary, and the court's involvement might reduce tensions by helping to manage a failing partnership between the local authority and the parents.

What would post-order review by the court achieve?

An important question to be asked in all these decisions is: What is post-order review by the court likely to achieve? To answer this we must look at the reasons for non-fulfilment of the plan across the board. These reasons include child factors (age, vulnerability and the child's wishes and feelings), family factors (parental problems, contact and relationship difficulties, particularly where there were sibling groups) and organisational factors (a shortage of suitable carers and staff, together with the scarcity of some placement resources and the demands of the child protection system). These factors usually acted in combination with each other. It can reasonably be argued that courts would not be able to remedy any of these matters – especially if the main reason for non-fulfilment of the plan was a lack of resources. (See Thorpe and Clarke 1998.)

If the plan has to be changed because the child or carer does not want it, this calls into question the reason why the plan was made in the first place. Is the answer to improve the quality of plans? Some suggestions have already been made about how care planning might be improved; but in some cases where the plan failed, the children's guardian and other participants in care proceedings had taken a calculated risk because they wished to give the child a chance of achieving what appeared to be in his or her best interests. To do otherwise would be to sacrifice these interests in favour of a 'safe' plan that lent itself to fulfilment but excluded some gains. There is no merit in defensive practice, whose main object is to safeguard decisions from legal challenge.

The role of the reviewing officer

At the same time the child's wishes and feelings can provide an excuse for poor practice, in the same way as the resource argument does. Social services are accountable, and risks must be monitored and managed if the trust of the court is not to be eroded. A form of post-order review that gives the courts a supervisory function in relation to social services would infringe the principles of the Children Act 1989, and there are many reasons why it should not be undertaken (Dewar 1995; Hayes 1996); but the introduction of a reviewing officer into the system, even with a tenuous connection to the courts, may offer advantages if the considerable difficulties inherent in such an appointment can be resolved. Practical difficulties would include the allocation of time and money in a situation of resource restrictions – and more importantly there is the question of how far an officer working within the social services agency itself can be perceived as genuinely independent. However, the advantages are first that initial decisions can be made and plans kept under review with full knowledge of the many 'obstacles' to success. Second, the reviewing officer will be able to monitor breakdowns as well as delays in finding placements. Current debates suggest that the courts are most concerned about cases where the care plan is not implemented because of a change of mind on the part of the local authority or because of lack of resources. In our study this might apply to the fifteen children who never entered the placement, but it cannot apply to the 25 children whose placement broke down. Remedies must be found for children in need of stability and permanence because they are 'in transit' from one placement to another.

The importance of welfare outcome

We have, however, argued that due attention should be paid to welfare outcome. If welfare outcome is treated as the ultimate test of success rather than plan fulfilment, which cases would be chosen for special treatment? It might appear that no action was needed in the case of the sixteen children who managed to make good progress in our study despite the fact that their plans were not fulfilled; but what of the fifteen who made poor progress in fulfilled placements? Could these results have been improved? If so, we must rely on the regular system of in-care reviews to ensure that their needs are met. None of these children would have been selected for post-order review in a system that had plan fulfilment as one of its screening mechanisms, even if the main criterion for review by the court was a potential breach of human rights, because they did not pass the first hurdle. On the other hand once we have uncoupled plan implementation from welfare, either in the form of the seven LAC dimensions or in some other form that is based on human rights, care plan fulfilment ceases to be the main goal and it can drop out of sight altogether unless strenuous efforts are made to keep it in view. Such an outcome would be damaging – not least because children have a right to reasonable certainty about their futures.

The question of agency accountability runs through and beyond these debates. It is a question with which courts are heavily and inevitably involved; but it is only by courts and social services working in partnership that the balance between plan fulfilment and children's welfare can be achieved.

Monitoring the implementation of care plans: messages for policy and practice

- Collect information centrally in the local authorities to monitor plan implementation rates (placement, contact and services).
- Both generally and in individual cases, document the reasons why plans are not implemented successfully; but avoid blaming the child.
- Record how long it takes for children to reach the intended placement, and the reasons for any change of plan.
- In charting children's welfare outcomes, try to record evidence of progress or deterioration as well as the standard reached.
- Monitor carefully small children waiting for adoptive placement, out-of-control teenagers and cases of home placement.
- Note the interaction of child, family and organisational factors. Can staff allocations be better used?
- Review the local authority's use of independent visitors and children's advocates. Is there a need to increase these safeguards?
- Seek to preserve the independence of the reviewing officers.
- Remember that the social services department is accountable for its actions.
- Develop ways of distinguishing cases where the plan is difficult to implement from the more serious cases where there is a potential breach of human rights.

Final conclusion

This study set out to investigate the role and effectiveness of the care planning framework set up by the Children Act 1989. Besides clarifying the ingredients of a good plan, the study has uncovered much about the workings of courts and social services, both pre- and post-order, and the detailed tracking of individual cases has resulted in a variety of recommendations for policy and practice. On a much deeper level, however, the study has been exploring the links between procedural and substantive justice.

The care planning framework introduced by the Children Act 1989 was basically a procedural framework, designed to make it easier for courts to make well-founded decisions in care order cases. This procedural framework was intended to facilitate substantive justice in the form of a care order, which would ultimately result in the child's achievement of a good welfare outcome. (This is implicit in the welfare principle, which is the driving force of the Act itself.)

At the time when our study began, there were concerns that drift and delay in implementing plans might lead to poor outcomes, but a great deal of interest was also being expressed in the idea of testing out the implementation of care plans for procedural reasons. In other words, it was seen as necessary that courts should have faith in social services to carry through the commitments they had undertaken if the care planning framework was to be seen as viable, and research was one of the mechanisms that would bring this information to light. Since the advent of the Human Rights Act, however, there has been a greater tendency to see the plan itself as dispensing substantive benefits – benefits to placements, contact arrangements and services to which children and their parents or carers may have a moral right if not actually a legal right – and there is a growing feeling that if these benefits are denied, the conduct of social services is open to challenge. With the development of the Quality Protects initiative, too, the question of welfare outcome has acquired a higher profile, lending new strength and meaning to the welfare checklist in court, and some consideration of the Looking After Children dimensions of welfare is inseparable from the planning decisions.

For reasons of procedural and substantive justice, the implementation of the care plan presented to the court is now more important than ever before. The study has shown that fulfilment of the care plan on its own cannot guarantee progress for children, nor is it the only means by which a good outcome may be achieved; but nevertheless its implementation is strongly linked to children's future welfare, and it is an essential part of making care orders work.

Appendix 1:
Notes on the statistical analysis

Some of the children in the sample were related to others. In order to take account of possible correlations between the responses of children from the same family, therefore, all analyses used robust standard errors adjusted for the clustering of children in families. (The sandwich estimator of the standard errors was used; see for example Binder, 1983.)

Many of the outcome measures, including welfare progress and welfare status, were measured on an ordinal scale with a small number of categories. For example, welfare progress was measured on a scale from 0 to 7. Since we cannot assume a normal distribution for such ordinal responses, ordinal logistic regression was used to model the relationship between these variables and potential predictors such as age and plan implementation. Categories that occurred very rarely in the sample were merged with other categories. For example, for welfare progress, categories 0 to 3 were merged.

Ordinal logistic regression models the probability of a child falling into a particular category of the outcome as a function of a number of explanatory variables or predictors. The effect of each explanatory variable is measured by an odds ratio that is the multiplicative effect the variable has on the odds of falling into the higher categories instead of the lower categories. An important assumption of the model is that these odds ratios do not depend on where the ordinal scale is split to define high versus low categories. For example, if in a proportional odds model for welfare progress the odds ratio for plan implementation is estimated as 2, this means that the odds of falling into categories 5 or above are twice as great for those children whose plan was implemented as for those whose plan was not implemented. The same is true for the odds of falling into categories 6 or above or 4 or above, and so on. For continuous predictors, the effect of the predictor on the ordinal outcome is measured as the odds ratio associated with an increase in the predictor by one unit. Although this odds ratio may not be constant over the range of the predictor, for instance, the effect of a one year increase in age may be different for 3- and 4-year-olds when compared with 14- and 15-year-olds, the sample is not large enough to estimate the relationship in detail. The overall odds ratio can therefore be viewed as an average effect of a one year increase in age.

Other tests were as follows. We computed Kendall's tau-b to assess the correlation between two ordinal variables. (Here we did not present p-values because they are not valid for clustered data.) Linear regression was used to model the relationship between the total deficit score and a number of explanatory variables.

All analyses were carried out using the statistical package Stata (StataCorp., 1999. Stata Statistical Software: Relase 6.0. College Station, TX: Stata Corporation).

Appendix 2:
Standardised tests

The Strengths and Difficulties Questionnaire

The Strengths and Difficulties Questionnaire (SDQ) is a one-page behavioural screening questionnaire. It has 25 items, which are divided between five scales of five items each covering conduct problems, hyperactivity, emotional symptoms, peer problems and prosocial behaviour. All but the last area are summed to produce a total difficulties score. In addition, a one-page 'impact supplement' asks about the chronicity of symptoms and the respondent's evaluation of their impact. The SDQ has been adapted for use with parents and teachers (for children aged between 4 and 16 years) and with young people themselves (between 11 and 16 years).

The SDQ is a well-validated psychometric instrument, which has been shown to be effective at discriminating psychiatric 'caseness' in children and young people and to be somewhat better than the Child Behaviour Checklist (CBCL) at detecting certain difficulties such as hyperactivity and attention deficits. Furthermore, mothers preferred the questionnaire to the CBCL (Goodman and Scott, 1999). The 'impact supplement' has been shown to be a valid complement to the SDQ proper – indeed it provided a better level of discrimination of psychiatric 'caseness' than the SDQ (Goodman, 1999). The SDQ has been included in the recent Department of Health 'Children in Need' assessment packs and social workers are being encouraged to use it within their assessments. A particular advantage for both the practitioner and the researcher is that the SDQ gives a useful indication not only of the level of difficulties in emotional and/or behavioural functioning but also the nature of the difficulties (conduct, peer problems, and so on). We also chose the SDQ because it has the advantage of identifying and measuring strengths as well as difficulties, and this seemed to fit well with our conceptual model.

The General Health Questionnaire

The General Health Questionnaire (GHQ) is a widely used and well-validated measure of psychological–psychiatric problems (Goldberg and

Williams 1991). It was originally developed as a screening instrument for identifying potential cases of mental illness and was used as the first stage of a two-stage assessment process to pick up those with high scores. The diagnosis would then be made via a second stage semi-structured standardised interview, which would confirm or refute the presence of mental illness; but it has also been used as a proxy to estimate the prevalence of mental illness without the interview. (Much depends on the threshold chosen.) It has been used widely in studies by psychologists and physicians as a 'measure of psychological distress'.

There are four versions of the GHQ. We opted for the GHQ 12, which is used both as a screening instrument for mental illness and as a measure of psychological distress. The advantages are that it can be slipped into large-scale surveys and avoids questions with physical aspects (such as weight loss), as these aspects may introduce bias. It only takes two minutes to complete and its most justifiable usage is to identify and compare the proportions of people in given groups with a raised threshold. As can be seen from the material presented on parents on carers, the data was occasionally analysed using different thresholds in order to study the results.

References

Ahmed, S., Cheetham J. and Small, J. (1986) *Social Work with Black Children and their Families*, London: Batsford

Ainsworth, M., Blehar, M., Waters, E. and Wall, S. (1978) *Patterns of Attachment*, Hillsdale, NJ: Erlbaum

Alderson, P. (2000) *Young Children's Rights: Exploring Beliefs, Principles and Practice*, London: Jessica Kingsley

Bailey, S., Thoburn, J. and Wakeham, H. (2002) 'Using the "looking after children" dimensions to collect aggregate data on well-being', *Child and Family Social Work*, Vol. 7, pp. 189–201

Balloch, S., McLean, J. and Fisher, M. (1999) *Social Services: Working Under Pressure*, University of Bristol: Policy Press

Barker, S., Beckett, C., Borthwick, S., Cullen, D., Plumtree, A. and Spencer, M. (1999) *Contact in Permanent Placement: Guidance for Local Authorities in England & Wales and Scotland*, London: British Agencies for Adoption and Fostering

Barn, R., Sinclair, R. and Ferdinand, D. (1997) *Acting on Principle: An Examination of Race and Ethnicity in Social Services Provision for Children and Families*, London: British Agencies for Adoption and Fostering

Barth, R. P. and Berry, M. (1988) *Adoption and Disruption: Rates, Risks and Responses*, New York: Aldine de Gruyter

Bebbington, A. and Miles, J. (1989) 'The background of children who enter local authority care', *British Journal of Social Work*, Vol. 19, No. 5, pp. 349–68

Berridge, D. (1994) 'Foster and residential care reassessed: a research perspective', *Children and Society*, Vol. 8, No. 2, pp.132–50

Berridge, D. and Cleaver, H. (1987) *Foster Home Breakdown*, Oxford: Blackwell

Biehal, N., Clayden, J., Stein, M. and Wade, J. (1995) *Moving On: Young People and Leaving Care Schemes*, London: HMSO

Bilson, A. and Barker, R. (1995) 'Parental contact with children fostered and in residential care after the Children Act 1989', *British Journal of Social Work*, Vol. 25, pp. 367–81

Binder, D. A. (1983) 'On the variances of asymptotically normal estimators from complex surveys', *International Statistical Review*, Vol. 51, pp. 279–92

Booth, M. (1996) *Avoiding Delay in Children Act Cases*, London: Lord Chancellor's Department

Bourton, A. and McCausland, J. (2001) 'A service for children and a service for the courts: the contribution of guardians ad litem in public law proceedings', *British Journal of Adoption and Fostering*, Vol. 25, No. 3, pp. 59–66

Bowlby, J. (1988) *A Secure Base*, London: Routledge

Brandon, M., Thoburn, J., Lewis, A. and Way, A. (1999) *Safeguarding Children with the Children Act 1989*, London: The Stationery Office

Brent Borough Council (1985) *A Child in Trust: The Report of the Panel of Inquiry into the Circumstances surrounding the Death of Jasmine Beckford*, London Borough of Brent

Broad, B. (1999) 'Kinship care: enabling and supporting child placements with relatives and friends', in British Agencies for Adoption and Fostering *Preparing for Permanence: Assessment, Preparation and Support*, London: British Agencies for Adoption and Fostering

Brophy, J. (1999) *Expert Evidence in Child Protection Litigation*, London: The Stationery Office

Brophy, J. (2000) 'Race' and ethnicity in care proceedings: implications from a national survey of cases containing expert evidence, *Adoption and Fostering*, Vol. 24, No. 2, pp. 70–2

Browne, K., Davies, C. and Stratton, P. (1988) *Early Prediction and Prevention of Child Abuse*, Chichester: John Wiley & Sons

Bullock, R., Gooch, D. and Little, M. (1998) *Children Going Home: The Reunification of Families*, Aldershot: Avebury

Butler, I. and Payne, H. (1997) 'The health of children looked after by the local authority', *Adoption & Fostering*, Vol. 21, No. 2, pp. 28–35

Byrne, S. (2000) *Linking and Introductions: Helping Children Join Adoptive Families*, London: British Agencies for Adoption and Fostering

Cabinet Office (2000) *The Prime Minister's Review of Adoption*, London: Performance and Innovation Unit, Cabinet Office

Carr-Hill, R., Dixon, P., Mannion, R., Rice, N., Rudat, K., Sinclair, R. and Smith, P. (1997) *A Model of the Determinants of Expenditure on Children's Personal Social Services*, Centre for Health Economics, York: University of York

Children Law UK (2002) *Care Plans – the Way Ahead*, conference report, London: Children Law

Clark, A. and Sinclair, R. (1999) *The Child in Focus: The Evolving Role of the Guardian Ad Litem*, London: National Children's Bureau

Cleaver, H. (2000) *Fostering Family Contact: A study of Children, Parents and Foster Carers*, London: The Stationery Office

Cleaver, H., Unell, I. and Aldgate, J. (1999) *Children's Needs – Parenting Capacity*, London: The Stationery Office

Department of Health and Social Security (1985) *Social Work Decisions in Child Care: Recent Research Findings and their Implications*, London: HMSO

Department of Health (1991a) *Patterns and Outcomes in Child Placement: Messages from Current Research and their Implications*, London: HMSO
Department of Health (1991b) *The Children Act 1989: Guidance and Regulations*, London: HMSO
Department of Health (1996a) *Focus on Teenagers: Research into Practice*, London: HMSO
Department of Health (1996b) *Reporting to Court under the Children Act: A Handbook for Social Services*, London: HMSO
Department of Health (1998a) *Adoption – Achieving the Right Balance*. Local Authority Circular, LAC(98)20
Department of Health (1998b) *Care Planning and Court Order Study*, London: DoH
Department of Health (1998c) *Caring for Children Away from Home: Messages from Research*, Chichester: John Wiley & Sons
Department of Health (1998d) *Modernising Social Services*, Cm 4169, London: The Stationery Office
Department of Health (1998e) *Quality Protects: Transforming Children's Services*. Local Authority Circular, LAC(98)28
Department of Health (1999a) *Adoption Now: Messages from Research*, Chichester: John Wiley & Sons
Department of Health (1999b) *Care Plans and Care Proceedings under the Children Act 1989*. Local Authority Circular, LAC(99)29
Department of Health (1999c) *Framework for the Assessment of Children in Need and their Families*, London: DoH
Department of Health (1999d) *The Government's Objectives for Children's Social Services*, London: DoH
Department of Health (2000a) *Adoption: A New Approach*, London: DoH
Department of Health (2000b) *The Children Act Report 1995–1999*, Cm 4579, London: The Stationery Office
Department of Health (2001a) *The Children Act Now: Messages from Research*, London: The Stationery Office
Department of Health (2001b) *The Children Act Report 2000*, London: DoH
Department of Health (2002a) 'Children looked after in England, 2001/2002', *Statistical Bulletin*, Vol. 22
Department of Health (2002b) *Fostering for the Future: Inspection of Foster Care Services*. London: DoH
Department of Health Personal Social Services Local Authority Statistics (1998) *Children Looked After by Local Authorities: Year Ending 31 March 1998 England*. London: DoH.
Dewar, J. (1995) 'The courts and local authority autonomy', *Child and Family Law Quarterly*, Vol. 7, No. 2, pp. 15–25

Fahlberg, V. (1994) *A Child's Journey through Placement*, London: British Agencies for Adoption and Fostering

Farmer, E. and Owen, M. (1995) *Child Protection Practice: Private Risks and Public Remedies*, London: HMSO

Farmer, E. and Owen, M. (1998) 'Gender and the child protection process', *British Journal of Social Work*, Vol. 28, No. 4, pp. 545–64

Farmer, E. and Parker, R. (1991) *Trials and Tribulations: Returning Children from Local Authority Care to their Families*, London: HMSO

Farmer, E. and Pollock, S. (1998) *Sexually Abused and Abusing Children in Substitute Care*, Chichester: John Wiley & Sons

Farmer, E., Moyers, S. and Lipscombe, J. (2002) *The Fostering Task with Adolescents*, report to the Department of Health

Fortin, J. (1999) 'The HRA's impact on litigation involving children and their families', *Child and Family Law Quarterly*, Vol. 11, No.3, pp. 237–55

Fratter, J. (1996) *Adoption with Contact*, London: British Agencies for Adoption and Fostering

Freeman, P. and Hunt, J. (1998) *Parental Perspectives on Care Proceedings*, London: The Stationery Office

Gibbons, J. ed. (1992) *The Children Act 1989 and Family Support: Principles into Practice*, London: HMSO

Goldberg, D. and Williams, P. (1991) A *User's Guide to the General Health Questionnaire*, 2nd edition, Windsor: NFER/ Nelson

Goodman, R. (1999) 'The extended version of the Strengths and Difficulties Questionnaire as a guide to psychiatric caseness and consequent burden', *Journal of Child Psychology and Psychiatry*, Vol. 40, No. 5, pp. 791–9

Goodman, R. and Scott, S. (1999) 'Comparing the Strengths and Difficulties Questionnaire and the Child Behaviour Checklist: is small beautiful?', *Journal of Abnormal Child Psychology*, Vol. 27, No. 1, pp. 17–24

Goodman, R., Meltzer, H. and Bailey, V. (1998) 'The strengths and difficulties questionnaire: a pilot study on the validity of the self-report version', *European Child and Adolescent Psychiatry*, Vol. 7, pp. 125–30

Greenland, C. (1987) *Preventing CAN deaths*, London: Tavistock

Grimshaw, R. and Sinclair, R. (1997) *Planning to Care: Regulation, Procedure and Practice under the Children Act 1989*, London: National Children's Bureau

Harter, S. (1990) 'Self and identity development', in S. Feldman and G. Elder (eds) *At the Threshold: The Developing Adolescent*, Cambridge, MA: Harvard University Press

Harwin, J. and Forrester, D. (2002) *Parental Substance Misuse and Child Welfare: A Study of Social Work with Families in which Parents Misuse Drugs or Alcohol*, interim report to the Nuffield Foundation

Harwin, J. and Owen, M. (2002) 'A study of care plans and their implementation and relevance for re W and B and re W (care plan)', in The Rt Hon Lord

Justice Thorpe and C. Cowton (eds) *Delight and Dole: The Children Act 10 Years On*, Bristol: Family Law/Jordan Publishing

Hayes, M. (1996) 'The proper role of courts in child care cases', *Child and Family Law Quarterly*, Vol. 8, No. 3, pp. 201–16

Hester, M. and Radford, L. (1996) *Domestic Violence and Child Contact Arrangements in England and Denmark*, Bristol: the Policy Press

Hilgendorf, L. (1981) *Social Workers and Solicitors in Child Care Cases*, London: The Stationery Office

Hill, M., ed. (1999) *Signposts in Fostering: Policy, Practice and Research Issues*, London: British Agencies for Adoption and Fostering

Hill, M., Lambert, L. and Triseliotis, J. (1989) *Achieving Adoption with Love and Money*, London: National Children's Bureau

Hornby, H., Zeller, D. and Karraker, D. (1995) *Kinship Care in America: A National Policy Study*, Portland, Me: University of Southern Maine, Edmund S. Muskie Institute of Public Affairs

House of Commons Health Committee (1998) *Children Looked After by Local Authorities: second report from the Health Committee*, Session 1997–98 (HC 319; vol II), London: The Stationery Office

House of Commons Social Services Committee (1984) *Children in Care, Volume 1*. London: HMSO

House of Lords judgement (2002) *In re S (FC); In re S and others; In re W and others* (First Appeal) (FC); *In re W and others* (Second Appeal) (Conjoined Appeals), 14 March

Howe, D. (1995) *Attachment Theory for Social Work Practice*, Basingstoke: Macmillan

Howe, D. (1998) *Patterns of Adoption*, Oxford: Blackwell Science

Hunt, J. and Macleod, A. (1999) *The Best-Laid Plans: Outcomes of Judicial Decisions in Child Protection Proceedings*, London: The Stationery Office

Hunt, J., Macleod, A. and Thomas, C. (1999) *The Last Resort: Child Protection, the Courts and the 1989 Children Act*, London: The Stationery Office

Ivaldi, G. (2000) *Surveying Adoption: A Comprehensive Analysis of Local Authority Adoptions 1998/1999*, London: British Agencies for Adoption and Fostering

Iwaniec, D. (1995) *The Emotionally Abused and Neglected Child*, Chichester: John Wiley & Sons

Jackson, S. (1989) 'Education of children in care', in B. Kahan (ed.) *Child Care Research, Policy and Practice*, Hodder & Stoughton/Open University

Jackson, S., ed. (2001) *Nobody Ever Told Us School Mattered*, London: British Agencies for Adoption and Fostering

Jackson, S. and Thomas, N. (1999) *On the move again? What Works in Creating Stability for Looked-after Children*, Ilford, Essex: Barnardo's

Local Government Management Board (1992) *The Quality of Care: Report of the Residential Staffs Enquiry Chaired by Lady Howe*, London: Local Government Management Board

London Borough of Lambeth (1987) *Whose Child?*, report of the panel appointed to inquire into the death of Tyra Henry, presented to the London Borough of Lambeth by Elaine Arnold et al., London: London Borough of Lambeth

Lord Chancellor's Department, Children Act Advisory Committee (1995) *Annual Report 1994/5*, London: LCD

Lord Chancellor's Department, Children Act Advisory Committee (1997a) *Final Report*, London: LCD

Lord Chancellor's Department, Children Act Advisory Committee (1997b) *Handbook of Best Practice in Children Act Cases*, London: LCD

Lowe, N. (2001) 'Children's participation in the family justice system – translating principles into practice', *Child and Family Law Quarterly*, Vol. 13, No. 2, pp. 137–58

Lowe, N. and Murch, M. (2002) *The Plan for the Child: Adoption or Long-term Fostering*, London: British Association for Adoption and Fostering

Lowe, N., Murch, M., Borkowski, M., Weaver, A., Beckford, V. and Thomas, C. (1999) *Supporting Adoption: Reframing the Approach*, London: British Agencies for Adoption and Fostering

Maluccio, A. N., Ainsworth, F. and Thoburn, J. (2000) *Child Welfare Outcome Research in the United States, the United Kingdom and Australia*, Washington, DC: CWLA Press

Marsh, P. and Peel, M. (1999) *Leaving Care in Partnership: Family Involvement with Care Leavers*, London: The Stationery Office

Masson, J. and Harrison, C. (1999) 'Rebuilding partnerships with parents of looked-after children', in J. Masson, C. Harrison and A. Pavlovic (eds) *Lost and Found: Making and Remaking Working Partnerships with Parents of Children in the Care System*, Aldershot: Ashgate/Arena, pp. 105–25

Masson, J. and Oakley, M. (1999) *Out of Hearing: The Representation of Children by Guardians and Solicitors in Public Law Proceedings*, Chichester: John Wiley & Sons

Masson, J., Harrison, C. and Pavlovic, A. (1999) *Lost and Found: Making and Remaking Working Partnerships with Parents of Children in the Care System*, Aldershot: Ashgate/Arena

McCann, J. B., James, A., Wilson, S. et al. (1996) 'Prevalence of psychiatric disorders in young people in the care system', *British Medical Journal*, Vol. 313, pp. 1529–30

McFadden, E. J. (1998) 'Kinship care in the USA', *Adoption & Fostering*, Vol. 22, No. 3, pp. 7–15

Millham, S., Bullock, R., Hosie, K. and Haak, M. (1986) *Lost in Care: The Problems of Maintaining Links Between Children in Care and Their Families*, London: Gower

Monck, E., Reynolds, J. and Wigfall, V. (2003) *The Role of Concurrent Planning*, London: British Agencies for Adoption and Fostering

Mullender, A., ed. (1991) *Open Adoption*, London: British Agencies for Adoption and Fostering

Mullender, A., ed. (1999) *We are Family: Sibling Relationships in Placement and Beyond*, London: British Agencies for Adoption and Fostering

Murch, M., Lowe, N., Borkowski, M., Copner, R. and Griew, K. (1993) *Pathways to Adoption: Research Project*, London: HMSO

O'Hagan, K. (1993) *Emotional and Psychological Abuse of Children*, Buckingham: Open University Press

O'Halloran, K. (1999) *The Welfare of the Child: The Principle and the Law*, Aldershot: Ashgate, Arena

Owen, M. (1992) *Social Justice and Children in Care*, Aldershot: Avebury

Owen, M. (1999) *Novices, Old Hands and Professionals: Adoption by Single People*, London: British Agencies for Adoption and Fostering

Packman, J., Randall, J. and Jacques, N (1986) *Who Needs Care? Social Work Decisions about Children*, Oxford: Basil Blackwell

Packman, J. and Hall, C. (1998) *From Care to Accommodation: Support, Protection and Control in Child Care Services*, London: The Stationery Office

Parker, R. A. (1971) *Planning for Deprived Children*, Harpenden: National Children's Home

Paton, J. (2002) 'Adoption', in The Rt Hon Lord Justice Thorpe and C. Cowton (eds) *Delight and Dole: The Children Act 10 years On*, Bristol: Family Law/Jordan Publishing

Phillips, J. (1997) 'Meeting the psychiatric needs of children in foster care: social workers' views', *Psychiatric Bulletin*, Vol. 21, 609–11

Pinkerton, J. (1994) *In Care at Home: Parenting, the State and Civil Society*, Aldershot: Avebury

Plotnikoff, J. and Woolfson, R. (1994) *The Children Act 1989: Timetabling of Interim Care Orders*, study for the Social Services Inspectorate, Department of Health

Pringle, M. K. (1974) *The Needs of Children*, London: Hutchinson

Quinton, D. and Murray, C. (2002) 'Assessing emotional and behavioural development in children looked after away from home', in H. Ward and W. Rose (eds) *Approaches to Needs Assessment in Children's Services*, London: Jessica Kingsley

Quinton, D. and Rutter, M. (1988) *Parenting Breakdown: The Making and Breaking of Intergenerational Links*, Aldershot: Avebury

Quinton, D., Rushton, A., Dance, C. and Mayes, D. (1998) *Joining New Families: A Study of Adoption and Fostering in Middle Childhood*, Chichester: John Wiley & Sons
Rashid, S. P. (2000) 'The strengths of black families', *Adoption and Fostering*, Vol. 24, No. 1, pp. 15–22
Rhodes, P. (1993) 'Charitable vocation or proper job? The role of payment in foster care', *Adoption & Fostering*, Vol. 17, No. 1, pp. 8–13
Richardson, J. and Joughin, C. (2000) *Mental Health Needs of Looked After Children*, Royal College of Psychiatrists, London: Gaskell Publications
Rose, W. (2002) 'Two steps forward, one step back: issues for policy and practice', in H. Ward and W. Rose (eds) *Approaches to Needs Assessment in Children's Services*, London: Jessica Kingsley
Rowe, J., Cain, H., Hundleby, M. and Keane, A. (1984) *Long Term Foster Care*, London: Batsford Academic/British Agencies for Adoption and Fostering
Rowe, J., Hundleby, M. and Garnett, L. (1989) *Child Care Now: A Survey of Placement Patterns*, London: British Agencies for Adoption and Fostering
Ruegger, M. (2001) 'Seen and heard but how well-informed? Children's perceptions of the guardian ad litem service', *Children and Society*, Vol. 15, pp. 133–45
Rushton, A. and Dance, C. (2002) *Adoption Support Services for Families in Difficulty*, London: British Agencies for Adoption and Fostering
Rushton, A., Dance, C., Quinton, D. and Mayes, D. (2001) *Siblings in Late Permanent Placements*, London: British Agencies for Adoption and Fostering
Rutter, M. (2001) 'Psychosocial adversity and child psychopathology', in J. Green and W. Yule (eds) *Research and Innovation on the Road to Modern Child Psychiatry*, Volume 1, London: Gaskell and the Association of Child Psychology and Psychiatry
Schofield, G., Beek, M., Sargent, K. with Thoburn, J. (2000) *Growing Up in Foster Care*, London: British Agencies for Adoption and Fostering
Schofield, G. (2003) *Part of the Family: Pathways through Foster Care*, London: British Agencies for Adoption and Fostering
Scott, J. (1999) *Report of an Audit of the Implementation of 'Looking After Children' in Year 3: 1997–1998*, Leicester: University of Leicester School of Social Work
Sellick, C. and Thoburn, J. (1996) *What Works in Family Placement?* Ilford, Essex: Barnardo's
Shaw, C. (1998) *Remember My Messages: the Experiences and Views of 2000 Children in Public Care in the UK*, London: The Who Cares? Trust
Shaw, M. and Hipgrave, T. (1983) *Specialist Fostering*, London: Batsford
Sinclair, I. and Gibbs, I. (1998) *Children's Homes: A Study in Diversity*, Chichester: John Wiley & Sons
Sinclair, I., Gibbs, I. and Wilson, K. (2000) *Supporting Foster Placements, Reports One and Two*, York: Social Work Research and Development Unit

Sinclair, I, Baker, C, Wilson, W. and Gibbs, I. (2003) *What Happens to Foster Children?* Final Report submitted to the Department of Health by the Social Work Research and Development Group, University of York

Skuse, T. and Evans, R. (2001) 'Directing social work attention to education: the role of the Looking After Children materials' in S. Jackson (ed.) *Nobody Ever Told Us School Mattered*, London: British Agencies for Adoption and Fostering, pp.172–90.

Social Service Inspectorate (1996a) *For Children's Sake: An SSI Inspection of Local Authority Adoption Services*, London: DoH

Social Services Inspectorate (1996b) *Inspection of Local Authority Fostering 1995–96: National Summary Report*, London: DoH

Social Services Inspectorate (1997) *An Inspection of Post-Placement and Post-Adoption Services*, London: DoH

Social Services Inspectorate (1998) *Someone Else's Children*, London: DoH

Social Services Inspectorate (1999) *Strategic Planning in Children's Services*, London: DoH

Stein, M. (1989) 'Leaving care', in B. Kahan (ed.) *Child Care Research, Policy and Practice*, Hodder & Stoughton/Open University

Stein, M. and Wade, J. (2000) *Helping Care Leavers: Problems and Strategic Responses*, London: DoH

Stevenson, O. (1998) *Neglected Children: Issues and Dilemmas*, Oxford: Blackwell Science

Sturge, C. in consultation with Glaser, D. (2000) 'Contact and domestic violence – the experts' court report', *Family Law*, September, pp. 615–29

Sykes, J., Sinclair, I., Gibbs, I. and Wilson, K. (2002) 'Kinship and stranger foster carers: How do they compare?', *Adoption & Fostering*, Vol. 26, No. 2, pp. 38–48

Thoburn, J. (1980) *Captive Clients: Social Work with Families of Children Home on Trial*, London: Routledge and Kegan Paul

Thoburn, J. (1994) *Child Placement: Principles and Practice*, 2nd ed., Aldershot: Arena

Thoburn, J. (1999) 'Trends in adoption and foster care', in O. Stevenson (ed.) *Child Welfare in the UK*, Oxford: Blackwell Science

Thomas, C. and Beckford, V. (1999) *Adopted Children Speaking*, London: British Agencies for Adoption and Fostering

Thomas, N. and O'Kane, C. (1998) 'The ethics of participatory research with children', *Children and Society*, Vol. 12, pp. 336–48

Thorpe, L. J. and Clarke, E. (1998) *Divided Duties: Care Planning for Children Within the Family Justice System*, Family Law/Jordan Publishing

Triseliotis, J. (2002) 'Long-term foster care or adoption? The evidence examined', *Child and Family Social Work*, Vol. 7, pp. 21–33

Triseliotis, J., Sellick, C. and Short, R. (1995) *Foster Care: Theory and Practice*, London: Batsford

Triseliotis, J., Borland, M., Hill, M. and Lambert, L. (1995) *Teenagers and the Social Work Services*, London: HMSO

Triseliotis, J., Borland, M. and Hill, M. (2000) *Delivering Foster Care*, London: British Agencies for Adoption and Fostering

Tunstill, J. and Aldgate, J. (2000) *Services for Children in Need: From Policy to Practice*, London: The Stationery Office

Utting, W., Baines, C., Stuart, M., Rowlands, J. and Vialva, R. (1997) *People Like Us: The Report of the Review of the Safeguards for Children Living Away from Home*, London: The Stationery Office

Wade, J., Biehal, N., Clayden, J. and Stein, M. (1998) *Going Missing: Young People Absent from Care*, Chichester: John Wiley & Sons

Wagner, G. (1988) *Residential Care: A Positive Choice*, London: HMSO

Ward, H. (1995) *Looking After Children: Research into Practice*, London: HMSO

Ward, H. and Skuse, T. (2001a) *Looking After Children: Transforming Data into Management Information; Report from First Year of Data Collection*, Loughborough and Dartington: Loughborough University and Dartington Social Research Unit

Ward, H. and Skuse, T. (2001b) 'Performance targets and stability of placements for children long looked after away from home', *Children & Society*, Vol. 15, pp. 333–46

Wedge, P. and Mantle, G. (1991) *Sibling Groups and Social Work: A Study of Children Referred for Permanent Substitute Family Placement*, Aldershot: Avebury

Index